JAGUAR
XK120·XK140
XK150
Gold Portfolio
1948-1960

Compiled by
R.M. Clarke

ISBN 1 870642 414

Distributed by
Brooklands Book Distribution Ltd.
'Holmerise', Seven Hills Road,
Cobham, Surrey, England

Printed in Hong Kong

BROOKLANDS BOOKS

BROOKLANDS BOOKS SERIES
AC Ace & Aceca 1953-1983
AC Cobra 1962-1969
Alfa Romeo Alfasud 1972-1984
Alfa Romeo Alfetta Coupes GT.GTV.GTV6 1974-1987
Alfa Romeo Guilias Berlinettas
Alfa Romeo Giulia Berlinas 1962-1976
Alfa Romeo Giulia Coupés 1963-1976
Alfa Romeo Spider 1966-1987
Allard Gold Portfolio 1937-1958
Alvis Gold Portfolio 1919-1967
Aston Martin Gold Portfolio 1972-1985
Austin Seven 1922-1982
Austin A30 & A35 1951-1962
Austin Healey 100 1952-1959
Austin Healey 3000 1959-1967
Austin Healey 100 & 3000 Collection No. 1
Austin Healey 'Frogeye' Sprite Collection No. 1
Austin Healey Sprite 1958-1971
Avanti 1962-1983
BMW Six Cylinder Coupés 1969-1975
BMW 1600 Collection No. 1
BMW 2002 1968-1976
Bristol Cars Gold Portfolio 1946-1985
Buick Automobiles 1947-1960
Buick Riviera 1963-1978
Cadillac Automobiles 1949-1959
Cadillac Automobiles 1960-1969
Cadillac Eldorado 1967-1978
Camaro 1966-1970
Chevrolet Camaro & Z-28 1973-1981
High Performance Camaros 1982-1988
Chevrolet Camaro Collection No. 1
Chevrolet 1955-1957
Chevrolet Impala & SS 1958-1971
Chevelle & SS 1964-1972
Chevy II Nova & SS 1962-1973
High Performance Corvettes 1983-1989
Chrysler 300 1955-1970
Citroen Traction Avant 1934-1957
Citroen DS & ID 1955-1875
Citroen 2CV 1948-1988
Cobras & Replicas 1962-1983
Cortina 1600E & GT 1967-1970
Corvair 1959-1968
Daimler Dart & V-8 250 1959-1969
Datsun 240Z 1970-1973
Datsun 280Z & ZX 1975-1983
De Tomaso Collection No. 1
Dodge Charger 1966-1974
Excalibur Collection No. 1
Ferrari Cars 1946-1956
Ferrari Cars 1962-1966
Ferrari Cars 1969-1973
Ferrari Dino 1965-1974
Ferrari Dino 308 1974-1979
Ferrari 308 & Mondial 1980-1984
Ferrari Collection No. 1
Fiat-Bertone X1/9 1973-1988
Fiat Pininfarina 124+2000 Spider 1968-1985
Ford Automobiles 1944-1959
Ford Fairlane 1955-1970
Ford Falcon 1960-1970
Ford Mustang 1964-1967
Ford Mustang 1967-1973
Ford RS Escort 1968-1980
Honda CRX 1983-1987
High Performance Escorts MkI 1968-1974
High Performance Escorts MkII 1975-1980
High Performance Mustangs 1982-1988
Hudson & Railton Cars 1936-1940
Jaguar Cars 1957-1961
Jaguar Cars 1961-1964
Jaguar XK120 XK140 XK150 Gold Portfolio 1948-1960
Jaguar MK2 1959-1969
Jaguar E-Type Gold Portfolio 1961-1971
Jaguar E-Type 1966-1971
Jaguar E-Type V12 1971-1975
Jaguar XJ6 1968-1972
Jaguar XJ6 Series II 1973-1979
Jaguar XJ6 & XJ12 Series III 1979-1985
Jaguar XJ12 1972-1980
Jaguar XJS Gold Portfolio 1975-1988
Jensen Cars 1946-1967
Jensen Cars 1967-1979
Jensen Interceptor Gold Portfolio 1966-1986
Jensen Healey 1972-1976
Lamborghini Cars 1964-1970
Lamborghini Cars 1970-1975
Lamborghini Countach Collection No. 1
Lamborghini Countach & Urraco 1974-1980
Lamborghini Countach & Jalpa 1980-1985
Lancia Stratos 1972-1985
Land Rover 1948-1973
Land Rover Series II & IIa 1958-1971
Land Rover Series III 1971-1985
Land Rover 90 & 110 1983-1989
Land Rover 90 & 110 1983-1989
Lotus Cortina 1963-1970
Lotur Elan Gold Portfolio 1962-1974
Lotus Elan Collection No. 2
Lotus Elite 1957-1964
Lotus Elite & Eclat 1974-1981
Lotus Turbo Esprit 1980-1986
Lotus Europa 1966-1975
Lotus Europa Collection No. 1
Lotus Seven 1957-1980
Lotus Seven Collection No. 1
Marcos Cars 1960-1988
Maserati 1965-1970
Maserati 1970-1975
Marcos Cars 1960-1988
Mazda RX-7 Collection No. 1
Mercedes 190 & 300SL 1954-1963
Mercedes 230/250/280SL 1963-1971
Mercedes 350/450SL & SLC 1971-1980
Mercedes Benz Cars 1949-1954
Mercedes Benz Cars 1954-1957
Mercedes Benz Cars 1957-1961

Mercedes Benz Competition Cars 1950-1957
Metropolitan 1954-1962
MG TC 1945-1949
MG TD 1949-1953
MG TF 1953-1955
MG Cars 1957-1959
MG Cars 1959-1962
MG Midget 1961-1980
MGA Collection No. 1
MGA Roadsters 1955-1962
MGB Roadsters 1962-1980
MGB GT 1965-1980
Mini Cooper 1961-1971
Morgan Cars 1960-1970
The Morgan 3-Weeler Gold Portfolio 1910-1952
Morgan Cars Gold Portfolio 1968-1989
Morris Minor Collection No. 1
Olosmobile Automobiles 1955-1963
Old's Cutlass & 4-4-2 1964-1972
Oldsmobile Toronado 1966-1978
Opel GT 1968-1973
Packard Gold Portfolio 1946-1958
Pantera 1970-1973
Pantera & Mangusta 1969-1974
Plymouth Barracuda 1964-1974
Pontiac Fiero 1984-1988
Pontiac GTO 1964-1970
Pontiac Firebird 1967-1973
Pontiac Firebird and Trans-Am 1973-1981
High Performance Firebirds 1982-1988
Pontiac Tempest & GTO 1961-1965
Porsche Cars 1960-1964
Porsche Cars 1964-1968
Porsche Cars 1968-1972
Porsche Cars in the Sixties
Porsche Cars 1972-1975
Porsche 356 1952-1965
Porsche 911 1965-1969
Porsche 911 1970-1972
Porsche 911 1973-1977
Porsche 911 Carrera 1973-1977
Porsche 911 SC 1978-1983
Porsche 911 Turbo 1975-1984
Porsche 914 Gold Portfolio 1969-1976
Porsche 914 Collection No. 1
Porsche 924 Gold Portfolio 1975-1988
Porsche 928 1977-1989
Porsche 944 1981-1985
Reliant Scimitar 1964-1986
Riley 1½ & 2½ Litre Gold Portfolio 1945-1955
Rolls Royce Silver Cloud 1955-1965
Rolls Royce Silver Shadow 1965-1980
Range Rover Gold Portfolio 1970-1988
Rover 3 & 3,5 Litre 1958-1973
Rover P4 1949-1959
Rover P4 1955-1964
Rover 2000 + 2200 1963-1977
Rover 3500 1968-1977
Rover 3500 & Vitesse 1976-1986
Saab Sonett Collection No. 1
Saab Turbo 1976-1983
Studebaker Hawks & Larks 1956-1963
Sunbeam Tiger and Alpine Gold Portfolio 1959-1967
Thunderbird 1955-1957
Thunderbird 1958-1963
Thunderbird 1964-1976
Toyota MR2 1984-1988
Triumph 2000-2.5-2500 1963-1977
Triumph Spitfire 1962-1980
Triumph Spitfire Collection No. 1
Triumph Stag 1970-1980
Triumph Stag Collection No. 1
Triumph TR2 & TR3 1952-1960
Triumph TR4.TR5.TR250 1961-1968
Triumph TR6 1969-1976
Triumph TR6 Collection No. 1
Triumph TR7 & TR8 1975-1982
Triumph GT6 1966-1974
Triumph Vitesse & Herald 1959-1971
TVR Gold Portfolio 1959-1988
Volkswagen Cars 1936-1956
VW Beetle 1956-1977
VW Beetle Collection No. 1
VW Golf GTi 1976-1986
VW Karmann Ghia 1955-1982
VW Scirocco 1974-1981
VW Bus-Camper-Van 1954-1967
VW Bus-Camper-Van 1968-1979
VW Bus-Camper-Van 1979-1989
Volvo 1800 1960-1973
Volvo 120 Series 1956-1970

BROOKLANDS MUSCLE CARS SERIES
American Motors Muscle Cars 1966-1970
Buick Muscle Cars 1965-1970
Camaro Muscle Cars 1966-1972
Capri Muscle Cars 1969-1983
Chevrolet Muscle Cars 1966-1972
Dodge Muscle Cars 1967-1970
Mercury Muscle Cars 1966-1971
Mini Muscle Cars 1961-1979
Mopar Muscle Cars 1964-1967
Mopar Muscle Cars 1968-1971
Mustang Muscle Cars 1967-1971
Shelby Mustang Muscle Cars 1965-1970
Oldsmobile Muscle Cars 1964-1970
Plymouth Muscle Cars 1966-1971
Pontiac Muscle Cars 1966-1972
Muscle Cars Compared 1966-1971
Muscle Cars Compared Book 2 1965-1971

BROOKLANDS ROAD & TRACK SERIES
Road & Track on Alfa Romeo 1949-1963
Road & Track on Alfa Romeo 1964-1970
Road & Track on Alfa Romeo 1971-1976
Road & Track on Alfa Romeo 1977-1984
Road & Track on Aston Martin 1962-1984
Road & Track on Auburn Cord & Duesenberg 1952-1984
Road & Track on Audi 1952-1980
Road & Track on Audi 1980-1986

Road & Track on Austin Healey 1953-1970
Road & Track on BMW Cars 1966-1974
Road & Track on BMW Cars 1975-1978
Road & Track on BMW Cars 1979-1983
Road & Track on Cobra, Shelby &
 Ford GT40 1962-1983
Road & Track on Corvette 1953-1967
Road & Track on Corvette 1968-1982
Road & Track on Corvette 1982-1986
Road & Track on Datsun Z 1970-1983
Road & Track on Ferrari 1950-1968
Road & Track on Ferrari 1968-1974
Road & Track on Ferrari 1975-1981
Road & Track on Ferrari 1981-1984
Road & Track on Fiat Sports Cars 1968-1987
Road & Track on Jaguar 1950-1960
Road & Track on Jaguar 1961-1968
Road & Track on Jaguar 1968-1974
Road & Track on Jaguar 1974-1982
Road & Track on Jaguar 1983-1989
Road & Track on Lamborghini 1964-1985
Road & Track on Lotus 1972-1981
Road & Track on Maserati 1952-1974
Road & Track on Maserati 1975-1983
Road & Track on Mazda RX7 1978-1986
Road & Track on Mercedes 1952-1962
Road & Track on Mercedes 1963-1970
Road & Track on Mercedes 1971-1979
Road & Track on Mercedes 1980-1987
Road & Track on MG Sports Cars 1949-1961
Road & Track on MG Sports Cars 1962-1980
Road & Track on Mustang 1964-1977
Road & Track on Peugeot 1955-1986
Road & Track on Pontiac 1960-1983
Road & Track on Porsche 1951-1967
Road & Track on Porsche 1968-1971
Road & Track on Porsche 1972-1975
Road & Track on Porsche 1975-1978
Road & Track on Porsche 1979-1982
Road & Track on Porsche 1982-1985
Road & Track on Porsche 1985-1988
Road & Track on Rolls Royce & Bentley 1950-1965
Road & Track on Rolls Royce & Bentley 1966-1984
Road & Track on Saab 1955-1985
Road & Track on Toyota Sports & G T Cars 1966-1986
Road & Track on Triumph Sports Cars 1953-1967
Road & Track on Triumph Sports Cars 1967-1974
Road & Track on Triumph Sports Cars 1974-1982
Road & Track on Volkswagen 1951-1968
Road & Track on Volkswagen 1968-1978
Road & Track on Volkswagen 1978-1985
Road & Track on Volvo 1957-1974
Road & Track on Volvo 1975-1985
Road & Track Henry Manney at Large & Abroad

BROOKLANDS CAR AND DRIVER SERIES
Car and Driver on BMW 1955-1977
Car and Driver on BMW 1977-1985
Car and Driver on Cobra, Shelby & Ford GT40
 1963-1984
Car and Driver on Datsun Z 1600 & 2000
 1966-1984
Car and Driver on Corvette 1956-1967
Car and Driver on Corvette 1968-1977
Car and Driver on Corvette 1978-1982
Car and Driver on Corvette 1983-1988
Car and Driver on Ferrari 1955-1962
Car and Driver on Ferrari 1963-1975
Car and Driver on Ferrari 1976-1983
Car and Driver on Mopar 1956-1967
Car and Driver on Mopar 1968-1975
Car and Driver on Mustang 1964-1972
Car and Driver on Pontiac 1961-1975
Car and Driver on Porsche 1955-1962
Car and Driver on Porsche 1963-1970
Car and Driver on Porsche 1970-1976
Car and Driver on Porsche 1977-1981
Car and Driver on Porsche 1982-1986
Car and Driver on Saab 1956-1985
Car and Driver on Volvo 1955-1986

BROOKLANDS MOTOR & THOROUGHBRED & CLASSIC CAR SERIES
Motor & T & CC on Ferrari 1966-1976
Motor & T & CC on Ferrari 1976-1984
Motor & T & CC on Lotus 1979-1983
Motor & T & CC on Morris Minor 1948-1983

BROOKLANDS PRACTICAL CLASSICS SERIES
Practical Classics on Austin A 40 Restoration
Practical Classics on Land Rover Restoration
Practical Classics on Metalworking in Restoration
Practical Classics on Midget/Sprite Restoration
Practical Classics on Mini Cooper Restoration
Practical Classics on MGB Restoration
Practical Classics on Morris Minor Restoration
Practical Classics on Triumph Herald/Vitesse
Practical Classics on Triumph Spitfire Restoration
Practical Classics on VW Beetle Restoration
Practical Classics on 1930S Car Restoration

BROOKLANDS MILITARY VEHICLES SERIES
Allied Military Vehicles Collection No. 1
Allied Military Vehicles Collection No. 2
Dodge Military Vehicles Collection No. 1
Military Jeeps 1941-1945
Off Road Jeeps 1944-1971
V W Kubelwagen 1940-1975

CONTENTS

Page	Title	Publication	Date
5	Jaguar Speedster	Autocar	Oct. 29 1948
6	Jaguars Re-Enter the 100mph Class	Motor	Oct. 27 1948
9	Jaguar Demonstration	Motor	June 1 1949
10	Jaguar 120 Does 132½ mph	Autocar	June 3 1949
11	My Favorite Sports Car...	Road & Track	March 1950
12	Jaguar XK120 Sports Car	Motor Trend	April 1950
15	XK120 Jaguar Super Sports Road Tests	Autocar	April 14 1950
18	The World's Fastest Sports Car — Jaguar	Speed Age	Oct. 1950
20	A Jaguar XK120 Coupé	Autocar	March 2 1951
24	The Jaguar XK120	Motor Sport	April 1951
26	The American Driver's Viewpoint Road Test	Road & Track	May 1951
29	XK Tune-up	Autocar	Aug. 17 1951
31	That Exciting New Jaguar	Autocar	July 13 1951
35	Earning Its Type-Number	Autosport	Jan. 11 1952
37	The Fitch-Jaguar	Autosport	May 1952
38	Jaguar Edurance Run	Autocar	Aug. 15 1952
39	Jaguar XK120 Coupé Road Test	Autocar	Oct. 17 1952
42	The Jaguar XK120C Road Test	Motor	Oct. 22 1952
45	Seven Days of Speed	Auto Topics	Nov. 1952
46	Jaguar Trial	Speed Age	Dec. 1952
51	Jaguar XK120M Road Test	Road & Track	May 1953
54	"M" Jag Road Test	Auto Sport	June 1953
56	Honourable Retirement	Autocar	July 10 1953
57	Road Testing the C-Jag	Auto Sport Review	July 1953
60	The Jaguar XK120 Drophead Coupé Road Test	Autosport	May 14 1954
63	Jaguar in Competition	Sports Cars & Hot Rods	Dec. 1953
66	The D-Type Jaguar	Autocar	Sept. 3 1954
72	Jaguar XK120 Becomes XK140	Motor	Oct. 18 1954
74	Fiercer Jaguars	Autocar	Oct. 15 1954
77	The 1955 Jaguars	Auto Age	May 1955
79	Coventry's Finest Formula — XK140 Road Test	Road & Track	June 1955
81	Jags Grab More Horses	Cars	July 1955
84	Notes on the 140	Sports Cars Illustrated	July 1955
86	Jaguar Over the Andes	Autocar	Aug. 5 1955
90	Soup for the Jaguar	Sports Cars Illustrated	Oct. 1955
93	The Jaguar XK140 Road Test	Autosport	Nov. 4 1955
95	Jaguar XK140 Coupé Road Test	Autocar	Dec. 9 1955
99	Jaguar Drivers Report	Motor Life	July 1956
101	Black Jaguar	Autocar	Aug. 17 1956
104	Jaguar XK140 is a Real Grand Turismo	Sports Car & Specials	Oct. 1956
107	XK "SS"	Motor	Jan. 30 1957
108	Jaguar XK140 MC Road Test	Sports Cars Illustrated	March 1957
113	The New Jaguar XK150	Autosport	May 24 1957
114	The New Jaguar XK150	Motor	May 22 1957
117	Looking in at Jaguar	Motor Sport	June 1957
119	The New Jaguar XK150	Road & Track	Aug. 1957
121	Jaguar's 24-Hour Parade	Speed Age	Oct. 1957
123	Jaguar XK150 Road Test	Road & Track	Nov. 1957
125	Jaguar XK150 Road Test	Autocar	Feb. 21 1968
129	An Open Two-Seater Jaguar	Motor	March 26 1958
132	Jaguar XK150S	Sports Cars Illustrated	Aug. 1958
135	Two Jaguar Roadsters Comparison Test	Road & Track	Sept. 1958
138	Luxurious Lightening Road Test	Speed Age	Oct. 1958
142	The Jaguar XK150 Road Test	Motor Sport	Oct. 1958
144	Jaguar XK150S	Sports Cars Illustrated	Dec. 1958
146	The 1959 Lister Jaguar	Motor Racing	Feb. 1959
148	Jaguar XK150 Road Test	Motor Racing	Nov. 1958
149	Jaguar XK150S Road Test	Autosport	June 5 1959
151	The Jaguar XK150S Fixed-Head Coupé Road Test	Motor	Aug. 19 1959
155	No Jagged Seams to This Velvet Glove Quick Test	Sports Car World	Oct. 1959
158	A Very Fast Car!	Motor Sport	Jan. 1960
160	The 3.8 Litre Jaguar XK150S Road Test	Autosport	June 17 1960
162	The Le Mans Jaguar	Motor	June 22 1960
164	The XK Series Jaguar Road Test	Road & Track	Sept. 1961
171	End of an Era	Autocar	March 5 1983
172	Re-Acquaintance with an XK120	Motor Sport	June 1986
174	Morgan Plus 8 v Jaguar XK140 — The Classic Alternative	Motor	Sept. 26 1987
176	Jaguar's Jewel Profile	Classic and Sportscar	June 1984

INTRODUCTION

"The memorable introduction of the Jaguar XK120 roadster at the 1948 Earls Court Automobile show created much more than a local sensation," reads the first line of one of the articles in this latest set of Brooklands reprints. Indeed it did, for the XK120 led on to a whole series of formidable sports cars bearing the XK designation which earned Jaguar a prominent and lasting place in the automotive Pantheon.

Yet, in many ways, the XK range was conceived by chance. The XK120 was drawn up hurriedly during 1948 when it became apparent that the new twin-overhead-camshaft engine under development for the forthcoming MK. VII saloon would form the ideal basis for a high-performance two-seater sports car. That car's vivid performance and, above all, its breathtaking styling made it an instant success. Jaguar found themselves deluged with orders, particularly from the sports-car-mad North American market.

The XK120 developed into an XK140 in 1954, and that in turn developed into an XK150 in 1957, each more potent and refined than the last. But the flowing lines of these cars were abandoned for 1961's E-type (or XKE, as the Americans called it), which drew its inspiration from the sports/racing cars based on the XK range. By the time the last XK Jaguar rolled off the production lines in 1961, over 30,000 had been made. They left behind a long series of sports and racing successes, and a legend which is reflected today in the huge sums of money paid by enthusiasts to restore examples of the XK range to the condition of their heyday in the 1950s.

Not every XK enthusiast of today lived through the 1950s, of course, and those who did not would find it hard to understand the magic of the XK name without reading the road tests and other articles written about the cars at the time. So here, in this new Brooklands Books Gold Portfolio, is a whole sheaf of such reading matter for the enthusiast, reprinted with the kind permission of Auto Age, Autocar, Autosport, Auto Sport Review, Auto Topics, Cars, Classic & Sportscar, Motor, Motor Life, Motor Sport, Motor Trend, Road & Track, Speed Age, Sports Car & Specials, Sports Car World, Sports Car & Hot Rods and Sports Cars Illustrated.

Brooklands Books were originally conceived to meet this need felt by enthusiasts for contemporary written material about their cars, and the series has grown over the years into its present familiar and well-respected format which covers a huge range of titles. The accessibility of the material these books contain is appreciated by more than just enthusiasts, as well: motoring writers invariably reach first for the relevant Brooklands volume when in search of material for a historical piece. So it is pleasing to be asked to write the introduction to the latest volume in a series I have relied on for years. I am confident that this book's readers will enjoy these articles as much as I have — and will return to them again and again as I shall no doubt need to do in the years to come!

James Taylor

NEW CARS DESCRIBED

A well-proportioned body gives the new Jaguar Super Sports two-seater very fine lines. There is a choice of two engines, the four-cylinder being the production version of Lt.-Col. Goldie Gardner's record engine.

Jaguar Speedster

Super Sports Two-seater: 160 b.h.p. from a Twin o.h.c. Engine

THERE is an exciting new Jaguar to thrill the fast-motoring fans. It is a two-seater with new high-efficiency twin-overhead camshaft engine. The chassis follows the lines of the recently announced Jaguar Mark V saloon, but it has a shorter wheelbase, and the rigid straight-sided box-section frame needs no cruciform and economises in weight. Independent front suspension with wide-base wishbones and torsion bar springs is fitted. There will be a choice of six-cylinder 3½-litre and four-cylinder 2-litre engines, and perhaps the most surprising matter is the relatively low price, £988 plus purchase tax £275 3s 11d, total £1,263 3s 11d, irrespective of engine size.

When Lt. Col. Goldie Gardner recently established the new 2-litre class record of an easy 176 m.p.h., he had in his car a four-cylinder prototype of the new engine, which was modified to a 10 to 1 compression ratio and developed over 140 b.h.p. These new X.K engines have been designed to incorporate the most advanced yet well-proved points of technical knowledge. The design really starts with a massive crankshaft having journal bearings of 2¾ inches in diameter, made of 65-ton steel, and suitably counter-weighted. This shaft is carried in seven bearings on the Six, three on the Four, and the bearings are supported in webbed walls in the monobloc casting of cylinders and crankcase. This block is well ribbed for rigidity, and there is a strong tie between the bearings and the head.

Now comes a very important part of the design. The detachable cylinder head is made of a high tensile strength aluminium alloy, the combustion chambers are of hemispherical shape, and the valves are overhead and set at an angle of 70 degrees, with the sparking plugs offset between them. The valve seats are of a special high-expansion cast iron alloy and are shrunk into position. The inlets are larger than the exhausts, and the exhaust valves are made of corrosion-resistant Austenitic steel. The induction system and combustion chambers were designed in collaboration with H. Weslake and Company to achieve the maximum filling of the cylinders through the wide range of engine speed, to ensure adequate turbulence in order to obtain smooth combustion without high pressure rises, and with effective scavenging during the exhaust stroke. As the cylinders are adequately filled, it is possible to obtain a high power output without recourse to a high compression ratio.

For an engine to be able to rev freely, it is essential that the valve mechanism should have as small reciprocating weight as possible. Hence the X.K has been given twin overhead camshafts, with the cams operating upon the hard crowns of light floating piston-like tappets working in guides. The valve stem bears upon the underside of the piston, and clearance adjustment is set by small pads or "biscuits" of selected thickness. Lubrication of this valve gear is cleverly arranged so that the pistons and cams are in an oil bath, but the valve stems are guarded from swamping by means of a draining gallery. The twin camshafts are driven by a very neat arrangement of two-stage twin chains.

An extra large oil pump picks up oil through a floating filter and delivers it through a full-flow filter to all bearings, right up to the gudgeon pins through tubes in the light alloy connecting rods. From a high-pressure pump the water flow is directed across the cylinder head, and the block is controlled at constant temperatures by a restricted circulation.

SPECIFICATION

Engine.—6 cylinders, 83 × 106 mm (3,442 c.c.); 4 cylinders, 80.5 × 98 mm (1,995 c.c.). Overhead valves, hemispherical combustion chambers, twin overhead camshafts; two-stage duplex chain drive. Counterweighted steel crankshaft; 7 bearings for Six, 3 bearings for Four. Pump lubrication with floating and full-flow filters. Pump water circulation. Twin S.U. carburettors. Compression ratio 7 to 1. Six, 160 b.h.p. at 5,000 r.p.m. Four, 95 b.h.p. at 5,000 r.p.m.

Transmission.—Single-plate clutch. 4-speed gear box with synchromesh on 2, 3, 4. Central change. Gear ratios: Six: Top 3.634, third 4.98, second 7.23, first 12.3 to 1. Four: Top 4.09, third 5.57, second 8.1, first 13.79 to 1. Hardy Spicer open propeller-shaft and hypoid bevel final drive.

Suspension.—Front independent; wishbones and torsion bar. Rear, half-elliptic.

Brakes.—Girling hydraulic two-leading-shoe.

Steering.—Burman re-circulating ball.

Fuel System.—15-gallon tank. Twin S.U. fuel pumps.

Wheels and Tyres.—Pressed steel disc wheels with Dunlop 6.00 × 16in tyres; wide-base rims.

Electrical Equipment.—12-volt Lucas with 64 ampère-hour battery. Flush-fitted head lamps.

Main Dimensions.—Wheelbase, 8ft 6in. Track (front), 4ft 3in; (rear), 4ft 2in. Overall length, 14ft; width, 5ft 11in; height, 4ft 2in. Ground clearance, 7½in. Unladen weight; Six, approx. 22 cwt. Four, approx. 21½ cwt.

This is the 3½-litre six-cylinder engine which can be supplied in the new speed model.

Reprinted from "The Motor," October 27 1948

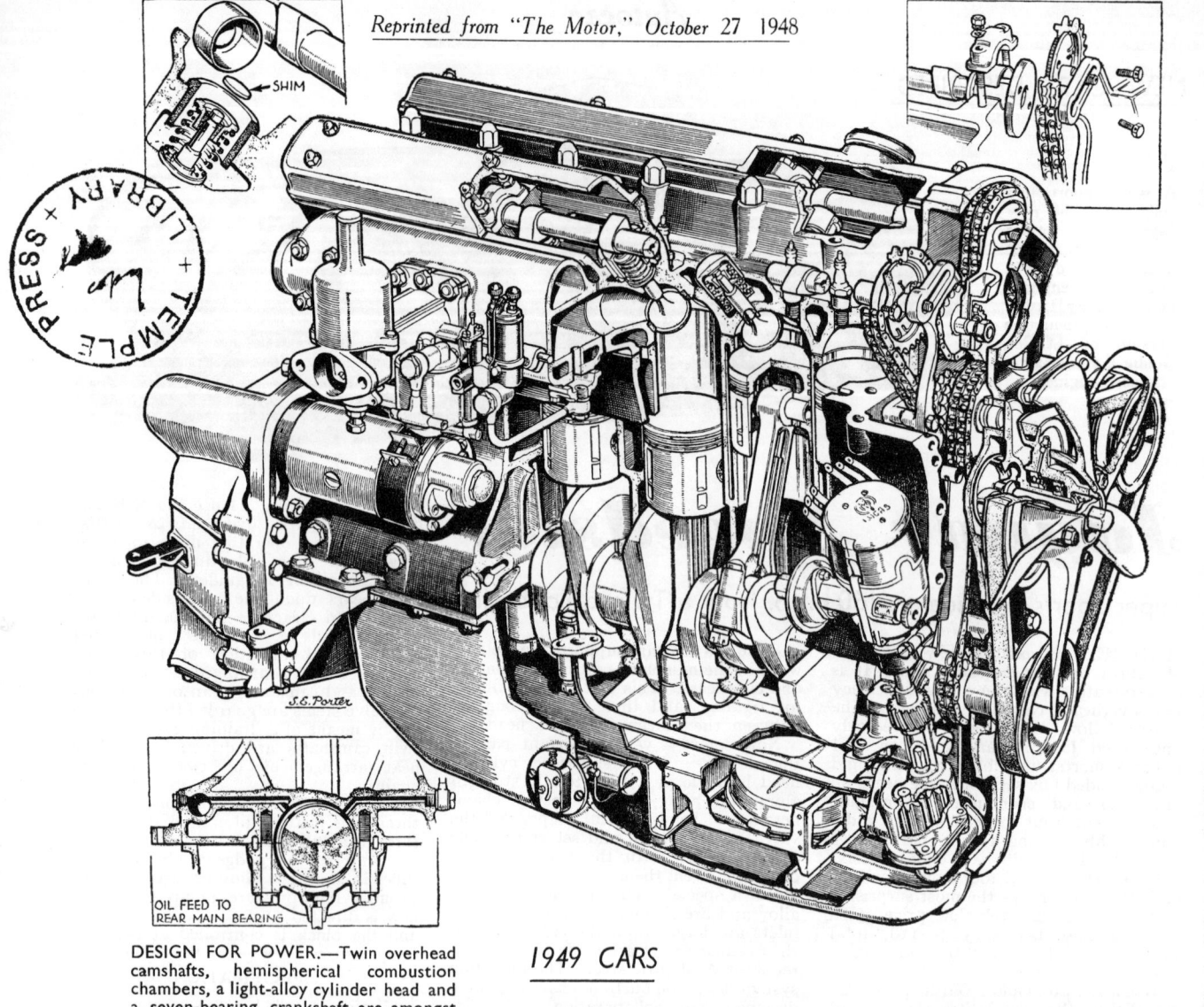

DESIGN FOR POWER.—Twin overhead camshafts, hemispherical combustion chambers, a light-alloy cylinder head and a seven-bearing crankshaft are amongst the notable features of the new 3½-litre six-cylinder Jaguar engine which develops 160 b.h.p. A four-cylinder edition of 2-litre capacity is also available.

1949 CARS

JAGUARS RE-ENTER

WHEN, scarcely a month ago, Lt.-Col. A. T. Goldie Gardner, M.C., broke various International Records in the 2-litre class at speeds ranging up to 176.649 m.p.h. and it was announced that the engine used was an unblown prototype Jaguar unit, the knowing ones wagged their heads and said that it would not be long before the Jaguar concern would supplement its range of saloons with a model to take the place of the famous Jaguar "100" of pre-war days. And when, in a speech introducing the new saloons on September 30, Mr. W. Lyons, managing director of Jaguar Cars, Ltd., made a direct reference to the intention to produce a sports car, the suspicion became a virtual certainty. What was not generally anticipated was that the new sports model would be at the Motor Show.

The engine used by Goldie Gardner was a four-cylinder twin-overhead camshaft 2-litre unit and a production edition, developing 95 b.h.p. at 5,000 r.p.m., forms one of the alternative engines fitted to the new car. The other is precisely similar in general design but is of the six-cylinder type and of 3½-litre capacity, with the exceptionally high output of 160 b.h.p. at the same speed. Apart from gear ratios, the cars are otherwise identical and both are priced at the astonishingly low basic figure of £988, which is the same as the price of the saloon.

These new models are known as the "XK 100" and "XK 120" respectively, the "XK" being the type designation of the new engine and the figures representing a close approximation to the maximum speeds of which the cars are claimed to be capable.

The chassis used is a modified and slightly abbreviated version of the new i.f.s. type employed for the recently announced saloon models and the open two-seater coachwork is thoroughly post-war and extremely attractive in a way at once satisfying to the modernists and acceptable to those of more conservative tastes.

* * *

As the two new cars are identical in general form and differ in engine specification principally in the number, bore and stroke of their cylinders, it is proposed for simplicity to devote this detailed description to the 3½-litre car and to refer readers to the data panel for information regarding the dimensions and performance factors of the 2-litre type.

To the general design of the chassis (engine, of course, excepted) it is not proposed to devote much space here, since a very comprehensive description was included in "The Motor" as recently as October 6, and

Motor Show Surprise is a Striking Two-seater Sports Car with Entirely New Twin o.h.c. Engine available in 6-cylinder 3½-litre (160 b.h.p.) and 4-cylinder 2-litre (95 b.h.p.) Form.   Price £988

the sports edition differs in little except dimensions and gear ratios. The frame has been shortened 18 ins. and narrowed proportionately to give a slight crab track as opposed to the opposite layout on the saloon edition. For comparative purposes, the wheelbase and track measurements of the two versions are appended, the saloon dimensions being given in parentheses in each case:—Wheelbase, 8 ft. 6 ins. (10 ft.); front track, 4 ft. 3 ins. (4 ft. 8 ins.); rear track, 4 ft. 2 ins. (4 ft. 9 ins.).

These changes, allied to light coachwork, should make for even better handling properties as well as effecting a very considerable saving in weight. The latter is given as 22 cwt. in dry form and this results in the exceptionally high power/weight ratio of 145 b.h.p. per ton.

110 at 5,000

Obviously, high gearing is to be expected with a power/weight ratio of this order and a top of 3.643 to 1 has been chosen, backed by a close third and second. Calculations show that peak engine speed (5,000 r.p.m.) is equivalent to 110 m.p.h., 80.5 m.p.h., 55.5 m.p.h. and 33.0 m.p.h. respectively on top, third, second and bottom (the speed on the latter being rather interesting in the light of its possibilities at traffic lights in built-up areas!). It is worth noting, however, that although the actual peak speed is 5,000 r.p.m., the power curve is almost flat at the top end, the output remaining very close to the maximum from 4,900 r.p.m. to 5,400 r.p.m.

Although the peak speed of the engine is high, special attention has been paid to obtaining a good low-speed torque and this characteristic, coupled with the unusual litres-per-ton-mile figure of 4,250 based on the dry weight, should give outstanding top-gear performance throughout the range, although, with a handy remote control gear lever and close supporting ratios, owners

he 100 m.p.h. CLASS

will have no excuse for hanging on to top when in a real hurry.

The bore/stroke ratio is 1 to 1.28, and this, in conjunction with the axle ratio used, gives the high cruising speed of just on 80 m.p.h. at 2,500 ft. per minute piston speed. Peak piston speed is 3,490 ft. per minute and the fast-revving potentialities of the engine are matched by ample evidence of the greatest care having been taken to achieve sustained reliability at high speeds, no concessions having been made to cheapness of production at the expense of this aim.

Thus, a particularly rigid crankcase is used and the crankshaft is a massive forging with main bearings bracketing each big end. The large diameter of the mains (2.75 ins.) and big-end journals (2.086 ins.) not only provides a large bearing area but also gives a considerable sectional overlap between adjacent bearings which adds considerably to the stiffness of the shaft. Counterweights are used for balance (the shaft is, of course, balanced statically and dynamically) and an interesting design detail is that, by means of large-diameter drillings sealed with suitable plugs which are frozen in position, the big-end journals are considerably lightened; the drillings (which are diagonal) serve the additional function of sludge traps.

Lubrication is, of course, on the full force-feed principle and each main receives an individual supply from the main oil gallery which runs the length of the crankcase and draws its supply direct from the gear-type pump via a Tecalemit filter. The mains have eccentric grooves machined in their housings behind the steel-backed white-metal bearing shells, thus enabling lubricant to be fed to each bearing at four points. The big ends are fed from the adjacent mains and the supply is then carried on to the little ends via copper pipes

JAGUAR DATA

Model	"XK 120" Sports	"XK 100" Sports
Engine Dimensions:		
Cylinders	6	4
Bore	83 mm.	80.5 mm.
Stroke	106 mm.	98 mm.
Cubic capacity	3,442 c.c.	1,995 c.c.
Piston area	50.4 sq. ins.	31.6 sq. ins.
Valves	Overhead (twin o.h. camshaft)	Overhead (twin o.h. camshaft)
Compression ratio	7 to 1	7 to 1
Engine Performance:		
Max. b.h.p.	160	95
at	5,000 r.p.m.	5,000 r.p.m.
Max. b.m.e.p.	140 lb./sq. in.	140 lb./sq. in.
at	2,500 r.p.m.	3,000 r.p.m.
B.h.p. per sq. in. piston area	3.175	3.01
Peak piston speed, ft. per min.	3,490	3,220
Engine Details:		
Carburetter	Two SU horizontal	Two SU horizontal
Ignition	12-volt coil	12-volt coil
Plugs: Make and type	Champion NA8	Champion NA8
Fuel pump	Two SU electric	Two SU electric
Fuel capacity	15 gallons	15 gallons
Oil filter (make, by-pass or full flow)	Tecalemit full-flow	Tecalemit full-flow
Oil capacity	3 gallons 1 pint	1 gallon 7 pints
Cooling system	Pump, fan and thermostat	Pump, fan and thermostat
Water capacity	3 gallons 1½ pints	1½ gallons
Electrical system	Lucas 12-volt c.v.c.	Lucas 12-volt c.v.c.
Battery capacity	64 amp./hrs.	64 amp./hrs.
Transmission:		
Clutch	10-in. Borg and Beck	10-in. Borg and Beck
Gear ratios:		
Top	3.643	4.09
3rd	4.98	5.59
2nd	7.23	8.1
1st	12.3	13.79
Rev.	12.3	13.79
Prop. shaft	Hardy Spicer	Hardy Spicer
Final drive	Hypoid	Hypoid
Chassis Details:		
Brakes	Girling hydraulic (2 LS on front)	Girling hydraulic (2 LS on front)
Brake drum diameter	12 ins.	12 ins.
Friction lining area	184 sq. ins.	184 sq. ins.
Suspension:		
Front	Independent (torsion bar)	Independent (torsion bar)
Rear	Semi-elliptic	Semi-elliptic
Shock absorbers	Hydraulic	Hydraulic
Wheel type	Bolt-on disc	Bolt-on disc
Tyre size	6.00 × 16 ins.	6.00 × 16 ins.
Steering gear	Burman high-efficiency	Burman high-efficiency
Steering wheel	18 ins.	18 ins.
Dimensions:		
Wheelbase	8 ft. 6 ins.	8 ft. 6 ins.
Track:		
Front	4 ft. 3 ins.	4 ft. 3 ins.
Rear	4 ft. 2 ins.	4 ft. 2 ins.
Overall length	14 ft.	14 ft.
Overall width	5 ft. 1 in.	5 ft. 1 in.
Overall height	4 ft. 2 ins.	4 ft. 2 ins.
Ground clearance	7½ ins.	7½ ins.
Turning circle	—	—
Dry weight	22 cwt.	21½ cwt.
Performance Data:		
Piston area, sq. ins. per ton	45.8	29.4
Brake lining area, sq. ins. per ton	167	171
Top gear m.p.h. per 1,000 r.p.m.	22	19.6
Top gear m.p.h. at 2,500 ft./min. piston speed	79.3	76.5
Litres per ton-mile, dry	4,250	2,840

NEW STYLING. — This three-quarter front view of the new Jaguar sports model gives a good idea of the modern frontal treatment and good aerodynamic form.

fitted into special channels formed in the connecting rods. Thus the little ends are lubricated under pressure and are not dependent on oil mist. The gudgeon pins are of the fully-floating type, retained in the Aerolite pistons by circlips, and the top rings are chromium-plated to increase bore life.

The valves are set at an angle of 70 degrees in the hemispherical combustion chambers and seat on austenitic cast-iron inserts (which have a high coefficient of expansion) in the aluminum alloy cylinder head. They are operated by twin overhead camshafts (of cast iron with chilled cams for hard wear) through the medium of piston-shaped tappets which slide in cast-iron guides and serve to take the side thrust. Dual springs are used and adjustment is by means of hardened steel biscuits of appropriate thickness under the heads of the hollow tappets.

Lubrication of each camshaft is by means of a pressure feed to the four steel-backed white-metal bearings, surplus escaping into a well which is formed in the head casting. This oil bath, into which the cams just dip, serves to lubricate the cams and tappets, drain holes being arranged to maintain the correct level.

A two-stage duplex roller chain drive is used to operate the camshafts, the primary chain (which is tensioned by a spring-blade tensioner with a fibre block adjacent to the opposite run to damp out flutter) conveys the drive to an intermediate pair of sprockets. Thence a further chain, which passes over both camshaft sprockets and an idler interposed between, completes the drive. The idler sprocket is eccentrically mounted for chain adjustment.

Service Subtleties

In order to avoid the need for disturbing the timing when the head is removed for decarbonizing, the central boss of each camshaft sprocket is provided with a threaded extension so arranged that when the sprocket is unbolted from the camshaft flange it is retained in position by a special cast bracket which is slotted to receive the boss. The thread on the latter enables the sprocket to be firmly bolted to the bracket whilst work proceeds. By this means chain removal is avoided and the chain cannot become disengaged from its sprockets.

Initially, the timing is set at the factory by means of a serrated adjustment incorporated in the composite camshaft sprockets, these consisting of an inner portion which bolts on to the camshaft flange and an outer portion which carries the teeth and fits over serrations on the inner part. The outer portion is located axially by a flange and a circlip, but there is no need to disturb this adjustment during routine maintenance.

The valve layout allows of particularly free port design, each cylinder having separate ports leading direct into the manifolds. The exhaust ports are of elongated section adjacent to the valves with the double object of providing easy flow and reducing the amount of heat transferred to the guides.

On the inlet side of the head (the design of which incorporates Weslake patents) the ports are shaped to promote gas swirl for efficient combustion and smooth slow-running characteristics and they mate with a cast light-alloy manifold to which the two horizontal S.U. carburetters are bolted direct, an interesting point being that the manifold is water-jacketed throughout its length; owing to the use of a thermostat, normal running temperature is rapidly attained after a cold start and remains more constant than is the case with the more usual exhaust-heated hot-spot arrangement.

Cooling and Lubrication

A centrifugal pump and five-blade cast-aluminium fan are incorporated in the cooling system and water from the radiator is fed to a special internally cast duct in the exhaust side of the block, whence it passes upwards to the head, where special care has been taken to provide ample water spaces round the exhaust valves; the flow is then across the head to the inlet side and, via the inlet manifold jacket, back to the radiator. Static water is employed in the cylinder jackets (which are continuous round each bore).

Some details of the lubrication system have already been given and it remains only to mention that special provision is made for ensuring a copious supply of lubricant to the timing chains, that filtering precautions include the use of a float-type pick-up to ensure sludge-free oil as well as the use of a full-flow Tecalemit filter bolted to the off-side of the crankcase, and that the aluminium alloy sump is ribbed internally as well as externally for cooling purposes. A refinement which will be appreciated is the fitting of an electric level gauge connected to a dial on the facia board.

This item gives a key to the equipment, which is on the usual lavish Jaguar scale. The facia is dominated by a large-dial 120-m.p.h. speedometer and a matching rev. counter, and other instruments include petrol and oil gauges, ammeter, thermometer and clock. A detail item of note is an electrically operated reserve tap with a warning light to remind the driver when the car is running on the reserve supply.

The body, which is aluminium panelled on a laminated ash frame, is intended solely as a two-seater with ample space in the extended tail for luggage appropriate to Continental touring. Access to this space is via a top-hinged rear panel which also discloses a spare wheel compartment below the luggage floor.

Of the styling of the car, nothing need be said here, since the photograph tells its own attractive tale, but it is worth drawing attention to the head lamps, which are of larger size than is frequently the case when these items are built-in. The hood is arranged to disappear into an aperture between the seat squab and the tail, where it is concealed by a neat fabric cover.

Altogether, the Jaguar "XK 120" is quite one of the most interesting new models to be seen at the Show and one which (with the "XK 100") is a very fitting successor to previous sports models of this marque.

★ New Jaguar Achieves Over 132 m.p.h. Using Normal Fuel and Equipment

JAGUAR TEAM.—W. H. Hassan, Development Engineer (left) and W. M. Heynes, Director and Chief Engineer, chat with driver R. M. V. Sutton, seated in the car which achieved the remarkable speeds given below. For the fastest runs a metal wind deflector, supplied as standard, replaced the glass windscreen.

JAGUAR DEMONSTRATION

THE TIMED RUNS

Distance	Hood and Screen	1st Run (m.p.h.)	2nd Run (m.p.h.)	Mean speed (m.p.h.)
Flying mile	Up	125.698	127.098	126.448
Flying mile	Down	131.916	133.283	132.596
Mile (Standing start)	—	—	—	86.434
Kilometre (Standing start)	—	—	—	74.168

DRIVING a standard unsupercharged XK 120 Jaguar sports two-seater on Monday last, R. M. V. Sutton covered a flying mile of the Jabbeke motor road just outside Ostend at a mean speed of 132.596 m.p.h. The runs were made under the auspices of the Belgian Automobile Club who were responsible both for measuring the course and for the actual timing.

The object of these runs was two-fold. In the first place, claims for ultra-high maximum speeds are always treated with some degree of suspicion in view of the common vagaries of speedometers and the virtual impossibility of accurate tests of maximum speeds in excess of 100 m.p.h. in this country

In the second, a Continental road test of another marque carried out by "The Motor" in 1946 led to some controversy, as a result of which the manufacturer concerned arranged an observed test on the Jabbeke motor road with the object of obtaining independent confirmation, backed by the official time-keeping of the Belgian Automobile Club. As readers will remember, the figures obtained (which included a mean speed of 110.8 m.p.h. over the mile) more than substantiated the road-test results obtained by this journal.

At the time (July, 1947), this 110.8 m.p.h. represented the highest officially timed speed put up by any current standard production car and the performance established what has come to be regarded as the Blue Riband of the sports-car world. Last Monday's Jaguar demonstration (which was witnessed by a party of Press representatives) was aimed at capturing that honour.

The use of the Jabbeke motor road was peculiarly appropriate, since part of the development of the XK 120 engine may be regarded as having taken place on this road, when Lt.-Col. A. T. Goldie Gardner, M.C., broke various International Class E (2-litre) records last September, using a prototype of the four-cylinder, 2-litre power unit now employed for the XK 100 Jaguar.

The XK 120 engine is of basically similar design but of six-cylinder type with a bore and stroke of 83 mm. and 106 mm. (3,442 c.c.). Twin o.h. camshafts are used and, on a compression ratio of 7 to 1, the power output is 160 b.h.p., giving a power/weight ratio (dry) of 145 b.h.p. per ton.

The car was running in standard form with the higher of the two optional axle ratios—unsupercharged, of course. The ratio used was 3.27 to 1 which gave maximum revs. on the fastest of the runs of 5,200 r.p.m. in top gear. The weight of the car is 22 cwt. and normal Dunlop tyres were used, whilst the fuel was Shell put in the car from a pump the previous day under the observation of the Royal Belgian Automobile Club. It was the normal Belgian standard grade of approximately 74 octane.

After a bright early morning the sky clouded over shortly before the runs were due to start. Some rain fell on the Ostend section of the "run-in" to the timed stretches but fortunately the latter remained dry. This wet on the course was, however, responsible for considerable wheelspin on the initial run with the car open and the first run of 129.817 m.p.h. was repeated when a speed of 131.916 m.p.h. was recorded, thus giving the remarkable mean of 132.596.

A large number of local spectators turned out to watch the run and a loudspeaker van kept spectators informed of the proceedings in both French and English. A very notable feature of the car was its absolute steadiness at maximum speed and also its quietness. Mr. W. Lyons, the Jaguar Chief, flew over to witness the run, accompanied by Mr. W. M. Heynes, the Chief Engineer.

After the timed runs were over, Sutton demonstrated the flexibility of the car by driving past the spectators at a speed of approximately 10 m.p.h. in top gear.

The Jaguar was running throughout with a detachable undershield which can be obtained from the factory as part of the car's equipment. With the hood down the windscreen was replaced by a Uni-screen, which is a small metal deflector provided by Jaguar as standard equipment for competition purposes.

The ivory Jaguar flashes past the spectators' cars as it starts a run over the measured mile.

JAGUAR 120 DOES 132½ m.p.h.

FASTEST EVER BY A FULLY EQUIPPED CATALOGUE MODEL

ON Monday morning one track of the famous Jabbeke-Aeltre motor road in Belgium was closed to traffic and one of the first production batch of the new 3½-litre Jaguar super sports two-seaters was taken out by R. M. V. Sutton, the company's chief test driver, for a series of runs timed by the R.A.C. of Belgium. Representatives of the Continental Press were there and a party of British journalists had been flown out from England.

With the hood down and the standard competition screen in position, the car achieved a mean speed of 132.596 m.p.h. over the flying mile, with a best run of 133.283 m.p.h. By this bold demonstration of faith in the product, Jaguars have established their car as the world's fastest unsupercharged catalogue model with full touring bodywork. Indeed, it is very doubtful whether any standard model in catalogue condition, even with the aid of a supercharger, has ever recorded such speeds over a measured distance.

Conditions at the middle of the long straight were perfect, with still air, bright sunshine and some humidity from early morning showers, which had fortunately failed to wet the timed stretches. Wheelspin was experienced on the getaway at one end of the course, however, owing to a local but very heavy shower which had wetted a portion of the track, and these runs were subsequently repeated with an appreciable improvement in speed.

The car ran first in full touring trim with hood and side-screens erected, and using the undershield now available. With a low hum from the exhaust which gave little indication of the power from the 3½-litre engine, it flashed over the measured mile in 28.64 sec, returning in 28.29 sec, giving a mean speed of 126.448 m.p.h.

The hood and side-screens were then taken down and the large V windscreen was replaced by the small competition screen included in the standard equipment. With the tonneau cover in place the car then streaked over the mile in 27.01 sec, equal to 133.23 m.p.h. The highest speed recorded during the morning was on its outward run over the kilometre in 16.77 sec, which gave 133.388 m.p.h. The returning runs were only slightly slower.

Sutton then did a series of standing-start runs over the kilometre and mile, the best times recorded being 29.91 sec and 41.50 sec respectively. Immediately after the conclusion of the runs the extraordinary top gear flexibility of the car was demonstrated, and it was then turned over to the Press representatives who were able to drive it and assure themselves of its tractability and excellent road manners.

These runs will rank as Belgian sports car records, subject to confirmation, and when the car returned to Ostend the cylinder head was removed so that the Belgian authorities could satisfy themselves that the engine was, in fact, the 3½-litre, twin-camshaft, six-cylinder unit with 7 to 1 compression ratio, as described in the catalogue. It was run on Shell fuel of 74-octane and Shell X100 motor oil bought from a public garage the day before, and after the run the seals on fuel and oil fillers were broken and samples taken to provide confirmation.

Before the British party returned to England there was a civic reception and a luncheon at Ostend where Mr. "Bill" Lyons, managing director of Jaguar Cars, Ltd., revealed that the engine of the new Jaguar was originally conceived by chief engineer Heynes and his team at fire-watching sessions during the war.

The low price of the Jaguar 120 created a sensation when it was announced. Now the performance figures win it new headlines. In England the car costs £988 plus £275 3s 11d tax. Most of them will go abroad, but a few will be delivered in England this year.

JAGUAR 120 SPEEDS

Touring trim with hood and side-screens erected.

	m.p.h.
Flying kilometre: Mean time 17.67 sec,	126.594
Flying mile: Mean time 28.47 sec,	126.448

With hood stowed and competition screen fitted.

	m.p.h.
Flying kilometre: Mean time 16.90 sec,	132.362
Flying mile: Mean time 27.15 sec,	132.596
Standing kilometre: Mean time 30.16 sec,	74.168
Standing mile: Mean time 41.65 sec,	86.434

MY FAVORITE SPORTS CAR...

NO. 3 OF A SERIES

by Clark Gable

I'm generally a man of few words (especially written words) but when requested that I say something about my new Jaguar XK-120 I must confess I felt like trying to outdo Webster. To call the XK "My Favorite Sports Car" is putting it mildly.

I've always been a bug on cars, especially fast ones. From Duesenbergs to and thru souped-up popular makes, I've owned and/or driven most of them. Many were fast but hard to handle on the turns; some lacked the acceleration that one feels should accompany speed; others were uncomfortable, uneasy, cumbersome, or otherwise undesirable from one standpoint or another. The XK has, so far as I've encountered, none of these drawbacks.

When the 120 was first announced, I was driving a Mark IV Jaguar so I already knew what the name implied. The general appearance and specifications of the car were enough to make me want it like a child wants candy. I wasn't alone in wanting an XK-120, but I was fortunate to be among the early birds in becoming an owner.

As this was shortly after the car had set a world record of over 132 miles per hour for stock production cars, I lost no time in seeing just what mine, which I KNEW was strictly stock, would do. So, I decided to try a clocked run at one of the dry lakes here in Southern California. To

make a long story short, we went through the measured mile course at (the studio will probably cut this out) 124 mph (*the studio didn't—ed.*). Though the run was timed only by stop watch, it satisfied me.

There were no fancy extras, no specials, no preparatory tuning for this run, so I can't go into any of the technological aspects of special cams, manifolds, carburetors, gear ratios, and the like, but I can and will describe what, to my way of thinking, is a masterpiece of design and construction for a production car. The engine is a twin overhead camshaft six-cylinder Jaguar engine of 3442 cc (210 cu. in.) displacement having a bore of 3¼" and a stroke of 4-3/32 inches. The block is of high grade cast iron, the head—aluminum alloy with spherical combustion chambers. Pistons are aluminum with steel connecting rods coupled to a seven main bearing crankshaft. She puts out 160 HP at 5000 RPM on the tach (and will turn 5300 in a pinch) and is vibrationless and noiseless at all speeds. So much for the unit that makes the XK move the way it does.

I can say, without reservation, that the car is the easiest handling vehicle I have maneuvered at any speed or condition. There isn't the slightest feeling of exceptionally high speed one generally has in smaller automobiles—in fact, for a sense of security at high speed I prefer the Jag regardless of size. As for maneuverability, I'll stack the cornering abilities of the XK against anything I've ever driven. I have put her into as many types and kinds of slides as I know without once having the fear or uneasiness I generally have about whether I'm going to come out in one piece or not. Such characteristics can only mean to me that the car is superbly designed as to steering geometry, weight distribution, braking power, suspension (which is torsion bar on the front and semi elliptic leaf on the rear), and chassis rigidity.

Of course, many of you will say that there can't be "a real live dream car"— one that has absolutely no faults or undesirable qualities—and you'll be right. Some of the things I don't particularly like are the 12 volt system, the non-American screw thread system with its odd size nut and bolt heads, and the lack of a provision for cool air in the cockpit. But to get the thrill of real sport motoring a fellow has to make some sacrifices and if these minor items are all that are required in my case I'll gladly make room for them—until some American manufacturer can give me the same performance, comfort, and price.

ENTHUSIASTS attending the Automobile Show at Earls Court, London, England, late in 1948, were unanimous in their acclaim of an entirely new entry in the sports car field. Combining meticulous mechanical design with a well balanced graceful appearance, the XK-120 Super-Sport Jaguar is the outstanding achievement of a distinguished marque.

Outstanding qualities of acceleration and maximum speed are combined with many things appreciated in a really high performance car. The seats afford a degree of comfort close to luxury. The flexible suspension allows a soft, though controlled, ride with the utmost stability and control while cornering. It is of special credit to the Jaguar that the brakes will bring the car to a stop from speeds above 100 mph. Designed from the ground up for maximum performance and efficiency, nothing has been overlooked, and no compromises have been made that would affect the performance of this remarkable new car.

In this new design the first feature to consider is the frame, because upon it, to a great degree, depends the road performance of the car in regards to stability and good steering. This frame is the result of careful designing and is one of the most rigid to be used. It consists of box-section side members, which are straight in both planes, eliminating torsional deflection from direct bending loads. These side members reach their maximum cross-section in the area just forward of the cowl. Forward of the rear axle a decided kick-up is apparent, allowing ample room for axle movement incidental to a flexible suspension, and which also provides a low level for the floor. The front crossmember is a straight, heavy box-section in the same plane as the side members, providing the utmost rigidity and ensuring a solid mounting for the front suspension units. Frame twist or corner-to-corner stiffness is obtained by a central cruciform member. The entire unit is assembled by electric arc welding.

The independent front suspension, while along conventional lines, is of particular interest. The principle used is of unequal length lateral wishbones, and longitudinal torsion bars. The lower wishbone consists of a large "I" beam section, which carries the load from the wheel to the torsion bar. The latter is attached at the fulcrum point below the frame. A tubular strut, running from the outer end of the "I" beam diagonally forward to an attach point beneath the front crossmember, completes the lower wishbone and relieves the beam from the fore-and-aft loading caused by braking. The upper wishbone is anchored to a bracket above and outboard of the frame. The outer ends of the wishbones are ball sockets, which carry the swiveling assembly. This serves a dual purpose in completing the suspension link and steering movement.

This effective construction provides against lateral movement of the wheel since a single, instead of a double, joint forms the side of the steering parallelogram. The ball pins are hard chrome plated and the seats are a special graphite bronze. This combination is able to withstand hard usage and retain a low coefficient of friction. The ball sockets are self adjusting to compensate for wear. The torsion bars are made of silico manganese spring steel, splined at both ends, and are proportioned to ensure that stresses are low. The torsion bar mounting is free of any bending loads set up by braking, the rear mount containing an adjustable stop.

This suspension design provides a soft ride; however,

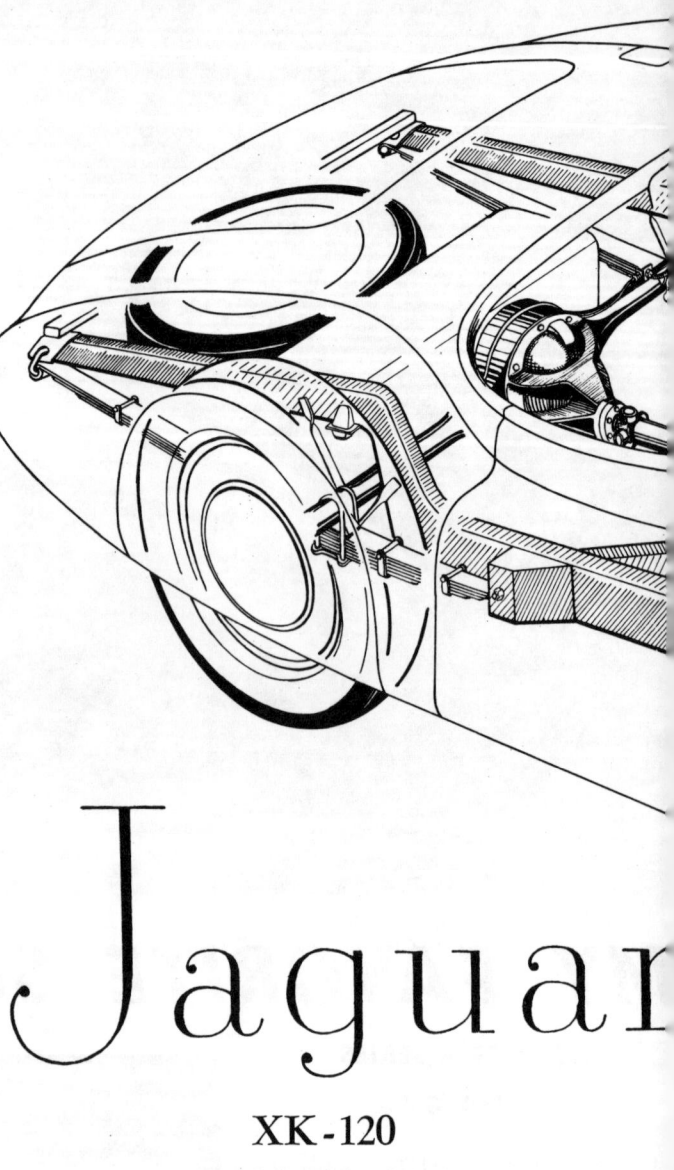

Jaguar
XK-120
SPORTS CAR
by Robert N. Hoeppner

it retains the road-holding and cornering stability characteristic of previous Jaguar cars. Girling telescopic hydraulic shock absorbers are used to obtain the necessary damping. They are mounted in a manner becoming ever more popular, angular, in which the bottom is attached far out on the "I" beam of the lower wishbone, and the top to a bracket incorporated in the upper wishbone mount. This method of shock mounting, in conjunction with the torsion bar stabilizer, reduces to a great extent side sway or roll.

Burman circulating ball-type steering is used, giving a positive but light control with three turns from lock to lock. The gear box is so mounted that the pitman arm movement corresponds to an idler lever on the opposite side of the frame. Connecting these levers and the steering arms of the wheel spindles are three links forming an articulated tie-rod, in which the outer links coincide geometrically with the suspension wishbones.

Designed to offer minimum air resistance, the body is

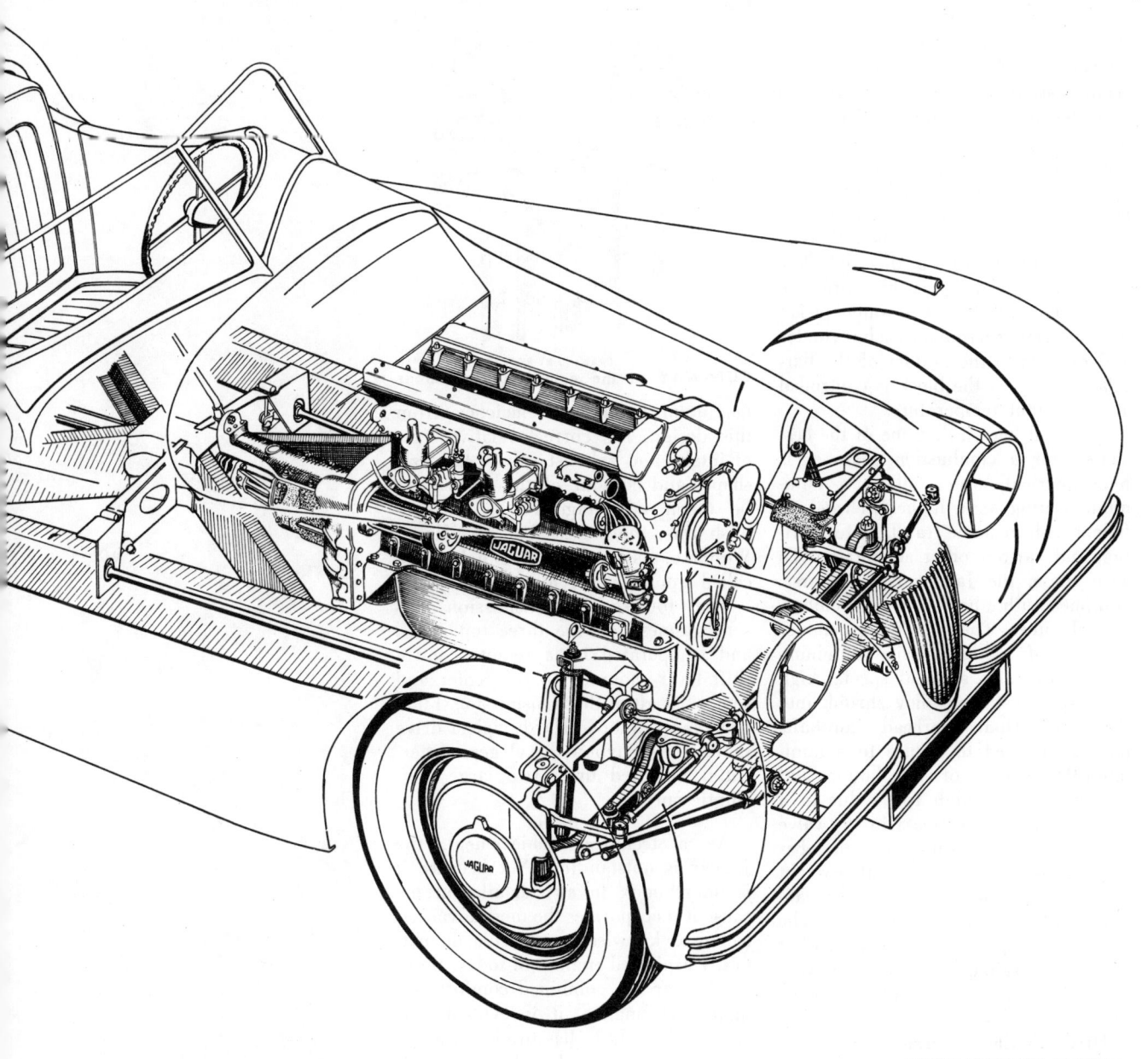

DRAWING BY ROBERT N. HOEPPNER

thoroughly streamlined, and its low build is immediately noticed. The absence of excessive chrome trim adds to the beauty, as this well-balanced and correctly proportioned design needs no excess adornment. The body is constructed of aluminum paneling over a stressed framework. The wide doors are carried on concealed front hinges, with door handles being installed in the interior only. The cockpit contains ample room and the ultimate in comfort for a sports design. Seats are of generous size and are independently adjustable for leg room. In combination with an adjustable telescopic mount for the steering wheel, the ideal driving position is readily available. The interior of the body, doors, side panels, and seats are upholstered in two shades of leather, beige and dark brown. The instrument panel and dashboard are similarly covered. Instrumentation and minor controls are grouped in a central panel, containing a large tachometer and speedometer to the right and left sides with the ammeter, oil pressure, water temperature, fuel gauge and clock located in the middle.

The heart of this new Jaguar is an exceptionally well-engineered design. Upon opening the hood you are greeted by highly polished aluminum overhead camshaft covers, the enameled triple branch exhaust manifold to the left, and the twin S.U. carburetors and fuel pumps on the right. The engine has everything that experience has found necessary to render high performance with reliability and be able to withstand prolonged periods of full power output.

The bore-stroke ratio of 1.27 gives a piston speed of 3,750 ft. per minute at maximum bhp or 5400 rpm. The counterbalanced crankshaft is of generous size, having journals of 2¾ inches diameter. It has maximum rigidity due to the overlap of the crank pins in the webs. Seven large main bearings, well backed by numerous internal webs, support the crankshaft. Assuring a long, trouble-free life for the engine, the lubrication system is more than adequate to care for prolonged full power output. The oil pump is a large gear-type that supplies a generous volume of oil

Jaguar XK-120 Sports Car

through oversize galleries and lines to all bearings. The balance of the main reciprocating parts are of interest, in that the aerolite aluminum alloy pistons have chromium-plated top rings that will increase the life of the cylinder bores. Connecting rods vary from the usual in that they are also of a light alloy. Engine cooling is well taken care of, incorporating directed flow across the head by a high-pressure pump. The block has a water jacket that entirely surrounds each cylinder and extends to the bottom of the barrels. Cooling of the block is controlled at a constant temperature.

It is well known that one of the best shapes for a combustion chamber is hemispherical, which allows a minimum heating area, higher thermal efficiency, short flame travel, better porting, and various other advantages. To gain these, the Jaguar is, of course, equipped with a hemispherical combustion chamber. The detachable cylinder head is of a high tensile aluminum alloy with valve seats of special high expansion cast iron alloy shrunk into the head. Dual overhead camshafts have been used to reduce to a minimum the problem of valve bounce and spring surge at high rpm's due to a heavy reciprocating mass in the valve operating mechanism. The cam lobes operate directly upon featherweight piston-type tappets installed in a manner similar to the Offenhauser. The cams and tappets operate in oil baths; however, drainage galleries prevent valve stems from receiving an excess of oil.

Drive to the overhead cams is by means of a two-stage, duplex roller chain, providing a simple, reliable, and quiet method of operation. To obtain

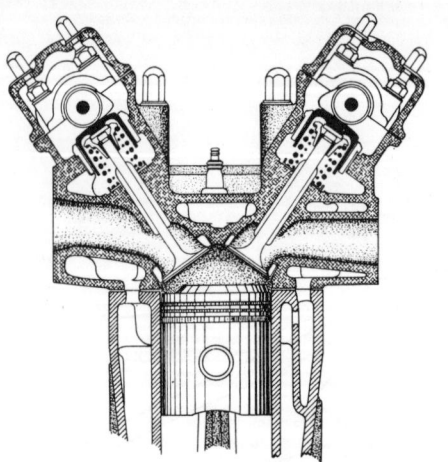

DRAWING BY ROBERT N. HOEPPNER
CUTAWAY of the combustion chamber

maximum volumetric efficiency from this design, the correct relative sizes of intake and exhaust valves, the size, shape, and contour of the ports must be taken advantage of. To accomplish this, the services of Mr. Harry Westlake, a specialist in this field, were called upon, with remarkable success.

The four-speed transmission has synchro-mesh on the three top gears, and is operated by a remote control shift lever mounted in the center and somewhat aft of the transmission. Final drive is by an open Hardy Spicer drive shaft, and a hypoid bevel gear differential mounted upon two large half-elliptic springs.

Conclusion

As a technical achievement, the Jaguar is outstanding. Not because it is unorthodox in any detail, but because it incorporates the most advanced technical knowledge available on naturally aspirated engines of today. Since the Jaguar has combined comfort and high performance, it is evident that Jaguar Cars, Ltd., has produced a car that will be honored and admired by motoring enthusiasts for many years to come.

The Autocar ROAD TESTS

DATA FOR THE DRIVER

JAGUAR XK120

PRICE, with sports two-seater body, £988, plus £275 3s 11d British purchase tax. Total (in Great Britain), £1,263 3s 11d.

ENGINE: 25.6 h.p., (R.A.C. rating), 6 cylinders, overhead valves, (twin overhead camshafts), 83 × 106 mm, 3,442 c.c. Brake Horse-power: 160 at 5,100 r.p.m. Compression Ratio: 8 to 1 (7 to 1 alternative). Max. Torque: 195 lb ft at 2,500 r.p.m. 22 m.p.h. per 1,000 r.p.m. on top gear.

WEIGHT: 26 cwt 0 qr 7 lb (2,919 lb). LB. per C.C.: 0.85. B.H.P. per Ton: 122.78.

TYRE SIZE: 6.00 × 16in (Dunlop Road Speed) on bolt-on steel disc wheels.

TANK CAPACITY: 15 English gallons. Approximate fuel consumption range, 13–17 m.p.g. (21.7–16.6 litres per 100 km.).

TURNING CIRCLE: 31ft 0in (L and R). Steering wheel movement from lock to lock: 2$\frac{6}{10}$ turns. LIGHTING SET: 12-volt.

MAIN DIMENSIONS: Wheelbase, 8ft 6in. Track, 4ft 3in (front); 4ft 2in (rear). Overall length, 14ft 5in; width, 5ft 1½in; height, 4ft 4½in. Minimum Ground Clearance: 7⅛in.

ACCELERATION

Overall gear ratios	From steady m.p.h. of		
	10–30 sec	20–40 sec	30–50 sec
3.64 to 1	7.8	7.5	7.8
4.98 to 1	5.6	5.4	5.9
7.22 to 1	4.0	4.1	4.4
12.29 to 1	2.9	—	—

From rest through gears to:—

	sec		sec
30 m.p.h.	4.0	80 m.p.h.	19.0
50 m.p.h.	8.3	90 m.p.h.	25.9
60 m.p.h.	12.0	100 m.p.h.	35.3
70 m.p.h.	15.5		

SPEEDS ON GEARS:

(by Electric Speedometer)	M.p.h. (normal and max)	K.p.h. (normal and max)
1st	28—34	45.1—54.7
2nd	54—60	86.9—96.6
3rd	76—90	122.3—144.8
Top	115 (Maximum within distance available)	185.1 (Maximum within distance available)

Speedometer correction by Electric Speedometer:—

Car Speedometer	Electric Speedometer m.p.h.
10	9.0
20	20.0
30	30.0
40	39.5
50	48.5
60	58.0
70	68.0
80	78.0
90	87.0
100	96.0

WEATHER: Dry, mild; wind light to negligible.

Acceleration figures are the means of several runs in opposite directions.

Described in "The Autocar" of September 2, 1949, and December 17, 1948.

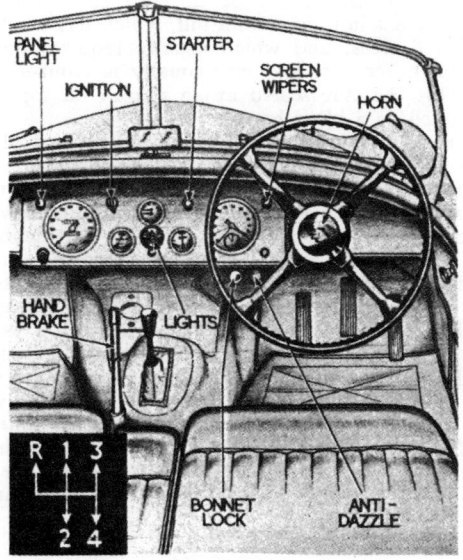

The flush-sided body is as clean as it could possibly be in keeping with the requirements imposed by the practical considerations so evidently studied by the makers. Note the air entry vents low at the front.

No. 1403 . . . . . 3½-LITRE XK120 JAGUAR SUPER SPORTS

"NO, it's not a racing car," was an answer that had to be given several times to small boy admirers of the Jaguar XK120 while it was with *The Autocar* for Road Test. Perhaps there are others who do not appreciate that this stupendous car of the sleek appearance is primarily a very fast, tractable touring car and not "a racer," even though examples of the model have appeared with great success in sports car events, notably the Production Car Race at Silverstone last August.

Fresh in mind, too, will be that remarkable performance on the Belgian motor road in 1949, when one of these cars, running with an undershield, which is optional equipment, and fitted with a racing type windscreen, which, again, is available, achieved 132.6 m.p.h. over a flying mile and 126 m.p.h. with normal windscreen and hood and side screens erected, thus making the XK120 indisputably the fastest series production car in the world. Owing to the virtual impossibility of attaining such speeds in England at present, ultimate possibilities as regards maximum speed have been taken as read, in view of that officially certificated performance, which was witnessed by a member of the technical staff of this journal; but readings up to 117 have been seen on this present occasion on a speedometer only 4 per cent fast at an indicated 100.

In trying to convey in a word-picture the supreme position which the XK120 two-seater occupies, there is a temptation to draw from the motoring vocabulary every adjective in the superlative concerning the performance, and to call upon the devices of italics and even the capital letter!

It has a power-to-weight ratio which gives it the heels of any car produced in series; better than 122 b.h.p. per ton is an extraordinary figure for a production car. There is the astonishing fact to keep in mind that it is listed at the same home market price as the 3½-litre Jaguar saloon, though unfortunately the home enthusiast is all but barred from buying the XK at present. Whilst a full 100 m.p.h. can be treated as a timed acceleration test, and only sufficient breathing space is needed to see 110, 115 m.p.h., and more, on the regular production car as now issuing from the Coventry factory in some numbers, it is also remarkably docile and capable of being driven on top gear at 10 m.p.h.

Nothing like the XK120, and at its price, has been previously achieved—a car of tremendous performance and yet displaying the flexibility, and even the silkiness and smoothness of a mild-mannered saloon.

The heart of this astonishing versatility is a 3½-litre six-cylinder twin overhead camshaft engine that develops 160

This partly overhead view gives a fine impression of the classically simple flowing lines of the XK120. A detachable tonneau cover is supplied, to cover either both seats or the passenger seat alone. The strip running round the top of the doors and above the facia is softly padded under a leather exterior.

ROAD TESTS ... continued

b.h.p. at 5,100 r.p.m. with astonishing smoothness, and maintains that figure on a flat peak of the power curve towards the 6,000 r.p.m. mark. This power unit is a British achievement in which everyone in this country interested in cars of high performance may well take pride. Indeed the XK is a prestige gainer for Britain's engineering as a whole and car engineering in particular. During a test of some 700 miles, at the beginning of which it was brand new and by no means run-in, it necessarily received some merciless treatment, but showed no sign of losing tune, used very little oil and did not at any time record above 80 deg C water temperature.

More than usually, study can be commended of the performance figures in the accompanying data panel. These show an ability to reach very high speed in phenomenally short spaces of time (notably from rest through the gears to a genuine 100 m.p.h. in not much more than half a minute—33.5 sec was the best recording), and also top gear acceleration, even from speeds as low as 10 and 20 m.p.h., of an order associated with the best of biggest engined saloons designed for top gear performance. Yet the XK-120 runs on a top gear ratio as high as 3.64 to 1; 3.27 to 1 is available optionally.

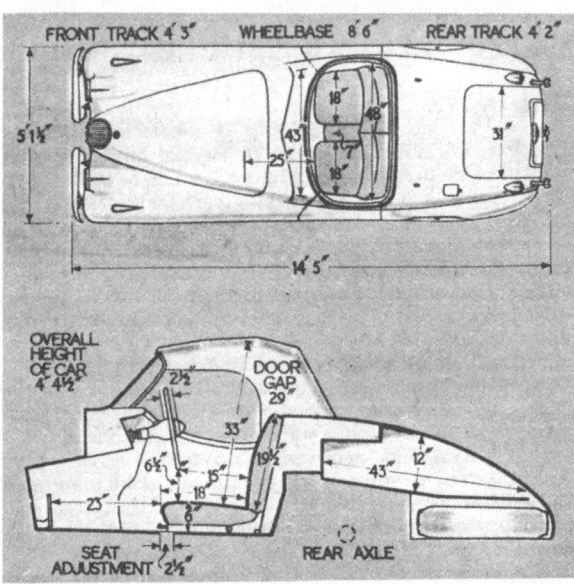

Measurements in these scale body diagrams are taken with the driving seat in the central position of fore and aft adjustment and with the seat cushions uncompressed.

The practical nature of the XK120 is again underlined by the useful size of the luggage compartment, unobstructed by the spare wheel, which is carried below. The light in the lid operates when the side lamps are on. The fuel filler is a quick-action flap embodied in a panel to the left of the luggage locker opening and is locked by a key.

Dual Character

Truly this is two cars in one. It can be handled quietly with very little use of the gears if the driver is in a lazy mood. Press the right foot hard down, however, and a different car is revealed. A snarl comes into the exhaust note, though never excessive noise, and on a familiar road the bends and even the landmarks seem to have been redesigned overnight, and placed much closer together than had previously been realized!

Still further illustration of the top gear powers was provided on a 1 in 9-maximum hill, which has one bend of nearly 90 degrees, and which usually requires third and second on other cars and occasionally is climbed on top gear. This the XK scaled at 40 m.p.h. on top until it was baulked on a blind bend.

The usual 1 in 6¼ hill of these tests became almost a Shelsley Walsh affair—after dark, for the sake of the greater safety factor implied with head lights in use. Probably with rushing tactics even this gradient could have been scaled on top gear, certainly fast on third, but deliberately second was used to give maximum performance on a hill which is far from straight. The extraordinary rate of 58 m.p.h. by corrected reading was reached on this quite severe hill, where to climb at even 35-40 m.p.h. is exceptional. The driver concerned at this stage, familiar with this hill over the past twenty years in most of the world's makes and models, feels that he will need to live long before he improves on that performance, or, indeed, on most of the recordings put up by the XK during this test.

Even town traffic is a pleasure in it, because the driver can nip in and out swiftly without ever becoming a nuisance

to others because of noise. Minutes can be clipped off customary times even for short journeys, whilst on longer runs the average speed is limited only by the enterprise of the driver and the traffic encountered. The cruising speed is as fast as you can drive it. Given the right conditions, the average speed of a lifetime could obviously be achieved —and the driver rest on his laurels for evermore.

The control is exactly as one would wish with such a car—firm but light steering, highish geared, with sufficient caster action, allowing of a quick swerve with complete safety; and suspension which ties the car down and yet is thoroughly comfortable. It is well damped by telescopic hydraulic shock absorbers for the torsion bar independent front suspension, and big hydraulic dampers for the half-elliptics at the rear. With normal tyre pressures of 25 lb per sq in the riding is in every way comparable with that of the best independently sprung cars of today.

Yet the XK can be hurled round bends with quickly increasing confidence, and, as was particularly shown by a few fast laps of an unofficial circuit on a disused airfield, extremely fast cornering is achieved with no more than tyre scream and the body leaning over so far but no farther, so to speak, in a way which does not cramp the driver's style. For the high-speed part of the test the Dunlop Road Speed tyres were inflated to 35 lb per sq in, as recommended for sustained faster work. The riding is then harder, as would be expected, but still is not harsh.

Brakes and Gear Change

The Lockheed hydraulically operated brakes are given a tough task on such a car, but with the special linings used on this model they did not fade and at all times the driver felt that the speed was under control, whilst the brakes could be used hard with safety at high speed. The central gear change is by a short, rigid lever which is placed rather too far back to be ideal at a close driving position, though the movements are pleasing. The synchromesh for second, third and top does not intrude. Very fast downward changing is achieved without beating the synchromesh, by employing the old double-declutching technique, or more leisurely changing is made smoothly and quietly, taking full advantage of the synchromesh. Third gear is silent and can be used with tremendous effect for alternate deceleration and acceleration on a winding road.

The car that has been handled in succession by *The Autocar's* "high-speed flight," each member of which has unstinted praise for the performance, represented the first of the production examples with a steel body. Experience

Not the most flattering portrait of the Jaguar, but one which emphasizes that it is designed as a car for normal use, and has serviceable, stoutly made all-weather equipment, which is not difcult to put up and down. The hood is attached to the windscreen frame by over-centre clip fixings. The rear wheel spats are easy to remove and replace, there being no awkward clip fixings to deal with.

has been had also of one of the earlier aluminium-bodied cars that ran at Silverstone last year, the bulk of the present testing being carried out on the production car. Independent weighing showed, contrary to expectation, the steel-bodied car to be some 40 lb *lighter* than the early example, in the running trim as tested.

This production car had left-hand drive as for the U.S.A. and elsewhere, and the high compression ratio of 8 to 1 intended for high octane fuel available in some countries. Part of the test, including recording the performance figures, was carried out on 80-octane petrol, as available to the factory for test work. On 80-octane there was practically no pinking, and then only at low speed, and even on normal Pool petrol (approximately 70-octane) the pinking was not violent and running on did not occur.

A first-press start from cold was obtained on every occasion, and without sign of temperament or need for warming up, as used to be expected of a really high-performance engine.

So much needs to be said of this car of cars on the road that little detail can be given regarding the bodywork and equipment. Elbow room is adequate, and the separately adjustable front seats, upholstered in fine-quality leather, give suitably upright positions and good support to the shoulders. Driving vision is good, with a very satisfactory view of both wings, although a short to medium-height driver would prefer the top of the telescopically adjustable steering wheel to be lower.

The mirror view is good. There is useful luggage space and good provision for carrying oddments is made in wide pockets in the thickness of the doors. The head lamp beam is useful up to, say, 90 m.p.h. on known roads.

Control department of the left-hand drive export-specification car that has been tested by "The Autocar." The hand brake lever is of the fly-off type, very convenient and practical. The rev counter (on the left) reads to 6,000 r.p.m. and the speedometer to 140 m.p.h. Oil pressure and water temperature are combined in the central upper dial. The instrument board is leather covered. Pressure on the lower black knob on the right gives an indication of engine oil level. The door catches are operated by leather pulls and the doors can be locked from inside, which is unusual in an open car.

Glimpse of the twin overhead camshaft six-cylinder engine which provides so remarkable a performance. The twin S.U. carburettors are without air cleaners. The supporting strut could be easier than it is to reach after the bonnet has been opened by freeing the safety catch low down at the front. The sparking plugs are perfectly accessible, mounted vertically in the well between the two 70-degree camshaft covers. The oil filler is thoroughly well placed in the left camshaft cover, and against the left bonnet side is seen the reservoir for the hydraulic brake system fluid.

The World's Fastest Sports Car—Jaguar

By STANLEY GARDNER

THERE is little evidence to discount the Coventry, England, Jaguar Cars, Ltd's. claim that they produce, in the XK 120, the world's fastest sports car.

In fact, this company can rightfully claim the title to practically every classification to which automobiles are regulated.

It seems that the Jaguar people had three goals to reach, in their post war car. Speed, eye appeal and pocketbook. The speed is now a matter of official record. Eye appeal is a matter of personal taste, but judging from the "ohs" and "ahs," at the various auto shows wherein the "Jag," as it is popularly known, has been shown, that objective has not only been reached, but surpassed. And as for the pocketbook, the price of $3,945 for the two seater XK 120—the replica model—is within the reach of many persons with serious intentions towards romantic motoring. The XK 120 is the most expensive of the Jaguar line.

Jaguar was well known before the war. The model 100, of pre war days, was so named because it fell into the 100 MPH speed class. Therefore, it was but a mild shock when Lt. Col. A. T. Goldie Gardner, M.C., broke various international records in the two litre class at speeds ranging up to 176.649 MPH, and it was announced that the engine used was the unblown prototype Jaguar unit. This was September 1948.

Gardner, who will be remembered as the tanned and angular Britisher who made himself a popular person in the pits at Indianapolis this spring, had used a four cylinder, twin overhead camshaft, two litre engine, developing 105 BHP at 5,400 RPM. This model is still undergoing exhaustive tests, but has not yet gone into production, while the accepted power plant of the new XK 120 is of six cylinder 3½ litre, 160 BHP, capacity.

The latter set-up, on May 30, 1949, achieved a speed of 132.6 MPH, using pump gasoline, in a road test at Jabbeke, Belgium. With Leslie Johnson driving, the same model flashed over the line as the winner at the 100 mile stock car race at Silverstone, and later captured its class, with Johnson driving, at Palm Beach Shores, Florida last January. The Sports Car Club of America awarded this model a special prize for the best performance by a British car.

Americans owning this car read like a listing of sportsmen of the Blue Book and filmdom. A few are Jim Kimberly of Kleenex, Briggs Cunningham, Charles E. Bedford of Standard Oil, Jack R. Vanderbilt, Alfred duPont, D. Cameron Peck, Brookes Stevens, Eric Dunn, Lowell Neicker, Thorne Donelly, Clark Gable, Robert Montgomery, Dick Powell and Gary Cooper.

With Jags becoming a regular sight along the American highway, it would be well to examine this car, relative to the performance and appointments one may expect when making a purchase.

Detailing the two seater type XK 120, we find a chassis of torsion bar suspension in front and semi-elliptic leaf springs in the rear. Telescopic type shock absorbers, front and rear, and 6.00x16 tires. The car uses Lockheed hydraulic brakes.

Steering is the much debateable 3¼ turns, lock to lock, with the turning circle 31 feet. Fuel tank is 14 gallons, with a 25 gallon tank optional, and oil capacity is 25 pints. Transmission holds four gears and a reverse.

Engine specifications include six cylinders, bore 83 MM, stroke 106 MM, cubic capacity 3,442 CC and piston area 50.3 square inches. With twin overhead cams, the unit operates in a forced oil bath, with drainage designed to prevent valve stems from over lubrication. The cylinder barrels are separated with water spacing all around, reaching to the foot and keeping heat distortion at bay.

The engine is kept light by using detachable heads of a special aluminum alloy. Pistons also are of aluminum alloy, with chrome plated top rings, thus increasing the life of the cylinder bores.

When the hood is opened, there is a sight to delight the eye of the enthusiast —a section full of overhead camshaft engine with nicely polished aluminum

Above: Leslie Johnson flashes across the finish line at England's Silverstone Speedway at better than 120 mph in his Jaguar XK120, to win the 100 mile stock car race.

Below: The beautiful 3½ litre XK120 super sports two seater with its luggage accommodations, cockpit interior and full all weather equipment.

covers. Stove enamelled triple branches of exhaust manifolds are on the left and twin carburetors and fuel pumps are on the right. Most components to which one must reach, for tuning, are high up and easily accessible.

Ground clearance is 7⅛ inches, over-all width 5 feet, 1½ inches, and height is 4 feet, 4½ inches. The seat is adjustable.

Coloring: one has the choice of nine major colors, with their variations and matching interior.

Many private and registered performance tests have been made of the XK 120, a compilation of which gave some startling figures. Using four opposite runs, an average speed of 124.6 MPH was obtained on a flying half mile. Maximum speed in third gear was 90, and in second was 62. A standing quarter mile was reached in 17 seconds and the car climbed from 0 to 100 MPH in 27.3 seconds. In accelleration tests, by 10 MPH stages, the pick-up was uniform to 80 MPH, reached in 15.7 seconds, then 20.1 for 90 and 27.3 for the century.

Fuel consumption is rather startling in such a high speed performance. An unexpected 27.5 MPG was realized at 30 MPH, and 22 at 60 MPH. At 100 MPH, the consumption was at the rate of 13 MPG.

It would be well to point out, in these tests, that instruments were checked as being 10 per cent fast at 30 MPH, eight per cent at 60, and so on. This is no deterrent when comparison is made with American makes, as most performance data is given with the standard instruments, which deviate to a like percentage.

The advantage of such speedometer readings, long criticized, still has not been eradicated, and although the backers of import models are loud in their criticism of this fallacy, the trick is hardly unknown abroad. To strike a complete

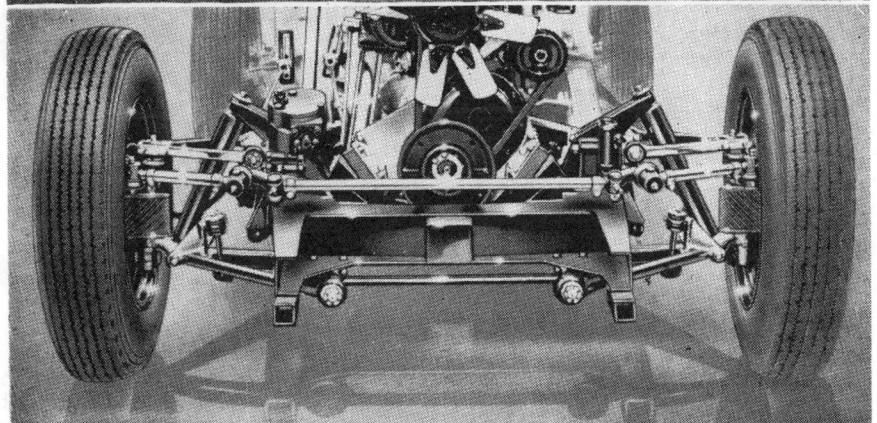

Top: Leslie Johnson takes a turn at Silverstone at better than 100 mph in his XK120. Note damage from a tangle with another car.

Center: The Jaguar Mark V uses the I.F.S. system, incorporating wishbones and torsion bars.

Right: Side view of the Jaguar XK120 four-cylinder engine.

picture for the average reader, who is a quick and careless reader at best, the same false readings must be quoted. It would be unfair to either model to quote otherwise. The only fair testings are those against the watch over measured distance, such as the Belgium run, and it makes this record all the more amazing.

Fast, though it is to an extreme degree, the Jaguar is a comfortable touring machine. When tire pressures are normal, the suspension is extremely comfortable. Driving position emphasizes the car's intent to roadster characteristics.

That is the world's fastest sports car— the Jaguar XK 120.

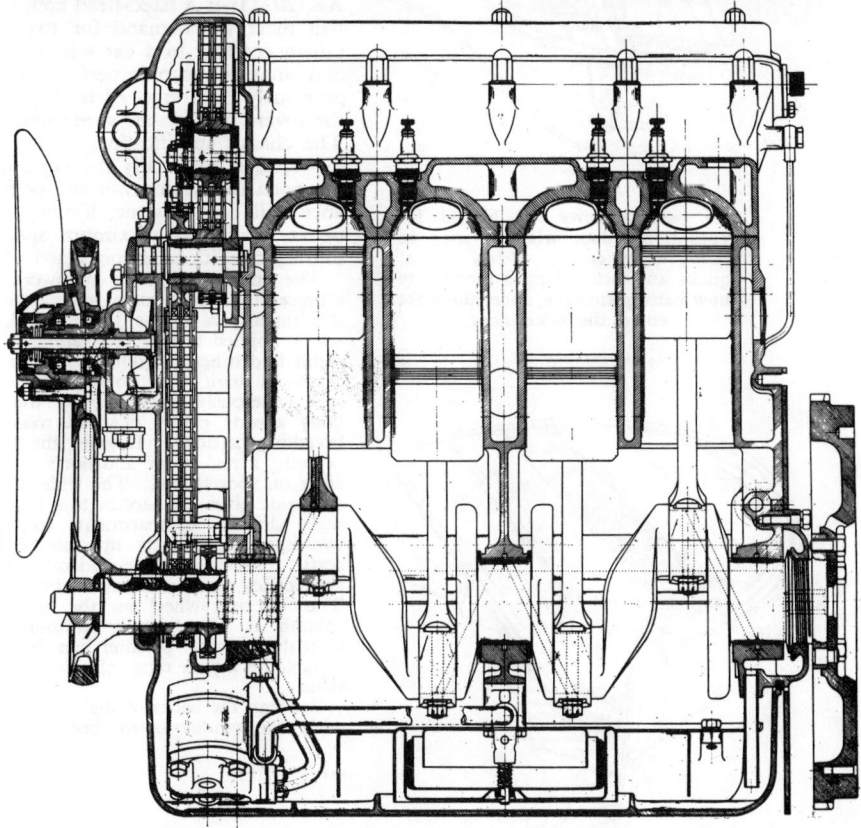

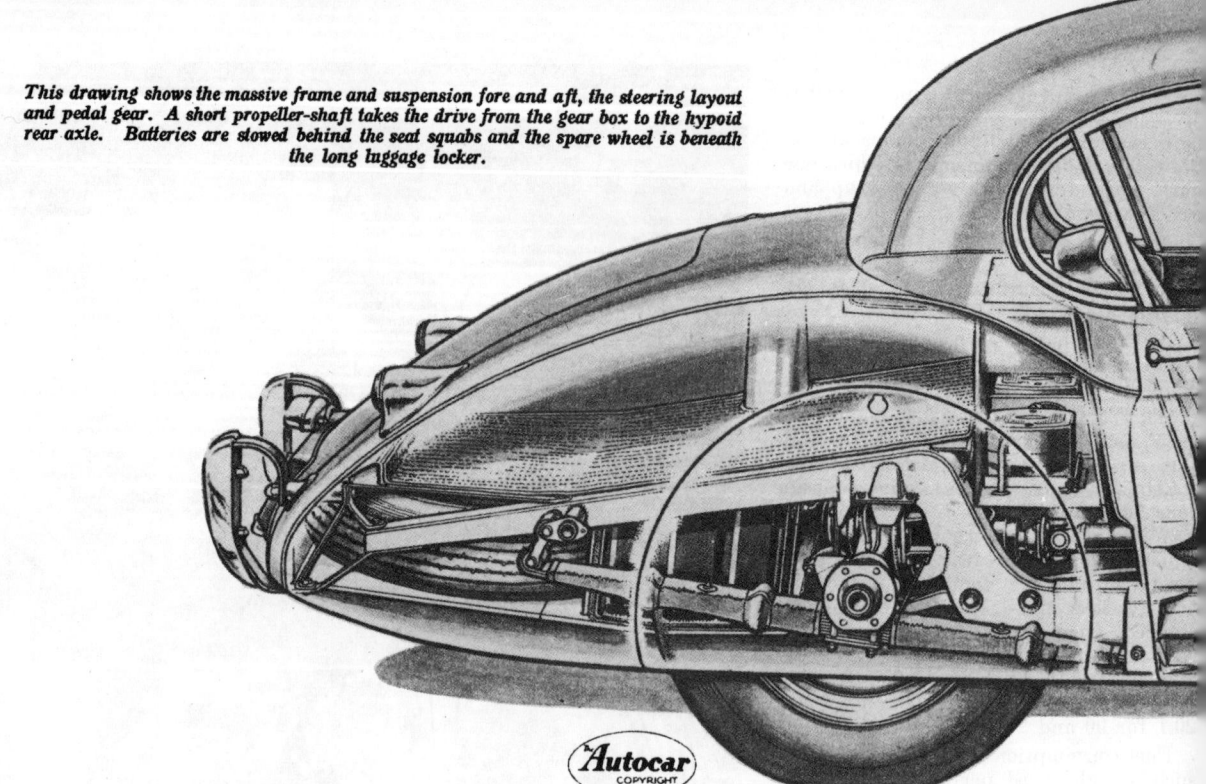

This drawing shows the massive frame and suspension fore and aft, the steering layout and pedal gear. A short propeller-shaft takes the drive from the gear box to the hypoid rear axle. Batteries are stowed behind the seat squabs and the spare wheel is beneath the long luggage locker.

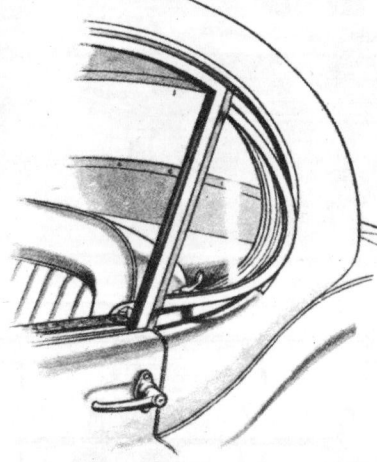

The rear windows are hinged for ventilation; door windows may be wound right down. Below: Seat squabs and locker hinged forward to show battery stowage under the front end of the locker floor.

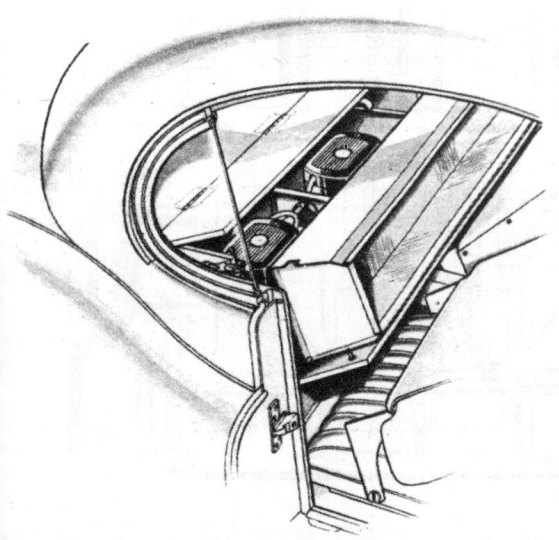

A Jaguar XK12

MAKING its first bow to the public at the Geneva Show, opening on March 8, will be a new model of the famous Jaguar XK120. It is a fixed-head coupé, and will meet the demand for two-seater saloon comfort in a car whose terrific and amazingly supple performance has previously been enjoyed to the full by the lovers of open-air speed motoring. The chassis specification, as might be expected, is materially the same as for the open two-seater, but the performance will be the same, if not a trifle better, so far as maximum speed in touring conditions is concerned.

The lines of the new coachwork have a graceful distinctiveness, a suggestion of the upper part of the Jaguar Mark VII saloon applied to the XK contours. The result is distinctly striking and attractive. With its high and sloping windscreen and generously curved roof, the new body affords plenty of head room and breathing capacity. It gives the feeling of being a real coupé and not a cramped affair on sports lines. The wide door on each side gives easy access to a large and wide driving compartment, containing two large and deeply upholstered chair seats. These are independently adjustable for leg reach, and have tilting squabs. The steering wheel on the well-raked column is telescopically adjustable, so that the driving position can be made suitable for a wide range of human dimensions.

Between the backs of the seats and the wide rear window of the body is a platform of considerable size for the odd ments of a long journey. This platform however, is rather more than it appear at first sight. There is a lid along the front of it which gives access to a locke practically the full width of the interio of the body. And that is not all. If the seat backs are tilted forward, this whol locker can also be tilted forward, to dis close the batteries nestling in a compart ment beneath.

The tail of the car contains a luggag locker of considerable size, wide an long. This can be seen in the large sec tional drawing, which also shows ho the spare wheel is carried below th locker floor, and the position of the larg fuel tank.

Ventilation

Particular attention has been paid t the ventilation of this coupé body i order that it may be satisfactory in h climates. The windows on each side ar divided into three sections. The wid centre section is operated by windin handle, to drop flush into the door. Bot the triangular front section and the curve rear section are centrally hinged, and ca be opened a short way to act as extrac tors, or a long way to act as air scoops An interior heater is fitted.

Upholstered in pleated leather, an equipped with figured walnut instrumen panel and cappings, the interior is i excellent taste. This is a car for re motoring; hence the speedometer an rev. counter dials are large and round. I fact, all the dials are round, and the posi tions of the needles can be seen in

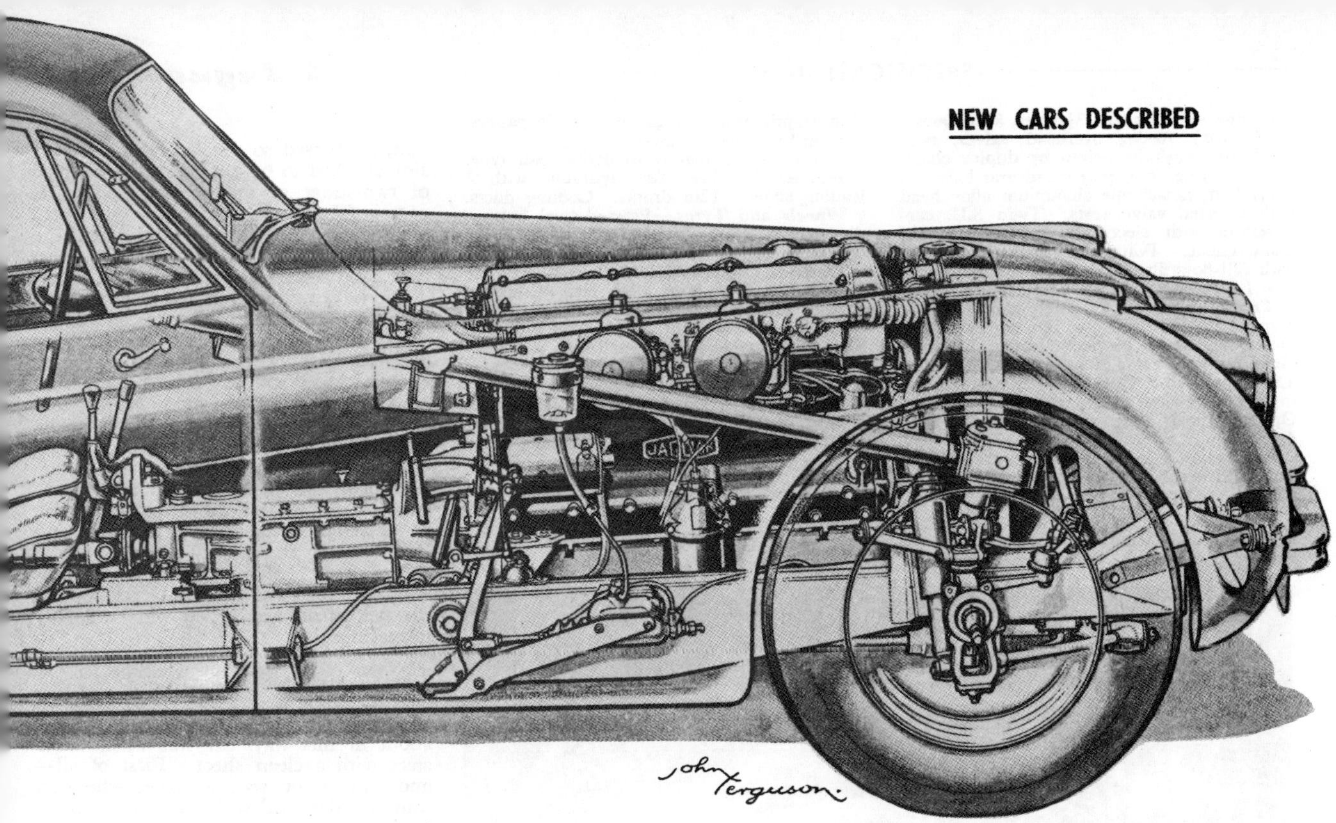

NEW CARS DESCRIBED

Coupé: FIXED-HEAD TWO-SEATER OF STRIKING LINE

ash. In the same way, the secondary ontrol knobs are not set in a confusing w, but are well apart so that the esired one can be found instantly.

Similarly again, the gear change lever central, well back in the car and ready hand, whilst the hand brake lever close y has the racing type of catch; that is say, the ratchet comes into use only hen the knob on the top is pressed own. In the scuttle on the opposite de to the steering column is a locker ith a lid. The centrally placed driving irror is of fair size and in conjunction ith the large rear window it gives an usually good field of rearward view. he pedal plates are unusually large, the edals being adjustable for leg reach; bber bellows prevent heat or fumes

from issuing into the body through the slots. Wide sun vizors are hinged in the roof.

So often and so thoroughly has the general mechanical design of this quite outstanding British car been described that it might seem almost superfluous to go over the matter again. It is not, however. Anyone and everyone who has had the good fortune to handle the XK120 on the road cannot fail to have noticed that it possesses certain marked characteristics which are superbly satisfying, and these need relating to the design behind them. That immense turn of speed is almost by the way. It is not the essence of the car's charm, which really lies in the smooth flexibility of the engine, the light but precise steering, the comfort of the

suspension, and the stability shown under all conditions of handling.

Well acquainted with the strength of public interest in the "Jag XK," the writer felt that it would be fascinating to find out from the designer himself what "makes the engine tick" so admirably. He therefore called on Mr. W. M. Heynes, the chief engineer of the Jaguar company, and the gist of his answers to many questions was as follows:

From the beginning, the engine now in the XK was conceived as an engine for a saloon—as it now is in the Jaguar Mark VII—and there was no thought of sports cars and competitions. Long life was to be put first, and high power output second. But when the engine was made, and before it was put into full produc-

The beautiful wing line of the open model has been retained and the coupé top styled in harmony with it.

SPECIFICATION

Engine.—6 cylinders, 3½ litres, 83 × 106mm (3,442 c.c.) 70-deg overhead valves, twin overhead camshafts driven by duplex chain. Seven-bearing counterweighted and balanced crankshaft, detachable aluminium alloy head with inserted valve seats. Twin S.U. carburettors with electrically controlled automatic choke. Forced oil feed throughout, with full-flow filter. Compression ratio 7 or 8 to 1. 160 b.h.p. at 5,000 r.p.m.

Transmission.—Dry single-plate clutch. 4-speed single-helical gear box with synchromesh. Ground gears. Needle bearings. Gear ratios: First 12.29, second 7.22, third 4.98, top 3.6 to 1. Hardy Spicer needle bearing propeller-shaft to hypoid bevel final drive. Optional final drive ratios 3.27; 4.0; and 4.3 to 1.

Suspension.—Independent front suspension with wishbones and torsion bar springs. Newton telescopic hydraulic dampers. Half-elliptic rear springs enclosed in gaiters. Girling hydraulic dampers.

Steering.—Burman recirculating ball type.

Brakes.—Lockheed full hydraulic with 2 leading shoes. 12in drums. Cooling ducts.

Wheels and Tyres.—Pressed-steel bolt-on disc wheels, with Dunlop 6.00 × 16in Road Speed tyres.

Electrical Equipment.—Lucas 12-volt de luxe, 64 ampère-hour batteries. Constant voltage control. Flush-fitting head lamps, wing lamps, stop light, reversing light, twin rear lights, panel light, twin horns and twin screenwipers.

General Dimensions.—Wheelbase 8ft 6in. Track (front) 4ft 3in, (rear) 4ft 2in. Overall length, 14ft 5in; width, 5ft 1½in; height, 4ft 5½in. Ground clearance 7½in. Turning circle 31ft. Unladen weight 25½cwt (2,856lb) approx.

Tank Capacity.—15 gallons.

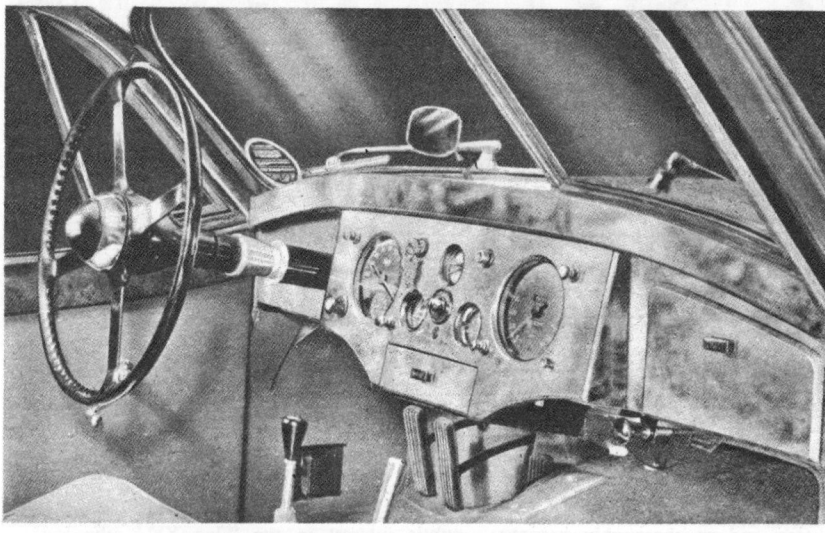

Instruments meant to be read, in a polished wood facia, and a convenient gear lever and hand brake.

Seats give the support necessary in a high performance car and are of the considerable fore and aft depth which gives comfort on a long journey.

tion, it showed so much promise that it almost asked to be put into a sports type of two-seater so that it could show its paces. There was, perhaps, a fair world market for such a car, but even the optimists in the company did not guess how good a market it was going to prove.

Anyway, a few dozen sports cars round the world in different hands, not under works supervision, would provide an excellent test of the soundness of the engine. And so the XK120 came into being, to show, as everybody knows, that it was the fastest production car in the world, and to prove a tremendous success in competitions and actual racing. Moreover, the engine proved that it was entirely suitable for the original purpose of its design, installation in a saloon, and into a saloon it has now gone.

No doubt before long *The Autocar* will Road Test the Mark VII saloon, and the performance recorded will be highly interesting.

Valve Evolution

The actual design of the engine came about in this way. It was intended to start with a clean sheet. First of all—and this is, or was, a secret—the new unit was designed with the very latest in push-rod-operated valves. But experience with that prototype produced the opinion that this system of valve operation had been advanced to the limit of its possibilities, and that a change was needed. Hence it was decided to take a stride and go over to hemispherical combustion chambers with 70-degree overhead valves, camshaft operated, which with scientific porting can give an exceedingly high power output on reasonable fuel consumption; in short, high efficiency. Moreover, push rod overhead valves can never be quite as quiet as a well-designed overhead camshaft system.

Now the advantages of the overhead camshaft can be these. In the push rod and rocker system for each valve there are (neglecting the sliding of the valve stem and of the cam follower or tappet in their respective guides) three places where rolling friction is taking place—the two ball ends of the push rod, and the pivot of the rocker; there are two places where scrubbing friction exists; the cam on the follower and the rocker end on the valve stem. The rocker end, incidentally, puts a side thrust on the valve guide.

Where there is movement there must also be slight clearance, even if only for lubrication. And when there is friction there will be wear, however small. Moreover, the inertia of the many reciprocating parts imposes a considerable load on these points. Hence the push rod and rocker system has many places from which a growing clearance may add up, necessitating frequent adjustment or producing noise.

But if the camshaft is situated above the valve, and an inverted piston-like cam follower is positioned as a guide, with its under-face in contact with the valve stem, then there is only one place where scrubbing friction occurs, between cam and follower, and only two places where clearance exists; that is, between cam and follower, and follower and valve stem. Inertia is reduced to a minimum, and there is no side thrust on the valve guide. Further, the necessary strength of the valve spring is reduced, and length of the valve stem and of the spring can be

Coupé : continued

A view of the car in profile gives a striking impression of the low build of the XK120 coupé.

shortened, giving another slight gain against inertia. Consequently the wear, or the building up of clearance, is so slow that adjustment is needed only when the valve itself has worn down its head or its seat.

In the XK engine there is a hard steel washer, or "biscuit," between the head of the valve stem and the under-face of the follower; these biscuits are manufactured in a range of thicknesses, and provide the necessary setting of the clearance when the engine is being built or overhauled.

One feature of the XK arrangement is that the guides for the followers are part of a tray or ledge in the head casting, in which fresh oil is maintained at a predetermined level and lubricates the cam, the follower face and the follower guide. It is decidedly interesting to observe that the theory of this valve system is borne out in practice, for the XK engine maintains its tune for particularly long periods without need of adjustment.

Design Detail

There are many special points in the aluminium alloy RR 50 cylinder head of this engine. The holding down studs are carefully spaced, four of them equidistant from each cylinder barrel, so that the risk of distortion from improper stud tightening is reduced. The valve seats are of high expansion cast iron, and are inserted into the head by a freezing process. The tappet guides are of chill-cast iron, also inserted. Incidentally the inlet valves, which are slightly larger than the exhausts, are made of silicon-chrome steel, and the exhaust valves of austenitic steel.

It is easy to give a general description of the cylinder head and valve arrangement in terms of "70-degree o.h.v. set in hemispherical combustion chambers, with the inlet ports on one side and the exhausts on the other." But in actual fact this head embodies the solution of many scientific difficulties, and has been worked out in collaboration with Weslake and Co., Ltd. A description of these mysteries would be beyond normal understanding; suffice it, therefore, to say that the result of the design is to give the highest possible gas flow, especially at low valve lift, and the correct degrees of turbulence and swirl. And in this matter lies part of the secret of the smooth flexibility of the engine. (A detailed description appeared in *Automobile Engineer* for July, 1950).

The arrangement of the cross water flow through the cylinder is also interesting. The cool water enters the head directly opposite each exhaust valve seat, flows around the seat, onwards around the sparking plug bosses, over and around the inlet valve seat, and thence out. The water spacing is most carefully proportioned so as to avoid pockets, and to use a high speed flow. The cylinder barrels are jacketed to the foot, and the circulation of the water in these jackets is partly thermo-siphon, the object being to maintain as even a temperature as possible.

Reducing Friction

With the attainment of head and valves to give maximum output, the designer is confronted with another problem, to ensure that the "applied mechanics" in the engine have dealt faithfully with the structure and the moving parts, so that as little as possible has been lost in friction, distortion, or vibration. The XK engine was given a very substantial crankshaft with seven bearings, $2\frac{3}{4}$in in diameter, and webs and crankpins to match. But it is of small avail to have a hefty crankshaft unless you support it rigidly, and that led to a cylinder block and crankcase in which there are many virtues. In the first place, interior vertical webs run right down from the bosses of the cylinder head studs to the bosses of the main bearing studs. The case is divided at the level of the crankshaft centre line, and the walls of the main bearing supports are heavily ribbed in every necessary direction. Not only that, but on one side of the foot of the crankcase there is an end-to-end channel section rib, and on the other a similarly intended tubular rib, which is also the main oil gallery. No doubt the engine owes a good deal of its success and its smoothness to this rigidity of crankshaft and cylinder block. Research has shown that the XK requires considerably less power to motor it round than is usually the case; in short, mechanical losses are relatively small.

Reference to the main oil gallery at the side of the crank chamber brings up another point. The oilways in this engine are all of relatively large bore. The object is to obtain a good flow of oil at a low velocity, whereby frothing is avoided. To the same end, sharp edges and corners in the oilways are avoided.

These are a few of the special points of the design, and they serve to show that the success of the engine is not the result of any one particular feature, but of a choice of good features in an engine designing recipe, and a most thorough attention to every detail, large or small. There is no doubt that the success of this recipe will be borne out in the coupé.

Tools are clipped in position on each side of the luggage locker, which also houses the spare wheel. There is a useful light on the inside of the lid.

"Motor Sport's" Impressions of that Much-Discussed Car—

THE JAGUAR XK 120

[MOTOR SPORT copyright.
LEFT.—Another busman's holiday, when the Editor exchanges typewriter for XK 120. He discovers he isn't nearly as fast at Brands Hatch as Stirling Moss but enjoys himself for all that !
ABOVE.—A further shot of the Jaguar on this exciting one-mile circuit.

AFTER going along to Henly's showrooms, appropriately situated at the head of Great Portland Street, formerly known as the "Street of Cars," to snatch a pre-view of the new fixed-head coupé on the Jaguar XK 120 chassis, I was able to fulfil a long-standing ambition and take away for test an open XK 120. This remarkable Jaguar made its appearance 2½ years ago and since then many and varied have been the Pressmen who have tried it. Perhaps the fact that MOTOR SPORT has not done so sooner is so that we can have the last word—at all events, our test coinciding with the release of a newer model, it rather seems so.

First impressions of an unfamiliar fast car are not always the most favourable, and so it was with this XK. The snug hood and rigid side-curtains were erect when I took over, and as the reassurances of "Lofty" England were cut off abruptly as he stood upright I realised that I was alone in the maelstrom of London's rush hour traffic in England's fastest standard car. Naturally no self-respecting motoring journalist wants to loiter in such a vehicle, but as I pressed strongly along I was embarrassed to discover the great distance my throttle foot had to travel to encounter the brake pedal and a bit put out at the way the Jaguar wallowed and howled its Dunlops when deflected from the straight ahead—you have to be used to sailing small boats to master this chap, I thought.

But the response to the throttle was magnificently stimulating and that of the brakes likewise, when I could find them. It was almost immediately apparent, too, that the 3½-litre, twin-cam 160-b.h.p. engine, like a bank clerk, is quite devoid of temperament. I left it idling all the while we were in the Bayswater traffic hold-ups and I poodled along at 500 r.p.m. in top gear without upsetting the mixture or lubricating the sparks. When a gap appeared—my word, how we made use of it.

So to the A30 Arterial, where people roaring homeward in the extreme right hand groove were perplexed, sometimes peeved, to receive a reminder from the Jaguar's *very* polite horn, so that we could get on with *our* motoring. The way we left everything behind will long live in my memory.

Thus to familiar roads, where I discovered many new corners—the same as I did on first driving a Morgan "4/4" after long spells in family saloons, only now these corners were *acute* !

At first I felt alarmed at the idea of hurrying along the twisty bits in a car so softly sprung, for the XK 120 is that all right. It gives a most creditably comfortable ride over atrocious roads. You can hear the suspension links, anti-roll bars or whatever they tie the wheels to the chassis with these days, chattering to themselves over the rough bits and if, even at a crawl, you lock over hard on a loose-ish surface, the outer front wheel scrubs in a manner I met pre-war in the Mk V Bentley and V12 Lagonda, when really supple springing on really rapid cars was in its infancy. The Jaguar also rolls freely and dips its nose if you anchor at all sharply, then " breasts the waves " as you accelerate. But I realised how well the wheels followed the surface contours and later, when I negotiated twisty roads at advanced throttle openings, I was surprised how correctly geared the Burman-Douglas steering seemed, although in fact it asks 3¼ turns lock-to-lock whereas usually I fret at anything lower than 2. Indeed, the Jaguar " holds in " splendidly round fast bends and is exceedingly stable on wet roads.

A part explanation of this is the exceedingly generous steering lock, so handy for turning the XK 120 round in narrow places—if ever anyone wants to ply for hire in London streets in one of these cars Scotland Yard certainly won't find any fault with the lock; it's immense! The rest of the explanation seems to be the accuracy of control. In spite of its rolling tendencies the XK comes to heel decently, so that you know just how much wheel work will be needed under given circumstances and the steering accurately interprets the driver's desires. The wheel, rather thick-rimmed, has its spokes placed properly, the vivid castor-action is both useful for straightening-up hands-off after acute corners and takes all backlash out of the steering, while only the slightest tremors are transmitted through the wheel. Whip an XK through the " chicane "-type of bend and you will quickly appreciate that, if " disconnected " in the modern manner, the steering is very good. It is also reasonably light, although at racing speeds one is conscious of holding the car against the powerful castor action. The seats and steering column adjust to give a good position, although the seat squab leans back a trifle too far for a truly alert posture.

Rev. up the engine and pleasing sounds come from the exhaust, but the outstanding impression left by this wonderful car is its combination of extravagant performance and silent, effortless functioning, exhaust sound vanishing at about 2,500 r.p.m. So easily does the XK 120 go about its task that at first a newcomer behind its long alligator bonnet is a trifle disappointed. As he glances at the speedometer needle showing 65 or so he wonders, where is this great speed they speak of ? Then he reflects that the speedometer is mostly only consulted as the car is eased through corners and that afterwards the immense acceleration, still with no display of effort, thrusts the car forward into the eighties and nineties in a refreshingly brief space of time. Even driving the Jaguar as essentially a top-gear car, 90 m.p.h. becomes commonplace in between dodging the lorries along any main or secondary road, so great is the accelerative ability. No particular speed can be cited as the cruising speed—rather do you make a series of hawk-like swoops past slower traffic, punctuated by firm applications of the brakes to tuck you safely behind prevailing obstructions. It is all tremendously exhilarating—that is the word!—and accomplished so easily that after hundreds of miles you never even begin to feel blasé. The "quick" steering and this smooth, unending surge of acceleration brings familiar towns and villages quite astonishingly close together.

The 12-in. Lockheed brakes normally do their stuff admirably, too. With only light pressure and small travel on the pedal (I soon found it wasn't really inaccessible) truly powerful, progressive, snag-free retardation is available, without which the XK 120 wouldn't be half the car it is. I write "normally," because I did come up against rather disconcerting fade. I had braked hard from about 90 m.p.h.—one is so seldom *under* 70 or 80 in this car—for a minor cross-roads and entered some narrow lanes, which I took at about 50, braking for the incessant corners. All of a sudden I found almost all anchorage had evaporated, just as if I'd wetted the shoes in a water-splash, only I hadn't. The harder I pressed the more negative was the effort, until negotiation of a congested high-street at 20 m.p.h. constituted quite an adventure. By this time you could *smell* how hot the drums and linings were from the cockpit. After I had had lunch temperatures (and tempers) were normal again and the brakes as good as ever. Now this fading did not occur in really fast main road driving luckily, but I can now sympathise with XK 120 drivers who have slapped the straw during a sports car race or come down an Alp a thought too quickly.

This suave Jaguar was so enormously quick from one place to another that to plot its true performance seemed somewhat pointless. In any case, it was in absolutely standard trim, with the 7 to 1 compression ratio instead of 8 to 1 and the low 3.64 to 1 axle ratio, and, of course, no undershield. The engine "pinked" almost inaudibly on "Pool," started from stone cold instantaneously and ran straight up into "the red "—well over 5,000 r.p.m.—without the slightest anxiety. It was silk-smooth to 4,000 r.p.m., a bit rough beyond that, vibration travelling up the gear-lever at 4,500 r.p.m. and above. Speedometer readings of 40, 70 and 100 m.p.h. were realised in the indirect ratios of 12.29, 7.22 and 4.98 to 1. I suspect the speedometer was optimistic and 90 m.p.h. the true maximum in third gear. Normally, of course, I started in second, went almost at once into third, stayed there up to 70, then got going in top. How easily speed builds-up in the 3.64 to 1 top ratio is illustrated by a casual run down past Frensham Ponds from Farnham, when, baulked on the "run-in," I nevertheless got up to 4,300 r.p.m. along the undulating straight beside the lake. This represents about 97 m.p.h., although the speedometer said 110. Later I saw 120 m.p.h. recorded along a mile or so of straight road and colleagues using the Southend Arterial "clocked" 130. This represents a true 120 m.p.h. and I would put the genuine two-way maximum at approximately 110 m.p.h. The surge of acceleration from 80 m.p.h. onwards is, perhaps, more exhilarating than those impressive maximum speeds. The real punch comes in at about 50 in this gear, but this is no hardship, for the gear-

---

THE JAGUAR XK 120 TWO-SEATER

Engine : Six cylinders, 83 by 106 mm., 3,442 c.c.; 7 to 1 compression-ratio. 160 b.h.p. at 5,200 r.p.m.
Gear ratios : First, 12.29 to 1; second, 7.22 to 1; third, 4.98 to 1; top, 3.64 to 1.
Tyres : 6.00 by 16 Dunlop Road Speed on bolt-on steel disc wheels.
Weight : Approx. 25½ cwt., without occupants.
Steering ratio : 3¼ turns, lock-to-lock.
Fuel capacity : 15 gallons; Range approx. 180-200 miles.
Wheelbase : 8 ft. 6 in.
Track : 4 ft. 3 in. front; 4 ft. 2 in., rear.
Overall dimensions : 14 ft. 5½ in. by 5 ft. 2 in. by 4 ft. 4½ in.
Price : £988 (£1,263 3s. 11d. with purchase tax).

PERFORMANCE DATA :

Speeds in gears :
  1st ... 40 m.p.h.
  2nd ... 60 m.p.h.
  3rd ... 90 m.p.h.
  Top ... 120 m.p.h.
Acceleration through gears :
  0- 30 m.p.h. in 2.8 sec.
  0- 60 m.p.h. in 9.0 sec.
  0- 80 m.p.h. in 14.9 sec.
  0-100 m.p.h. in 25.4 sec.
Brands Hatch flying lap (anticlockwise) : 1 min. 0.5 sec.
Makers : Jaguar Cars, Ltd., Coventry, England.

---

change is delightful to use—reminiscent of that of a "TD" M.G.—and from a crawl things happen very satisfactorily indeed when you open up in third.

Its pedal rather far to the right, the clutch functions as a Borg and Beck should; there is ample room for your left foot.

For a car good for 100 m.p.h. almost anywhere the XK 120 is notably docile in conception and demeanour. It runs very cool, the water temperature mostly below 60 degrees C. Oil pressure builds to 40 lb./sq. in. as the revs. rise. The facia is devoid of masses of switches and dials; it even incorporates a cigar lighter (fancy smoking a *cigar* in an XK !). There is one of those *wonderful* petrol gauges that becomes an oil-level indicator when you press a button. The oil part always read "full" while I had the car; alas, not so the "petrol" indicator, for speed costs money and we only seemed to be doing about 13-14 m.p.g.

This is a snug car, too, when hood and side bits are unfurled, absolutely suited to taking the popsie to—well, to the pictures. Open, the big screen gives excellent protection even at 100 m.p.h., at the expense of a bit of a blind spot created by its centre support. Even torrential rain blows clear of the occupants over 40 m.p.h. Both wings are easily visible and the rear-view mirror is excellent for those built-up areas where they do not *disguise* their police cars. Actually, Jaguar drivers are the least likely to exceed speed limits; for example, I took a great pride in doing a genuine 10 m.p.h. for the entire length of the police diversion so limited in Farnham, to the amusement of the policeman on point duty; after all, only moments before I had seen the speedometer at 110, and could get it there again many times before reaching London.

Lack of cubby holes is compensated for by excellent flap-covered door pockets, the door "pulls" and internal locks are nicely done, the doors shut "expensively" and getting in and out couldn't be easier. The lines of the car are superb, and the hood stows away neatly. Minor grumbles —a draught about my feet, the irritation of speedometer and rev.-counter needles moving in opposite directions and a craving, unsatisfied, for an oil thermometer, direction indicators when the car was enclosed, a fuel range greater than 200 miles (15 gallons—only about five hours running time in an XK), and some means of knowing whether "side lamps on" had been selected correctly with the single rotary lamps switch—in which connection, isn't it rather droll that they tell you when the headlamps are full on but nothing about your nav. lamps ?

A few rattles intruded but the gears are well behaved. Having to unlock a flap before you can refuel has mixed blessings. I was spared a radio and heater, liked very much the fly-off handbrake, and found the headlamps (foot-dipper) penetrating, if a thought "uppish." The big luggage locker is useful, too—and in case anyone asks what this and similar "amenities" have to do with *real* sports cars, let me say that the very rapidity and driving pleasure afforded by such cars makes them appropriate for long-distance touring.

Before parting with the car it was subjected to some very hard laps of Brands Hatch, after which it completed some very enjoyable miles in Kent with only slightly more free-movement of the brake pedal and a trace of an oil-leak from the gearbox to indicate how hard it had been driven. It never boiled and on the circuit only slight brake-fade intruded.

By the high quality of its finish and appointments alone the XK 120 represents very good value for money. Its very liberal speed and acceleration, accomplished with such willing ease, are unrivalled and to drive this Jaguar is to enjoy an experience at once unique and embracing one of the highest pinnacles of modern motoring.—W.B.

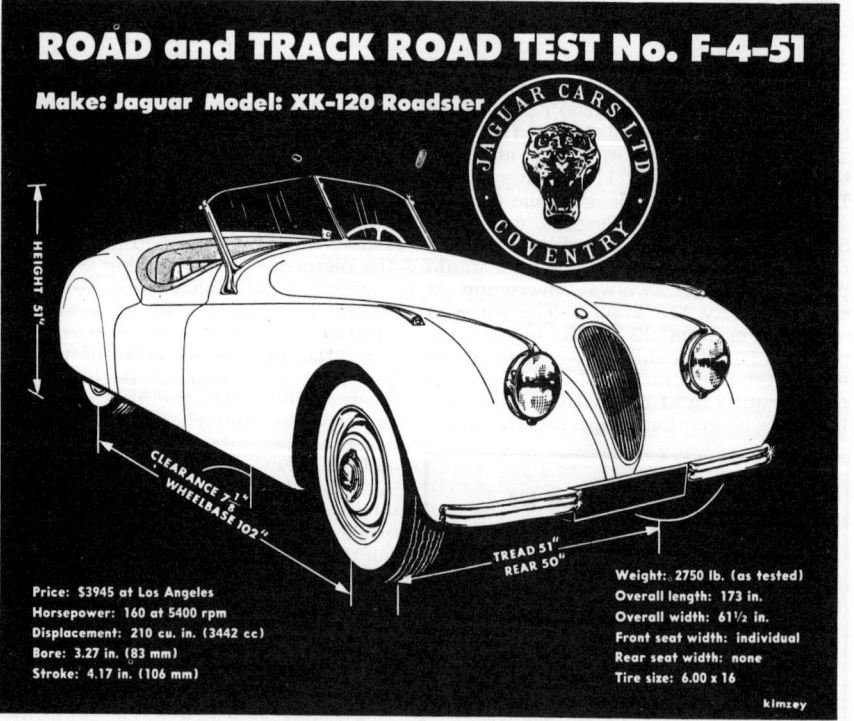

ROAD and TRACK ROAD TEST No. F-4-51
Make: Jaguar Model: XK-120 Roadster

HEIGHT 51"
CLEARANCE 7½"
WHEELBASE 102"
TREAD 51"
REAR 50"

Price: $3945 at Los Angeles
Horsepower: 160 at 5400 rpm
Displacement: 210 cu. in. (3442 cc)
Bore: 3.27 in. (83 mm)
Stroke: 4.17 in. (106 mm)

Weight: 2750 lb. (as tested)
Overall length: 173 in.
Overall width: 61½ in.
Front seat width: individual
Rear seat width: none
Tire size: 6.00 x 16

kimzey

PERFORMANCE FIGURES

ACCELERATION
Standing ¼ Mile - 18.3 sec.
0-50 mph - 7.5 sec.
0-60 mph - 10.1 sec.
0-70 mph - 12.6 sec.

MAXIMUM SPEED
Flying ¼ Mile - 123.2 mph
Opposite Direction - 120.0 mph
Average - 121.6 mph

The fifth of a series of road tests of foreign and American automobiles from the American driver's viewpoint

MR. A. REPORTS

Driving the Jaguar XK-120 is an experience not soon forgotten—one expects much and is not disappointed. Like any really good automobile, it is much easier to list the faults than the virtues.

Unquestionably, the XK-120 has performance far and above any stock American make, but due to the engine size being less than that of a Chevrolet, the torque is not high at low engine speeds. The four forward ratios are well chosen, and when used properly to take full advantage of the 160 horsepower available, the car can reach 70, 80 or even 100 honest mph in a very short time. The engine is smooth and unobtrusive all the way to its recommended maximum of 6000 rpm . . . it starts instantly and idles reliably but not regularly.

Purely personal grievances concern the too nearly vertical steering wheel which has a protruding horn (I managed to hit it fairly often when making 90° corners). The brake pedal pressure seemed almost too low, but this is probably a question of getting accustomed to the car. Likewise, the gear shifting lever seemed slightly awkward compared to the M.G. (with which I am familiar). In particular, the necessary travel from neutral seemed different for each gear and it would take considerable practice to master really snappy changes.

Suspension is all that could be desired for a very fast long distance touring machine . . . very comfortable, yet much stiffer springing and less roll than found on American family cars.

I particularly liked the modern styling and the excellent performance. Foot pedals seem a little high, but the seats are excellent, and the general quality of the interior appointments calls for considerable praise. Several XK-120 owners tell me that the interior is not exactly dry in rainstorms, but the new "hard top" coupe will satisfy those who demand comfort even at the expense of losing the features of open-air motoring.

MR. B. REPORTS

The Jaguar XK-120 is by far the fastest car yet tested by *Road and Track*, a two-way average speed of 121.6 mph being attained. Considering the daily use of this car for city traffic driving and the complete lack of special tuning, the fact becomes even more remarkable.

Altho the Jaguar XK-120 has enjoyed much popularity in the United States, some people have been inclined to doubt its high speed ability. For this reason, we were particularly anxious to obtain a top speed figure on this car. To assure strict compliance with stock status, the 5,000 mile tune up, by Joe Thrall of International Motors, was personally observed. Removing the windshield and fitting an aero-screen (optional extra) was the only alteration to the standard delivered form. (For ordinary use, we positively do not recommend driving without windshield. Both the driver and photographer turned a deep blue from the early morning desert cold.) The 121.6 mph average was obtained with the standard 3.64:1 rear axle ratio and not the 3.27:1 ratio used on the official Jabbeke Road record run in 1949. Unlike the XK used in the Belgian run, the *Road and Track* test car used no underpan or tonneau cover. Two men were in the car and the run was at an elevation of over 3,000 feet.

At top speed, the Jaguar has a steadiness usually associated only with a race car and gusts of wind have little or no effect on stability. Steering and roadworthiness of the Jaguar would be difficult to improve. The excellent seating position, combined with fast (3¼ turns lock to lock), positive steering, recirculating ball type, produces a cornering ability unequalled by any car tested to date.

The Jaguar brakes are extremely powerful, requiring rather low pedal pressure, and did not display any tendency to fade (apparently only severe braking, such as during a road race, tends to bring about fade on the XK). While the cooling is adequate under normal conditions, traffic driving brings a rise in engine temperature.

The Jag went up a 32% grade in 2nd gear at 42 mph. This is 20 mph faster than the MG, and 30 mph faster than the Studebaker. The speedometer was only moderately optimistic, being 2.4 mph fast at 50 mph and 4.8 mph fast at 70 mph.

Apart from the rather awkward appearance presented with the top in place, weatherproofing is not up to the standard of the average roadster or convertible and rain finds its way in at various points.

Both interior and exterior finish are excellent. Instrumentation is quite complete, including such unusual, but welcome, items as an oil level gauge and a warning light which blinks on and off as fuel becomes low. Luggage accommodations are rather small. However, two good size suitcases may be accommodated in the luggage compartment, which is not entirely weather-tight. Storage of tools in the trunk is another praiseworthy feature, . . . included are such items as extra spark plugs, gaskets, and water hoses, each item having its individual clip, thus providing secure and accessible stowage.

Performance, smoothness, appearance and price of the Jaguar XK-120 make it one of the best sports car values on the market today.

MR. C REPORTS

The "XK" is remarkably smooth . . . for a fast car. Surprisingly, one can use 4th gear almost exclusively—in the "family sedan" manner—and yet, when the occasion demands, rocket ahead in 2nd or 3rd. Normal starts from rest are in 2nd gear, with more than ample acceleration. In 1st gear, care must be taken to avoid burning rubber on dry pavement. The clutch is smooth and easy to operate, as are the other controls.

The body work and paint (on the test car) was not up to usual Jaguar quality . . . sheet steel fenders must sacrifice some stiffness in order to achieve lightness. The metallic paint used on most of the examples seen is not very attractive by American standards.

Watching the high speed runs of the XK, it seemed to be making those remarkable speeds with little or no effort and with relative silence. Incidentally, when it was approaching from over a mile away, the sound in the crisp desert air was not unlike that of a jet plane.

I agree with many who feel that this car looks much better with the fender skirts removed. The resulting interruption of streamlining might cut the maximum speed slightly. The homely top has been mentioned by the others and is probably on Jaguars' book of future modifications, along with new bumpers to provide more adequate protection. It's a shame that a little space isn't available for emergency passengers behind the seats . . . a la Simca Sport.

It is a car I'd love to own—but not unless I also owned a family transportation car.

MR. X REPORTS

Sleek as a Kentucky Derby winner, as desirable as a beautiful woman, and faster than the wind . . . that's the Jaguar XK-120. Here is a sports car with real personality. Your morale receives a terrific boost as soon as you sink into the comfortable leather seats.

The heavy exhaust note sets the mood for a ride with a thrill. Altho it takes a bit of

Altho the XK-120 rolls slightly on corners, it handles beautifully with its quick positive steering. Windscreen was substituted during tests. Don Parkinson, well-known driver, helped with tests.

High speed corners (up to 100 mph) were taken with the Jag under complete control.

practice to "play" the gears, the shift lever has an ideal form and location. From low, a slight rear-end bump and a tire screech announced departure for high speed in a hurry.

A real surprise is that smooth acceleration in hand at *any* speed. Even at 90 or 100 mph, there is an immediate response to the throttle. And best of all, the engine sounds quite happy at the century mark . . . yes, this is truly a high speed motor car . . . and one that can be driven at terrific speed all day—and like it!

The expression, "It takes corners as if on rails," is often heard, but can really be appreciated in the Jaguar. If you drive with "the seat of your pants" you actually get the sensation of being stabilized by rails. Real 90° crossed-arm turns can be made, aided by an almost vertical steering wheel and fast ratio. Very sharp corners can be taken at surprising speeds before a slide (which is quickly corrected) begins. Wider curves can be taken at Grand Prix speeds with complete stability and confidence.

Faults are few: larger instrument faces (tach and speedo are big), a more graceful weathertight top, and non-fade brakes.

Oh yes, brakes . . . altho they can be faded in racing, they are real honeys in traffic.

So you think I am enthusiastic over the XK? Well, so is everyone else, and besides, I'm sold . . . I want a Jaguar XK-120!

JAGUAR
wins First Alpine Gold Cup ever awarded in Europe's most gruelling Trial

To crown his achievements in a long series of successes, Trials driver Mr. Ian Appleyard has become the first to gain the Golden Coupe des Alpes, an award of the highest merit for completing three successive Annual Alpine Trials *without the loss of a single mark*. This outstanding feat has been achieved on the same Jaguar XK120 car which has now exceeded a mileage of 45,000 and with which Mr. Appleyard has gained over 40 awards in major International competitions. Measure of its reliability is emphasised by the fact that out of 95 entrants only 23 cars finished this arduous Alpine course, out of which Jaguars gained 1st, 2nd, 3rd and 4th places in their class, and returned fastest times of the day in five out of the six timed tests.

Write for details to Distributors for *States West of Mississippi*: Charles H. Hornburg, Jr., 9176 Sunset Boulevard, Los Angeles, Cal. *Eastern States*: The Hoffman Motor Car Co., Inc., 487 Park Avenue, New York, 22, and at Esquire Building, South Water Street, Chicago.

JAGUAR
XK SUPER SPORTS

What the XK can do has been shown by Ian Appleyard, here seen on the top bend of Rest-and-Be-Thankful.

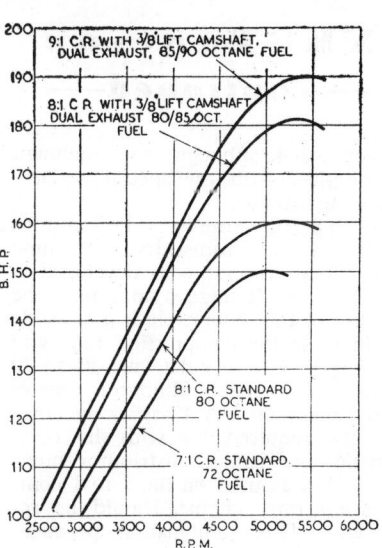

With various standard stages of tune the horse power developed by the XK can be increased from 150 b.h.p. at 5,000 r.p.m. to 190 b.h.p. at 5,400 r.p.m.

XK Tune-up

MAKER'S ADVICE ON HOW TO MAKE A JAGUAR WIN!

JUDGED by its competition results from the first time that it appeared, there is no question that the Jaguar XK120 is capable of winning events when it is in a perfectly standard form. However, the phrase "good enough" will never apply to competition work, and there is no doubt that individual owners wish to improve their cars in order to increase their chances of success. To respond to this desire, Jaguar Cars, Ltd., have very wisely produced a service bulletin entitled *Tuning Modification on XK120 Cars for Competition Purposes*, which was briefly mentioned in *The Autocar* of June 22.

Jaguar's are to be congratulated on making public such information. Apart from improving the performance of the cars in no uncertain manner, it also indicates the limits to which one can go without making major structural alterations.

Probably the most important engine "mod" is made possible by pistons providing compression ratios of 7, 8, and 9 to 1, but the manufacturers stress the point that no satisfactory increase in performance can be obtained by raising the compression ratio beyond 7 to 1 unless a fuel of octane rating higher than 72 is available. However, an improvement in performance can be obtained with 70 octane fuel and a 7 to 1 compression ratio by fitting $\frac{3}{8}$in lift camshafts (the standard camshaft being $\frac{7}{16}$in lift); but to carry out this modification it is necessary to reduce the length of the valve guides and also the tappet guide inserts in order to give the necessary clearance for the increased valve lift.

To improve getaway from standstill and low gear acceleration a lightened flywheel (reduced by about 8lb) is available. It is, of course, necessary to have the crankshaft—complete with its damper, new flywheel, and clutch—balanced as a unit. The special crankshaft damper has a steel inertia disc designed to stand up to the increased engine speed. With these modifications, and with RF needles in the S.U. carburettors, a further increase in horse power is obtained.

In countries where 80 octane fuel is available it is advantageous to increase the compression ratio to 8 to 1 by fitting grade F pistons; also to change the sparking plugs to Champion NA 10 and replace the distributor (No. 2747) with unit No. 2748. Actually the only modification to the distributor unit is the fitting of different centrifugal advance springs, and although some may consider that this spring change is a fairly simple matter, the manufacturers feel that for a high-performance vehicle the advance curve on the complete distributor should be checked before it is fitted to the engine. In consequence they recommend that a new distributor unit should be used. For racing purposes the manual says that the vacuum advance unit should be

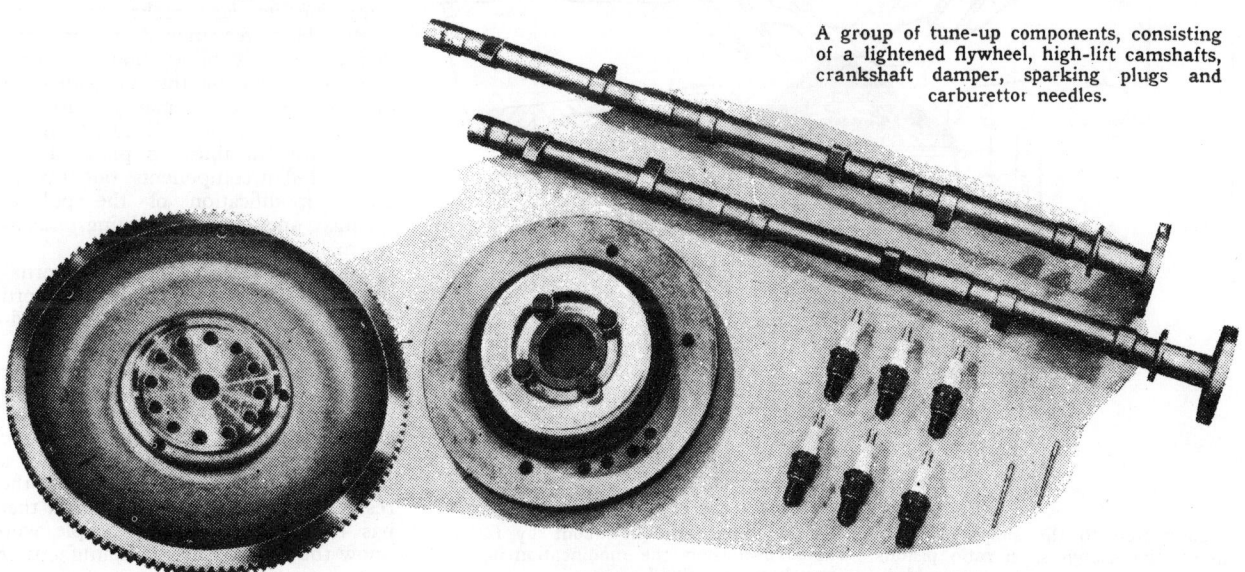

A group of tune-up components, consisting of a lightened flywheel, high-lift camshafts, crankshaft damper, sparking plugs and carburettor needles.

XK Tune-up
—continued—

disconnected, although this equipment is supplied with the special replacement distributor.

With 8 to 1 compression ratio pistons and $\frac{3}{8}$in lift camshafts something better than 180 b.h.p. is developed at 5,300 r.p.m. If there is no limit to the quality of fuel obtainable it is possible to increase the compression ratio still further to 9 to 1 and to use 85 to 90 octane fuel. RB carburettor needles and Champion NA 12 sparking plugs are also required, but with this combination the standard distributor (number 2747), as used on the 7 to 1 compression ratio engine, should be replaced. This combination produces around 190 b.h.p. at 5,400 r.p.m.

To obtain the best performance for engines with any of the above modifications it is advantageous to fit a dual exhaust system, and in this the two branches (each catering for three ports) are extended right through the silencer, which is, in fact, two silencers built in one. Unfortunately it is not possible to fit both pipes through the hole in the frame cross member (as with the single pipe used on the standard system) and in consequence the pipes are led below the frame member. This reduces the ground clearance of the car by approximately two inches, but this disadvantage is partially offset if the road springs are replaced by a special set of competition components which increase the stiffness by approximately 20 per cent and consequently give a firmer ride for high-speed work.

To transmit the increased horse power made available by tuning, a new clutch assembly which is balanced and specially tested for high-speed operation should be used. In conjunction with this unit a solid clutch centre plate, designed to stand up to strenuous racing start conditions, should also be fitted.

Front torsion bars and rear leaf springs can be supplied to give approximately a 20 per cent increase in suspension stiffness.

Other recommended engine modifications consist of the removal of the water thermostat unit to allow a more direct flow of coolant and the fitting of a manually operated switch for the starting carburettor so that carburation is controlled by the driver and not directly by temperature as with the standard car.

Four different axle ratios are available, ranging through 3.27 to 1, which gives 145 m.p.h. on top gear at 5,800 r.p.m.; 3.64 to 1, which produces 139 m.p.h. at 5,800 r.p.m. and is the standard ratio; and two higher ratios, 3.92 to 1 and 4.3 to 1, giving 121 m.p.h. and 112 m.p.h. respectively at 5,800 r.p.m. The low ratio (3.27 to 1) axle is recommended only for very fast circuits having straight sections of approximately three miles in length.

Stoppers

Not content with just making the engine go more quickly, Jaguar's have tackled the question of making the car stop under racing conditions also—a matter of utmost importance on a fast car whether it be used on the roads or for competition work. One finds that the manufacturer's recommendation is to leave the brakes alone, as they say that best results will be obtained by using the standard brake drums and shoes. However, they do recommend that increased cooling should be provided by removing the hub caps and the rear wheel cover plates. Also, for long races it is possible to fit linings which are $\frac{1}{4}$in thick in place of the standard $\frac{3}{16}$in components, but this requires modification of the pull-off springs and micro-adjusting mechanism.

To save weight on the body alternative seats upholstered in Bedford cord can be supplied and also racing windscreens and cockpit cowling.

As to the cost of this quite comprehensive list of modifications, to "go the whole hog" would cost about £160, which cannot be considered excessive when it is realized that this is not a hit-and-miss method of tuning, but the result of much development work that has been carried out by people who know the car as only the manufacturer can.

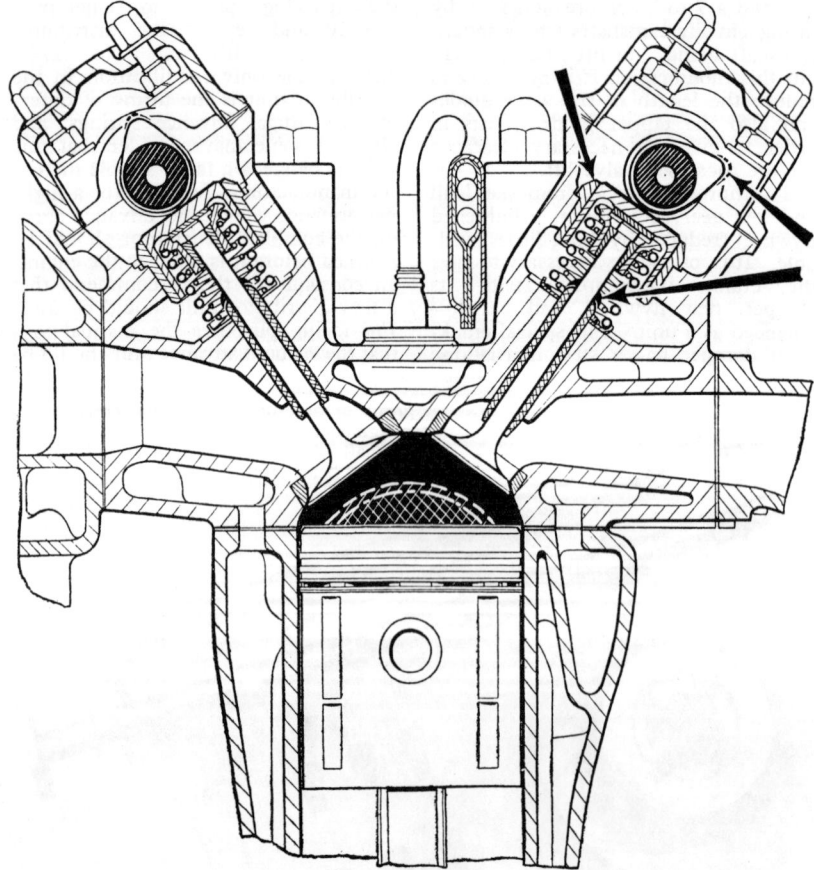

Modification to the shape of the combustion space brought about by fitting alternative compression ratio pistons. The arrows show the modification necessary when high-lift camshafts are fitted.

NEW CARS DESCRIBED

That Exciting New Jaguar

FULL DETAILS OF THE 3½-LITRE XK120 TYPE C

ALREADY it will have been realized that the designation Type C denotes a fresh version of the famous XK120, intended purely for competition and racing purposes. It consists of standard XK components rearranged in a different short and rigid triangulated steel tube frame, with special suspension and steering suitable for actual racing. The normal XK120, as was explained when that car was first introduced, was never intended as a racing car. It was to be one of the fastest open two-seater production cars offered to the public, and to that end it was given comfortable suspension and a flexible ease of performance which would appeal just as much to the experienced driver who enjoys the thrills of handling a tremendous acceleration, as to the devotee of ultra high speed. The XK120 leaped straight into popularity. It has proved to be so good that it quickly found a way into all kinds of competition, and has scored an impressively long series of successes.

As a result of this, owners, particularly in America, began to take the XK120 into competition with specially prepared lightweight "hot rods," when naturally it was handicapped by the weight of its luxury as a fast road touring car. Requests began to come in from the U.S.A. for information on tuning the XK120 to higher speeds still, which, of course, can be done, as explained in the Jaguar Service Bulletin No. 95 (reference to which was made in *The Autocar* of June 22). But it was decided that, if enthusiasts really wanted to go in for all-out catch-as-catch-can sports car races and competitions, the best thing was to give them a lightened new version of the XK120 made for the job, and for that job only, which meant a chassis suitable for speeds of 150 m.p.h. or more, and for handling at ultra high speeds.

And so, about eight months ago, design for the Type C was put in hand. It is a stark competition car. Its seating accommodation is limited, it is not provided with hood or screens, it has only one door, on the driving side, and the amenities normally desired for general touring purposes have been dispensed with, in order to assist in reducing weight. It is not a dual-purpose car like the standard XK120. It will be put into limited production only, and it is not likely to be available for the home market in the foreseeable future. But what it has done already is to win a classic race first time out, the 24 Hours at Le Mans, against the best that the world can produce. (Impressions of the winning car appeared in *The Autocar* last week.) The price of the XK120 Type C will not be known until overseas deliveries can be made.

In laying out the design of the chassis, the primary consideration was to improve the ratio of power-to-weight by reducing the weight of the whole car and increasing the power output of the engine, in order to gain in acceleration as well as higher speed. In order to express these gains to the best advantage in competition and racing, the cornering ability had to be stepped up, and that entailed a stiffer but not a heavy frame construction, quicker and more positive steering, and a more controlled suspension.

Coming now to details, the engine is the same, in general, as the well-known 3½-litre six-cylinder 83×106 mm (3,442 c.c.), as shown in the specification. It has, however, the tuning modifications which are described in the service bulletin, and which include an 8 to 1 or 9 to 1 compression ratio according to the fuel which will be used. Different pistons are fitted to suit the different ratios. Both inlet and exhaust camshafts have high-lift cams, the ignition timing is advanced, and a special distributor head is used. The needles used in the carburettor are special, and "hot" sparking plugs are fitted. A lighter flywheel is used, and also a special high-speed crankshaft damper. A dual exhaust system is an

The steering wheel has a telescopic column for adjustment. On the facia the two main instruments are speedometer and rev counter of large size. The rev counter reads up to 6,500 r.p.m., and the section between 5,700 and 6,500 is coloured red. On the left of these are the ignition switch and ammeter, and on the right the fuel gauge and oil and water gauges. The gear lever is central and is carried on a shorter tunnel than in the XK.

All the front panelling hinges up to give remarkable accessibility.

The Jaguar XK120 C

briefest time, that is enough, and doors can be reduced to one, and that only a shallow affair.

This quite simple aspect has a very definite bearing on the design of the frame as a whole, because it allows room for a structure of increased vertical height just at a point where rigidity is much needed, but is apt to be lacking, on most open two-seater cars with two doors. With these points in mind the Type C frame can be studied. Perhaps the easiest way to grasp the meaning of the forest undergrowth of steel tubes which appear in the sketch of this frame is to consider first the central part, around which the scuttle is situated. It will be seen that there is a tubular centre section framework more or less in the shape of a rectangular box lying laterally across the structure. This centre section is triangulated in three directions, laterally, horizontally, and longitudinally. The legs of the driver will be inside this box, and the front of it will be closed off with a steel bulkhead to divide it from the engine compartment, and to add stiffness.

Projecting forward from the centre section there is on each a triangulated girder of steel tube, forming, as it were, a horizontal pyramid. The outer side of each pyramid is also diagonally braced in the vertical plane. The apexes of the two pyramids are joined by the front cross-member structure, consisting of upper and lower box section laterals, and a V-shaped centre piece. This structure is further braced by an aft cross tube at the top, and diagonal foot bracings. Top and bottom of the front cross-member structure are brackets which provide the anchorage for the lateral links of the front independent suspension, and the lower bracket on each side contains the front end of the longitudinal torsion bar, the tail of which is adjustably located in a bracket on the lower cross tube of the main centre section of the frame. It will be seen that this construction provides for rigidity between the front cross-member component and the centre section in every direction,

Rear suspension: The axle casing is located by underslung longitudinal links, the fulcrums of which are attached to a transverse torsion bar spring. The triangular torque-reaction member, on the right side above the axle end, prevents lateral movement, and, being at maximum distance from the axis of the propeller-shaft, imposes the maximum resistance to lift and spin of the right side wheel.

important feature. The clutch has a special assembly, with a solid centre and linings riveted and cemented to the plate, to deal with racing starts. Much of the work of increasing the power output of the engine was carried out in conjunction with Mr. Henry Weslake.

When a car is to be capable of exceedingly high speeds it is essential that the construction be as rigid as possible, otherwise it will be difficult to control with that precision which the driver needs on curves and corners, and may also be uncertain during maximum acceleration and maximum braking. With the intention of providing this rigidity and at the same time not being too heavy, the Type C frame is a structure quite different from the more orthodox XK, and is a very interesting design. When laying out a touring car the designer has to consider the comfort of the occupants, not only for riding, but also for the simple matter of getting easily in, and subsiding gracefully into an armchair seat. That means doors. But when designing a competition or racing car, so long as the driver can leap hurriedly in, and compose himself for action in the

Frame of the Jaguar XK120C, which combines lightness with most carefully planned rigidity. The design of this structure is explained in the description.

lateral, vertical, longitudinal, "lozenge," and torsional. In the space between the pyramids the engine is mounted.

Now to look backwards from the main centre section: It will be seen that the lower longitudinal tubes of the forward part continues rearward to a tubular cross-member, in which the torsion bars of the rear suspension are housed. Triangulated tubes run down from the top of the centre section to meet this cross-member, and are further braced with diagonals. Running diagonally upwards and rearwards on each side are box section members, joined at the top by a cross tube, the space between them being filled by a steel bulkhead with a large slot in it for the tail of the propeller-shaft and the nose piece of the final drive case. It will be noticed that from the front cross-member to the centre of the back cross-member there are channel section runners, plentifully perforated for lightness. These, too, are diagonally braced, and carry the steel flooring. They also serve as "anti-lozenge" ties.

This frame needs a little explanation because it is unusual in shape. The part behind the centre section is the place where the driver has his bucket seat, with its back adjacent to the slotted bulkhead. The X-shaped members on each side occupy the space where the doors of an ordinary car would be situated, so at this point the frame retains its strength, and is fully triangulated right up to the point where the back axle is attached. There is reached another very interesting part of the design, the rear suspension.

The rear axle is a tubular type with an offset hypoid bevel final drive, and an open propeller-shaft with Hardy Spicer needle roller-bearing universal joints. Below each end of the axle casing is a downwardly depending bracket, at the foot of which is a link

A multiplicity of small tubes forms the main structure of the new type C Jaguar. Rack and pinion steering, mounted to the rear of the wheel centre lines, is operated from the steering column via a universal joint. Fresh cool air is conveyed to the twin S.U. carburettors by means of a large duct of rectangular section. Behind the rear damper can be seen the reaction member which enables the torque developed by the engine to assist in keeping both rear wheels on the ground, thereby considerably improving the getaway from rest.

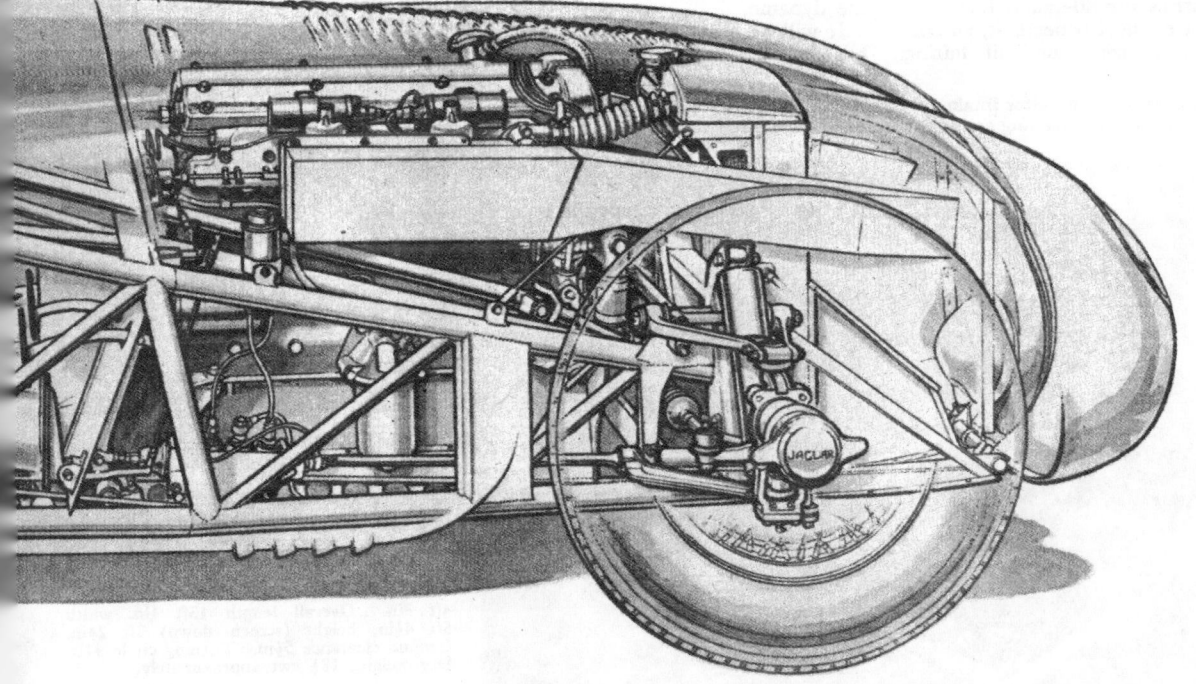

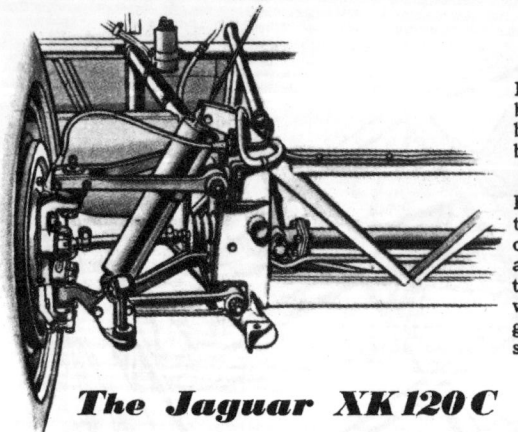

Left: Front suspension, with wide-based wishbones, longitudinal torsion bars and large Newton dampers, behind which the rack and pinion steering gear can be seen.

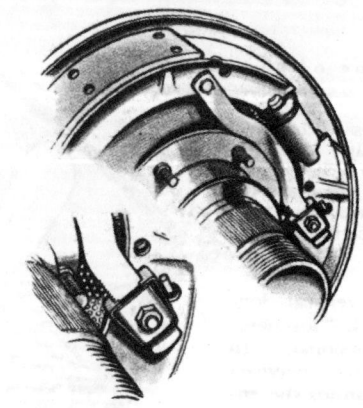

Right: Automatic adjustment of the Lockheed brakes. The shoes are coupled by a tie bar; one end slides, and has a fine tooth ratchet passing through a housing. The ratchet is free when the shoes are expanding but engages on the nearest tooth when the shoes move into the "off" position.

The Jaguar XK120C . . . continued

running forwards to a fulcrum anchorage at the back of the frame, these anchorages being attached to the ends of the rear cross tube of the frame as already described. The fulcrum of each link is splined to the outer end of a torsion bar spring, concealed in the cross-member and anchored in the centre of it. The foot of a telescopic hydraulic damper is attached towards the end of each link, and the head of the damper is hinged to the end of the upper lateral tube of the back of the frame structure. Hinged above the axle on the right-hand side, that is, just behind the driver, is a wide triangular link, with its fulcrum parallel to the axle, and its apex hinged to the back of the frame. This is the torque reaction member, and the purpose of mounting it to one side is to reduce the lift of the axle on one side when violent accelerations of the car are taking place; otherwise one rear wheel tends to lift and spin. The drivers in the race were enthusiastic about the effectiveness of this component.

The structure of the frame appears to end suddenly with the after bulkhead behind the driving compartment. Actually there is a subsidiary tail frame attached to this bulkhead, in a manner rather like the outrigger mounting of an engine in an aircraft. The tail frame carries the 40-gallon fuel tank, and a spare wheel beneath it, all concealed in a streamline tail fairing.

The whole outfit is relatively easily removable.

Similar in principle to that of the XK120, the independent front suspension consists of lateral wishbones and longitudinal torsion bar springs, controlled by large size 2in diameter Newton telescopic hydraulic dampers. The outer ends of the wishbones have spherical sockets which embrace ball heads at the top and bottom of the stub axle "fork," so that this fork becomes the steering swivel as well as forming the strut between the ends of the wishbones. The details of the Type C suspension are shown in one of the sketches, and it may be noted that the lower wishbones are somewhat shorter than on the XK, with a wider base. The two independent systems are cross coupled by a torsion anti-sway bar. Another material difference is that a rack and pinion steering gear is used. The purpose is to provide a light and direct steering which is quick in action. The steering wheel has a telescopic adjustment, and the column has a universal joint at the foot.

Built into the bonnet top are two ducts, with orifices which flank the radiator. One of these ducts conveys fresh frontal air under wind pressure to the filter box of the twin S.U. carburettors; the other plays cool air on the dynamo.

It will be observed that the Type C has a body designed in accordance with the modern ideas of fairing, or streamlining. Mr. William Heynes, the engineering director of the Jaguar company, expressed to *The Autocar* the view that this fairing was a very material help in achieving the very high speed of which the cars are capable. He pointed out that the streaks of dust showing on the outside of the body after the race are practically in straight lines along the length of the car, which is an indication that air eddy currents are not being caused.

Although a car of this variety does not need to have much accommodation, the Type C has one or two recesses, notably in the hollow of the door and on the opposite side, also on the right side below the bonnet. The battery is carried below the door, and the tools below the second seat if one is is position. If there is no seat a leather tonneau cover streamlines the opening of the cockpit.

SPECIFICATION

Engine.—6 cylinders 83 × 106 mm (3,442 c.c.). Overhead valves at 70 degrees operated by twin overhead camshafts driven by two-stage Duplex chain. Large valves have Austenitic seats in aluminium alloy detachable cylinder head. Aluminium alloy pistons, steel connecting rods, counterweighted crankshaft in seven 2⅜in steel-backed bearings. Pump water circulation. Full-flow Tecalemit oil filter. Twin horizontal S.U. carburettors. Twin exhaust system. Hemispherical combustion chambers. Compression ratio 8 to 1 for 80 octane fuel, gives 200 b.h.p. at 5,800 r.p.m. 9 to 1 ratio for 85 octane fuel gives 210 b.h.p. at 5,800 r.p.m.

Transmission.—Borg and Beck dry single-plate clutch with solid centre and bonded riveted lining. 4-speed synchromesh gear box with central lever. Overall gear ratios, normal 3.31, 4.51, 6.59, and 11.2 to 1; close ratio box, 3.31, 3.99, 5.78, and 9.86 to 1. Axle ratios available, 2.9, 3.31, 3.54, 3.75, 3.92, 4.09, and 4.27 to 1. Final drive by Hardy Spicer propeller-shaft to hypoid bevel axle with semi-floating shafts.

Suspension.—Independent front with wishbones and torsion bar springs. Special controlled rear with torsion bar springs and torque reaction couplings. Newton hydraulic dampers back and front.

Brakes.—Lockheed hydraulic, 2 L.S. front. Self adjusting. 12in drums.

Steering.—Rack and pinion. Adjustable wheel.

Wheels and Tyres.—Dunlop Road Racing, 6.50 × 16in on knock-off wire wheels with light alloy rims.

Electric Equipment.—Lucas 12 volt, Lucas coil; 40 ampère-hour battery. Champion N.A.10 or N.A.12 sparking plugs.

Fuel System.—40-gallon rear tank; two S.U. electric pumps.

Main Dimensions.—Wheelbase 8ft. Track 4ft 3in. Overall length 13ft 1in, width 5ft 4½in, height (screen down) 3ft 2½in. Ground clearance 5½in. Turning circle 31ft. Dry weight, 18½ cwt approximately.

Ducting over the carburettor intakes matches up with an air intake duct built into the bonnet panelling and taking in fresh air at the front of the car.

The author in the XK 120 Jaguar, with which he achieved a mean speed of 132.596 m.p.h. for the Flying Mile on the Jabbeke-Aeltre road near Ostend, in 1949.

EARNING ITS TYPE-NUMBER

How the Jaguar XK 120 Justified the Belief of its Designers that it was one of the World's Fastest Sports-Cars

by
R. M. V. SUTTON

THE Jaguar XK 120 is today world-famed as one of the fastest, if not *the* fastest production car, and its numerous successes in competitions are too well known to need any repetition. Yet at one time, like any other new model straight from the drawing board, its potency had yet to be discovered, and it may be of interest to describe the early tests.

It will be recalled that the car made a successful début at the 1948 Motor Show, where, although universally admired, doubts were expressed in some quarters as to whether performance would match the appearance. We, at the works, knew that it was outstanding, but had only a somewhat vague idea of the maximum speed we might expect, so the obvious thing was to find out. It was most desirable that, having named the car XK 120, that figure in terms of m.p.h. should be attained, and we confidently hoped it would be exceeded.

Now, a manufacturer's claims for speed are of no value unless backed up by independent witnesses, and it was decided to take the car to the Jabbeke-Aeltre road in Belgium where Goldie Gardner has put up so many records, and arrange for officially timed runs to be carried out under the auspices of the R.A.C. and the R.A.C. of Belgium. The British Press were also invited to be present, and a 27-seater plane was chartered to fly them over. It would indeed have been a catastrophe had the car failed to do its stuff before the assembled multitude, so preliminary tests were carried out in this country.

There was, however, one little matter which was secretly worrying me. My fastest ever speed had been achieved in the dim and distant past; 1928 to be precise, when I clocked 112 m.p.h. at Brooklands on a Lea-Francis.

If there are any ex-Leaf exponents who think this is an exaggeration, I would inform them that the three special short wheelbase work's cars (known as The Lobsters) fitted with No. 9 Cozette blowers could, and did, attain this speed, along the Railway Straight.

But this is by the way.

Now 20 years is a long time, and another 20 m.p.h. or so on the top of 112 m.p.h. quite a considerable step, and although I had kept my hand in to a certain extent by driving moderately fast cars in the interim, I had not exceeded my speed of a score years earlier, and I must confess to having some doubts as to my ability to cope.

It was essential that both the car and myself should be tried out before proceeding to Belgium, so I set out early one spring morning for a road where a five-mile straight was available.

I must admit that while waiting for the dawn at a transport café, consuming numerous cups of tea, I was a little apprehensive as both the car and myself were unknown quantities. Still, it was encouraging to know that no traffic would be met with on that particular road, but discouraging in the extreme to think that, in the event of "an unfortunate incident" no help would be at hand for a long time.

However, as soon as I let in the clutch all traces of nervousness vanished. That first run certainly felt fast—very fast indeed, the road appearing to taper off to the width of a footpath, and I remember involuntarily ducking my head, as the telegraph wires, which crossed at one point, appeared to bear down upon me. A quick glance at the rev. counter showed the speed to be over 125 m.p.h., but I was quite comfortable and the car held the road perfectly.

The second and third runs gave the impression of being slower, as I had time to read all the instruments and make mental notes, yet now that the engine and transmission had thoroughly warmed up, the rev. counter recorded a speed of over 130 m.p.h.

Feeling quite satisfied, I returned to the café for more tea, which somehow tasted much better than before, and I was able to report to the works that all was well with the car; but what was of more importance to my mind, I had renewed confidence in myself. It may have been due to the superb way in which the car handled, but I was surprised to find that I felt less conscious of speed than I had been at 112 m.p.h. so many years before.

On my return to the works the Design Department appeared to be a little sceptical, so I repeated the run a few days later, this time with a mechanic.

So far so good, but the speed had, as yet, only been estimated by rev. counter, and the next step was to stage a dress rehearsal on the actual road in Belgium and time the car over a mile.

Mr. "Wally" Hassan, Jaguar's Development Engineer and my immediate chief, was unfortunately indisposed and unable to accompany us, so I set out with one mechanic; none other than Jack Lea who had ridden with me in the 1930 T.T. and yet for some unknown reason, was willing to be my mechanic again.

Apart from part of the carburetter falling off in London (incidentally this was the only spare required throughout the tests) and embarking on the wrong boat, an error fortunately discovered in time, the journey to Ostend was uneventful, and we installed ourselves in one of the most palatial hotels.

This was a mistake, and we soon realized that if we had all our meals in this establishment, there would be no money with which to buy petrol, and very little for beer. Accordingly each day saw us sinking lower and lower in our choice of restaurants, until we finally finished up in little back street estaminets, where the food was surprisingly good in spite of their somewhat unprepossessing exteriors.

Naturally we took the first opportunity to inspect the Jabbeke-Aeltre road, which was ideal for our purpose, comprising two carriage ways, divided by a grass verge, and stretching dead straight for more miles than we required. The concrete surface was also very good, although unbelievably slippery when wet.

M. Wybo, who had assisted Goldie Gardner, was very helpful and came out with us, bringing the marking boards for the mile and kilometre. Fortunately he knew where their sockets were hidden in the grass, which saved us having to crawl on hands and knees for several kilometres. The official run, which, as I shall describe, took place a few weeks later, was of course, electrically timed and the road closed, but as this is a luxury which cannot be afforded very often, we had to be content, for the rehearsals, with hand timing on an open road.

I was told, before leaving Coventry, that very little traffic would be met with, but found this far from being the case. Every morning as soon as the inevitable fog had dispersed, lorries and cars rolled up by the score, many of them pulling up to watch the Jaguar, which did not help matters. However, we put in several runs at around 130 m.p.h. for the mile, and felt fairly satisfied.

On returning to the works it was

OFFICIAL SPEEDS
In Open Form

	Flying Mile		Flying Kilometre	
	M.P.H.	K.P.H.	M.P.H.	K.P.H.
North Run	131.916	212.290	131.355	211.391
South Run	133.283	214.490	133.388	214.660
Mean	132.596	213.390	132.362	213.017

Standing Mile (Mean) 86.434 m.p.h.
Standing Kilo (Mean) 139.100 k.p.h.

Hood and Sidescreens Erected

	Flying Mile		Flying Kilometre	
	M.P.H.	K.P.H.	M.P.H.	K.P.H.
North Run	125.698	202.290	126.095	202.931
South Run	127.253	204.790	127.038	204.545
Mean	126.448	203.490	126.594	203.735

decided to raise the axle ratio from 3.6 to 3.2, as with the former, revs were rather near the danger limit and it was thought that, besides playing for safety, the higher ratio would result in slightly increased speed, but as a matter of fact the practice and official runs were almost identical. It says much for the car that, apart from changing the axle ratio, no other work was carried out.

Wally Hassan had now fully recovered, and by virtue of his position and qualifications as a driver, was entitled to drive the car himself. This, however, he refused to do, saying that as I had done the spade work, it was only fair that I should have the credit, but that he would come over with us to assist in the organization and preparation of the car. This was indeed a most generous sporting gesture, and one that I shall never forget.

We returned to Belgium a few days before the "The Day", and, profiting by our previous mistake, stayed in a modest but pleasant hotel at Bruges, which, apart from the smell of the picturesque canal, is a delightful old city.

Fortunately, there was very little work to be done on the car, and we were able to amuse ourselves on "The Dodgems" at one of the most colossal fairs I have ever seen, occupying the whole of the Grande Place. I am afraid we made rather a nuisance of ourselves, and were informed by the proprietor, as he switched off the current, that, if we could not drive properly, we had better keep away.

It was part of the demonstration to run on pump petrol, and the day before the event the tank was drained and filled up with Shell petrol under observation, the filler cap, etc., then being sealed. We scanned the weather forecasts with no little anxiety, as unlike most record attempts when one can wait days or weeks for suitable conditions, this "show" had to be run to a strict schedule, as in addition to laying on the timekeepers, gendarmerie, etc., the guests were being flown over, and had to return that afternoon. However, the gods were extremely kind to us. Just before the commencement there was a veritable cloudburst at each end of the road, but the section we were using remained as dry as a bone. The Belgium R.A.C.'s organization was most efficient; dozens of gendarmes rolled up, and in a very short time one carriageway was closed, a mile of wiring laid down, and the timekeepers and loudspeaker vans took up their position.

The electrical timing apparatus was actuated by a cotton thread stretched across the road, which, on breaking, in addition to starting watches, operated another instrument which recorded the time on a tape. This was inserted in yet another gadget something like a cash register, and the time came out printed on a ticket, to three places of decimals, and announced as soon as I had completed each run. No argument. No fuss.

The first runs were carried out with hood and sidescreens erected. These, together with the windscreens were then removed, the latter being replaced by a small cowl, and a tonneau cover fitted. As I wished to be absolutely certain of attaining peak r.p.m. before entering the measured mile I took a run of 2½ miles, but I was actually up to my maximum within a mile. Everything went according to plan, and for those interested in such things, I append the official speeds.

The photographers and film people got busy after it was all over and I had a close-up taken from a car travelling alongside at a speed which was supposed to be over 130 m.p.h., but was actually something under 30 m.p.h. Unfortunately, this section of film was spoiled, as, on being developed it was noted that I was smoking a cigarette with what looked like two inches of ash on the end!

We felt quite satisfied with the results and adjourned for a celebration lunch, while the Press party departed very happily to catch their plane.

I returned to the works the next day, and while I did not expect to find the flags out, was rather taken aback when welcomed by a senior member of the drawing office staff, who had been putting in some hectic work on his slide rule, with the words, "And *why* were you so slow?" Had he prefaced that remark by saying "Good morning", I should not have taken quite such a dim view about it.

THE FITCH-JAGUAR

By JOHN FITCH

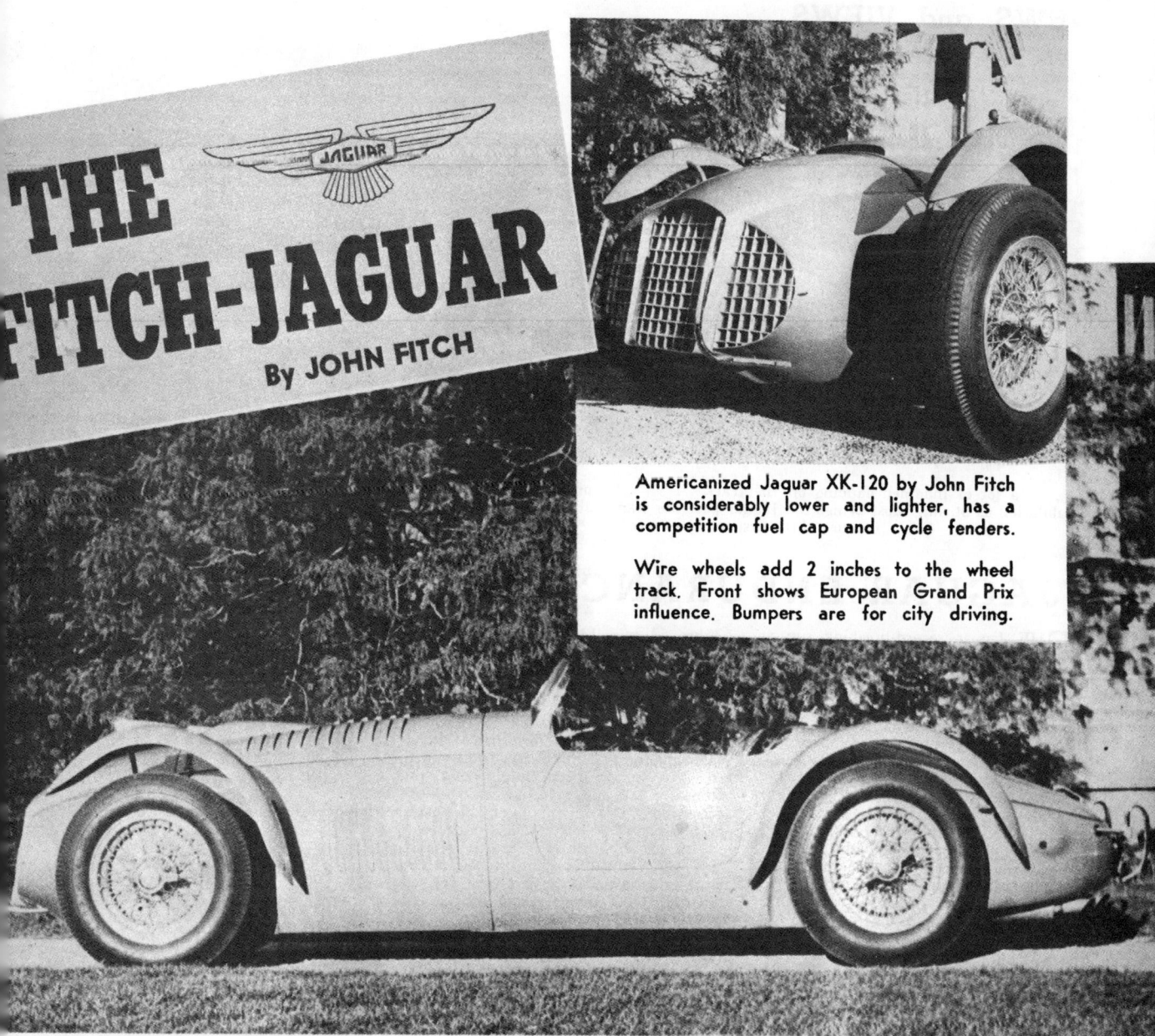

Americanized Jaguar XK-120 by John Fitch is considerably lower and lighter, has a competition fuel cap and cycle fenders.

Wire wheels add 2 inches to the wheel track. Front shows European Grand Prix influence. Bumpers are for city driving.

WE call this special Fitch-Jaguar the "Le Mans" model because the prime means of obtaining performance, the light body, is the same method used by the majority of Le Mans winners of the past; Bentley, Bugatti, Lagonda, Talbot, etc. Also, Coby Whitmore, popular illustrator from Briarcliff, New York, and the owner for whom the car was built, hopes to enter it at Le Mans.

The Le Mans Fitch Jaguar was designed as a competition car to suit the special conditions of U.S. sports car racing. Our courses being short and permitting relatively low average speeds, our greatest concern was for light weight, hence high acceleration, and the interests of streamlining by use of an enveloping body were sacrificed to this on the premise that a cycle fendered body can be built lighter than the enveloping type. Our prediction is supported by the fact that XK 120 C is 150 pounds heavier than the Le Mans in spite of the lighter tubular frame. Incidentally, the LeMans was built before the XK 120C made its famous first appearance.

THERE is little difference under the skin between the Le Mans Fitch-Jaguar and the standard XK 120. The box frame is identical and undrilled. In front the torsion bars were simply adjusted to the lighter load and the rear springs were re-arched. A new twenty gallon gas tank was built to fit behind the seats and in front of the rear axle. The stock radiator was relocated lower and forward of the frame. A large expansion tank and filler was placed high behind the fire wall. Seats and steering wheel were both lowered and the "seat" is very comfortable thanks to foot wells in the floorboard . . . plenty of room for the left foot. Alfin aluminum drums and wire wheels complete the alterations, the wire wheels increasing the track by 2 inches.

The handling characteristics are completely different. The reduced load has relatively stiffened the springs and shocks and practically eliminated the tendency to lean or sway.

The net weight is 2100 pounds as compared to 2900, more or less, of the production model. Reduced weight equals power added, and I would say the equivalent in performance to the "Le Mans" would be the standard Jaguar with a healthy 220 B.H.P. available. The "Le Mans" is a delight to drive; it has smooth manners and boulevard docility as family traits, but enhanced by an almost Grand Prix authority when requested.

NEWS and VIEWS

"... a lot of madmen dancing on the track ..." The pit staff display their jubilation as Stirling Moss brings the Jaguar past the stands at Montlhéry after the capture of the first world's record.

JAGUAR ENDURANCE RUN

THE Jaguar record-breaking run at the Montlhéry track near Paris, referred to in last week's issue, has now reached its end. Although all the objectives were not attained, four world's records and five international Class C records were captured, all at speeds in excess of 100 m.p.h.

A fixed-head Jaguar XK120 coupé was the car used; it was in standard trim except for certain modifications that are all available to Jaguar owners as optional extras. These included high-lift camshafts, twin exhaust system, 25-gallon fuel tank, oversize sump, and knock-off wire wheels; the higher optional compression ratio (8 to 1) was used, together with the highest of the available axle ratios. The run was initiated by Leslie Johnson, who had as co-drivers Bert Hadley, Stirling Moss and Jack Fairman; Jaguars prepared the car and provided the team of mechanics, and Desmond Scannell, secretary of the B.R.D.C., looked after the organization and acted as team manager, assisted by "Mort" Morris-Goodall.

On Monday, August 4, at 4 p.m., the car got under way for the attempt; but after only 12 hours' running a thrown tyre tread damaged a wing and severed a battery lead. A halt was therefore called for repairs, and the attempt was re-started at 4 p.m. on the following day, Tuesday, August 5. The car began to lap at between 105 and 110 m.p.h. with no difficulty at all, and the first two days passed almost without incident. A feature of the run was the employment of two-way Pye radio communication between car and pit.

First real excitement came at the end of the third day, when the following message was sent to Stirling Moss, who was then driving: "If you see a lot of madmen dancing on the track, pay no attention to them; just go on for three more laps and then come in." The occasion for the display of madness was the capture, at 4 o'clock on Friday afternoon, of the first world's record—72 hours at an average speed of 105.55 m.p.h. This also constituted a Class C record. At 2 o'clock that morning the Jaguar had also broken the Class C record for 10,000 kilometres, in 57 hrs 54 min 13$\frac{19}{20}$ sec, at an average speed of 107.031 m.p.h. The previous 10,000 kilometre record had been held by a Delahaye, with an average of 104.7 m.p.h.; and the 72-hour record was pulverized, for since 1937 it had stood at 89.33 m.p.h. to the credit of a ladies' team in a Matford.

During the first three days some rather fast driving had been indulged in, the record lap being covered by Stirling Moss at a speed of 121.28 m.p.h., and the average being kept at 110 m.p.h.

With the first world's record secured, there was a stop of 12 minutes, when the sump, gear box and rear axle were drained and refilled and the car generally checked over, but without any change of tyres. Instructions were given to hold lap times down to 55 to 57 sec, which corresponded to about 3,600 r.p.m., but still held the car a safe distance above the existing records.

Next to fall was the four-day (96-hour) world's and Class C record, at 101.17 m.p.h.; and this was followed by the 15,000 kilometre record in the same categories, at 101.94 m.p.h. Just before the completion of 10,000 miles, however, came trouble, in the shape of a broken rear spring on the left-hand side; but the car was kept running until this distance had been exceeded, and the records were duly secured at 100.65 m.p.h. Then the spring was replaced during a three-hour pit stop; but, since the spare spring had not been carried on the car, by the rules no further records could be claimed. However, it was decided to continue for the full seven days and nights, to demonstrate that the average speed could be maintained.

On Tuesday, August 12, at 4 p.m., the Jaguar completed its momentous run of seven days and seven nights, having covered 16,851.73 miles at an average speed of 100.31 m.p.h. Leslie Johnson was at the wheel for the final laps. At Dover on Wednesday afternoon, the Mayor of Dover and Mr. W. Lyons, managing director of Jaguar Cars, Ltd., welcomed the team at the quayside to the civic reception held in honour of the Jaguar's achievement.

All the records referred to are, of course, subject to official confirmation.

The XK120 coupé has very graceful flowing lines. The front wing line sweeps right back through the doors to blend into the rear wing curves. Ventilators are fitted in the body sides

JAGUAR XK120 COUPE

SEVERAL years ago Jaguar Cars designed a six-cylinder twin overhead camshaft engine with a capacity of 3½ litres. This engine was a winner right from the start. It was first fitted to the XK120 open sports two-seater, which was an instant success. It has a very high performance, a sound chassis layout, and it is also very good value for money. Later, the same engine was fitted to a new six-seater saloon known as the Mark VII, and this has proved one of the few large saloon cars road tested by this journal that has recorded a mean maximum speed of over 100 m.p.h. The Mark VII is also extremely good value for money, and at the last London Show, when it was first exhibited, the question on the lips of very many people was: "How do Jaguar's do it for the price?"

Although these two models will meet the needs of a very large proportion of the high-speed motoring public there are some people who require a vehicle that has saloon car comfort coupled with high speed, but who want a car dimensionally smaller than the Mark VII saloon. Consequently the XK120 two-seater fixed head coupé was produced. This model is in effect an XK chassis and body with a metal top and full doors in place of the hood and side screens. A left-hand drive special equipment version of this model has recently been road tested by *The Autocar*.

The coupé can perhaps be likened to a well-trained racehorse, inasmuch as it is extremely powerful yet very willing and docile; but, on the other hand, it must be controlled and treated with respect if the best results are to be obtained. The outstanding impression after having driven this car for more than 2,000 miles is of the way it goes, and keeps on going. Even after a high-speed Continental journey, and also a complete road test on a Belgian motor road, the car had no

DATA

PRICE (basic), with fixed head coupé body (and special equipment), £1,255.
Not available in Great Britain.
Extras: Radio £33.
Heater, standard equipment.

ENGINE: Capacity: 3,442 c.c. (210 cu in).
Number of cylinders: 6.
Bore and stroke: 83 x 106 mm (3.268 x 4.173 in).
Valve gear: twin overhead camshafts.
Compression ratio: 8 to 1.
B.H.P.: 180 at 5,300 r.p.m. (B.H.P. per ton laden 118).
Torque: 203 lb ft at 4,000 r.p.m.
M.P.H. per 1,000 r.p.m. on top gear, 21.3.

WEIGHT (with 5 gals fuel), 27 cwt (3,037 lb).
Weight distribution (per cent): 47.5 F; 52.5 R.
Laden as tested: 30.6 cwt (3,422 lb).
Lb per c.c. (laden): 0.95.

BRAKES: Type: F, Two-leading shoe. R, Leading and trailing.
Method of operation: F, Hydraulic. R, Hydraulic.
Drum dimensions: F, 12in diameter, 2¼in wide. R, 12in diameter, 2¼in wide.
Lining area: F, 103.5 sq in. R, 103.5 sq in. (135 sq in per ton laden.)

TYRES: 6.00—16in.
Pressures (lb per sq in): 25 F, 25 R (normal); 35 F, 35 R (for fast driving).

TANK CAPACITY: 14 Imperial gallons.
Oil sump, 25½ pints.
Cooling system, 25½ pints.

TURNING CIRCLE: 31ft 0in (L and R).
Steering wheel turns (lock to lock): 2¾.

DIMENSIONS: Wheelbase 8ft 6in.
Track: 4ft 3in (F); 4ft 2in (R).
Length (overall): 14ft 5in.
Height: 4ft 5½in.
Width: 5ft 2in.
Ground clearance: 7½in.
Frontal area: 17.13 sq ft (approx.).

ELECTRICAL SYSTEM: 12-volt, 64 ampère-hour battery.
Head lights: Double dip, 48-48 watt.

SUSPENSION: Front, independent; wishbones and torsion bars and anti-roll bar. Rear, half-elliptic springs.

PERFORMANCE

JAGUAR XK120 COUPÉ (Special Equipment Model)

ACCELERATION: from constant speeds. Speed, Gear Ratios and time in sec.

M.P.H.	3.77 to 1	5.16 to 1	7.48 to 1	12.73 to 1
10—30	7.9	5.6	4.1	2.9
20—40	7.7	5.4	4.0	—
30—50	7.3	5.3	4.2	—
40—60	7.4	5.6	4.8	—
50—70	7.9	6.0	—	—
60—80	8.1	6.7	—	—
70—90	9.3	8.7	—	—
80—100	10.9	—	—	—

From rest through gears to:

M.P.H.	sec
30	3.3
50	7.5
60	9.9
70	13.7
80	17.1
90	22.1
100	28.2

Standing quarter mile, 17.3 sec.

SPEED ON GEARS:

Gear		M.P.H. (normal and max.)	K.P.H. (normal and max.)
Top	(mean)	120.5	193.9
	(best)	121	194.7
3rd	...	72—90	116—145
2nd	...	49—60	79—97
1st	...	26—36	42—58

SPEEDOMETER CORRECTION: M.P.H.

Car speedometer	10	20	30	40	50	60	70	80	90	100	110	120
True speed	10	21	29	41	50	60	70	80	90	100	111	121

TRACTIVE RESISTANCE: 23.7 lb per ton at 10 m.p.h.

TRACTIVE EFFORT:

	Pull (lb per ton)	Equivalent Gradient
Top	300	1 in 7.5
Third	400	1 in 5.5
Second	525	1 in 4.1

BRAKES:

Efficiency	Pedal Pressure (lb)
94 per cent	125
83 per cent	100
64 per cent	70

FUEL CONSUMPTION:
16.2 m.p.g. overall for 169 miles (17.8 litres per 100 km).
Approximate normal range 14-18 m.p.g. (20.1-15.7 litres per 100 km).
Fuel, Belgian premium grade (approximately 80 octane).

WEATHER: Dry surface; wind very slight.
Air temperature 58 degrees F.
Acceleration figures are the means of several runs in opposite directions.
Tractive effort and resistance obtained by Tapley meter.
Model described in *The Autocar* of March 2, 1951.

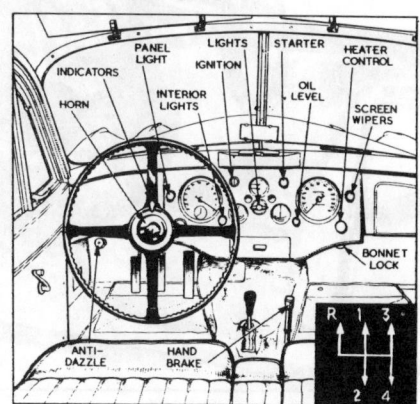

The simple and compact radiator grille, together with the powerful built-in head lamps, produces a very graceful frontal appearance to this fine car. Below the two-piece bumper are air intakes for ventilation of the under parts and brakes.

This view shows the extremely low build of the car. The lines of the roof and the luggage locker are well balanced and retain a family likeness that is shared by other models. The car provided for test—the special equipment model—had wire wheels, and when these are fitted the cover panels for the rear wings are removed.

feeling of tiredness, nor was there any noticeable falling off in its sprightliness. This ability to go and keep on going can also be applied to the chassis components and, in reverse, to the brakes, which will stop and keep on stopping. Those fitted to this particular model are Lockheed hydraulically operated (with automatic adjusters at the front), and during the whole time that the car was on test no manual adjustment was made to the brakes, nor was there any apparent increase in free pedal travel.

The six-cylinder twin overhead camshaft engine is extremely flexible in spite of the tuning modifications, which include a high compression ratio of 8 to 1, high lift cams, a lightened flywheel and dual exhaust systems. Although on British Pool fuel a certain amount of pinking was experienced, on Belgian premium grade fuel this was almost completely eliminated, and some measure of the engine flexibility can be appreciated from the fact that it was possible to accelerate from 7 m.p.h. up to over 120 m.p.h. on top gear with the car carrying two people. In the accompanying table a mean maximum speed of 120.5 m.p.h. is quoted, with a best speed of 121 m.p.h. This makes the XK coupé's Road Test performance just about the fastest to be recorded since the mean maximum method of speed recording has been re-adopted by *The Autocar* since the war. Further, although the Jabbeke road in Belgium was used for the performance tests there was other traffic about and consequently the *ultimate* maximum speed was not obtained. Before this could be achieved with safety it would be necessary to close the road. Under normal road conditions it is, of course, not possible, or desirable, to use the ultimate maximum speed often, but the fact that there is sufficient power available to propel this car at such a speed also gives it superb acceleration, a quality that makes it extremely pleasant to drive and enables long distances to be covered very quickly. The average speed for a journey depends entirely on road conditions and the ability of the driver.

The general proportions, weight distribution and layout make it an extremely stable vehicle, and one that can be cornered very fast with a feeling of complete confidence. On Alpine roads and passes the car is completely at home and responds to every wish of the driver. There are very few cars indeed that can pass an XK coupé that is really in a

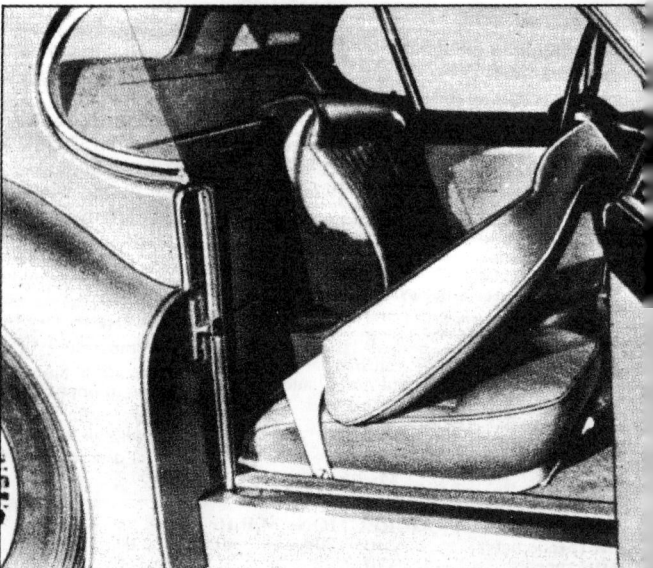

Owing to the low build of the body there is a large tunnel enclosing the gear box, yet the body is sufficiently wide to permit adequate leg-room. The facia panel is well finished in polished wood, while the instruments are recessed to prevent their causing reflections in the windscreen.

Both the separate seats hinge forward to gain access to the battery compartment and also to a small locker (shown with its lid in the open position). Hinged quarter lights are fitted both in front of and behind the main door window.

The locker is divided into two compartments, the lower one housing the spare wheel and some of the tools, while the tyre pump and tool roll are carried in the luggage compartment.
An interior light is fitted to the locker lid.

Measurements in these ⅛in to 1ft scale body diagrams are taken with the driving seat in the central position of fore and aft adjustment and with the seat cushions uncompressed.

hurry. The steering is light and very positive, and has good self-centring action, yet very little shock or kick is transmitted back to the steering wheel. The car as a whole has the very desirable quality of a slight amount of under-steer, and this again further inspires confidence and increases its stability.

The four-speed gear box, with synchromesh on top, third and second gears, is operated by a centrally placed remote control lever. This is well placed and very positive. The synchromesh is very effective and not easily beaten. Although it has some 180 b.h.p. to transmit, the clutch is smooth to operate and the pedal action is pleasantly light. The torsion bar independent front suspension, in conjunction with what may be called a conventional type of half-elliptic rear suspension, results in an extremely good ride—one that gives an impression of tautness rather than floppiness. On some types of stone setts a considerable amount of rumble could be heard, while on Belgian *pavé* the ride appeared quite hard if the high-speed tyre pressures were used, yet was quite comfortable with the normal touring-type pressures. At high speeds the car feels extremely stable and there is no suspicion of wander. The brakes (with a separate master cylinder for each pair of drums) are extremely effective and no noticeable fade was experienced either on the road or during the peculiar conditions of performance testing.

Seating and Controls

With such an excellent engine and chassis, perhaps the main criticism of the car, from the viewpoint of the driver principally concerned, is of the driving position and the arrangement of the foot-operated controls. But it must be realized that with a car of this type, in the interests of performance it is necessary to reduce the frontal area to a minimum; consequently, the overall height must be as low as possible, and this factor alone makes it very difficult to adopt what may be termed an ideal position, more especially for a tall driver. The seat squab is, however, well positioned and gives good support; the cushion, too, is comfortable, but a little more support for the driver's leg muscles would be appreciated.

The throttle pedal is well placed, but the brake pedal is much closer to the driver, and it is necessary to move the foot back from the throttle before the brakes can be applied, and this also makes the heel and toe type of gear change a little difficult. In the left-hand drive model submitted for the test there is ample room for the driver's left foot when it is not operating the clutch pedal. The fly-off racing type hand brake lever has a very good leverage ratio and is conveniently placed, yet it could, with advantage, be placed a little farther forward. The minor controls are well positioned on the facia panel, and include a switch for the heater which is standard equipment.

The interior is simply but tastefully trimmed in leather and polished wood, a combination that results in a very pleasing appearance. On a car of this type the luggage capacity is often very limited in order to keep the overall dimensions compact, and at first glance it appeared that the XK coupé came into this category, yet it should be recorded that by careful packing a considerable amount of luggage can be carried if the suitcases are of the right size and shape. There is a small locker behind the seats, while the tray between the rear squab and the rear window also provides extra carrying space. The body interior can be illuminated by two lights mounted in the trim. The head lamps earn full marks in that they are very powerful and have an exceptionally good beam and spread of light. They are dipped by means of a foot-operated switch mounted on the toeboard. The horns, too, are very powerful and have a penetrating yet pleasing note.

Starting from cold was at all times instantaneous and the mixture strength is controlled automatically, so that no separate choke control is fitted. This device proved to be quite satisfactory, yet gave the impression at times that it was not cutting out quite quickly enough.

When it is realized that this car, capable of speeds in excess of 120 m.p.h., coupled with startling acceleration (as reference to the data panel will reveal), has a basic price of £1,140, or, in the case of the special equipment model tested, £1,255, some idea of its exceptional value for money will be gained. This fact, coupled with the built-in ability to withstand a great deal of hard work without protest, makes it a very desirable car. With the XK coupé it is the driver and the road that are the limiting factors, and not the car.

The twin overhead camshaft engine and its auxiliaries completely fill the space under the bonnet. The coil is mounted on the right-hand side behind the twin S.U. carburettors.

The Motor Continental Road Test No. 9C/52—

Make: Jaguar
Makers: Jaguar Cars Ltd., Coventry
Type: XK 120C 2-seater

Dimensions and Seating

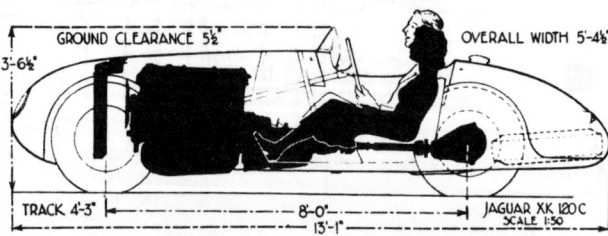

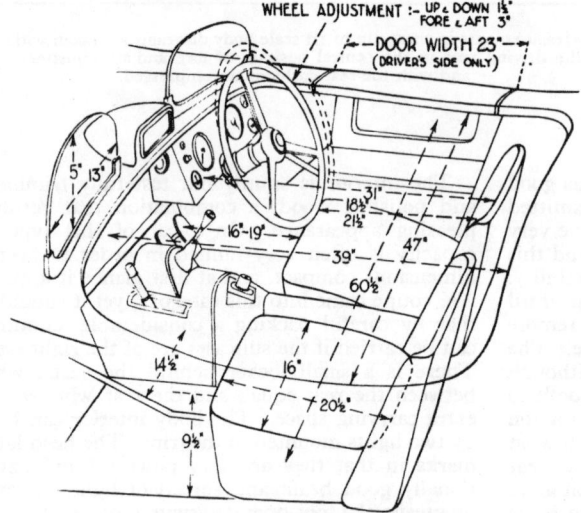

NOT TO SCALE

In Brief

Price £1,495 plus purchase tax £832 1s. 1d. equals £2,327 1s. 1d.
Capacity ... ... 3,442 c.c.
Unladen kerb weight ... ... 20 cwt.
Fuel consumption ... 16 m.p.g.
Maximum speed ... 143.7 m.p.h.
Maximum speed on 1 in 20 gradient ...approx. 132 m.p.h.
Maximum top gear gradient 1 in 6.8
Acceleration:
  10-30 m.p.h. in top ... 7.3 secs.
  0-50 m.p.h. through gears 6.1 secs.
Gearing:
  25 m.p.h. in top at 1,000 r.p.m.
  90 m.p.h. at 2,500 ft. per min. piston speed.

Specification

Engine
Cylinders 6
Bore ... ... 83 mm.
Stroke ... ... 106 mm.
Cubic capacity ... ... 3,442 c.c.
Piston area ... ... 50.4 sq. in.
Valves ... ... 2 o.h. camshafts
Compression ratio 8.0/1
Max. power ... ... 200 b.h.p.
  at ... ... 5,800 r.p.m.
Piston speed at max. b.h.p. 4,030 ft. per min.
Carburetter ... ... 2 S.U. horizontal
Ignition ... ... Lucas coil
Sparking plugs ... ... Champion NA10
  (soft, NA8; hard, NA12)
Fuel pump ... ... 2 S.U. electrical
Oil filter ... ... Tecalemit full-flow

Transmission
Clutch ... Borg & Beck 10 in. s.d.p.
Top gear (s/m) 3.31
3rd gear (s/m) 3.99
2nd gear (s/m) 5.78
1st gear 9.86
Propeller shaft ... ... Hardy Spicer
Final drive ... ... Hypoid bevel

Chassis
Brakes ... Lockheed hydraulic (2 l.s. front)
Brake drum diameter ... ... 12 ins.
Friction lining area ... ... 188 sq. in.
Suspension:
  Front: Torsion bar and wishbone I.F.S., with anti-roll torsion bar.
  Rear: Torsion bars and rigid axle.
Shock absorbers ... Newton telescopic
Tyres ... ... Dunlop Racing
  (Front, 6.00 - 16. Rear, 6.50 - 16)

Steering
Steering gear ... ... Rack and pinion
Turning circle ... ... 33 feet
Turns of steering wheel, lock to lock... 2¼

Performance factors (at laden weight as tested)
Piston area, sq. in. per ton 42.0
Brake lining area, sq. in. per ton ... 157
Specific displacement, litres per ton mile 3,440

Fully described in "The Motor," July 18, 1951.

Test Conditions

Cool, windy weather, with rain, except during standing start acceleration tests. 80-octane petrol. Driver and passenger in car, except during maximum speed tests run with half cockpit covered. Car tested on Ostend-Ghent motor road (smooth concrete surface).

Test Data

ACCELERATION TIMES on Two Upper Ratios

	Top	3rd
10-30 m.p.h.	7.3 secs.	6.4 secs.
20-40 m.p.h.	6.8 sec.	5.5 secs.
30-50 m.p.h.	7.2 secs.	5.8 secs.
40-60 m.p.h.	7.5 secs.	5.8 secs.
50-70 m.p.h.	7.5 secs.	6.1 secs.
60-80 m.p.h.	7.9 secs.	5.9 secs.
70-90 m.p.h.	8.0 secs.	6.3 secs.
80-100 m.p.h.	9.2 secs.	7.2 secs.

ACCELERATION TIMES Through Gears

0-30 m.p.h. ... ... 3.2 secs.
0-40 m.p.h. ... ... 4.3 secs.
0-50 m.p.h. ... ... 6.1 secs.
0-60 m.p.h. ... ... 8.1 secs.
0-70 m.p.h. ... ... 10.1 secs.
0-80 m.p.h. ... ... 12.2 secs.
0-90 m.p.h. ... ... 16.2 secs.
0-100 m.p.h. ... ... 20.1 secs.
0-110 m.p.h. ... ... 24.4 secs.
Standing Quarter Mile ... 16.2 secs.

FUEL CONSUMPTION

30.0 m.p.g. at constant 30 m.p.h.
30.0 m.p.g. at constant 40 m.p.h.
28.5 m.p.g. at constant 50 m.p.h.
26.0 m.p.g. at constant 60 m.p.h.
23.0 m.p.g. at constant 70 m.p.h.
20.0 m.p.g. at constant 80 m.p.h.
16.5 m.p.g. at constant 90 m.p.h.
15.0 m.p.g. at constant 100 m.p.h.
Overall consumption for 480 miles, 30 gallons, equal 16 m.p.g.

HILL CLIMBING (at steady speeds)

Max. top gear speed on 1 in 20 ... approx. 132 m.p.h.
Max. top gear speed on 1 in 15 ... approx. 125 m.p.h.
Max. top gear speed on 1 in 10 ... 100 m.p.h.
Max. gradient on top gear ... 1 in 6.8 (Tapley 325 lb/ton)
Max. gradient on 3rd gear ... 1 in 5.6 (Tapley 395 lb/ton)
Max. gradient on 2nd gear ... 1 in 3.7 (Tapley 585 lb/ton)

BRAKES at 30 m.p.h. (damp road)

0.80g retardation (= 37½ ft. stopping distance) with 125 lb. pedal pressure.
0.66g retardation (= 45½ ft. stopping distance) with 100 lb. pedal pressure.
0.48g retardation (= 63 ft. stopping distance) with 75 lb. pedal pressure.
0.21g retardation (= 143 ft. stopping distance) with 50 lb. pedal pressure.

MAXIMUM SPEEDS

Flying Mile (timed under very adverse conditions).
Mean of two opposite runs ... 143.711 m.p.h.
Best time equals ... ... 144.404 m.p.h.

Speed in Gears (at 5,700 r.p.m. recommended normal limit).
Max. speed in 3rd gear ... 119 m.p.h.
Max. speed in 2nd gear ... 82 m.p.h.
Max. speed in 1st gear ... 48 m.p.h.

WEIGHT

Unladen kerb weight ... 20 cwt.
Front/rear weight distribution ... 50/50
Weight laden as tested ... 24 cwt.

INSTRUMENTS

Speedometer at 30 m.p.h. ... accurate
Speedometer at 60 m.p.h. ... 3% fast
Speedometer at 90 m.p.h. ... 1% fast
Distance recorder ... 2½% fast

Maintenance

Fuel tank: 40 gallons. **Sump:** 19 pints, S.A.E. 30. **Gearbox:** 2¼ pints, S.A.E. 30. **Rear axle:** 3 pints Shell S3497. **Steering gear:** Grease lubricated. **Radiator:** 25¼ pints (2 drain taps). **Chassis lubrication:** By grease gun every 2,500 miles to 12 points. **Ignition timing:** 5° b.t.d.c. (static). **Spark plug gap:** 0.022-0.025 in. **Contact-breaker gap:** 0.012-0.015 in. **Valve timing:** I.O., 15° b.t.d.c.; I.C., 55° a.b.d.c.; E.O., 55° b.b.d.c.; E.C., 15° a.t.d.c. **Tappet clearances (cold):** Inlet, 0.006 in.; exhaust, 0.010 in. **Front wheel toe-in:** ⅛ in.–3/16 in. **Camber angle:** 1½°. **Castor angle:** 3° positive. **Tyre pressures:** 40-45 lb., front and rear, for high-speed driving. **Brake fluid:** Lockheed Racing Green. **Battery:** 12-volt, 40 amp/hr. **Lamp bulbs:** 12 volts. Headlamps, 45/36-watt, yellow; tail and stop lamp, 6/18-watt (Lucas No. 361); side, number plate and under-bonnet inspection lamps, 6-watt (Lucas No. 989); instrument lamps, 2.2-watt (Lucas No. 987).

Ref. B/35/52.

—The JAGUAR XK120C

An Extremely Fast and Docile Car Intended for Advanced Competition Work

The Jaguar 120C model is the fastest car yet road-tested. Allied to a maximum mean speed of 143 m.p.h., which was obtained in most unfavourable circumstances, is the ability to cruise at over two miles a minute wherever the roads permit.

THE road test of the Jaguar 120C presented several problems. This model was first introduced in 1951 and immediately received international prominence as a result of an outstanding victory at Le Mans. It was, however, made abundantly clear at the time by the Jaguar Company that unlike the well-established 120 model the "C" version represented a car designed entirely for competition motoring and not in any sense to be confused with the touring version which had already shown itself capable of more than 124 m.p.h. in our hands.

By late summer of 1952 the Jaguar 120C model began to emerge from the Coventry factory in sufficient quantities to merit the description "steady production" and it therefore seemed desirable that steps should be taken to carry out a normal road test of this interesting machine.

Safe and comfortable transportation for two people must form an essential part of any sports car however spartan, so it was decided to combine a maximum speed run on a closed motor road in Belgium with a drive to the Nurburgring in Germany and a subsequent passage over some of the major Autobahnen in Europe.

The weather proved most unpropitious during the preliminary trials and the conditions under which the maximum speed tests were made rendered it prudent to time the car electrically with only the driver aboard, rather than the two-passenger method normally adopted by this journal. Dry spells fortunately intervened for long enough to make the acceleration figures thoroughly representative and when a crew assembled in Brussels to drive the car to Germany they did so with the satisfactory knowledge that the Jaguar had averaged a mean speed of over 143 m.p.h. and in so doing had established certain Belgian sports car records.

The problem of the crew's luggage stowage at first appeared to be an insurmountable one. The 40-gallon petrol tank occupies the whole of the tail, and the two cockpit seats have no appreciable space behind them, but the body sides which constitute the driver's door and the passenger's elbow room proved so commodious that all the impedimenta of a prolonged trans-Continental journey could be housed therein leaving additional room for a quantity of waterproof clothing rendered necessary by the absence of hood and normal windscreen.

The many thousands of enthusiastic motorists who have watched the 120C in numerous races may have considered the vehicle far removed from the comforts of civilization but, in fact, bearing in mind the necessity for maximum possible performance from such a car, the amenities are attractive and well-planned. The driver and passenger sit well inside the Jaguar and despite pouring rain very little road dirt penetrates even when the car is driven fast. There is a certain snugness in the cockpit and the engine provides just sufficient warmth to give an impression of well-being which is greatly amplified as soon as the wheels commence to turn.

Flexible and Viceless

Let there be no mistake. The Jaguar 120C justifies absolutely the overworked term of thoroughbred. A stranger taking over the car for the first time at the height of a Brussels rush hour finds a docile and tractable machine completely without

The 120C has a very striking and attractive appearance. The door, which is mounted on the driver's side, gives easy access to the cockpit and the aero screens provide surprisingly adequate protection. The engine is rendered remarkably accessible because the whole of the front envelope of the car can be swung forward. Details of chassis frame, steering and suspension can also be studied in the photograph on the right.

The driver sits well inside the car and is thus protected from dirt and dust to a surprising degree. The large filler cap gives access to a 40-gallon petrol tank. Forward visibility is good and the general comfort and finish of the cockpit is of a high order.

Jaguar XK 120C - Contd.

temperament, ready to trickle through the traffic and proceed along slippery pavé and wet tramlines with most of the silence and comfort of the modern touring car. The astonishing flexibility of the 120C is best appreciated by a study of the performance data. It is sufficient here to say that second and third gears cope with any situation from walking speed to 100 m.p.h., and within a very few hours of first acquaintance the experienced driver feels well able to travel at speeds in excess of 120 m.p.h. whenever the road and traffic conditions render such motoring prudent.

The highest praise must be given to the steering characteristics of the Jaguar. This rack and pinion mechanism is not only light and responsive but sufficiently high-geared for the driver to change direction more by wrist action rather than arm movement. Additionally the car must be one of the truest "straight-line runners" the world has yet seen.

Planned Accessibility

We have stressed that the 120C is basically a racing car and accordingly the equipment is planned to meet the exacting needs of international contest. The accessibility of the entire engine when the front end of the body is raised could hardly be better. Incidentally, when this is done, under-bonnet lights come into action in case they are needed, and there is no part of the power unit which cannot be tackled in the minimum of time. The bonnet is secured by two straps and three fastening levers. The position of the side handles calls for some criticism because their quick operation will almost certainly remove a large area of skin from the fingers. Another matter for some comment is the cup-like guide tube for the sump dip-stick, because this is in the slipstream of any road dirt and soon attracts more grit around the orifice than is desirable.

Instruments are confined to essentials. The large matched dials of the revolution counter and speedometer are placed where they can be seen in a split-second glance. Other instruments comprise an ammeter, oil pressure gauge, fuel contents indicator and water temperature recorder. A very desirable attachment to the car under test was an additional switch on the right-hand side of the body which brought into action, until reset, the horns of the car, thus leaving the driver free to deal with other matters when overtaking at very high speeds. This switch is supplemented by a normal horn button placed so that either the driver or the passenger can reach it quickly and on the left-hand side of the scuttle there is a group of separate lighting switches. The headlight dipping control is mounted on top of the gearbox cover and a large anti-dazzle driving mirror gives a good rearward view from its cowled position amidships. The car has an ingenious permanently attached zip-fastened tonneau cover which shrouds the passenger's side of the cockpit when this is not in use. In addition to the aero-screen available for the driver, a similar model can be mounted on the left-hand side of the car for the passenger. Both bucket seats look alike but are somewhat different in construction. That of the driver is exceptionally luxurious and although a little narrow across the hips, gives excellent support in the right places and is high enough from the floor of the car to overcome the unpleasing impression of sitting with legs stretched straight out in front. The passenger seat covers a large tool box wherein lies all the necessary equipment for wheel changing and other deeds, but this makes the cushion very shallow and considerably less comfortable than the driver's version. The passenger also sits a little higher than the driver and so needs goggles at any speed in excess of 50 m.p.h. It is noteworthy that the driver can achieve double this figure without having to protect his eyes in this manner.

The 40-gallon tank does not appear materially to affect the handling of the car, whether it is full or nearly empty, and at the end of 500 miles' extremely hard driving a check showed that the Jaguar had consumed no appreciable amount of oil or water. A noteworthy example of the attention to detail is the provision of drilled extremities on the petrol and oil filler caps so that these may be sealed whenever race regulations require. The car ran on first-grade pump fuel of Belgian as well as German quality and did so without audible protest. There was no tendency to "run-on" even when heavy traffic of a large industrial town raised the coolant temperature some 15 degrees above its normal 55° C. Despite the small-capacity battery, the engine never failed to start at the first touch of the button—the car being left in the open each night.

The really excellent road holding qualities of the Jaguar were exercised during some fast runs on the Nurburgring. Only on the one significant straight could top gear be employed for any distance, and the demands made upon the brakes, particularly on the downhill section, were deliberately rendered excessive. Although the pedal pressure was high, brake fade was practically non-existent and at no time did the engine, despite its severe thrashing, show the least loss of tune. Apart from a curiously rasping exhaust note which could be heard only momentarily at a little above 2,000 r.p.m., the 120C is a very quiet car, and workmen patching the road surface on the German racing circuit were in some danger of being caught unawares, particularly where their viewpoint was thought to be sufficiently good to obviate the customary warning signal indicating road maintenance. After the long climb towards the Karussell the circuit is shaded by fir trees, and here a damp surface retained from overnight rain gave ample indication that the 120C is a very stable car in the wet.

High-Speed Controllability

Subsequently the test of the Jaguar was transferred to a famous motor road and it was here that its remarkable ability to cruise in the neighbourhood of 120 m.p.h. with sharp bursts of acceleration up to 135 m.p.h., demonstrated the great ease with which the car can be directed when running fast. The steering is neither light nor heavy but so instantly obedient to wrist movement that a piece of timber which had fallen from a lorry was avoided at near maximum with so little effort that the incident passed unnoticed to the passenger. As the speed climbs beyond the 130 mark the car does tend to feel a little light, but a curious sense of becoming faintly airborne is offset by no loss whatever in directional control. At such speeds there is no shake or even tremble in the body, nor is there anything to indicate that much higher speeds would not feel equally safe to the occupants of the car.

The driving of the Jaguar XK 120C on the motor roads of Europe is in fact a great and memorable experience, and tribute must be paid to the designers and executives who have made possible such a fine contribution to British automobile engineering.

The adjustable steering column with its permanently attached tommy bar and the carefully cowled rear mirror are indicative of the attention to detail bestowed by the designers of the 120C. Instruments are reduced to a minimum and are easy to read. A surprising amount of soft luggage may be stowed in the body space alongside the passenger and the permanently attached tonneau cover protects an empty passenger seat when required. The good-looking and practical covering over the floor and gearbox can also be seen.

SEVEN DAYS OF SPEED

Jaguar coupe averages 100.31 mph for a week

Leslie JOHNSON, A YOUNG BRITISH engineer, is probably better known for his sports car driving (at least to this side of the Atlantic) than he is for his engineering projects. One of his pet ideas for which he had "pitched" some time bore fruit a few weeks ago.

Johnson had lapped the badly patched and disintegrating Montlhery (France) track for one hour in 1951 coming up with a fast 131.83 mph average for the hour. His car, for that run, was a stock XK-120 Jaguar, and he was immediately impressed with the possibility of making a much longer run with the same make. This had become almost a fixation with him when he finally convinced the Jaguar company that a seven day and seven night run was not an unreasonable project. The only fly in the ointment was that he wanted to average 100 mph for the one week period!

When the record run started, there was no deliberate intention of attacking the existing distance records, but there was always the possibility that a few of them would fall by the wayside if the car did not. This turned out to be true as, at the end of three days, with the Jaguar coupe still going strong, the 107.31 mph average had thoroughly smashed the 10,000 kilometer record that had stood in International Class "C" (3000-5000 cc) since 1934. In rapid succession, the car went on to take the Class "C" records for three days, 15,000 kilometers, four days, and the 10,000 mile mark.

Unfortunately, shortly after the four day record was set up, the choppy circuit took its toll. The Jaguar broke a rear spring. If, in accordance with the FIA International Regulations for an event of this kind, a spare spring had been carried on the car, the run could have continued to establish new records. However, a pit stop had to be made to fit a new part and the official records (other than timing) were halted.

Leslie Johnson, and his excellent team of co-drivers, Stirling Moss, Jack Fairman, and Bert Hadley were determined to run the full seven days at 100 mph so the run continued. Spelling each other every three hours, these four men ended in a blaze of glory as they established an average of 100.31 mph for the entire week including the repair stop. No other car has ever approached this mark!

The car itself was a XK-120 Coupe with wire wheels, a 40-gallon fuel tank, a larger oil sump, and a 2.9:1 rear end ratio. One other practical modification was the addition of a Pye two-way radio telephone. The entire run was made on Shell 80-octane fuel.

The four drivers pose after their record run. Left to right: Hadley, Johnson, Moss, and Fairman

Stirling Moss gets a verbal handshake from the crew as he sets a new record for the 72-hour run

The Jaguar coupe rests after its 16,851-mi. run. Extra road lamps and the hood straps were added as safety factors. Note the everpresent British Racing Drivers Club emblem on the door

Speed Age Presents:
Jaguar Trial

MORRIS B. CARROLL, JR.

Beginning a new monthly department ... testing of sports cars ... with one of the world's most famous marques.

Text and Photos by

MORRIS B. CARROLL, JR.
SPEED AGE FEATURE WRITER

ALTHOUGH a newcomer on the sports car scene when contrasted with such marques as the MG and the Alfa-Romeo, the Jaguar XK120 has already set more than its share of records, excited many an admiring feminine glance, been road-tested to death and the distraction of the reader, and touched off more than one argument relative to its roadability and value as a competition car. There's little doubt that, delivering for $4,039 in New York, it offers more dependable miles per hour per dollar than any other car in the world.

Introduced in London at the Earl's Court Auto Show in 1949 and first placed in production in 1950, it is certainly one of the most bug-free designs in automotive history. Since 1949, only nine engineering changes have been necessary. Included in these are such minor items as a change from a three to four-terminal horn relay, the addition of anti-rattle springs to the brake shoes, and a change from castellated nuts and cotter pins to plain nuts and lock washers.

Seating two in comfort and three (good friends and slender) in a pinch, the car is obviously designed for speeds far in excess of those now on most statute books. From the plain white figures on the black faces of the purposeful-looking instruments to the stubby centrally mounted gear change lever, everything denotes speed and efficiency combined with the utmost in comfort—a rare combination. Typical and illustrative of this is the steering wheel—four spring steel spokes for maximum safety combined with a quick four-inch in-and-out adjustment so that the most comfortable driving position is available. Housed under that sleek hood, or bonnet as the English would have it, is a six-cylinder 210-cubic inch, double overhead cam engine that puts out 160 horsepower at 5200 RPM. Couple this to a total weight of 3,000 pounds and the weight/power ratio figures out to just under 19 pounds/HP—low enough to make this car the master of anything it's likely to meet on the road.

Much of the high horsepower rating is derived from the ex-

The Jaguar's instrument panel is complete and well arranged with a tachometer, fuel and oil level gauge, oil pressure gauge, ammeter and an accurate speedometer. Headlight switch is in center, with ignition warning light below.

The sleek lines decrease frontal area and reduce rear-end turbulence. Holes in wheels of this Jaguar are not standard.

tremely simple and efficient valve porting which, in combination with the now well-known hemispherical combustion chambers, squeezes every possible ounce of energy from each charge. Two of the very simple and efficient S. U. carburetors supply the mixture and a dual exhaust manifold carries away the burnt gases. It is unfortunate that on the standard models the exhaust manifolds discharge to a single muffler and tailpipe, thus robbing the engine of some five to eight horsepower. Factory modified, competition models carry a dual system.

The pistons, of course, are of a low expansion aluminum alloy and are available to give alternative compression ratios of 7, 8, or 9 to 1. The 8 to 1 pistons are normally fitted to cars delivered in this country while the 9 to 1 ratio is fitted to the modified models.

The overhead camshafts are driven by two roller chains and the valves are not adjustable except by varying the thickness of the shims between the ends of the valve stems and the cam lobes. The frame is of the box type with such rigidity that the car can actually be driven with only one front wheel. We made this test last winter and found that with the right front wheel removed and the car resting on three wheels, the maximum twist in the frame was 3/32 of an inch.

The rear axle is conventional Hotchkiss drive with the center line of the axle mounted two inches forward of the center of the 44-inch semi-elliptic springs. Rear shocks are Girling PV7 piston type, double acting.

Front suspension is by torsion bar, adequately snubbed by Newton telescopic hydraulic shocks. Both front and rear shocks can be refilled if necessary.

The upper A frame and the lower control arm terminate in ball joints which handle the up and down motion of the suspension as well as the rotary motion due to steering, thus eliminating the need for king pins with their attendant friction and wear. This arrangement, while not new on the Continent, has not been used on a production car in this country until adopted by Lincoln for the '52 models. With its minimum of unsprung weight it is undoubtedly responsible for the fine handling qualities of the Jaguar as well as those of the Lincoln (SPEED AGE, June 1952).

Steering is remarkably light, entirely free from play and with a ratio of three turns lock to lock. This is too fast if you are accustomed to American cars, just about right for most driving, but a bit slow for competition.

Speaking of competition, let's take a turn around the new one-and-one-half mile road course at Thompson, Conn. which util-

Excellent weather protection is provided. Top is raised and lowered by hand, eliminating weight and higher cost.

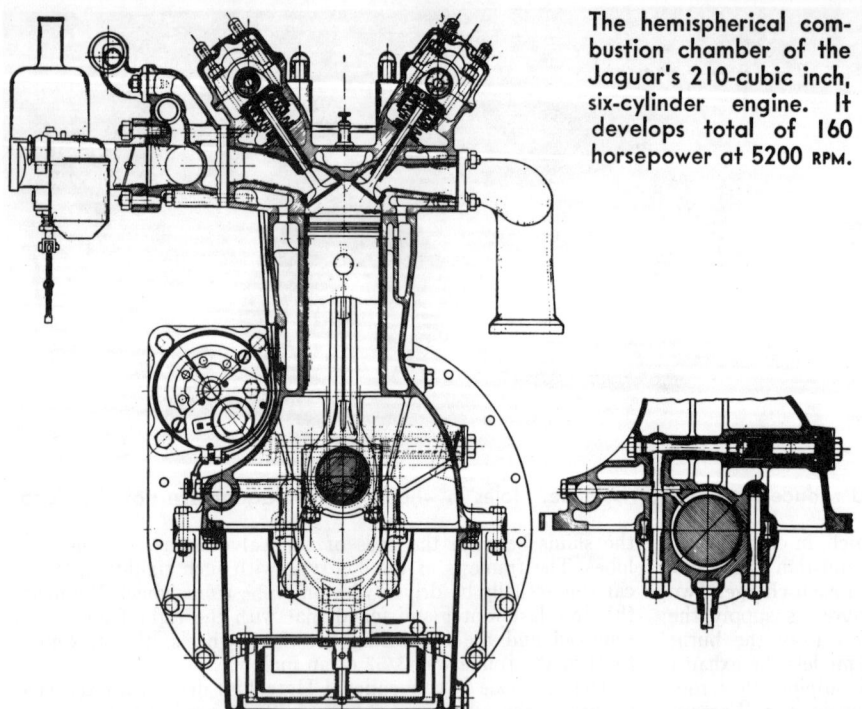

The hemispherical combustion chamber of the Jaguar's 210-cubic inch, six-cylinder engine. It develops total of 160 horsepower at 5200 RPM.

Jack fits in socket in frame and raises both wheels on side being jacked.

izes about half of the existing banked track, cuts off to the left and up a hill, then drops down sharply and goes to the right into a one-half mile straight. Then comes a 90-degree turn followed immediately by one of 80 degrees which leads back to a hard left turn into the straight in front of the grandstand.

Crossing the starting line at about 65 MPH in third gear, the throttle will be left open until we come into the banked turn at about 72 MPH. A quick, light stab at the brake pedal and an equally quick twist of the wheel will slow the car to a little over 60 and set up the drift. We'll control the rate of turn with the throttle, noting that the bank has mysteriously flattened out and that the smell of rubber is strong (and expensive!).

Coming out, there's just time to floor it again and head to the left up the hill with the speedometer reading 90. There's a bit more speed available but with those bumps as the road bends to the right we'll ease off a bit, stick close to the right, and brake heavily with the right heel while the right toe revs the engine up to 5500 RPM as we shift down into second. Then ease off on the gas to add engine braking to the regular brakes, position the car for the turn, back on the accelerator and take it through under power. Shift back to third down the straight and let 'er go.

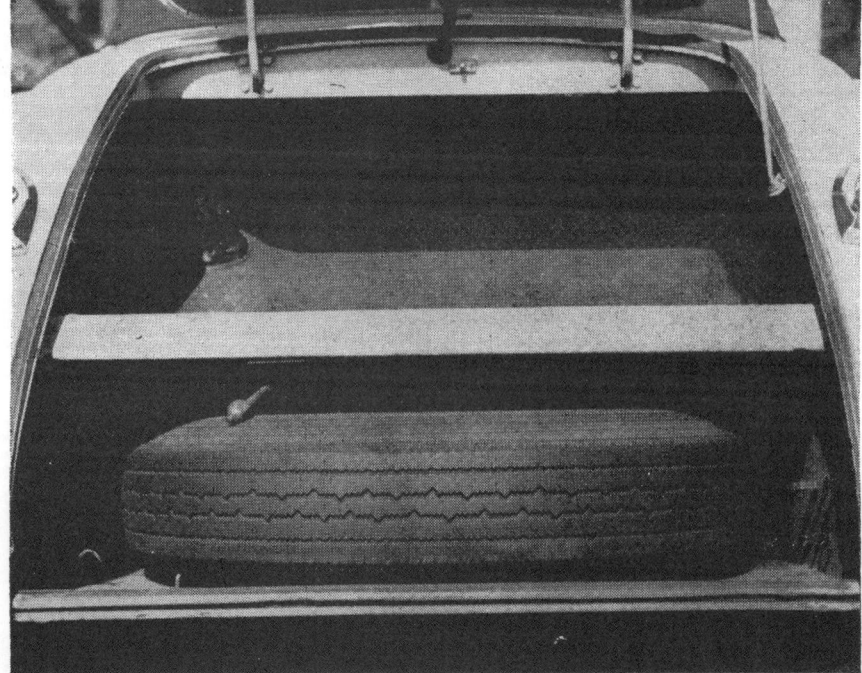

Trunk is 36 inches wide and 40 inches deep, providing greater than usual sports car luggage space. At upper left is gas tank filler pipe protector.

This straight is too short for top gear so we'll wind to 6000 RPM and then repeat the braking and downshifting pattern as we come into the two fast turns at the end of the straight.

Swing wide, then cut close to the inside, let it go a bit wide as we come out of the first half then put your foot in it and aim for the flagman on the inside of the second half. The car will drift beautifully on the smooth surface and we'll come out at about 5800 RPM (60 MPH), shift to third and head for the hard left. Hit the brakes, gas and clutch simultaneously, shift into second then back down hard on the gas as we power through close to the inside and let it drift to the outside as we come out so that full advantage may be taken of the slight drop as the road comes back into the track. Wind out in second at the near end of the grandstand, shift to third and repeat for nine more laps.

The Jaguar was not designed for this type of course which pays heavy dividends for acceleration and relatively little for roadability and top speed. Overheating on any course where top gear cannot be used is a severe problem and the car's excessive weight (for a competition car) severely limits its acceleration.

At the recent SCCA races held at Thompson, I was not a little chagrined to be passed not only by a 1939 B.M.W. but also by a blown MG. A little thought bears out the conclusion that the power available is not nearly as important as the power to weight ratio. This is particularly true on a short course.

Short courses are the rule rather than the exception in this country and consequently the Jag's competitive record can't compare with that of the Allard or Cunningham. On the other hand, if you're a purist and insist that a sports car must be in daily use between races, the Jaguar becomes the fastest sports car ever produced.

About this point we come to the fa-

Jaguar Trial

vorite question, 'how fast will it go?' That appeared to be an impossible question to answer without a test strip but one has been located and aside from the fact that runs have to be made at night, it's a perfect set-up.

Two runs were made in each direction to compensate for any slight gradient (there was no wind) giving an average of 126.47 MPH with the best run at exactly 127 MPH. The factory-advertised 132.6 MPH was not expected inasmuch as this car was equipped with the standard 3.64 rear end gears and the factory run was made with a 3.27-1 ratio. My runs were made with the top and sidescreens erected as other tests have shown the car to be fastest in this trim. Handling at these speeds was not noticably different than at others although it must be noted that the surface was extremely smooth in addition to the lack of wind.

The best zero to 60 time (using first and second only) was 8.8 seconds but the average of four tries came to 9.0 seconds. The standing quarter was not timed because suitable markers were lacking. I have, however, turned the standing quarter-mile in 18.3 seconds in competition and have found that other Jags, also unmodified, will post 17 seconds flat.

Stopping, Ettore Bugatti's famous remark to the contrary, is quite important and I find the Jag somewhat weak in this department. The brakes will stop the car in 171 feet, 6 inches from 60 MPH with the clutch pedal depressed but judicious use of the gears will reduce this distance by some 22 feet to 149 feet, 9 inches. When considering brakes for average use this is excellent but costs precious seconds when dueling with a Ferrari which can haul down from 60 MPH in 135 feet.

In competition, I find that the most serious brake trouble comes on courses such as Bridgehampton where speeds of 115-118 MPH are attained on the long straights. Braking down approximately once each mile from such speeds apparently imposes a greater load on the brakes than does the much more frequent braking from the slower speeds attained on courses such as Thompson.

Attempting to evaluate the braking problem and its effect upon lap times I would say that the lack of adequate brakes increases lap times by approximately two seconds per racing mile. This is more than three minutes in a one hundred mile race and becomes something to think about.

In all fairness to the manufacturer, the Jaguar is catalogued and represented as a fast touring car and not as a competition model. As a touring car the Jag is close to tops under all conditions. Over the road averages as high as 60 MPH can be maintained in 'during-the-week' traffic and the ease with which even the hottest American iron is left behind is unbelievable. Under 50 MPH the ride is definitely hard by American standards and 30 MPH on cobblestone road is downright uncomfortable. But over 50, particularly on the average blacktop road, I'm firmly convinced that it yields nothing in comfort to anything I've ever ridden in or driven.

In wet or snowy going, because of the comparatively stiff springs and lack of roll, the car will sideslip sooner than an American car under the same conditions. I do not consider this dangerous in the hands of an experienced driver for the Jaguar gives ample warning and a judicious application of power will bring you around in perfect safety. Here is the most valuable use of the quick steering ratio—it adds the controlled slide, or drift, to the repertoire of the skilled driver and there are times when it can be a mighty handy maneuver.

Fore and aft traction on snow and ice is fantastically good since 55% of the car's weight is concentrated over the rear wheels. I once lent the car to a friend to use on a skiing trip to Vermont and of course stowed a new set of chains in the trunk just in case. When the car was returned to me I was told it had been used to break out the driveway of the ski lodge after a six-inch snowfall and that chains hadn't been necessary because "that little car will go anywhere."

Luggage space is more than ample for two people if they can get by with three suitcases—one large and two of average size. My usual complement of luggage is two suitcases, each 19 x 14 x 7 inches, a 10 x 10 x 18 inches toolbox, the factory-provided spare parts kit (about 3 x 10 x 24 inches), a safety helmet, and other odds and ends.

On the debit side are several small but important items and at least one serious fault. Let's take the worst first.

Earlier I mentioned that only nine engineering changes had been made since the car first went into production—number ten should be the cooling system. Why, after three years and undoubtedly many complaints about heating up in traffic, the factory hasn't done something about this problem is a mystery to me. It's practically impossible to drive across town in New York in the summer without reaching the boiling point and if you get caught in a traffic jam just pull off the road, brother, you've had it.

Another problem, annoying at best and downright dangerous at its worst, is the windshield wipers. Powered by a single speed electric motor through an inaccessible cable drive, these devices are the antithesis of reliability. If the motor doesn't need brushes, the cable jams. The brushes are easily replaceable and can be obtained at any hardware store but the cable is behind the instrument panel and it's almost an hour's work, flat on your back, to get at it.

The ignition system is another weak point and I have reluctantly arrived at the conclusion that point life can be considered as 500 miles, maximum. I've tried all the tricks . . . replaced condensers, used refaced old points, set new points to a wider-than-standard gap to compensate for high initial wear on the rubbing block, and so on. The only result has been that replacement of points, considered a lengthy job because of the alleged inaccessibility of the distributor, has become a simple four minute operation, discounting the time required for resetting the timing.

As I find that I'm not alone in having this trouble I believe a magneto is the only satisfactory answer. I recently wrote the factory and mentioned a magneto. The comment was, "of course, you realize that the fitting of a magneto will not improve performance." Mebbe not, old chap, and mebbe one hundred bucks will buy a lot of points but my first spare hundred

Standard Specifications and Performance Data
Jaguar XK-120

Width of front seat measured
5 inches from back .... each 18 inches
Depth of front seat cushion .... 5 inches
Height of front seat cushion .... 18 inches
Front seat horizontal adjustment ...... 4 inches
Vertical distance wheel to seat .... 6 inches
Head room front seat .... 4 inches
Leg room front seat
 from front of cushion .... 25 inches

Engine Specifications
ENGINE:
Number of cylinders .... 6 in line
Valve Arrangement ..... Double overhead cam
Bore .... 3.267 inches
Stroke .... 4.170 inches
Displacement .... 209.9 cubic inches
Taxable horsepower 25
Brake horsepower .... 160 @ 5200 rpm
Maximum torque .... 195 @ 2500 rpm
Compression ratio (standard) 8/1
Compression ratio (optional) 7/1, 9/1
CRANKSHAFT:
Number main bearings 7

Chassis
FRAME:
Type .... Box section
WHEELBASE .... 102 inches
TREAD:
Front .... 51 inches
Rear .... 50 inches

WEIGHT:
Curb .... 3000 with full tank of gas
DIMENSIONS:
Overall Length .... 174 inches
Overall Width .... 62 inches
Overall Height .... 52½ inches
REAR AXLE:
Gearing .... Hypoid
Ratio .... 3.64 std., 3.27, 3.92, 4.3 optional
TRANSMISSION:
Conventional:
Number forward speeds 4
Overdrive .... No
Ratios: first 12.29
 second 7.22
 third 4.98
 fourth 3.64
FOOT BRAKES:
Drum diameter .... 12 inches
Material .... Cast-iron
Type .... Hydraulic
Linings .... Mintex M-14
STEERING:
Type .... Burman recirculating ball
Turns, lock to lock 3
Ratio 14/1
Wheel diameter .... 17 inches
Turning radius .... 15 feet 6 inches
ROAD CLEARANCE:
Minimum .... 7⅛ inches
SUSPENSION:
Front .... independent torsion bar
Rear .... semi-elliptic leaf
Shock absorbers .. Double-acting front and rear
TIRES:
Standard 6.00-16

(Oh, happy day!) will go for a magneto.

While I'm a mechanical, rather than an electrical, engineer, I feel that the wiring system is unnecessarily complicated. On the credit side, however, is the fact that it is a 12-volt system and the urge comes from two inexpensive six-volt batteries connected in series rather than by one high-priced 12-volt job. They are carried behind the seats.

The heater apparently was designed by someone who wintered in Florida and is totally inadequate for winter weather in the New York area. This, combined with the absence of defrosting equipment,

Because the changeover from Whitworth to S.A.E. threads is practically completed, American wrenches can be used for almost every nut and bolt on the car and the manufacturer has thoughtfully provided a complete set of wrenches in addition to a comprehensive set of spare parts to cover almost any emergency.

Most service stations welcome the chance to do a grease job on a foreign car and I have yet to find a man who will not willingly work from the comprehensive lube chart included in the owner's manual.

attempt will be made to rate utility, for example, on the same scale which I would use on something like the Plymouth Suburban.

Appearance .... Excellent
Performance .... Excellent
Roadability .... Excellent
Dependability .... Excellent
Availability of Service .... Good
Economy .... Good
Utility .... Good
Weather Protection ...... Fair

As far as competition is concerned, the car is excellent as a stepping stone to something like the Allard or Ferrari and, in a totally unmodified form, can be a source of much fun as well as good experience when run in the increasingly popular stock XK races.

The chances of even a class victory at venues such as Bridgehampton and Sebring are remote unless considerable modification is carried out. The Jaguar, however, does have the tremendous advantage of being able to absorb the pounding of a full season's racing with no preparation other than brake adjustment, carburetor cleaning, and the replacement of points and spark plugs. I know of no other sports car that offers so much high speed racing on top of normal driving for such a ridiculously small maintenance budget.

Snaps have been added to bottom of curtains to prevent flapping at high speed.

makes winter driving a bit on the rugged side unless one wishes to invest in a surplus Army flying suit and a set of fleece-lined boots.

Repairs are a rarely encountered problem and factory-authorized service and parts depots are located in every city of any size throughout the country. The instruction book, instead of being confined to upholstery cleaning instructions and repeated admonitions to take the car to an authorized dealer to have this or that minor operation performed, gets down to brass tacks and covers practically every detail from adjusting the points and carburetors to a complete overhaul.

Labor charges are comparable to those charged on the upper bracket American cars; two examples are replacement of clutch throwout bearing for $75 including parts and labor, and changing of differential ring and pinion gears for $40, labor only. The ring and pinion set sells for approximately $90, brake linings seem rather high at slightly over $30.

An overall evaluation of a sports car is difficult because its purchase and use is on an emotional basis and the usual standards of utility and economy of operation become of secondary importance. The evaluations I make are based on my knowledge of other sports cars and no

One of the most important considerations in the analysis of any sports car that is to be used for competition is the question of how fast it can lap any given course.

Lap times on courses which are open to the public for 364 days a year would be impossible to get, even for testing purposes. With this thought in mind, Ted Koopman and I have arranged to use the Thompson Raceway one and one half mile road track as a proving ground and all sports car road tests will include best time for a lap at speed. This course offers everything except a long straight but a comparison of the various lap times, by the same driver, should give a good idea of the relative potentialities of the cars tested.

My best lap in the Jaguar was 1:24.0 or an average of 64.28 MPH. ☆ ☆

"There's a wonderful car—for the man who's a mechanical genius!"

SPEED AGE

ROAD and TRACK ROAD TEST No. F-5-53
Jaguar XK 120M

SPECIFICATIONS

Wheelbase	102 in.
Tread—front	51 in.
—rear	50 in.
Tire size	6.00 x 16
Curb weight	3100 lbs.
—front	1500 lbs.
—rear	1600 lbs.
Turning circle	31 ft.
Turns lock to lock	2¾
Engine	6 cyl. in line
Valve system	double ohc
Bore & Stroke	83 x 106 mm.
	(3.268 x 4.173 in.)
Displacement	3442 cc
	(210 cu. in.)
Torque at 4000 rpm	203 ft. lb.
Horsepower at 5300 rpm	180
Compression ratio	8:1
Gear ratios—4th	3.77
—3rd	5.16
—2nd	7.48
—1st	12.73
Transmission— 4 speeds	3 syncro
Mph per 1000 rpm	21.3
Mph at 2500 ft./min. piston speed	76.6
Seating capacity	2
List price	$4460

TAPLEY READINGS

Pulling Power	Gear	Mph
547 lbs per ton	2nd	45
410 lbs per ton	3rd	50
307 lbs per ton	4th	57

Wind & Rolling Resistance (coasting)

19 lbs per ton at	10 mph	
29 lbs per ton at	30 mph	
72 lbs per ton at	60 mph	

PERFORMANCE

Test conditions: 60° F.; calm, dry night; 30 ft. below sea level; passengers, equipment weight, 335 lbs.

Top speed (avg.)	120.8
Fastest one way	123.3

ACCELERATION

0-30 mph	3.5 secs.
0-40 mph	5.2 secs.
0-50 mph	6.7 secs.
0-60 mph	8.5 secs.
0-70 mph	11.0 secs.
0-80 mph	14.9 secs.
0-90 mph	20.0 secs.
0-100 mph	25.3 secs.
Standing ¼ mile	16.66 secs.
Fastest one way	16.39 secs.
Standing ½ mile	26.6 secs.
Fastest one way	26.0 secs.

SHIFTING POINTS

From	1st	2nd	3rd
Mph	29	62	86

SPEEDOMETER ERROR

Speedometer	Actual
10 mph	11.8
20 mph	20.0
30 mph	29.0
40 mph	38.0
50 mph	47.9
60 mph	56.6
70 mph	66.6
80 mph	75.7
90 mph	84.9
100 mph	93.8
110 mph	103.3
120 mph	115.3

FUEL CONSUMPTION

Light traffic and 60/80 mph highway cruising — 15.2 mpg

Photographs by Chesebrough

The Modified Jaguar XK-120 Coupe offers high performance plus weather protection.

It may be argued that the scrutiny of a road test crew should be directed toward those automotive aspects which are mechanical and functional—and that aesthetic considerations are best left to symposia on styling and design.

Yet, the unblushing swank of the 1953 XK 120 Jaguar Modified Coupe demands consideration—if the precepts of honest reporting are to be observed. It has been rumored that Mr. William Lyons, General Manager of Jaguar Cars Ltd., was personally responsible for the design, but regardless of whose drawing board gave birth to the flowing lines, the Jaguar poses an amusing paradox. American women—for whom today's "mobile living room" cars are allegedly designed—seem the least able (of the two sexes) to withstand the appeal of the British hardtop. Performancewise the XK 120 is a man's car in the truest sense, yet its concours design and its feminine appeal result in a veritable "jewel box on a sports car chassis."

The car as tested had been driven 4100

What constitutes a sports car? The 1953 and 1938 Jaguars illustrate one difference of opinion. Front wheel of Dave Mitchell's XK had not yet been chromed when cars were photographed.

miles since new by its owner, Mr. Dave Mitchell of Pasadena, California, and was exactly as purchased, with the exception of especially attractive crushed-strawberry paint, chromed wheels and Mitchell mufflers. These latter were installed by the owner who, as proprietor of Mitchell's Muffler Shop, Pasadena, utilized his lengthy experience to fit a set of mufflers which not only proved quieter than the originals, but retrieved some of the ground clearance the company lost in adding a dual system on these special equipment Jaguars.

Performance ...

Perhaps the real charm of the Jaguar lies in its response to the driver's skill and proficiency, for this is a car with a dual personality. Driven as it asks, and using the three syncronized gears to the full, the acceleration is simply tremendous with "more performance than you will ever need". Yet the six cylinder dual overhead camshaft engine will give smooth acceleration in 4th gear from 15 to 120 honest mph and a lazy driver can even putter about town in high gear, using 2nd only for starting up from traffic lights.

But the XK-120M is a sports car, and its high efficiency engine is not as docile nor as quiet, as the family Buick. Smooth starts can be made in 2nd gear, with acceleration to 60 mph in less than 10 seconds. Third gear is well suited for town driving, and even out on the open highway offers brilliant acceleration. 60 to 80 mph for example, takes only 6 seconds, and this ratio is particularly well suited for "dusting off" 200 plus horsepower cars on mountain roads. Even at 88 mph in third (6000 rpm) the engine felt solid, smooth, and safe.

Fourth gear acceleration is interesting. Despite the special high lift camshafts which give a torque peak at 85 mph, the rate of acceleration in this gear is notably uniform at just under 4 seconds for each 10 mph increment from 15 to 85 mph. An unusual and very commendable state of affairs.

There is always a question about the best method of producing optimum standing start acceleration. Allowing the wheels of a large engined car to spin will more than likely waste split seconds getting off the mark. However, in accelerating the Jaguar (with its 3½ litres) wheelspin was freely indulged in so as to allow the engine to rapidly climb its torque curve. The results proved the theory of this technique which was used in this case by Bill Corey (who tuned the car, and who was asked to take over the acceleration runs because of his familiarity with the Jaguar gearbox).

The matter of cruising speed on this coupe requires some explanation. A piston speed of 2500 feet per minute is usually considered a safe limit for cruising a production passenger car engine. By modern standards the stroke of the Jaguar might be considered long (4.127 inches), but this has obviously been carefully considered by the Company engineers. Through rugged design, ample bearing area, good lubrication, adequate cooling, and the best materials and workmanship, the Jaguar engine has conclusively proven its ability to cruise at a piston speed of 3000 fpm with a durability equal to lesser engines at 2500 fpm. The cruising speed of this modified coupe can therefore be conservatively set at 92 mph.

Handling and comfort ...

The low car is exceptionally stable at all speeds. Fortunately for the sake of the tests, high gusty winds were encountered at highway cruising speeds. The wind seemed to slip over the car's flowing lines rather tha to buffet it about, and little attention neede to be paid to the steering under these co ditions.

The steering was in fact completely sati factory in every way and geared to give a excellent compromise between quickness an ease of driving on long trips.

The slight weight bias at the rear of th Jaguar Coupe shows up well on windir roads, there being neither over or understee up to the point where the rear end final "breaks away". Several sharp corners wer taken with the throttle open on 2nd gea Carelessness by the driver (or inexperience could make the rear wheels break tractio but a little familiarity with the car allo the driver to get through fast corners rapi ly and smoothly. This car has no vices, eve for the novice sports car driver.

The modified XK-120s, with their stiff front torsion bars and stiffer rear leaf sprin have a much more positive ride at all spee than the standard model—which brings up discovery made by the staff in previous tes and reconfirmed by the Jaguar. Without a tempting to change the convictions of t car buying public, the belief must be state that the comfort of soft suspensions is 75 illusory—at anything above boulevard speed While the stiff-sprung coupe did make i occupants aware of road discrepancies speeds under 25 mph, it cannot be said th passenger comfort was really jeapordize Furthermore, handwritten notes jotted dov at cruising speeds were fully as legible those made at a desk and a feminine pa senger applied lipstick without a trace smear; both operations are difficult in "sof vehicles. Furthermore, all other things equa stiffly sprung cars seem less fatigue produ ing on long trips, strange though it may seer

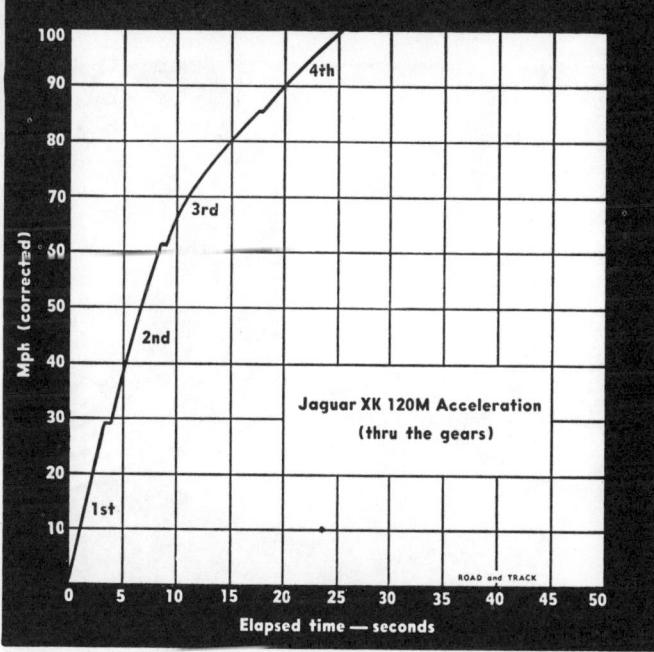

Racing style handbrake, large instruments, adjustable steering column, center gear shift, walnut paneling, and luxury of XK 120 Coupe.

Steep curve illustrates the tremendous acceleration potential of the Jaguar. "Jogs" in the curve indicate optimum shifting points.

No tests were run on the brakes, but experience with normal Jaguars has taught the staff that the 12 inch drums are more than adequate for anything short of all out road race competition. The car stopped quickly and easily and in a straight line under all test condition.

General Comments . . .

The view behind the wheel of the Jaguar brings the conviction that the designer was a shrewd psychologist. Whereas the coupe appears predominantly compact from the outside, the driver is mainly impressed with a feeling of unleashed power, engendered by the massive appearing hood and curving fenders. The seating position is good, as is the feel of the adjustable steering wheel. One of the test staff found that his legs bumped the steering wheel while operating clutch and brake pedal when the adjustable steering column was in forward position. "Full out" position resulted in some loss of elbow room. The solution was to leave the knurled handnut loose and to move the steering wheel in or out according to various driving conditions. Otherwise, the coupe provides plenty of room for both driver and passenger and 200/300 mile trips seem all too short.

The Modified Jaguar will outperform most production cars in the world today. When that fact is coupled with the high degree of comfort and beauty, the car tested seems to be a lot of car for the money. R.D.

Sid Brody, Beverly Hills, lowered his Jaguar seats and shortened clutch and brake pedals to accommodate his 6'5" height. Fender bulges house spare wheel, overnight bag.

Package shelf, radio speaker, rear quarter window and interior light.

"M" JAG

An ASR Road Test

By Barney Clark

THERE IS AN ugly rumor going around that Jaguar may alter the exhaust system on its Modified models, the XK-120 roadster and coupe. Dealers feel that some sensitive prospects are being frightened off by the Wagnerian music that comes through those twin pipes.

Now I am strongly opposed to this, for if there is any one thing that would tempt me to buy a M-type Jag it is the truly noble, soul-satisfying trumpeting that ensues when you depress what the British so aptly call the "loud pedal." It is an utterly distinctive sound—hard, taut, competent; the voice of a really potent high-performance sports car.

I am willing to concede that there may be souls so sluggish that this music fails to lift them, but I contend that these are more likely prospects for Buick Skylarks than Modified Jaguars. And it is true that the sound of an M-type—even at 30 miles per hour in high gear—rings "General Quarters" for every cop in the Western Hemisphere. Tickets you are bound to get—but it is worth it!

These conclusions were reached during the course of a road test of a Modified Jaguar hardtop coupe, a conservative little number painted a sort of Gantron red, with white sidewall tires. This car was the property of Kjell Qvale, proprietor of British Motor Car Distributors, Inc., San Francisco, who turned it over with the remark that: "Nobody has driven this car yet without getting a ticket—I think it's the color."

Nevertheless, we put the car on the road, in the midst of some of the nastiest, sloppiest, wettest weather available. Which is a good way to begin a road test of the hardtop coupe, for it points up the virtues of a vehicle that combines most of the sporting characteristics of the XK roadster with most of the com-

JAGUAR COUPE DATA

SPECIFICATIONS: Jaguar XK-120 Coupe (Modified) Test car from British Motor Car Distributors, San Francisco.

ENGINE:
Type: six-cylinder, double overhead cam.
Displacement: 3442cc.
Compression ratio: 8 to 1.
Bore and stroke: 83 by 106 mm.
Brake horsepower: 180 at 5300 r.p.m.

CHASSIS:
Frame: straight steel box-section.
Front suspension: Independent; wishbones with torsion bar springs.
Rear suspension: semi-elliptic leaf springs.

TRANSMISSION:
Central manual floor shift; four speeds forward; synchromesh on top three ratios. Single dry-plate clutch.

DIMENSIONS:
Wheelbase — 102 in.   Weight — 3022 lbs.
Rd. clearance—7½ in.   Length — 173 in.
Tread — front, 51 in.   Width — 62 in.
       rear, 50 in.   Height — 53½ in.

PERFORMANCE:
Acceleration from standing start:
0-30 m.p.h. — 3.4 sec.   0-80 m.p.h. — 18.9 sec.
0-50 m.p.h. — 8 sec.   0-90 m.p.h. — 24.7 sec.
0-60 m.p.h. — 10.4 sec   Stand. ¼-mile—17.5 s.
0-70 m.p.h. — 13.9 sec.   Top speed — 120.2 sec.

High gear acceleration:
10-30 m.p.h. — 7.2 sec.   50-70 m.p.h. — 8.4 sec.
30-50 m.p.h. — 7.2 sec.   60-80 m.p.h. — 10.2 s.

Mark of the M-type—wire wheels.

Rain for the road test only pointed up the virtues of the Jag coupe.

forts of home: wind-up windows, adequate heating, panoramic visibility to the rear (which the roadster doesn't have with the top up), freedom from wind roar, side-curtain flapping and drumming, and a modicum of protection in case you manage to stand one on its head.

Normally you might be able to add "no drafts" but it wasn't strictly true in the case of this sample: one of the chilliest little drafts in North America came helling out of the side ventilator and through the brake and clutch holes in the floorboards to converge on the driver's ankles.

FROM the start it was apparent that the Modified Jag is an even more desirable property than the standard XK version. As most of you ardent readers know, the M-type costs $395 more than the standard, bringing the total to $4460 for the coupe, less license and taxes. For the extra bite you get Rudge-Whitworth wire wheels all around, engine modifications that boost the horsepower from 160 to 180, and the aforementioned dual exhaust system. In high-bracket circles this is considered a bargain—and so it is, for the items purchased separately would run you at least double that.

The engine changes used to be considered strictly competition stuff and you might expect the M to be a bit hot for town driving. Not at all: Mr. Q's coupe moved off smooth as silk—no roughness at idle, no hawking and spitting while waiting for stoplights, no flat spots in carburetion. The steering was light and precise (more so than the standard edition), the shift through the four gears solid and quiet (you don't necessarily have to use low), the clutch firm but soft (though it still has that dreadfully long stroke characteristic of Jaguars).

So finally we get a shot at a little piece of straight road and plant the right foot firmly down—in second gear. Right NOW those six cylinders start blaring out "Ride of the Valkyries," somebody pulls the string on the catapult, the tach needle whips up to 5200 r.p.m. and, oops!—no more straightaway!

No straightaway means a curve and here the Modified reveals some of the changes Jaguar has made in the handling department. The steering is, oddly enough, easier than standard, but with less self-centering action. The front shocks and torsion bar springs have been beefed up slightly, so there is less roll and the front wheels seem to adhere a good deal better under really high-speed cornering. None of this affects the ride adversely—if anything, the M-type seems to ride better.

Though wet surfaces aren't the best in the world for testing maximum braking power, the coupe indicated that it is considerably better in the stopping

CONTINUED ON PAGE 170

HONOURABLE RETIREMENT

NUB 120 GOES TO A HOME IN THE JAGUAR COMPANY'S MUSEUM

IN the course of their useful lifetimes a limited number of competition cars have built up for themselves fame and reputations which are never forgotten. This was possibly more easily achieved in the past, when events were fewer and consequently more famous, and individual cars had less of a miasma of minor names to outshine.

Among the moderns, however, Ian Appleyard's white Jaguar XK120 can most certainly claim its place in the halls of fame. Acquired by the Appleyards in 1950, NUB 120 started its career by collecting almost every available trophy in the Alpine Rally of that year. Permanently enlisted as Ian's co-driver and navigator for this event and for every other in which the car competed was his wife, Patricia, elder daughter of Mr. W. Lyons, chairman of Jaguar Cars, Ltd. To illustrate the fact that this team made no gradual climb to the awards lists, a reminder of the trophies won in this event is interesting. Apart from the coveted Coupe des Alpes, the collection of subsidiary awards comprised *The Autocar* Trophy for the best performance by a British car, trophies for the fastest time of the day on the *autostrada* speed trial and the Col de Vars hill-climb, best performance in the Tre Croce hill-climb, best aggregate in the special tests, and—to cap it all—fastest time of the day in the acceleration, braking and manœuvrability tests held on the quayside at Cannes—not bad for a curtain-raiser!

In this event Appleyard skidded on the steep and loose-surfaced Col de Forclaz, and buckled a wing. A description of a run in the car after its return from the rally and without any attention was published in *The Autocar* of September 1, 1950.

With the bit securely under its bonnet, NUB 120 proceeded to prove that this was no isolated success produced by the kindly attentions of a flash-in-the-pan luck. Coupes des Alpes were won in 1951 and 1952 with the accompanying collection of subsidiary awards. These three successive Alpine Cup wins obtained for the Jaguar the first Golden Alpine Cup ever awarded. Further to enhance its reputation the Appleyard-Jaguar team scored successes in the 1951 Tulip Rally, the R.A.C. Rallies of 1951 and 1953, the Morecambe Rallies of 1951 and 1953 and the London Rally of 1951; in addition to these, there is a host of successes in club events too numerous to list.

After skidding on a corner on the narrow, treacherous Forclaz Pass in the 1950 Alpine Rally—the damage sustained is seen in this photograph—NUB 120 was able to continue, without losing marks, to make best individual performance.

The car has covered a total mileage of over 50,000 in competitions alone, apart from its daily use as the Appleyards' personal transport. Now, after three energetic years, NUB 120 is to go into honourable retirement; it is to be placed in the Jaguar company's museum. It is to be replaced by a similar XK120, again painted white, but bearing this time the registration number RUB 120. The first appearance of this successor will be in the Alpine Rally, starting today, Friday, July 10; with good driving and a measure of good fortune, it should run true to form, and may well bring as much fame to the registration of RUB 120 as its predecessor did to the similar combination, NUB 120.

Road-Testing the C-Jag

Setting up a smooth drift, the C-Jag whistles through a long curve.

By Alfred Coppel

LAST December at the Torrey Pines road race Phil Hill got there first with the most and scored a runaway victory with a Le Mans Jaguar. Now there are six of these projectiles on the West Coast and about twenty in all in the United States, and it's time to take a closer look at this remarkable machine.

If a driver were to be asked to design his own dream-car, it would be a car very like the C Jaguar. Most of the accepted ingredients are mixed in proper proportion in the C, and its few faults are not serious enough to remove it from the list of the world's great sports cars.

Yes, I said *sports cars*. The C, in spite of all its speed, is a docile, well-mannered beast that's almost as much at home in Sunday traffic as it is at Pebble Beach or Bridgehampton. And, of course, its looks make all the Skylarks and Caribbeans and Nineteen Fifty X's appear the pseudo-sports-cars they are.

Having struck the conventional blow at the Wrong Idea, let us climb aboard the Jaguar and fire up. A real experience is in the making.

We may as well start with a minor flaw. When one settles down in the driving seat of the C, and if one happens to be an average five foot ten, a periscope is needed. The first "modification" of my own C was the raising of the seat a full three inches. Thus elevated, I found I could see the road ahead— an essential, I believe. The wheel is adjustable for height and reach and the foot pedals are placed just where they need to be for fast heel-and-toe maneuvers.

There is a tubular frame member just under the seats that can be utilized very nicely for anchoring a safety-belt—a practice, by the way, that gives our English friends apoplexy. The Britons consider seat belts very dangerous.

The Jag's instrument panel is neat and severely plain. Two large dials are situated right in front of the driver—a 6000 rev tachometer

Dual exhausts are neatly recessed into side of car.

and a 160 mph speedometer. There is an ammeter, water temperature indicator, fuel gauge (for the 39-gallon tank), and a generator warning light. Instead of the hissing-demon type of electric choke fitted to normal Jags, there is a comforting, functional hand-choke. It is refinements like these that make one feel the master of his own soul aboard the C.

The driver sits within a rigid box of steel tubes, well within the body of the car.

THE tuned Jag engine (200 b.h.p. at 5800 rpm) catches quickly and easily, and, considering the severity of the camshafts, idles well at 800 to 1000 revs. The clutch is extremely stiff and it is either in or out, in true sports car tradition. Any attempt to slip it will result in juddering and, if you persist in abusing it, an ominous smell of hot lining. The gearbox is normal Jaguar, stiff while new, but soon relaxing so that shifting is like moving a hot knife through butter.

Okay, having settled down and fired up the slinky boat, we are ready to move out and have a go. The takeoff is sharp and positive, but if properly done, smooth. The Dunlop Racing tires are of the diamond tread pattern and they sound like a siren while the car is in motion. The whole machine has a whistling, effortless way of moving. The engine is quiet, responsive to the throttle. The worm and nut steering is quick and extremely positive (2½ turns from lock to lock). Road shocks are felt through this type of steering, and every pebble on the road is noticed—though not severely enough to disgrace the beautifully no-play steering.

The C is delivered with several gear ratios—from 3.31 to 1 all the way to 4.27 to 1. Mine is fitted with a 3.54, which figures to about 139 mph at 5800 revs—rather too high for our Western racing circuits but about right for the longer courses in the East.

Acceleration is excellent. If you make allowances for only 210 cubic inches, it is really quite remarkable. From a standing start to 100 mph takes just under 19 seconds. This isn't jump of the same order as a Cunningham or Cad-Allard, but it's damned close and with about half the displacement. An ordinary Jag or Jag Modified is completely outclassed by the C in the dig department. In fact, to race a C against ordinary Jaguars is, in my opinion, unfair competition—but let's not get started on *that*.

I DON'T know whether or not the gearbox ratios are the same in the C as in the normal Jag. I get the impression that they are closer, though this may be caused by the high rear-axle ratio. In any case, down-shifting is accomplished easily by double clutching.

Brakes are quite good, with not too much pedal pressure required, though I have no first-hand knowledge yet as to fade characteristics. The drums are

Portrait of a happy man—Al Coppel at the wheel of his C. He's graduated from 1500cc's.

Plain and functional dashboard is dominated by big speedometer (left) and 6500 rpm tach. Shift lever is just under driver's left hand. Seating is much better than on XK Jaguars. Below is the 200 hp engine, which uses standard Jag parts.

ROAD TESTING THE C-JAG

cast iron and they are shrouded within the wheel rims. Aluminum ribbed drums and proper vents for cooling would be an important improvement I suspect, particularly since the streamlining of the car is so good that you get almost no braking effect from air resistance. However, all four wheels can be locked at speed, and though I wouldn't suggest this as anything but a test, it is comforting to know that the braking system is good and potent.

Handling characteristics are *Italian*, and this I mean as a compliment. The C corners very like the Osca, which is fine cornering indeed. If the C has any advantage over the Allards, it is certainly in this department. The car hangs flat and true on the road, and one gets the feeling that the corner could have been taken much faster. There is a very slight understeer, which makes it just about perfect for setting a drift and getting around a turn fast and in complete control.

Over bumpy roads the C's extremely rigid boxed-tubular frame and crowned panel bodywork result in amazing absence of the rattles and drumming noises one usually associates with a competition car. The ride is firm, but not unpleasantly so. The four-wheel torsion bar arrangement seems to be the answer to four wheel independent suspension. An ingenious torque arm set-up on the rear axle holds the rear wheels down when negotiating tight corners and keeps wheel spin to a minimum.

AT HIGH SPEEDS the car has no tendency to wander, and I get the impression that stability in-

Shot through back window of ASR camera car, the C-type Jaguar shows its beautiful, road-hugging lines and clean simplicity of design. It looks what it is: a highly efficient road projectile.

creases at over 110 mph due to the shape of the nose section. There is none of that freakish airborne feeling some fast cars have at speeds over the century mark.

The windscreen is adequate for the driver's protection at any speed. In fact, unless you are traveling at 90 or better, goggles are not needed. The passenger, though, gets the full blast of the wind and it isn't fun when there are bugs in the air. For the man who actually uses a C as a working sports car, a full windscreen would be a must. The rear view mirror is an antiglare job that vibrates to the point of uselessness. A minor point, to be sure, but something to change before serious racing is attempted.

To sum it all up, I should say that the C Jaguar is about the finest sports car out of the foggy islands yet. It is the equal of Ferraris of comparable size and better constructed—and best of all, the price is right: $5860 plus the state and other taxes. It is my personal opinion that the car is worth $10,000 of anybody's money, and I can't see how Jaguar Cars does it. But they do and I'm not asking any questions.

There's a catch, of course—there always is. The Jaguar factory made only 50 cars and they are almost all sold. The day will come real soon when the owner of a C can name his own price and collect it, too. It isn't every day that a man can buy a sports racing car of Ferrari class and maintain it easily with parts available in every American city of over 50,000 population. Any time Jaguar wants to sell a million cars, all they have to do is make a normal roadster version of the XK-C. That's free advice—Coventry can take it from there.

C-TYPE JAGUAR
Specifications

Cylinders	6
Bore	83mm
Stroke	106mm
Displacement	3442cc
Piston area	50.4 sq. in.
Valve gear	DOHC
Compression ratio	8 to 1
Power at peak	200bhp at 5800 rpm
Piston speed at max. power	4030 rpm
Carburetion	2 SU sidedraft
Ignition	Lucas Coil and Dist.
Spark plugs	Champion NA 10
Fuel pumps	2 Lucas
Clutch	Borg and Beck 10 in. sdp
Prop shaft	Hardy Spicer
Final Drive	Hypoid bevel
Brakes	Lockheed hydraulic
Drum diameter	12 in.
Lining area	188 sq. in.
Suspension front	Torsion bar & wishbones
Suspension rear	Torsion bar & rigid axle
Dry weight	2100 lbs.

Performance

0-30 through gears	3.0 sec.
0-50	6.0 "
0-70	10.0 "
0-110	24.1 "
Standing quarter-mile	16.1 "
Max. speed (3.54 -axle)	139 mph
Front-rear weight distribution full load	50 front 50 rear

Headlight on the C-Jag is protected from the windstream.

HANDSOME: "In closed form", opines John Bolster, "it is the best-looking Jaguar that has yet been made". Performance of the XK 120 coupé is well up to its appearance with 120 m.p.h. attainable in complete ease and quiet.

JOHN BOLSTER TESTS THE JAGUAR XK

When the glamorous XK 120 first burst upon an astonished world, there were many sceptics. These could be divided into two classes, "it can't be done for the price", and "it won't last". Since then, Jaguars have been sold all over the world at a figure that would appear to invite certain bankruptcy, and yet the shareholders are more than happy.

How this advanced, twin-overhead camshaft luxury car can undersell smaller pushrod-engined machines, only Mr. Lyons can say. What I do know, from the experience of several of my friends, is that the XK is one of the hardest-wearing vehicles on the market. Thus, it carries on the tradition of the vintage years, when large British sports cars were built which could run almost for ever. The "Jag" can take it, and in the hands of all sorts of drivers, it has acquired a reputation for toughness that has never been surpassed.

The heart of a Jaguar is its engine. This unit has a counterbalanced crankshaft which runs on seven $2\frac{3}{4}$ in. journals in steel-backed bearings. The cylinder block-cum-crankcase is of cast iron, and the detachable head of aluminium. The valves are inclined at 70°, and rest on austenitic cast iron seats. They are operated by twin overhead camshafts through inverted pistons, and the drive is in two stages by duplex roller chains. Twin horizontal S.U. carburetters, with an electrically controlled easy-starting device, supply the mixture, and the rest of the specification follows the best modern practice.

MILE-EATER: "A long run in this car is a pleasure difficult to put into words". The Jaguar was controllable at all speeds on wet or dry roads, its steering steady and accurate.

A dry single-plate clutch transmits the power to a unit-mounted gearbox, with synchromesh on 2nd, 3rd and top. The Hardy-Spicer open propeller shaft is connected to a three-quarter floating hypoid rear axle. Long semi-elliptic rear springs, with Girling dampers, locate the axle and absorb the driving and braking torque.

The steel box-section frame, with box-section cross members, is of extremely solid construction. It is suspended in front on wishbones and torsion bars, with Newton telescopic dampers. The wishbone ends have ball joints, which perform the double duty of suspension links and stub axle swivels. A three-piece track-rod, with Burman box and slave arm, is mounted ahead of the wheel centres. The brakes are Lockheed hydraulic, and are supplied with cooling ducts.

The car which I have been using was a drophead coupé. With the top down, this model resembles the well-known open sports, except for the neatly folded hood under its closely fitting envelope. In closed form it is, in my opinion, the best-looking Jaguar that has yet been made. The head is padded and lined, and the operating mechanism is completely concealed. Compared with the open car, the whole interior is more luxuriously appointed, and the walnut dashboard, with large, round instruments, is a joy to behold. I must confess that the metal and plastic dashboard of the average modern car, with its dials of various tortured and non-functional shapes, is something that always saddens me. I am glad that Britain's best manufacturers still scorn this juke-box fashion.

On the road, the first thing one notices about the Jaguar is its delightful manners. The engine is quite astonishingly quiet, and I am glad to say that the exhaust is very well silenced—a virtue which I value highly. Even in London traffic, the 3.54 to 1 top gear may be used, and the car will pick up rapidly from a crawl. I once inadvertently started from rest in top gear, and the machine moved off easily without any apparent distress! If desired, almost any journey can be completed without touching the gear lever, so flexible is the powerful engine.

Nevertheless, a useful gearbox with well-chosen ratios allows 60 and 88 m.p.h. to be attained on second and third gears respectively. The short, central lever is ideally situated, and though it requires fairly firm movements at low speeds, the changes go through quite easily

120 DROPHEAD COUPÉ

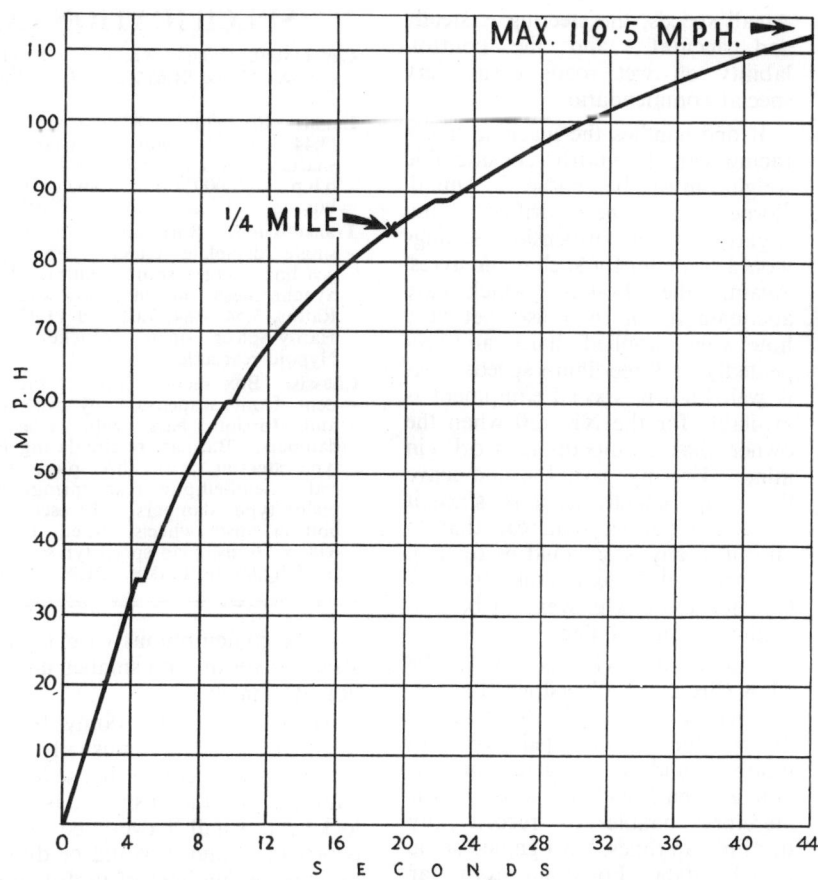

0-100 *M.P.H. IN 31 SECS.: Acceleration graph of the 26½ cwt. Jaguar drophead coupé.*

at the higher revolutions. The clutch is at all times smooth and well up to its work. The "fly off" hand brake was also much appreciated.

The other controls would benefit from a little re-positioning. The steering wheel is adjustable for length of column, but is, I thought, too close to the legs if a heavy overcoat be worn. The foot pedals, too, might be adjusted to give easier "heel and toe" for simultaneous braking and changing down. As, however, these trifling alterations could easily be made to suit the individual owner, this is not a serious criticism.

HEART OF THE JAGUAR: The famous 3½-litre twin o.h.c. six-cylinder XK 120 engine, which gives 160 b.h.p. at 5,000 r.p.m., and propels the 26½ cwt. coupé with contemptuous ease, permitting 100 m.p.h. cruising on half-throttle.

The seats are extremely comfortable, there is excellent forward vision, and the beautifully made body is free from objectionable wind noise at even the highest speeds. The rear quarters are somewhat blind, as is unavoidably the case with all convertible bodies, and the back window is smaller than that of a "hard top". The rear part of the hood can be zipped out separately to provide ventilation in tropical conditions. The body is watertight in the worst storms, and the heating and demisting work admirably. The doors open and close very easily, and there are no rattles.

This is one of the finest high-speed touring cars that has ever been made. The suspension gives a far smoother ride than the lighter type of sports car can provide, and the effortless, half-throttle cruising speed of 100 m.p.h. is a real pleasure. Even at a full 120 m.p.h. (126 on the "clock" of my particular car) the engine remains quiet and smooth.

At all speeds, the steering is steady and accurate, and the controllability on wet roads earns very special commendation.

If one handles the machine like a racing car, the fairly considerable weight must be borne in mind. Corners can be "drifted", but slightly harder suspension settings would be better for such manœuvres. Again, the brakes, which are adequate for normal use, get very hot when applied hard and repeatedly at three-figure speeds. As is well known, special equipment is available for the XK 120 when the owner has competition work in mind. For my part, I would leave this coupé exactly as it is, since it is such a perfect road car that to alter it in any way would be to spoil it. After all, Jaguars make the "C" type for those who want to be first at the chequered flag.

I drove the XK 120 round the Club Circuit at Silverstone, but unfortunately my visit took place during the recent spell of bad weather, and a thunderstorm was raging when I made my tests. I was therefore unable to record any startling lap times, but I gained some valuable data. For instance, the car proved utterly controllable on the corners, even when driven to its limit. The screen wipers ensured 100 per cent. visibility, and the brakes gave even retardation on the glassy surface.

A long run in this car is a pleasure that is difficult to put into words. Whether it is its complete indifference to all kinds of road surface, its silence and smoothness, or the feeling of always having more power in reserve, I know not. Suffice it to say that the miles melt away without the slightest effort, and one never makes oneself conspicuous by sounding like a racer. For those who can afford the higher petrol consumption, the 3½-litre engine

SPECIFICATION AND PERFORMANCE DATA

Car Tested. Jaguar XK 120. Drophead coupé. (Price £1,616 2s. 6d., including P.T.)

Engine. Six cylinders 83 mm. x 106 mm. (3,442 c.c.). Twin overhead camshafts. 7 to 1 compression ratio. 160 b.h.p. at 5,000 r.p.m. Twin SU carburetter. Lucas coil and distributor.

Transmission. Borg and Beck 10 ins. single dry-plate clutch. Four-speed gearbox with short central lever. Synchromesh on 2nd, 3rd and top. Ratios, 3.54, 4.84, 7.01 and 11.95 to 1. Hardy-Spicer open propeller shaft. Hypoid rear axle.

Chassis. Box section frame. Independent front suspension by wishbones and torsion bars with telescopic dampers. Burman re-circulating ball-type steering with three-piece track rod. Semi-elliptic rear springs with piston-type dampers. Pressed steel bolt-on disc wheels, fitted Dunlop 6.00 x 16 ins. road speed tyres. Lockheed hydraulic brakes. 2L.S. in front, 12 ins. drums, 208 sq. ins. lining area, ducted cooling to front brakes.

Equipment. 12-volt lighting and starting. Speedometer, rev. counter, ammeter, water temperature, oil pressure and fuel gauges. Electric clock. Heating and demisting. Windscreen washer. Flashing direction indicators.

Dimensions, etc. Wheelbase 8 ft. 6 ins., track, front 4 ft. 3 ins., rear 4 ft. 2 ins. Ground clearance 7 ins. Overall length 14 ft. 5 ins. Turning circle 31 ft. Weight 26½ cwt.

Performance. Maximum speed 119.5 m.p.h. Speeds in gears: 3rd 88 m.p.h.; 2nd 60 m.p.h.; 1st 35 m.p.h. Standing quarter mile 17.5 secs. Acceleration: 0-30 m.p.h. 3.5 secs.; 0-40 m.p.h. 5.3 secs.; 0-50 m.p.h. 7.1 secs.; 0-60 m.p.h. 9.5 secs.; 0-70 m.p.h. 12.5 secs.; 0-80 m.p.h. 16.9 secs.; 0-90 m.p.h. 23.3 secs.; 0-100 m.p.h. 31 secs.; 0-110 m.p.h. 40.9 secs.

Fuel Consumption. 14½ m.p.g.

gives a contemptuous ease to high-speed travel that no smaller unit can hope to match.

There is a fairly roomy boot in the tail, and an unusually large parcel space behind the seats. In addition to the usual dashboard locker, a small baize-lined drawer is provided, and it would be difficult to imagine any item of useful equipment that has been left out. Both seats are separately adjustable, and there are lights in the roof and boot.

The XK 120 coupé is strictly a 2-seater, but every comfort is provided for the driver and his passenger. Whereas an open sports model,

even with hood and sidescreens erect, is not an ideal every-day conveyance, this drophead coupé would be perfectly adequate for the one-car man, who must use his vehicle for business as well as pleasure. Furthermore, the lady of the house could take it to the shops without ever thinking about that potential 120 m.p.h. maximum.

This is a car of superb appearance, extremely high performance, and proved stamina, and it sells at a price that makes it—to say the least—a very attractive proposition. I can think of one improvement; let Jaguars fit a transparent bonnet, for it seems a shame to cover up the beauty of that shining, twin-camshaft engine!

(Above) The air cleaner for the XK 120 engine is mounted between the radiator block and the grille.

★

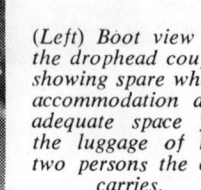

(Left) Boot view of the drophead coupé, showing spare wheel accommodation and adequate space for the luggage of the two persons the car carries.

Full details and specifications of the XK-120 Type C, that won the 1953 Le Mans road race.

JAGUAR IN COMPETITION

By HARVEY B. JANES

His lower lip grimly thrust forward, Duncan Hamilton drives the winning car at speed during the 1953 Le Mans race.

WHEN, in June of 1951, the final flag had been dropped at the close of the 24-hour Grand Prix at Le Mans, France, the sports-car world was startled and amazed to find that a Jaguar, driven by Peter Walker and Peter Whitehead, had emerged as the overall winner. Averaging 93.49 mph., the Jag had taken on the best the world had to offer in the way of specially built competition road cars and had run them into the ground. In the 24-hour period, the winning car had covered a total of 2,244 miles. Another Jag had set the lap record at a speed of 105.24 mph. And all this with a brand-new car—one never before seen in public, much less raced—the XK-120-C.

While there had been rumors that Jaguar was working on a specially tuned, super-light sports car designed to replace the standard XK-120 in competition, it had not been given much of a chance against the Talbots, Ferraris, Alfa-Romeos, Frazer-Nashes, etc. But now the big race was over, the results were in, and it was obvious that the new Jaguar was a car to be taken seriously after all. Almost immediately, the questions started to pour in.

"What kind of engine does it have?"

"What's the top speed?"

"How about the chassis?"

"Will the car be available to the public?"

"If so, how much will it cost?"

Bill Lyons, the head of Jaguar Cars, Ltd., was in all his glory. Here he was, at the top of the sports-car heap at last, and he was only too happy to release the details on his newest and most successful car, especially since it used the same basic six-cylinder, twin-overhead-cam engine that had made the stock XK-120 so famous. This engine had, of course, been modified until it developed a peak of 210 hp at 5,800 rpm, giving a top speed of better than 150 mph. As for the chassis, that had been entirely redesigned by the Jaguar technical staff, keeping in mind the multiple problems of power/weight ratios and handling qualities. Eventual chassis construction had been accomplished through the use of lightweight but rigid triangular steel tubing. The suspension on all four wheels was by torsion bars. To this was added a special hand-built body of aluminum which, with the addition of the rest of the running gear, etc., brought the total weight of the car up to approximately 2,175 lbs.

Within a few months of the '51 Le Mans race, the C-Jags were being delivered, in limited quantities, to known sports-car drivers in the United States and Europe, for

Tony Rolt takes his turn behind the wheel. Here he is seen piloting the Jaguar past a section of grandstands.

And then they change back again. Rolt prepares to quit the car during a short pit stop as Hamilton stands by.

about $5,800, and were blazing new trails to success.

The triumphs of the C-Jag continued with amazing regularity until the 1952 racing season, when the new Mercedes 300-SL sports cars came roaring out of Germany. With grim precision, the Mercedes team proceeded to win practically every major road race in Europe and America, culminating in a dramatic one-two victory at Le Mans despite frantic Jaguar efforts to add much needed mph to their cars. Actually the Jaguar efforts had been a bit too frantic and much too hurried, for while they did manage to streamline the cars a bit better, they neglected to include sufficient cooling vents, with the result that the cars got little air and overheated early in the race. It was a sorry sight to British eyes when the C-Jags all came limping into the pits, had their hoods opened by the pit crews, and shot geysers of boiling water and steam high into the air. Lyons and his associates were bitterly disappointed, but not completely licked yet. There was still next year, and they looked forward to sweet revenge on the Mercedes team.

But then the unexpected happened. At the end of the 1952 competition season, Mercedes went into its now-famous shell, announcing calmly that since they had already established the superiority of their cars beyond a shadow of a doubt, they no longer considered it necessary to race the 300-SL. What a bombshell! The Ferrari team was furious, challenging Mercedes to a match race on any European course. They were turned down with a smile. Other sports-car manufacturers, including Jaguar, felt equal pangs of frustration.

Nevertheless, having been deprived of their motive for revenge, the manufacturers went back to their shops with new determination. All sights were set on the 1953 Le Mans race and the order of the day was "beat Mercedes' record average speed of 96 mph."

A flood of new, ultra-fast sports cars appeared during the early part of the 1953 season, new course records were set, millions of dollars were spent, and as race day at Le Mans grew near, rumors were flying thick and fast.

"Will Mercedes show up at the last minute?"

"Is Pegaso finally going to run?"

"How about Cunningham, Alfa-Romeo, Ferrari?"

And there was some conjecture about Jaguar.

But as the cars began their practice sessions on the famous Le Mans course, a few days before the race, Mercedes still hadn't shown and it seemed as though the Alfa-Romeo "Disco Volante" was the car to beat, with Ferrari and Cunningham also in strong contention. To everyone's great surprise, the Jaguar team appeared with three cars that looked, outwardly at least, almost exactly like the C models that had won the 1951 race.

But when the actual race had begun, it was an entirely different story. Not only had the Jaguars been juiced up even further under the hood, they were armed with a fantastic new weapon—disk brakes. These allowed them to decelerate so abruptly that they were able to drive at speed 200 yards farther into the turns than their competition could. When the race had ended at four p.m. on Sunday afternoon, June 14, Jaguars had taken first, second, and fourth places, and the lead car, driven by Tony Rolt and C. Duncan Hamilton, had averaged an astounding 106 mph. This was the first time any car had won at Le Mans with a speed of over 100 mph. And it was doubtful if the Jaguars had opened up completely at any time during the 24 hours—they didn't have to, their brakes were that good.

The first observers at the practice sessions had been right; the cars were quite similar to those that ran in 1951. Changes, besides the disk brakes, included three Weber carburetors, beefed-up rear suspension, and a single new air duct on the hood. The cooling problem was so thoroughly licked that not a drop of water was added to any of the Jaguars during the entire race. Specifications of the new Le Mans XK-120-C Jaguar are as follows:

Power is supplied by the usual 3½-liter XK-120 engine displacing 3,442 cc. (210 cu. in.). Special racing pistons have been added. The twin overhead cams are somewhat

Hamilton (left) and Rolt are congratulated after their record win. Chief Jag engineer Heynes is at far right.

Jaguar is given the victory flag as it crosses finish line at the conclusion of the 24-hour endurance grind.

Tired but happy, the winning team of two drivers and two mechanics board their XK-120-C for ride to paddock.

hotter than stock. There are three Weber carburetors, an 8:1-compression head, a reinforced, seven-main-bearing crankshaft, and twin exhausts with a single outside muffler. Running on 80-octane fuel, the engine develops approximately 210 hp. at 5,800 rpm.

Transmission is accomplished through the use of a Borg and Beck dry single-plate clutch coupled with a four-speed synchromesh gearbox. Rear-axle ratios available include 2.9, 3.31, 3.54, 3.92, 4.09, and 4.27:1 and the final drive is by Hardy Spicer propeller shaft to a hypoid bevel axle with semifloating shafts.

Suspension in the front is the same as in the previous C-type Jaguars—wishbones and individual torsion bars. In the rear, however, special torque-reaction couplings have been added to the torsion bars, giving increased stability, especially during cornering and rapid acceleration. This additional equipment is being made available to the owners of older C-Jaguars.

The brakes, of course, are Dunlop disk, with Girling operating gear, and the steering is rack-and-pinion with the adjustable wheel that has become so popular in the stock XK models. The knock-off 16" wire wheels are fitted with Dunlop road-racing tires. Electrical equipment includes a Lucas 12-volt, 40-amp. battery, a Lucas coil, Champion spark plugs, and an S. U. electric fuel pump.

As for the dimensions of the car, the wheelbase is 96", the tread is 51", the overall length is 157", the width is 64½", and the overall height without the racing windscreen is a scant 38½".

Add to all this the special lightweight frame and body and you have the new champion of road racing. When you consider that Jaguar engineers, as it was discovered later, had designed an entirely new chassis for the race, which was not entered because it had not been sufficiently tested, the victory at Le Mans seems all the more convincing. Perhaps by next year the new car will be ready, or will we see the rumored 4½-liter engine? All we can do is look hopefully to the future and sweat it out. •

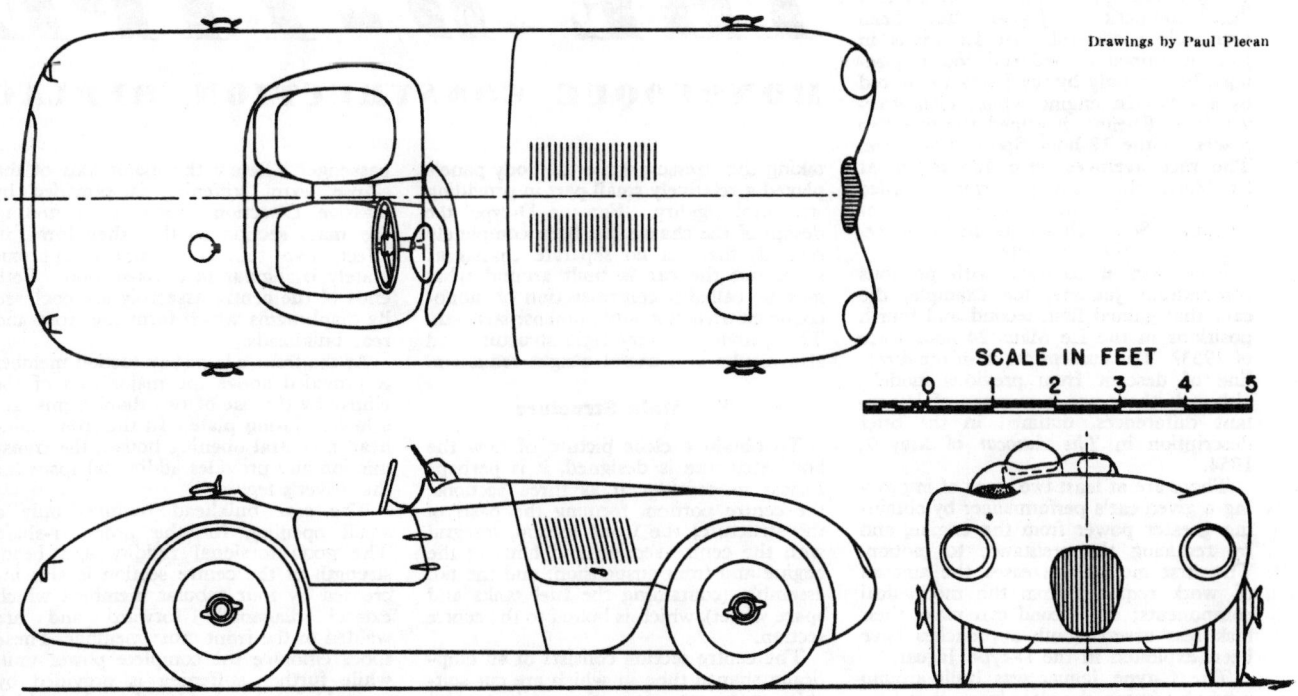

Drawings by Paul Plecan

SCALE IN FEET

INTERESTING COMPETITION CARS

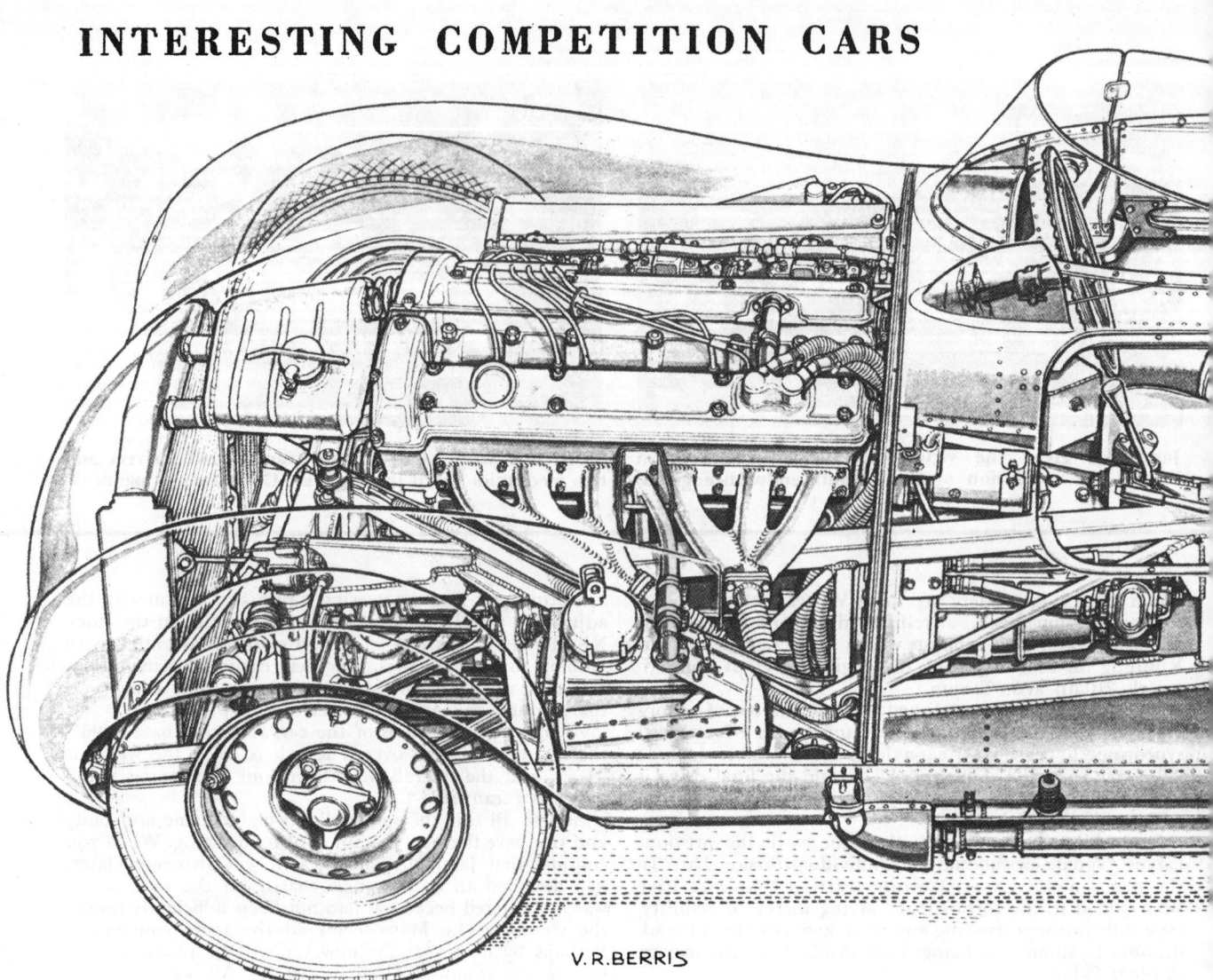

V. R. BERRIS

THE D-TYPE

MONOCOQUE CONSTRUCTION REPLAC[ES]

ON the two recent occasions when it has appeared in public, the new competition Jaguar has been extremely successful. At Le Mans in June it gained second and fourth placings, beaten only by the Ferrari powered by a 4,954 c.c. engine, while, soon afterwards at Rheims, it gained the first two places in the 12-hour Sports Car Race. The race averages were 105 m.p.h. at Le Mans (the winning Ferrari recorded 105.1 m.p.h.), and 104.55 m.p.h. at Rheims. So much for its performance, but what of the car itself?

How does it compare with previous competition Jaguars; for example, the cars that gained first, second and fourth positions in the Le Mans 24-hour Race of 1953? The current car is in the direct line of descent from previous models, although there are a number of important differences, outlined in the brief description in *The Autocar* of May 7, 1954.

There are at least two ways of improving a given car's performance: by obtaining greater power from the engine, and by reducing the resistance to motion. The first method increases the amount of work required from the mechanical components; the second can make their task less severe—both approaches have been exploited in the D-type Jaguar.

The C-type Jaguar was built around a tubular frame, the main frame members taking the stresses, while the body panels played a relatively small part in providing structural rigidity. For the D-type, the design of the chassis has been completely revised; there is no separate chassis as such, but the car is built around what may be called a centre-section of monocoque construction and immense strength. This provides a very rigid structure and also results in a useful weight reduction.

The Main Structure

To obtain a clear picture of how the body structure is designed, it is perhaps easiest to consider it as three sections; the centre portion, forming the basis of the structure; the front section, integral with the centre section and housing the engine and front suspension; and the tail assembly (containing the fuel tanks and spare wheel), which is bolted to the centre section.

The centre section consists of an elliptically shaped tube in which are cut suitable openings for the driver and passenger. Below the major axis of the ellipse, extra stiffening is provided by massive L-section pressings, riveted to the main section so that they form, in effect, two tubular members, approximately triangular in cross-section. Both ends of the centre assembly are enclosed by diaphragms which form the front and rear bulkheads.

At the front, a large box-section member is provided above the major axis of the ellipse by the use of two diaphragms and a lower closing plate. In the front bulkhead a central opening houses the transmission and provides additional space for the driver's legs.

The rear bulkhead requires only a small opening, for the propeller-shaft. The good torsional rigidity and beam strength of the centre section is also increased by four tubular members which extend diagonally forward and are welded to the front cross-member. These tubes embrace the complete power unit, while further stiffening is provided by two additional square-section tubes which

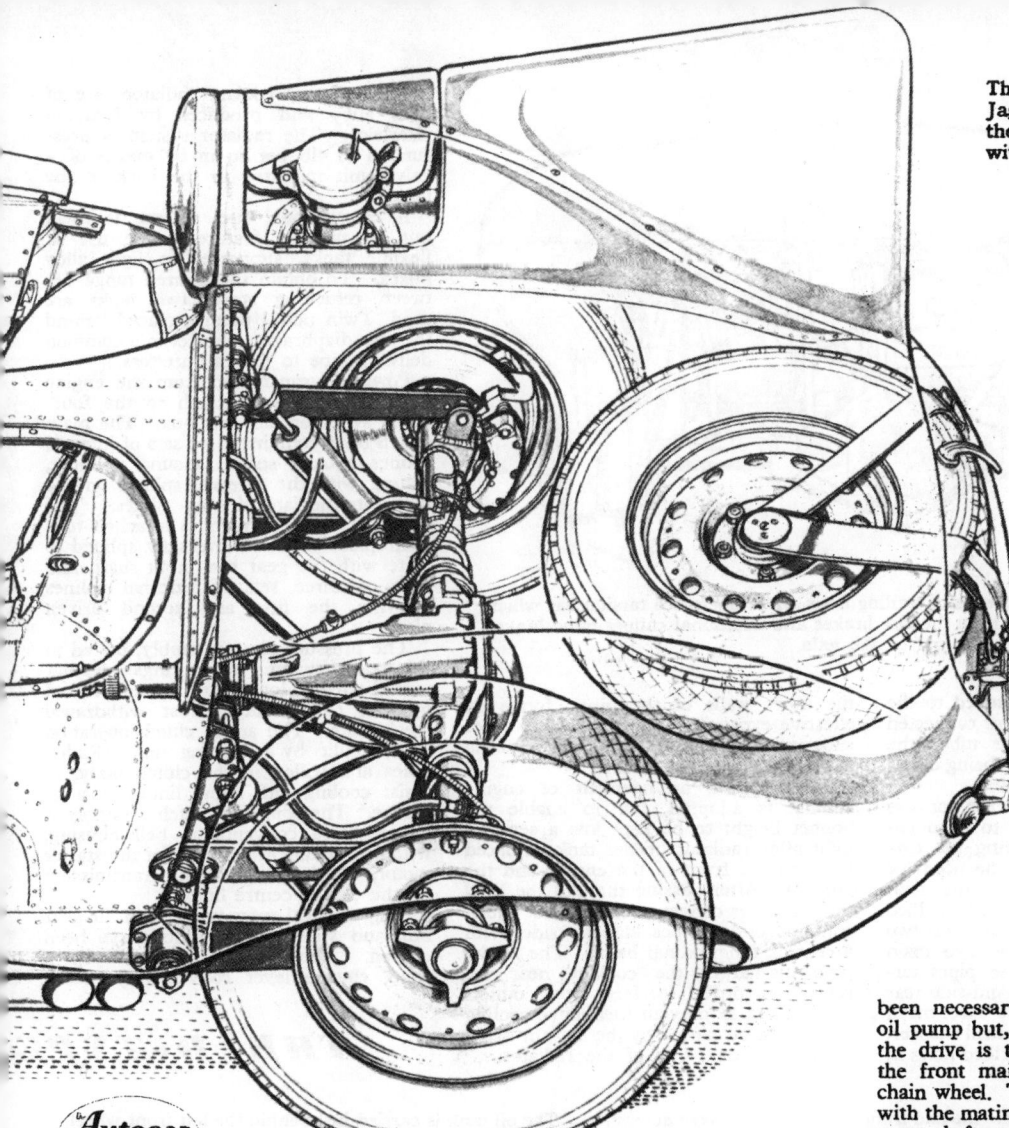

This drawing of the D-type Jaguar shows the layout of the major components together with the main structural members.

and the shaft itself is of EN16 steel.

The engine has no flywheel, but there is a substantial crankshaft torsional vibration damper at the front, and flywheel effect is produced by the mass of the triple dry-plate clutch and its housing, together with the starter ring which is pressed on the clutch assembly centre section.

The most noticeable difference in the appearance of the engine is caused by the change from wet to dry sump lubrication, made to reduce the height of the engine, the sump height having been halved. This not only enables the bonnet line to be lowered considerably without adversely affecting ground clearance, but also lowers the centre of gravity of one of the major masses.

It has, of course, been necessary to provide an additional oil pump but, as on the standard engine, the drive is taken from a gear between the front main bearing and the timing chain wheel. The crankshaft gear engages with the mating gear which drives a transverse shaft, operating the pressure pump on the right-hand side of the engine and the scavenge pump on the left-hand side.

Oil from the tank is drawn by the pressure pump and directed to the bottom of the oil cooler. Forced through the cooler, it passes along an external pipe to the crankcase where it lubricates the bearings via internal drillings in the normal way. Falling to the base of the sump, the oil is returned to the tank by a dual scavenge pump. It is, of course, necessary to make provision for rapid return of the oil to the tank to prevent build-up of lubricant at the base of the engine, and it must also be remembered that oil produces more resistance than air to crankshaft webs rotating at high speed.

With dry sump lubrication, one of the main problems is to prevent aeration of the lubricant, and on the Jaguar engine this has been accomplished by baffles inside the oil tank, with a breather pipe from the top of the tank connected to the crankcase.

As with the production engine, a light alloy cylinder head is used, with valve seat inserts for both inlet and exhaust valves. It has hemispherical combustion chambers and inclined valves, and the engine operates on a compression ratio of 9 to 1. To aid installation, the engine is inclined in the chassis at an angle of 8 deg to the left when viewed from the cockpit. The barrels of the three double-choke Weber carburettors are set at a similar angle to the vertical centre line of the engine, so that they are truly horizontal when the unit is installed. Six

JAGUAR
TUBULAR FRAME

run forward diagonally from the front of the bulkhead to meet in the centre of the front cross-member frame. They pass over, and are welded to, the two upper main frame tubes. The whole of the body structure is riveted and arc welded from magnesium alloy, the skin being of 18 gauge material.

Two transverse box-section members are secured to the rear diaphragm, and to these are attached massive vertical assemblies, each of two vertical plates riveted to a channel-section spacer, the whole forming box-section members housing the bearings of the trailing-link rear suspension.

The rear section of the body, which does not carry the main loads, is attached to the centre section by bolts around the periphery of the ellipse, while four additional bolts secure the rear assembly frame members to the rear suspension housing assemblies.

Although the D-type Jaguar is a completely new car, as many standard components as posible are utilized. For example, although the power unit has dry sump lubrication and develops more power than the standard XK 120 power unit, standard production castings are used for both block and cylinder head —a fact which speaks well for the basic design and layout of the engine and demonstrates to the owner of the normal production machine that his power unit is by no means operating near to the bone!

Developments in the XK 120 engine were outlined in some detail in the April 24, 1953, issue of *The Autocar*. It is, therefore, intended to explain quite briefly some of the subsequent modifications. All details of modifications are not at present available, for, with any competition machine, detailed development continues until it is superseded by a later model.

Engine Details

A single iron casting forms the cylinder block and crankcase, and the bores (which are relatively long, with a bore to stroke ratio of 0.778 to 1), are machined direct in the casting. The general layout of the crankcase is simple, and there is ample structural rigidity, produced by the internal webbing and the arrangement of the housings for the seven main bearings. The crankshaft and big-end bearings are of indium-coated lead-bronze bearings,

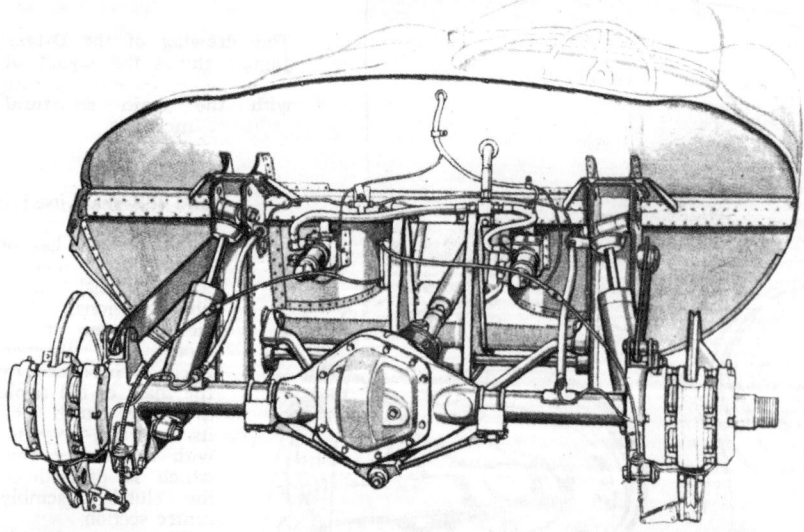

The rear suspension is by means of trailing links and a one-piece torsion bar which is anchored at the centre. Note the disc brakes and additional caliper hand brakes at each end of the axle.

tubular intake ducts are attached to the carburettor intake flanges, and connected by a large-diameter balance tube, the side walls of the intake tubes being cross-drilled at the appropriate points.

An intake duct in the bonnet conveys air from the radiator grille to an open-ended box which, surrounding the carburettor intakes, eliminates the need for pressure balancing pipes to the float chambers. The two three-branch, welded exhaust manifolds direct the gases via two short, flexible pipes into the two main outlet pipes. Just before the pipes terminate in front of the left-hand-side rear wheel, they are enclosed in a sheet-metal cover somewhat similar to a small silencer, which, in conjunction with drilled holes in the inner walls of the pipes, forms an effective expansion chamber and provides substantial mounting points for securing to the main body structure.

An orthodox arrangement of engine cooling is adopted, but to enable the bonnet height to be kept low a separate light alloy radiator header tank is placed between the front of the engine and the radiator. After passing through the head the coolant is conveyed to the tank which contains outlet pipes at each side, with a central, longitudinal baffle. The intake pipe discharges the coolant near the centre in order to feed both outlets equally and to prevent ineffective cooling that might be caused by the coolant being directed to one side of the radiator.

Both oil and coolant radiators are of light alloy and produced by Marston Excelsior. The radiator system is pressurized to 4lb per sq in by means of a valve unit mounted in the back of the tank.

A conventional fuel system is used, but an unusual feature is the use of flexible tanks, supported in light alloy boxes. To obtain the desired range between refuelling stops, two tanks are used. Twin petrol pumps, placed behind the rear diaphragm, connect to a common delivery pipe to the carburettors.

Power is transmitted from the engine via the triple-plate clutch to the four-speed synchromesh gear box. The main clutch body contains three sets of internal splines equally spaced around its bore, mating with the external splines on the two intermediate driving plates. The rear clutch driven plate is attached to a centrepiece which is internally splined to mate with the gear box input shaft, and contains three sets of external splines carrying the first and second driven plates.

The pressure plate assembly, bolted to the rear, contains six springs together with the toggle levers, which are operated by the ball-bearing thrust withdrawal mechanism. The actual clutch operation is hydraulic by a Girling unit. Radial holes are drilled in the clutch body, to assist cooling and allow lining dust to escape. The complete clutch assembly is housed in a conventional bell housing, with an opening at the back for the starter motor, which is above the transmission on the engine centre line.

Single helical gears are used in the gear box and special close ratios have been chosen. The gears are selected by a short change lever conveniently placed

THE D-TYPE

With the bonnet open the engine and front suspension are very accessible. The oil tank is carried just behind the left front wheel, while the small battery is placed in a similar position behind the right wheel. The large pipe running from the oil tank between the two exhaust manifolds is a breather which is connected to the engine.

The D-type engine can be distinguished by the very shallow sump used in conjunction with the dry sump lubrication system. The torsional vibration damper can be seen at the front of the engine behind the dynamo and water pump driving belts.

vide bearing housings for the trailing-link units. The top links are 16in long and of flat steel plate of approximately $2 \times \frac{1}{2}$in section. Rubber bushes are used for both the inner and the outer bearings. Metal bushes used for the lower bearings are $1\frac{1}{8}$in diameter, and are lubricated by grease nipples. Steel plates are also used for the lower links, and these have a similar centre distance to those above, so that a true parallelogram is formed.

To provide attachment of the lower links to the torsion bars, bearing units are riveted to the inner ends of the lower links; these are also bored to provide clearance for the torsion bar, and contain a larger diameter outer ring which is internally splined. The ends of the torsion bar, also splined, are of a much smaller diameter, so that, to connect the torsion bar to the rear links, rings are used which are externally splined to mate with the lower links and internally splined to connect with the torsion bar.

The single torsion bar used for the rear suspension has an enlarged centre section which is attached to a reaction plate bolted to the centre of the main body structure and containing arms which pass on each

just aft of the gear box unit. A small, flexible breather pipe extends forward and upward to the front of the main bulkhead.

From the rear of the gear box, a short Hardy Spicer propeller shaft continues the drive to the Salisbury rear axle. Except for a change in ratio and modified length of the axle tubes, this unit is similar to that fitted in the production XK. It has a hypoid final drive with a ratio of 2.79 to 1 and, with the tyres

JAGUAR .. continued

used at Le Mans, this gives a speed of 183 m.p.h. at 6,000 r.p.m. engine speed.

The front suspension is by upper and lower wishbones and longitudinal torsion bars. The inner fulcrum bearings are in line with the longitudinal centre line of the chassis, and rubber bushes form both upper and lower bearings; the front bushes are conical, while the rear ones are parallel. The upper wishbone—a one-piece forging—contains the ball housing at its outer end to permit the required movement for suspension and steering, while at the inner end there are two split bosses with pinch bolts.

The front boss is threaded internally, while a smaller diameter, plain section is provided for the rear one, the shaft which forms the top wishbone inner fulcrum having screwed and plain portions to mate with the wishbone. These two portions are concentric with the axis of the shaft, but the portions which pivot in the rubber bushes are eccentric, and the combined effect of the screw thread and eccentricity enables the wheel caster and camber to be adjusted after assembly.

With a number of torsion bar front suspensions, the bar supporting the weight of the car is concentric with the lower pivot point, but in the Jaguar layout, the front member of the lower wishbone assembly extends from its fulcrum point towards the centre of the car, forming a splined attachment for the bar which runs at an angle of $2\frac{1}{2}$ deg to the centre line of the car. This enables the bar to be changed without disturbing the main suspension components, but it also means that the suspension characteristics are modified slightly by the combined effects of bending and torsion. To adjust the height of the car, a vernier arrangement of splines is provided.

Rack and Pinion Steering

The steering arms, extending in front of the wheel centre line, are linked to the rack and pinion steering unit, which is placed fairly high in front of the main cross-member assembly. There is a universal joint in the steering column.

At the rear, the suspension consists of a live axle, trailing arms and a torsion bar. Two massive, box-section members attached to the main body structure pro-

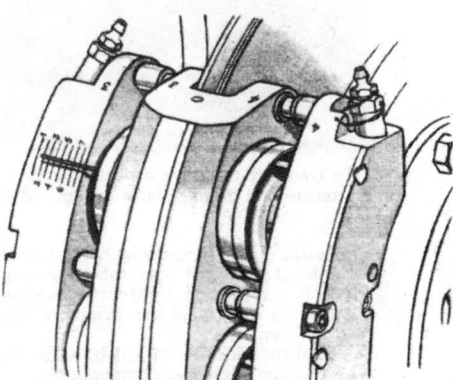

To enable the rate of wear of the brake friction pads to be determined during a race, a small visual indicator is provided with a pointer which lines up with a series of marks engraved on one of the caliper housings.

side of the propeller-shaft. The effective length from the reaction point to the splines is 20in. Under cornering conditions, the plates forming the suspension links are in torsion, increasing the roll stiffness of the car and necessitating the use of material for the links which will permit some flexibility.

To provide transverse location of the axle unit, an open A bracket is pivoted to the main structural members, the bearings being slightly forward of the link bearing line, while the apex of the A

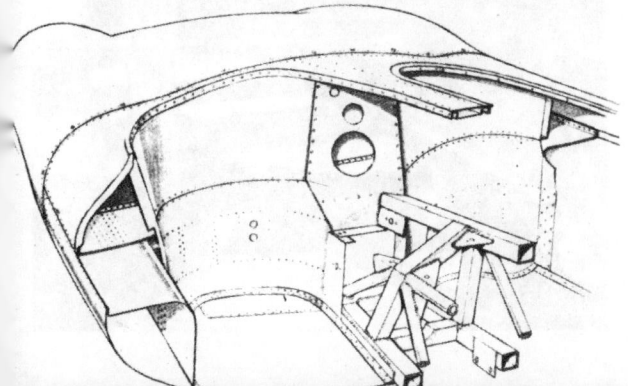

How the tubular frame members are united with the rear diaphragm plate. To provide extra clearance for the driver, a small diameter tube is used in place of a large square section one for the top right-hand member.

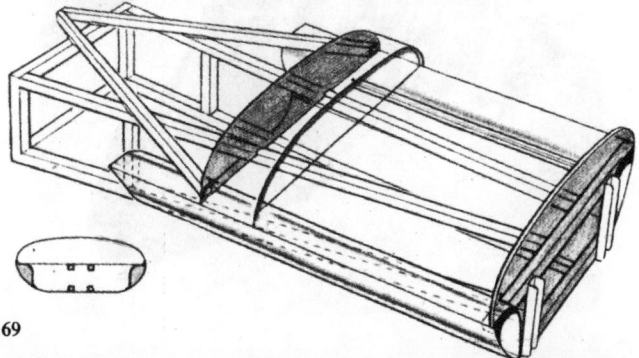

This sketch gives a diagrammatic representation of the main members which form the structure of the car; this complete magnesium-alloy structure has been carefully stressed to provide maximum rigidity with very light weight.

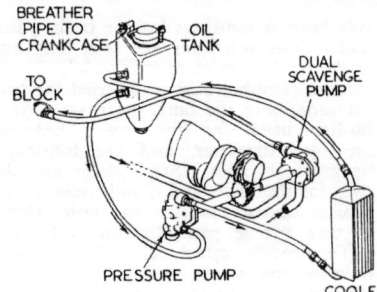

Engine lubrication: A cross shaft, gear driven from the front end of the crankshaft, provides the drive for the pressure and scavenge pumps.

attached to the lower link and bracketed to the main body structure. Built-in bump stops in the dampers consist of large rubber pads placed around the main damper spindle, which contact with the top of the main damper casing, while hydraulic rebound stops are also incorporated.

It was emphasized previously that one of the methods used to improve the performance of the new D-type car was to reduce wind resistance. When the drag of a car is reduced, so that it requires a relatively small b.h.p. to propel it at a high speed, it also requires extremely good brakes, since the retarding effect of air resistance has been reduced. As on last year's cars, Dunlop disc brakes are fitted to all four wheels. They have $12\frac{3}{4}$in diameter discs and three pairs of pads are used at the front, and two at the rear, to provide the required braking distribution. All the pads are $2\frac{3}{16}$in diameter, so that the total friction lining area for the foot brake is 45 sq in front and 30 sq in rear. To improve the brake life, the volume of the friction material has been increased by approximately 20 per cent since last year.

Structurally, the brakes consist of a caliper, machined from medium carbon steel, attached to a suitable flange on the front or rear suspension in the same way as the brake back plate is fixed on a drum-brake system. Bores in this caliper provide housings for the brake pads—which are circular blocks of brake lining material—so that torque reaction is taken by the caliper housing.

To eliminate the effect of disc distortion which might arise through deflection of the rear axle half-shafts when cornering, the rear brake pads are placed symmetrically about the horizontal axis of the wheel centre line. The brake discs are of mild steel, which is hard chromium plated to reduce the rate of wear.

THE D-TYPE

Under very arduous conditions, the temperature rise in and around the caliper area might cause the brake fluid to boil. To provide adequate cooling, the brake-operating cylinders—one for each pad, twenty cylinders therefore, being required—are arranged in the form of light alloy blocks, attached to the calipers by bolts and distance pieces to provide adequate air space. The outer end of each piston has a spherical seating so that slight tilting of the brake pad does not produce severe side loading on the piston. A normal type of rubber diaphragm seal is fitted towards the outer end of the piston to prevent foreign matter from reaching the cylinder bores. Drillings in the light alloy block take the supply pipes, while nipples are provided at convenient points to enable the system to be bled.

Automatic Adjustment

It is necessary to reduce to a minimum the movement required to bring the brake pads into contact with the disc, but at the same time to ensure that the pads are not rubbing when the brakes are not applied. If an unnecessarily large clearance were provided between pad and disc there would be an excessively long pedal movement before the brakes came into operation, owing to the large number of operating cylinders that are employed in this system.

To overcome this difficulty an ingenious system of retraction and automatic adjustment is provided to maintain

To transmit the drive a neat and compact triple plate clutch is used, and the two intermediate driving plates are splined into the centre portion of the clutch housing.

terminates in a bearing which is secured by a bracket to the axle tubes, serving not only to provide transverse location but also to determine the height of the rear roll centre.

The suspension is damped by CDR $4\frac{1}{2}$ type Girling telescopic dampers. At the front these are attached to the upper section of the front cross member at the top and the lower wishbone at the bottom, while the rear dampers are inclined transversely to clear the upper suspension links, the damper itself being

Left: Air scoops form part of the unsprung mass on the front suspension, and direct air over the front brake discs.

The front torsion bars are attached to an extension on the front portion of the lower wishbone, which is continued in past the fulcrum point.

only 0.010in to 0.015in clearance between the pad and the disc when the brakes are in the off position.

To apply the brakes, a dual hydraulic system is provided, with servo assistance by a Plessey pump driven, from the back end of the gear box, whenever the propeller-shaft is rotating. A simple hydraulic layout is used to operate the front brakes which, if necessary, can be applied without assistance from the servo, in the event of a failure occurring in the servo circuit.

With the servo in operation, the fluid is pumped from the header tank into the rear of the master cylinder, through four cross drillings into the hollow centre-

JAGUAR .. continued

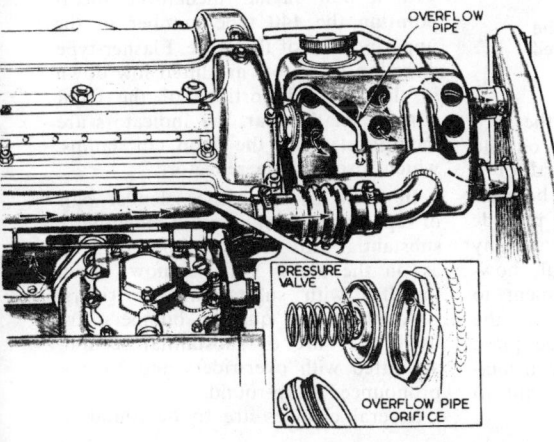

A baffle plate is fitted halfway across the radiator header tank to distribute the flow through both sides of the film block. The overflow pipe from the pressure valve runs out through the base of the header tank.

section of the rear portion of the piston, and out into another pipe which returns to the header tank. Whenever the car is in forward motion the fluid circulates in this way.

When the brakes are applied, the rear piston is forced against the main piston, applying the front brakes, and at the same time preventing the fluid from the servo pump returning to the header tank. The line pressure from the servo pump increases, and as this pipe is connected to the rear brakes they also are applied, and at the same time the build-up in servo pressure exerts a force on the back of the master cylinder piston which applies the front brakes.

The layout of the pistons in the brake master cylinder. An hydraulic servo is used.

Although it is necessary for the driver's foot to close the valve which increases the line pressure, the area so covered is much less than the area of the front brake master cylinder piston, and it is this difference which determines the servo ratio.

As the servo pump is driven from the output side of the propeller-shaft, it will be rotated in reverse whenever the car moves backward, and, unless precautions were taken, this might cause air to be drawn into the system.

A valve box is fitted between the input and output pipes from the pump, with a non-return valve so placed that pressure in the suction side of the pump causes the valve to open, providing a short open circuit between inlet and outlet sides of the pump. Two separate sets of mechanically operated calipers with triangular friction linings, fitted below the main hydraulically operated units on the rear brakes, are operated by a single cable connected to the handbrake lever by a pulley compensating mechanism.

To reduce weight, perforated disc light alloy wheels are used. They have a centre-lock fixing but, in place of the splined hub often used on a conventional centre-lock wheel, the wheel disc is attached to a steel centre portion by five bolts which have domed heads. These locate in holes drilled in the back flange of the hub and transmit drive or braking torque.

The cockpit is well laid out and is free from unnecessary equipment. It contains three instruments—a tachometer with an additional hand to record the maximum speed which the engine attains, an oil pressure gauge and a water temperature gauge. The steering wheel is adjustable and held on its splined column by a screwed clamp. In true racing tradition it has light alloy spokes and a neat wooden rim.

The curved plastic windscreen sweeps well round the sides of the cockpit, and the rear part of the body has a head rest just in front of the fuel filler cap and, to improve the direction stability under adverse wind

The fuel is carried in two flexible tanks which are neatly fitted into light alloy boxes in the tail of the car.

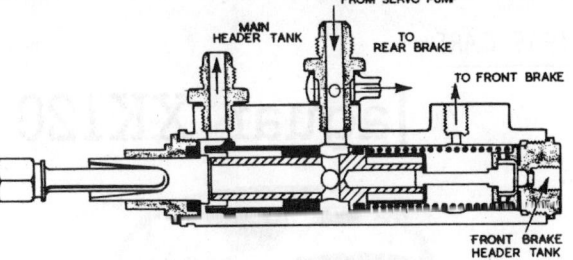

conditions, particularly at speeds of over 150 m.p.h., a tail fin which neatly blends into the driver's head rest.

SPECIFICATION

Engine.—6-cyl. 83×106 mm, 3,442 c.c. Compression ratio 9 to 1. 250 b.h.p. at 6,000 r.p.m. Maximum torque 242 lb ft at 4,000 r.p.m. Seven-bearing crankshaft. Hemispherical combustion chambers. Overhead valves operated by twin overhead camshafts.

Clutch.—Three plates, six springs. Hydraulically operated, ball-bearing withdrawal mechanism.

Gear Box.—Ratios: Top 2.79; third 3.57; second 4.58; first 5.98 to 1. Reverse 6.1 to 1.

Final Drive.—Hypoid bevel, ratio 2.79 to 1 (14:39). Two-pinion differential.

Suspension.—Front, independent, wishbone and torsion bars. Rear, trailing link and torsion bar. Suspension rate (at the wheel) front, 120 lb per in; rear, 120 lb per in.

Brakes.—Dunlop disc. Three-pad front; two-pad rear. Discs: front 12¾in diameter,

The starter ring is attached to the centre of the clutch casing; no normal flywheel is used, the necessary flywheel effect being obtained by the mass of the clutch and ring.

rear 12¾in diameter. Total lining area: 75 sq in; 45 sq in front.

Steering.—Rack and pinion. Eight-toothed pinion. 1¾ turns from lock to lock.

Wheels and Tyres.—Dunlop light alloy, perforated disc, centre-lock wheels. 6.50-16in Dunlop racing tyres on 5.00-16in rims.

Electrical Equipment.—12-volt; 40-ampère-hour battery. Head lamps, 48- or 60-watt bulbs.

Fuel and Oil System.—37 Imp. gallons in two flexible tanks. Oil capacity 3½ gallons.

Main Dimensions.—Wheelbase 7ft 6in; track (front) 4ft 2in; (rear) 4ft. Overall length 12ft 10in. Width 5ft 5½in. Height, at scuttle, 2ft 8in; at fin, 3ft 8in. Ground clearance 5½in under sump. Frontal area 10.85 sq ft. Turning circle 32ft.

1955 CARS

Jaguar XK120 Becomes XK140

Roomier, More Powerful, Better Steering, Firmer Suspension

BOLDER grille bars and sturdier bumpers distinguish the XK140 from the 120, this model being the hard-top coupé which has the roof extended rearwards to permit occasional extra seating, and wider doors.

IN a range of cars as successful as the Jaguar XK models, one does not expect to find fundamental changes and the cars which will be seen at Earls Court next week accordingly reflect the continued public approval of these types. Nevertheless, many detail changes will improve performance and handling, and at the same time adapt the bodywork to meet a wider range of need without in any way departing from the basic objectives of the XK range. In order to differentiate these new models and indicate the improved performance, they will in future be known as XK140 models.

In addition, the "D"-type competition model now goes into limited series production.

* * *

As with the new M-type Mark VII model described in *The Motor* last week, high-lift camshaft engines have been standardized. The new camshafts give a $\frac{3}{8}$-in. lift (in place of $\frac{5}{16}$ in.) and allow the engine to breathe more effectively at high speeds. In addition a Lucas oil ignition coil is now fitted. In its new form, the engine produces 190 b.h.p. at 5,500 r.p.m. compared with the previous 160 b.h.p. at 5,200 r.p.m.

To allow full use to be made of the improved performance, a close-ratio gearbox is now fitted, with a fractionally higher top gear and an appreciably higher bottom, the respective new ratios being 3.54 and 10.55 to 1 (in place of the former 3.64 and 12.29 to 1). As with the Mark VII, Laycock-de Normanville overdrive is available as an extra and a lower axle ratio is used in this case.

The new rack-and-pinion steering is of conventional design but with one important addition. As is well known, this system offers excellent responsiveness, the one drawback sometimes experienced being that, as it is completely reversible, road shocks may be transmitted to the steering wheel.

In the case of the XK140, the rack tube is mounted on brackets on the main chassis frame but, instead of a rigid mounting, a shallow bonded-rubber pad is interposed to provide sufficient shock absorption to take any kick out of the wheel without, however, allowing sufficient movement to make the steering spongy. On the pinion side, moreover, a bridge piece surrounds the base plate of the insulating pad, thus setting a safe limit to reaction movement.

As with the Mark VII, firmer front suspension has been adopted and the rate with $\frac{1}{16}$ in. larger diameter torsion bars goes up from 128 lb./in. to 154 lb./in.

Externally, the new cars have several distinguishing features. The front grille is of the same shape and size as before but now has bolder vertical bars, with a new Jaguar medallion, incorporating the 140 type number in the upper portion of the grille. Flasher-type direction indicators are fitted low down in the forward portions of the front wings. At the rear, the indicators are incorporated in the stop/tail lamps, which also include reflectors.

In place of the rather slender pair of separate front bumpers, a much more substantial full-width bumper (exactly as on the Mark VII), is now fitted, together with substantial over-riders.

At the rear, quarter bumpers are used; they are of substantial section, are fitted with over-riders and have a pronounced wrap-round.

Several changes are to be found in

JAGUAR XK140 DATA

Engine Dimensions		Chassis Details	
Cylinders	6	Brakes	Lockheed hydraulic (2LS on front)
Bore	83 mm.	Brake drum diameter	12 in.
Stroke	106 mm.	Friction lining area	208 sq. in.
Cubic capacity	3442 c.c.	Suspension : Front	Independent (torsion bar)
Piston area	50.4 sq. in.	Rear	Semi-elliptic
Valves	o.h.v. (twin camshafts)	Shock absorbers	Girling telescopic hydraulic
Compression ratio	8 to 1	Wheel type	Pressed-steel bolt-on
Engine Performance		Tyre size	6.00—16 (Dunlop Road Speed)
Max. power	190 b.h.p.	Steering gear	Rack and pinion
at	5,500 r.p.m.	Steering wheel	18 in.
Max. b.m.e.p.	151 lb. sq. in.	**Dimensions**	
at	2,500 r.p.m.	Wheelbase	8 ft. 6 in.
B.h.p. per sq. in. piston area	3.77	Track : Front	4 ft. 3 in.
Peak piston speed, ft. per min.	3,840	Rear	4 ft. 2 in.
Engine Details		Overall length	14 ft. 5 in.
Carburetters	Two S.U. horizontal (with automatic chokes)	Overall width	5 ft. 2 in.
Ignition	Coil	Overall height	4 ft. 4½ in. (hood up)*
Plugs : make and type	Champion NA8	Ground clearance	7½ in.
Fuel pump	Two S.U. electric	Turning circle	31 ft.
Fuel capacity	15 gallons	Dry weight	24 cwt.*
Oil filter (make, by-pass or full flow)	Tecalemit full-flow	***Performance Data** (2-seater)	
Oil capacity	22½ pints	Piston area, sq. in. per ton	42.0
Cooling system	Pump, fan and thermostat	Brake lining area, sq. in. per ton	174
Water capacity	22 pints	Top gear m.p.h. per 1,000 r.p.m.	22.7 (with o'drive : direct 19.6, o'drive 25.2)
Electrical system	Lucas 12-volt		
Battery capacity	64 amp.-hr.		
Transmission		Top gear m.p.h. at 2,500 ft./min. piston speed	81.7 (with o'drive : direct 70.7, o'drive 90.7)
Clutch	10 in. Borg and Beck		
	Standard With o'drive		
Gear ratios : Top	3.54 4.09	Litres per ton-mile, dry	3820 (with o'drive : direct 4410, o'drive 3430)
	(o'drive 3.19)		
3rd	4.28 4.95		
2nd	6.2 7.16		
1st	10.55 12.4		
Rev.	10.55 12.4		
Prop. shaft	Hardy Spicer		
Final drive	Hypoid bevel		

*NOTE—Data marked with an asterisk refers to the 2-seater. The fixed head 2-3 seater coupe has an overall height of 4 ft. 5½ in. and a dry weight of 25½ cwt. The drop-head coupe has an overall height (hood erected) of 4 ft. 4½ in. and a dry weight of 26½ cwt.
Special equipment models have an output of 210 b.h.p. and wire wheels.

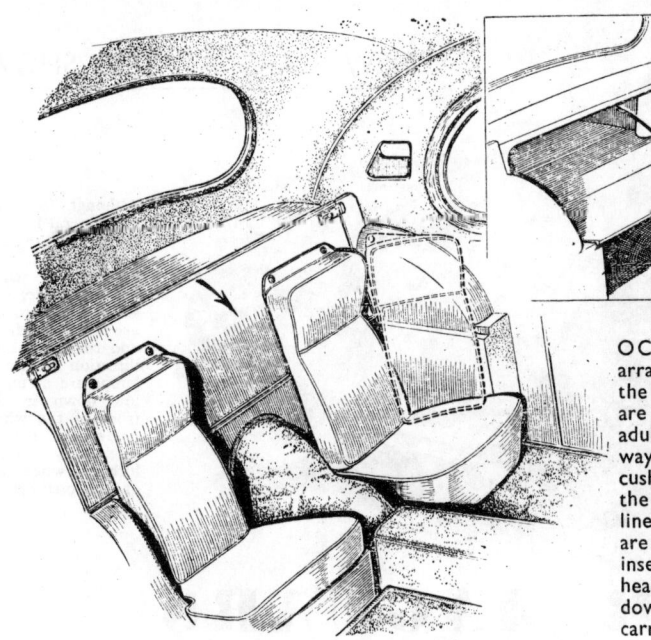

OCCASIONAL SEATING as arranged in the 2/3 seater edition the XK140. The two small seats are suitable for children but one adult can be carried sitting sideways; in this case, the spare back cushion is transferred to the side of the car (as shown in dotted outline.) For clarity the front seats are not shown in this drawing. The inset sketch shows how the bulkhead of the boot can be hinged down, when no passengers are carried in the rear, to extend the boot floor.

Jaguar XK120 becomes XK140 - - Contd.

the boot. The spare wheel is now housed below a hinged portion of the flat luggage floor, and more luggage space has been made available, when required, by hinging the bulkhead between the boot and the interior of the body along its bottom edge so that it can be swung forward and down to form a forward extension of the luggage floor.

On the two-seater and drop-head coupé, the floor length from front to rear is normally 41 in., but, with the bulkhead lowered, an extra length of approximately 8½ in. is available and this enables a reasonably-large suitcase (up to 7½ in. in depth) to be pushed forward beyond the normal limits of the boot. In this position, a suitcase occupies the space normally taken by the hood when it is folded. A similar plan is followed on the new fixed-head 2-3-seater coupé, but in this case the fold-down bulkhead is deeper, giving a luggage floor extension of approximately 10 in.

It was mentioned earlier that leg room has been increased and this has been achieved by moving the power unit forward 3 in. in the frame.

This completes the changes which apply to all models, but further improvements are to be found in the two coupé types. In the case of the drop-head model, small shallow cushions have been fitted in the rear so that young children can be carried. The cushions are of the sponge rubber type and can be removed when not required. Another detail which will be much appreciated, is the incorporation of spring assistance in the head linkage, the counterbalancing effect being sufficient to enable the head to be erected single-handed from the driving seat.

The new 2-3-seater fixed-head coupé is on the same lines as the old except that the roof has been extended backwards by approximately 6¾ in. to provide occasional extra accommodation.

This additional seating has been very ingeniously arranged. Backrests take the form of narrow upholstered sponge-rubber cushions, attached by press buttons, but pleated horizontally in such a way that they will fold forward with the bulkhead. Small seat cushions are used, one on each side of the transmission tunnel. These provisions are suitable for two children, or when one adult is carried, the unwanted back cushion can be buttoned to the side of the car to provide a corner seat.

The extended roof line of the new fixed-head coupé gives considerably greater window area and has also

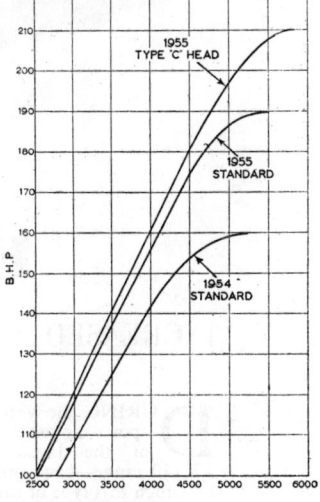

COMPARATIVE POWERS of the 1954 XK120, 1955 XK140 and the 1955 XK140 special equipment models; the latter, among other special features, have the C-type cylinder head.

enabled wider doors to be fitted. The door width has gone up from 32½ in. to 38 in.

All three types of the XK140 are offered in special equipment form, such cars having a C-type cylinder head, a dual exhaust system, an 8:1 or 9:1 compression ratio at option, wire wheels and fog lamps.

Finally, it has been decided to put the now-famous D-type Jaguar into limited series production in place of the former C-type. The special version of the XK engine used in this case develops 250 b.h.p. and the car is remarkable for its ingenious construction in which no separate chassis is used, the basis being a centre section of monocoque construction with integral extensions at the front to carry the engine and front suspension, and a bolt-on section at the rear which forms the tail assembly. Another very important feature is disc brakes which, after being proved on racing circuits, are now, at last, offered on a production model. This is claimed to be the fastest car in the world to be offered to the public in series production.

1955 JAGUAR PRICES

	Total.	Basic.
XK140 open sports	£1,598 8s. 4d.	£1,127 10s.
XK140 fixed-head coupé	£1,616 2s. 6d.	£1,140
XK140 drop-head coupé	£1,644 9s. 2d.	£1,160
Jaguar D-type	£2,685 14s. 2d.	£1,895

APART from bumper and grille changes, the two-seater models are little changed externally; this is one of the special equipment editions, with 210 b.h.p. engine, wire wheels and fog lamps.

NEW CARS AT THE SHOW

Although following the general lines of the XK120, the 140 has new front styling with a smaller radiator grille, and substantial bumpers are fitted both front and rear. Flashing direction indicator lamps are mounted low down in the front of the wings below the normal side lights. Centre-lock wire wheels are an optional extra.

FIERCER JAGUARS

INCREASED OUTPUT FROM XK ENGINE : OCCASIONAL SEATS IN COUPES

DURING the years of the post-war sports car renaissance the products of the Jaguar company — the XK120 range—have provided a yardstick by which this type of car has been judged. Since its introduction in 1948 the open two-seater has undergone very few changes, as have the other two models, the fixed-head and drop-head coupés which were introduced in 1951 and 1953 respectively. But in the sports car world the accent is on more performance, so not content to let matters rest, Jaguar have introduced a new range of cars with the type number XK140. As before, there is a choice of three models; open two-seater, and fixed-head and drop-head coupés. All models have improved engine performance and more body space, and in the two coupé models there is extra seating accommodation so that the cars now become a practical family proposition.

More Power

The power output of the six-cylinder twin-overhead-camshaft engine has been increased from 160 b.h.p. to a bench test figure of 190 b.h.p. at 5,500 r.p.m. This has been accomplished by increasing the valve lift from $\frac{7}{16}$in to $\frac{3}{8}$in by means of a change in the camshafts, and by detail improvements to the cylinder head to promote better breathing. The bottom end of the engine is basically unchanged, although detail alterations have been made. The crank chamber is simple in design and very stiff because of the bearing arrangement—one main bearing on each side of each crank throw. To cater for the increased power output, and at the same time to maintain the utmost reliability, steel main bearing caps replace the cast iron ones used previously. Although a sump shield is still fitted, the risk of damage is further reduced by replacing the cast light alloy sump with a pressed steel one. Other detail modifications to the engine include chromium plating on the chain tensioner to reduce wear, pre-packed bearings for the water pump to reduce maintenance, a narrow-section belt to drive the 22-ampère dynamo, and a cowled, eight-bladed fan to improve the cooling.

All three models are available in special equipment version with an engine developing 210 b.h.p. This further increase in output is obtained by enlarging the throat diameter of the inlet ports from $1\frac{3}{8}$in to $1\frac{1}{2}$in, but without increasing the valve size, which is $1\frac{3}{4}$in diameter. The exhaust valves have been increased from $1\frac{7}{16}$in to $1\frac{5}{8}$in diameter, while the port throat size has been enlarged from $1\frac{1}{4}$in to $1\frac{3}{8}$in diameter. All the ports are carefully cleaned up, particular attention being paid to matching the joints between manifolds and head, and in place of the single exhaust pipe there is a dual system.

To obtain the maximum benefit from the increased power output on both the standard and special equipment models, there is a new close-ratio gear box which enables higher speeds to be reached in the indirect ratios without over-revving the engine. The basic design

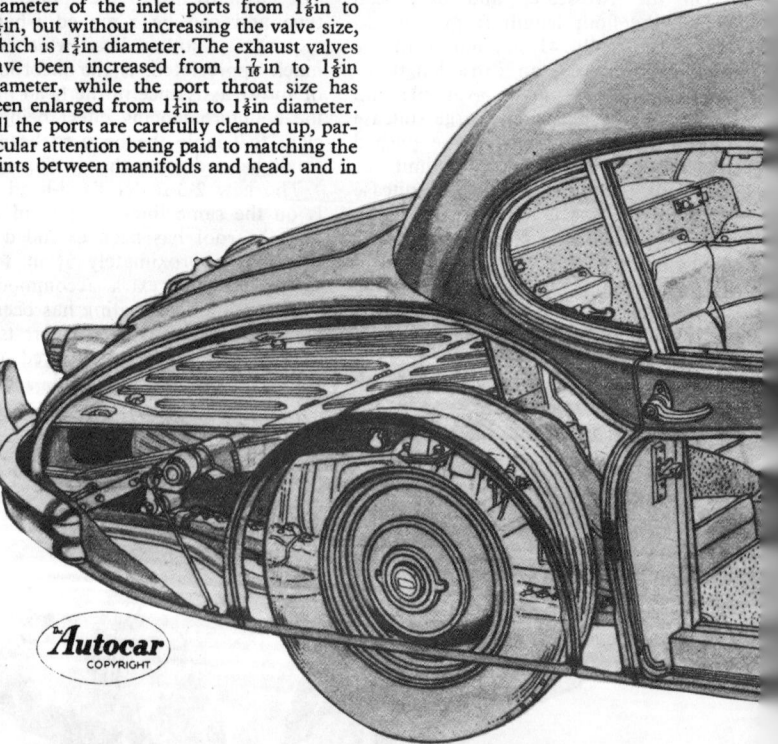

New features on the fixed-head coupé include rack and pinion steering, increased engine performance, and a modified bulkhead permitting more forward seating so that an adult or two children can be carried in the rear. The luggage locker has been modified, and access to the spare wheel is now via a trap-door in the luggage compartment. Substantial over-riders are fitted on the bumpers.

Bird's-eye view of the D-type Jaguar reveals the engine, the driving compartment and, hinged from the fin behind the driver's head rest, the fairing which covers the petrol filler cap.

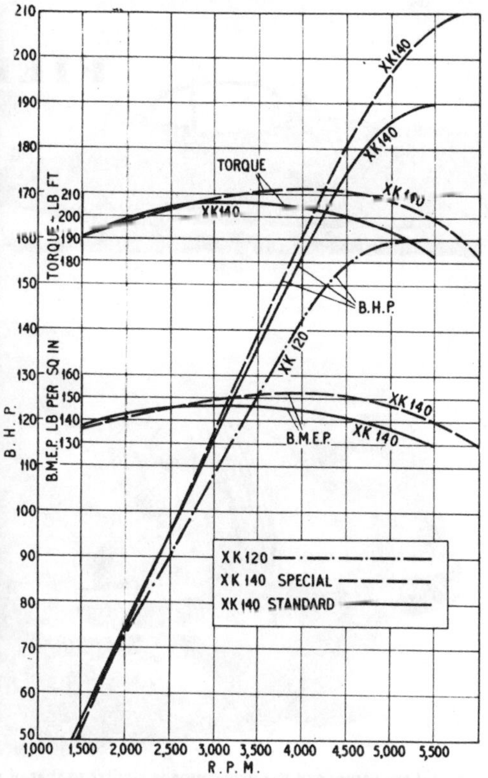

Performance characteristics for both the standard and special equipment versions of the XK140. For reference purposes the power output of last year's standard model is also included.

of the box is similar to that used on previous models, the change in ratios having been made by altering the constant-mesh gears. Previously confined to the Mark VII saloon, the Laycock-de Normanville overdrive unit can now be supplied as optional extra equipment, but for the XK140 range it is fitted with a manual control in the place of the semi-automatic control used on the Mark VII. On cars fitted with overdrive, the axle ratio is changed so that the car has better acceleration in the four normal gears.

The chassis has also been improved. As a result of experience gained in sports car racing the XK140s have rack and pinion steering. The front suspension torsion bars have been stiffened by increasing their diameter, and the understeer characteristic has been increased by repositioning some of the components. For example, the engine has been moved further forward, and the battery, previously located behind the seat back, is now in the engine compartment.

Repositioning the power unit has increased the amount of space inside the body on all three models, but to a different degree. On the open two-seater the facia and bulkhead have been moved forward 3in, and in place of a 4in adjustment on the seat slide, 7in is now provided. The body has also been raised an inch to give extra clearance between the steering wheel and the top of the seat. The seat back has been raised to give extra support, and the space previously occupied by the batteries is now available for extra luggage.

On the drop-head coupé the front seats have been repositioned similarly, the bottom of the facia has been lifted an inch,

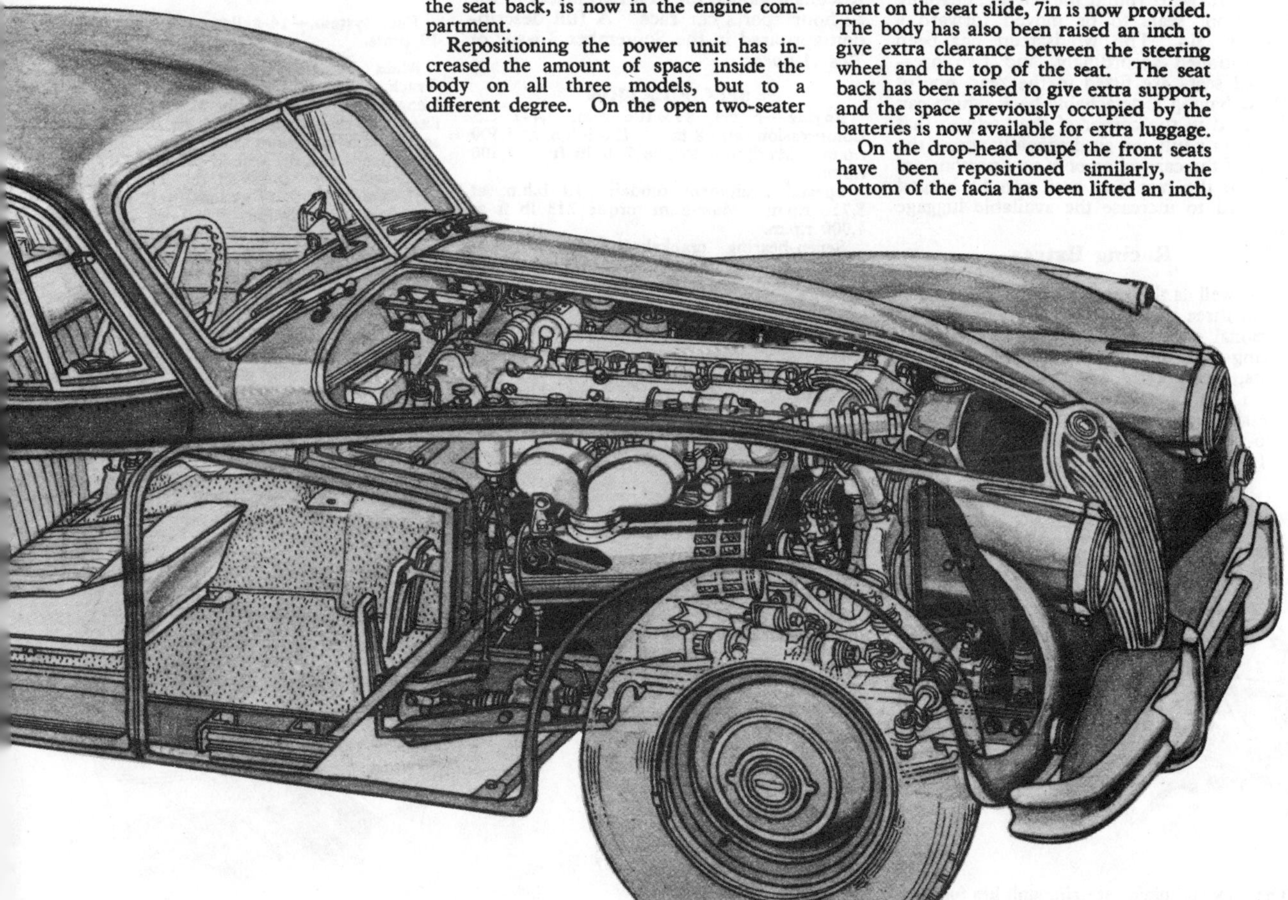

FIERCER JAGUARS ... continued

Frontal appearance of the new coupé is similar to that of the open two-seater. The windscreen has been moved farther forward, and the top part of the body extends farther back to provide the necessary space for the occasional rear seats.

and a pair of small occasional seats are provided in the rear. These are suitable for two children. On the fixed-head coupé there is even more interior space, as the sides of the main bulkhead have been swept forward round the engine, enabling the front seats to be moved forward a further 5in. The windscreen has been repositioned accordingly, and two occasional seats are fitted in the rear, one of these having a detachable back which can be fixed in the corner of the body so that an extra adult can sit diagonally across the rear of the car; when only two persons are carried the rear seat back can be hinged forward to increase the available luggage space.

Racing Extras

As well as the special equipment version of all three models, there are a number of optional extras available which include a racing-type clutch, competition bucket seats, racing tyres and tubes, lead-bronze main and big end bearings, 9 to 1 compression ratio pistons and, for the open two-seater, racing type windscreens.

In place of the C-type competition model, the new D-type car is now in production, as announced last week. This new sports-racing car has been seen several times this year; at Le Mans it gained second and fourth placings, and later at Rheims it gained the first two places in the 12-hour sports car race. A full description appeared in the September 3 issue of *The Autocar*.

SPECIFICATION

Engine.—6 cyl, 83 × 106 mm, 3,442 c.c. Compression ratio 8 to 1. 190 b.h.p. at 5,500 r.p.m. Maximum torque 210 lb ft at 2,500 r.p.m.

Special equipment model: 210 b.h.p. at 5,750 r.p.m. Maximum torque 213 lb ft at 4,000 r.p.m.

Seven-bearing crankshaft. Hemispherical combustion chambers. Inclined valves operated by twin overhead camshafts.

Clutch.—10in diameter single-plate. 12 springs. Carbon thrust withdrawal mechanism.

Gear Box.—Overall ratios: Top 3.54, third 4.28, second 6.2, first 10.55 to 1. Reverse 10.55 to 1. Synchromesh on top, third and second gears.

With overdrive: Overdrive 3.19, top 4.09, third 4.95, second 7.16, first 12.4 to 1. Reverse 12.4 to 1.

Final Drive.—Hypoid axle 3.54 to 1 (13 : 46). Four-pinion differential. With overdrive: 4.09 to 1 (11 : 45). Four-pinion differential.

Suspension.—Front, independent, longitudinal torsion bars, anti-roll bar; rear, half-elliptic leaf springs. Suspension rate (at the wheel): front 154 lb per in, rear 138 lb per in. Static deflection: fixed-head and drop-head coupés, front 4.65in, rear 4.7in; open two-seater, front 4.3in; rear 4.3in.

Brakes.—Lockheed, two leading shoe front; leading and trailing shoe rear. Drums: 12in diameter, 2¼in wide, front and rear. Total lining area: 207 sq in (103.5 sq in front).

Steering.—Rack and pinion. 3¾ turns from lock to lock.

Wheels and Tyres.—6.00-16in tyres on 5.5 × 16in rims. Five-stud steel disc wheels.

Electrical Equipment.—12-volt; 63 ampère-hour battery (two 6-volt batteries on fixed-head coupé). Head lamps, double-dip 60-36 watt bulbs.

Fuel System.—14-gallon tank. Oil capacity 19 pints.

Main Dimensions.—Wheel-base 8ft 6in. Track, front 4ft 3½in, rear 4ft 2½in. Length 14ft 8in, width 5ft 4½in. Height, fixed- and drop-head coupés, 4ft 7in; open two-seater 4ft 5½in. Ground clearance 7½in. Frontal area: fixed- and drop-head coupés 17.13 sq ft; open two-seater 16.99 sq ft. Turning circle 33ft. Weight (with 17 gallons fuel): drop-head and fixed-head coupés 3,080 lb; open two-seater 2,940 lb. Weight distribution: drop-head and fixed-head coupés 51.7 per cent front; open two-seater, 52.3 per cent front.

Price.—XK140 fixed-head coupé: £1,140, purchase tax £476 2s 6d, total £1,616 2s 6d. XK140 drop-head coupé: £1,160, p.t. £484 9s 2d, total £1,644 9s 2d. XK140 open two-seater: £1,127 10s, p.t. £470 18s 4d, total £1,598 8s 4d. XK140 Special Equipment Models: D-type: £1,895, p.t. £790 14s 2d, total £2,685 14s 2d.

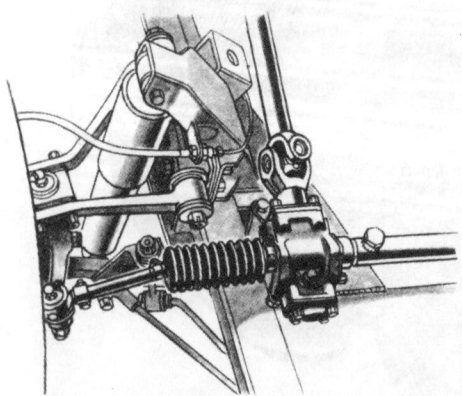

The rack and pinion steering unit lies forward of the centre line of the front wheels. The steering column has a universal joint.

When the rear panel of the rear seat is folded forward, increased space for luggage is provided.

This is the XK-140 coupe, newly enlarged to seat two adults and two children—or three adults. Wire wheels, a "C-type" engine are available.

FOREIGN CARS DESCRIBED:

the 1955 Jaguars

Roomier, faster and less expensive, these latest "Coventry Cats" are making a big bid for supremacy in the American market.

A WELL-KNOWN ex-president of the United States once said, "There's a time for planning and a time for action; the time for action is now!" Well, this seems to be the battle cry for another famous president—William Lyons of Jaguar Cars, Ltd. His long-planned and long-awaited line of new cars has finally been released to the public in this, the most competitive year in the history of the automotive industry—1955.

It would be interesting to speculate as to whether or not Mr. Lyons' long-range plans of a few years back included any sort of a model change in 1955. Was he "forced" into such a move by the pressures of competition or was it merely the next logical step? One thing is certain; his cars have been selling at an ever-increasing rate. Sales have climbed, in fact, until Jaguar is at this moment the largest-selling foreign car in the United States, regardless of price.

But even that isn't enough to satisfy Mr. Lyons. He is convinced that considering the tremendous potential car market in America, Jaguar sales up to this point have been only a fraction of what they might be. Most of the cars have sold to sports-car fans of a sort, and there are at best only a few hundred thousand of that strange breed. But there has been, at CONTINUED ON PAGE 78

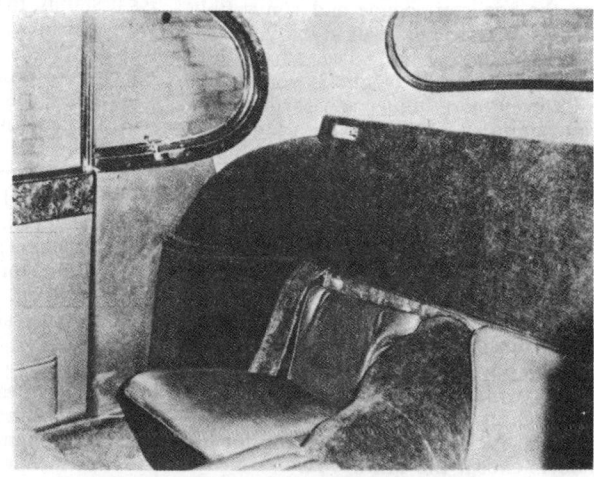
Rear compartment of the coupe looks like this. The small "occasional" seats are in new convertible model as well.

Body changes on the popular roadster line have been limited to new chrome trim, bumpers. Leg room is increased.

The 1955 Jaguars

the same time, a fringe of auto fans who like the speed and styling of sports cars all right, but who just aren't interested if they have to go back to an "old fashioned" manual transmission. And that is where the new Jaguar line comes in.

Since 1953, the Jag Mark VII sedan has been available with an American-manufactured Borg-Warner automatic transmission. The idea was to make it more competitive with the big U. S. luxury cars in its own price range. Apparently this plan worked out just fine, because for 1955 every one of the 10 models, in four basic body lines, can be had with the Borg-Warner unit as optional equipment. ($240.) Or, if you prefer, there is also the Laycock de Normanville overdrive for $160 extra.

But transmissions aren't the only big news this year. The standard power plant used in all models is a very warm, yet reliable, version of the famous XK-120 engine, now developing 190 hp at 5,200 rpm. Since the new designation for the roadster, coupe and convertible models is XK-140 instead of XK-120, the new engine is called simply the "XK," to show its origin. If you should want even more luxury and performance you can order a new XK-140 in the "M" series, with a special crankshaft damper, wire wheels, dual exhausts, two fog lamps and a set of windshield washers. And if that still doesn't satisfy you, the famous C-type engine—giving 210 hp—is featured in the new "MC" series.

Other prominent new mechanical features include increased diameter torsion bars, oil-filled ignition coils, larger radiators with eight-bladed fans, headlamps with special LeMans-type diffuser lenses, flashing-light traffic indicators and rack-and-pinion steering for all models except the Mark VII.

When it came to styling changes, Jaguar had a real problem on their hands. Since 1948, when the first XK-120 roadsters were produced, most people were agreed that the Jaguar was one of the most beautiful cars ever made. Its lines combined perfect streamlining and grace with a simplicity that was ageless. If the 1954 Jaguar was greeted with fewer "oohs" and "ahs" on the road than the 1948 model had received, it was only because the public had become a bit more accustomed to the car in six years.

Then why change it? Jaguar stylists wondered about this, too, and after much debate, they decided to compromise. The basic lines of the cars, they agreed, should not be altered. A completely new car might easily win many new fans for the Jaguar, but it would, at the same time, stand the chance of losing many of the original followers of the *marque*. So, the next best thing was to modify.

This was a much simpler task. The earlier Jags had been lacking in a number of departments, even in the eyes of the most avid enthusiast. There was, for instance, the problem of sufficient space, both for passengers and for luggage, in the Super Sports models. In the 1955 line this has been pretty well solved by the addition of two small "occasional" seats in the rear of the coupe and convertible models. Admittedly, these seats are only for children, but there is room for one fair-sized adult sitting across instead of fore-and-aft. This position is more comfortable in the coupe than it is in the convertible because the folding top in the latter takes up some of the room, and there frankly isn't much to spare. Leg room in both cars has been greatly improved in front—so much so that with the bucket seats all the way back, a six-footer cannot even reach the floor pedals. The same is true with the XK-140 roadster which, however, remains a two seater, probably to keep it light enough for sports-car competition. As it stands, the optional "MC" roadster, with 210 hp and just a little over 2,700 lbs. in weight, is the fastest Jaguar in the current production series.

Trunk space in all XK-140s has been increased and made more useable by virtue of the fact that a small "trap door" now leads from the trunk to the inside of the car, thus making allowance for extra-long packages.

Jaguar is much to be complimented for doing all this "stretching" without having extended the wheelbase of their cars. The over-all effect has been to make the vehicles much more practical while not affecting their outward appearance to any great degree. At the same time, there have been a number of minor external alterations, but these also tend to enhance rather than detract. The radiator grille has been made bolder and simpler and the chrome frames around the headlights have been redesigned. New, heavy wrap-around bumpers give the cars a more solid look and afford some much needed protection from bumps.

Prices on the XK-140 Super Sports run approximately $3,450 for the roadster, $3,795 for the hard-top coupe and the same price for the convertible. The "M" modifications, as described earlier, run to about $200 on each car and "MC" models cost an additional $150.

A Mark VII sedan with conventional transmission and the "M" engine as standard equipment is priced at $4,255; overdrive raises that to $4,415 and the Borg-Warner model costs $4,450.●

ENGINE: six-cylinder, twin overhead cams driven by a two-stage roller chain; bore, 83 mm; stroke, 106 mm; total displacement, 3,442 cc (210 cu. in.); 190 bhp at 5,200 rpm; compression ratio, 8 to 1; chrome-iron cylinder block with cooling by pump with by-pass thermostat control; cylinder head of aluminum alloy with hemispherical combustion chambers; aluminum alloy pistons with steel connecting rods; forced lubrication throughout by submerged pump with full flow oil filter and floating gauge intake; twin SU carburetors horizontally mounted with electrically-controlled automatic choke; 2¾-in. counterbalanced crankshaft carried in seven steel-backed main bearings.

TRANSMISSION: four-speed single helical synchromesh gearbox; ground teeth gears running on needle bearings; synchromesh on 2nd, 3rd and top. Gear ratios (XK-140); top, 3.54; 3rd, 4.84; 2nd, 7.01; 1st and reverse, 11.95. Ratios with overdrive: OD, 3.19; top, 4.09; 3rd, 5.59; 2nd, 8.11; 1st and reverse, 15.34. Gear ratios on Mark VII "M": top, 4.27; 3rd, 5.84; 2nd, 8.46; 1st and reverse, 14.43. Ratios with overdrive: OD, 3.53; top, 4.55; 3rd, 6.22; 2nd, 9.01; 1st and reverse, 15.35.

BRAKES: four-wheel hydraulic, Girling servo-assisted on the Mark VII and Lockheed on XK-140 models; brake drum diameter, 12 in.

WHEELS and TIRES: pressed steel bolt-on disk wheels on all models; Dunlop 6.00 x 16 tires on XK-140 models and 6.70 x 16 on the Mark VII. Wire wheels available on all XK-140 Super Sports.

STEERING: rack and pinion on XK-140 models and Burman recirculating ball-type on the Mark VII. All cars have adjustable steering wheels.

ELECTRICAL EQUIPMENT: Lucas 12-volt batteries; two-speed electrical windshield wipers; back-up lights; twin horns; oil coil ignition; heater and defroster.

SUSPENSION: Independent front suspension with torsion bars and transverse wishbones; Rear suspension by silico-manganese steel semi-elliptic leaf springs; telescopic shock absorbers all around.

DIMENSIONS: (XK-140) wheelbase, 102 in.: front tread, 51½ in.; rear tread, 50½ in.; over-all length, 176 in.; over-all width, 64½ in.; roadster height, 53½ in.; coupe and convertible height, 55 in.; ground clearance, 7⅛ in.; turning circle, 33 ft.; roadster weight, 2,744 lbs.; coupe, 2,856; convertible, 2,968.

(Mark VII) wheelbase, 120 in.; front tread, 56½ in.; rear tread, 58 in.; over-all length, 196½ in.; over-all width, 73 in.; height, 63 in.; ground clearance, 7½ in.; turning circle 36 ft.; weight, 3,696 lbs.

Coventry's Finest Formula:

$$\frac{\text{XK-140}}{\text{MC-210}} = 1955$$

For six years the Jaguar XK sports car has been the standard of comparison for performance and value in its field. When first introduced in 1949 the car was truly sensational, and although the company has pursued a policy of gradual improvement rather than radical change, the latest XK-140 sports roadster is still a car to be reckoned with.

One of the benefits of such a policy is that, whereas the original price (about $4000) seemed high to the average American, the price today—after a spectacular 1953 drop of up to $800—is not only lower in dollars but is also an even better value in comparison to the fantastic prices being asked for "middle-priced" U.S. sedans. Moreover, there is the remarkable record of owner satisfaction which stems not only from good service, but also from the fact that absence of model change has kept depreciation low.

It has been nearly four years since we tested a Jaguar roadster. Both the car and our road test procedure have advanced considerably in the interim. Accordingly, we elected to test the latest roadster in its most "deluxe" form, the XK-140MC, M for modified (which includes wire wheels, dual exhaust) and C for the C-type cylinder head. These options add $295 to the list price (included in our data panel price), and 20 bhp to the power output. An overdrive is also optional, but deliveries with this equipment are only just beginning.

After so long an interval between tests, it is difficult to make comparisons. The 1955 car seems easier to drive in traffic and there is more leg room. The shift lever seems "freer" but the left-ward bias of the pedals feels awkward, at least for a few miles. The engine is quieter and smoother than before with one exception. Under full throttle there is perhaps a shade of roughness as a result of the vastly increased horsepower (increased from the original 160 to 210 bhp). At very low rpm there was a faint tinkle with the foot pushed down hard, an indication that the engine tuning was near-perfect for local premium fuel.

One of the most anticipated innovations of the XK-140 is the new close-ratio gearbox, and it was disappointing to learn that most of the early '55 models, including our test car, came through with the old-type gearbox still installed. The old-type box was adequate but had a low gear designed for trials work and gave the feeling that revs were excessive for a normal brisk traffic start. The latest M-type exhaust system is nearly dead-silent, in marked contrast to the crackle of the earlier M-type mufflers.

As exhilarating as it is to drive a car such as this in traffic, only on the open road does it really begin to come to life. The new rack and pinion steering is without fault, but since a road test report is supposed to be objective, it should be mentioned that our two drivers disagreed on the castor return action. One felt that a high speed bend required too much force at the wheel rim to hold the car in the turn.

Riding qualities proved somewhat surprising. All Jaguar models for 1955 have the slightly stiffer springs used for some time on the M-type. Nevertheless the ride is very satisfactory, and as a matter of fact front end O.P.M. (oscillations per minute), a criterion of ride, appear to be almost unchanged, a result achieved by moving the engine about 5 inches farther forward and tilting the radiator to fit under the hood. When we first took over the car, tire squeal was rather easy to provoke, but after adjusting tire pressures to 30 psi in front and 35 psi at the rear the tires ceased protesting. The higher pressures made very little difference in riding qualities except on the most corrugated of surfaces. The Jaguar does have considerable roll in a hard corner, for a sports car, but the extra comfort of such springing is worthwhile to all but the toughest diehard, and a reasonable amount of roll is generally considered to be more desireable than none at all. The commencement of noticeable roll is a reliable indication of safe cornering speed and such a car as the Jaguar reduces "driver skill required"; it is in fact one of the easiest and safest automobiles to drive being built today.

Concerning the performance data, the figures tell much of the story. It is clearer than ever that only cars costing twice as much (or more) can improve on such times as 0-to-60 mph in 8.4 seconds, or a standing ¼ mile in 16.6 seconds. What the figures do not show is the consummate ease of obtaining the same readings again and again. Our acceleration tests are made with driver and observer in the car and every effort is made to get the best possible times; but we do not over-rev in the gears, do not

Small plaque on valve cover identifies "Type C" head.

ROAD & TRACK ROAD TEST NO. F-6-55
JAGUAR XK 140 MC ROADSTER

throw speed shifts. The Jaguar takes off best with a throttle setting of about 2500 rpm, and after the initial "chirp" from the rear tires the accelerator goes down hard. The clutch has a rather soft engagement, but even so the frame bottoms on the rubber bump stops when using this procedure. For some reason the test car objected to really brisk changes of gear, and in order to get the best out of the car it was necessary to accept a certain amount of "crunch" with each successive up-shift. The process seemed to do no harm but left the feeling that the syncronizers were not up to par.

Top speed runs were made with top and side curtains installed, and wind noise becomes noticeable as low as 40 mph; normal conversation ceases at about 75 mph. The timed top speed was a little below expectations, although the car was obviously in perfect tune, having been loaned to us by Jaguar Cars North American, Inc. The odometer read 2315 miles at the start of the high speed runs, and the car had experienced one hig speed roundtrip to San Francisco (The California Mille Miglia). While we believe that this is a fair evaluation of an MC type Jaguar, the mileage is perhaps insufficient to give a fair test of the best possible top speed. However, we also believe that 125 mph is close to the top limit for a strictly stock Jaguar MC roadster in full touring trim.

Results at the 1955 Daytona speed trials prove that this is so, for the best two-way average by a production type "M" Jaguar was 124.6 mph and a 1955 XK-140 recorded 119.68 mph. Record runs made by factory prepared cars give speeds as high as 141.51 mph, but commendable as such records may be, they bear little resemblance to results obtained on fully equipped production cars as sold to the general public. Nevertheless, it must be admitted that the new Jaguar is capable of cruising comfortably at any speed up to 100 mph, for as long as road conditions permit. The speedometer error on this car was, incidently, commendably accurate and read 120/121 mph during the best one-way timed run.

With performance per dollar excelled by no other car, the nicer details of finish and fittings on the XK roadster come as a pleasant bonus feature. The quality of finish is immediately apparent on the outside, but a look under the hood shows attention to detail that is in marked contrast to that found under a domestic product. The two seats are upholstered in genuine leather, with matching material on the instrument panel. The result is a very practical arrangement which does not seek to emulate a juke box and actually provides readable instruments with no annoying glare when driving top-down. With top and side curtains installed visibility is excellent for all normal driving. There are some drafts which could be eliminated by a little judicious bending of the curtain frames, but rear view visibility is almost nil and makes backing out of a parking lot an exciting chore. The rearranged and larger luggage compartment is a very worthwhile improvement, and most Americans will accept the larger and more massive bumpers as a necessary evil, for self-defense.

In our opinion the "standard of the world" has been, and still is, the Jaguar—in the sports car category.

SPECIFICATIONS

List price ("MC")	$3745
Wheelbase	102 in.
Tread, front	51.0 in.
rear	50.5 in.
Tire size	6.00-16
Curb weight	3135 lbs.
distribution	49.6/50.4
Test weight	3500 lbs.
Engine	6-cyl.
Valves	dohc
Bore & stroke	3.27 x 4.17 in.
Displacement	210 cu in. (3442 cc)
Compression ratio	8.00
Horsepower	210
peaking speed	5750
equivalent mph	133
Torque, ft/lbs.	213
peaking speed	4000
equivalent mph	92
Mph per 1000 rpm	23.1
Mph at 2500 fpm	83.1
Gear ratios (overall)	
4th	3.54
3rd	4.83
2nd	7.01
1st	11.95
R & T high gear performance factor	53.8

PERFORMANCE

Top speed	125
best run	121.1
average	120.3
Max. speeds in gears—	
3rd (5800)	98
2nd (5800)	68
1st (5800)	39
Shift points from— same as maximums	
Mileage	16/18 mpg

ACCELERATION

0-30 mph	2.7 secs.
0-40 mph	4.2 secs.
0-50 mph	6.5 secs.
0-60 mph	8.4 secs.
0-70 mph	12.1 secs.
0-80 mph	15.7 secs.
0-90 mph	19.6 secs.
0-100 mph	26.5 secs.
Standing ¼ mile— average	16.6 secs.

TAPLEY READINGS

Gear	Lbs/ton	Mph	Grade
1st	off scale	—	—
2nd	550	45	29%
3rd	400	52	20%
4th	280	65	14%

Total drag at 60 mph, 116 lbs.

SPEEDO ERROR

Indicated	Actual
30	30.1
40	38.4
50	48.0
60	57.6
70	67.8
80	78.0
90	88.4
100	98.6

JAGUAR XK 140 MC ROADSTER
acceleration through the gears

JAGS GRAB MORE HORSES

● JAGUAR XK140 drophead coupe poses elegantly outside famous Memorial Theatre, Stratford - on - Avon.

Performance even more exhilarating than hitherto may be expected from the new range of Jaguar XK140 sports models—plus looks and elegance now famous the world over.

With the coming of the cheaper 100 m.p.h. sports cars, some enthusiasts have come to forget the forerunner of the era — the XK Jaguars. The latest range from the famous Coventry factory, however, will certainly capture the market for those people who want fast and luxurious transport.

Known as the Jaguar XK140, the new models have more power, more passenger space, tougher characteristics and superior looks to the beautiful 120 series. Selling close to the £2,000 mark, the fabulous Jaguar must be the best sports car buy in the world today.

Just how the manufacturers can produce a car of the Jaguar's quality and sell it for anything less than £3,800 is nothing short of a miracle. Critics who obviously have never inspected one of Bill Lyons' cars say the Jags must be skimped somewhere along the line. To this I say "phooey". Every little piece of the Jag has been made and finished to equal the world's best.

The fact that the motor is a world beater has never been open to question. Outstanding performances at the Le Mans 24-Hours Race, dozens of production and sports car records, to say nothing of the countless wins and places gained throughout the world by the C and D type competition cars speak for themselves.

After World War Two, Detroit research engineers went to work to find the most efficient type of motor for passenger cars. They eventually

● RIGHT: SMARTER lines on new XK140 drophead result from new-type tail lights, wrap-around bumpers with hefty over-riders.

settled for a six cylinder, twin overhead cam job, between three and four litres capacity. The only thing which stopped such a motor going into production was the high cost, so that's why most American cars today have V8 motors.

Not long after these findings, Jaguars' came forth with the XK120, followed soon afterwards by the big Mark VII saloon, powered by the same 3½-litre twin overhead camshaft motor. Particularly embarassing for the American manufacturers was the Jags' modest price.

The XK140 motor has been stepped up 30 horse-power to 190 b.h.p. at 5,500 r.p.m. and the camshafts now give a lift of ⅜ inch, instead of 5/16 inch, to improve the engine breathing in the high rev. range. High dome pistons have increased the compression ratio to 8:1, but because of Australia's low grade petrol, hitherto, the cars coming here had a comp. ratio of 7:1 unless the customer requested 8:1.

Unless the high compression is fitted it follows that 190 b.h.p. would not be available from the motor, but it wouldn't be far short of it. With the coming of good fuel, high dome pistons could easily be obtained and fitted.

Another change which helps to extract the horses from the 3½-litre motor is a Lucas oil ignition coil.

To do justice to the improved output from the motor, the gearbox ratios have been made closer by fitting a 10.55:1 bottom gear, instead of 12.29:1 as in the XK120. Top gear is only a fraction higher in ratio and is now 3.54:1 instead of 3.64:1.

For about £60 extra, customers can order a manually operated Laycock - de - Normanville overdrive on top gear. With this fitted, the maufacturers have reduced the rear axle ratio slightly.

This gearing gives the overdrive model 19.6 m.p.h. per thousand revs in direct top and 25.2 m.p.h. in overdrive top. The model without overdrive gives 22.7 m.p.h. per thousand revs.

At 2,500 feet per minute piston speed, the standard car is travelling at 81.7 m.p.h. and the overdrive vehicle is doing 70.7 in direct top and 90.7 in the fifth ratio.

At the time of writing no performance figures were available, but taking into acount that the XK120 can accelerate to 30 m.p.h. in around three seconds and to 50 m.p.h. in about seven seconds, the XK140 should be an outstanding performer in its class.

I would be only guessing, but 130 m.p.h. seems likely as the maximum speed and even more with the overdrive model.

Fuel consumption should be better that 20 m.p.g. in normal driving conditions. Mark VII owners have frequently reported 22 m.p.g.

Completely new steering of the

● BELOW: NEW XK 140 roadster, capable of speeds up to 140 m.p.h., has heavier front bumpers with big over-riders, and different radiator grille.

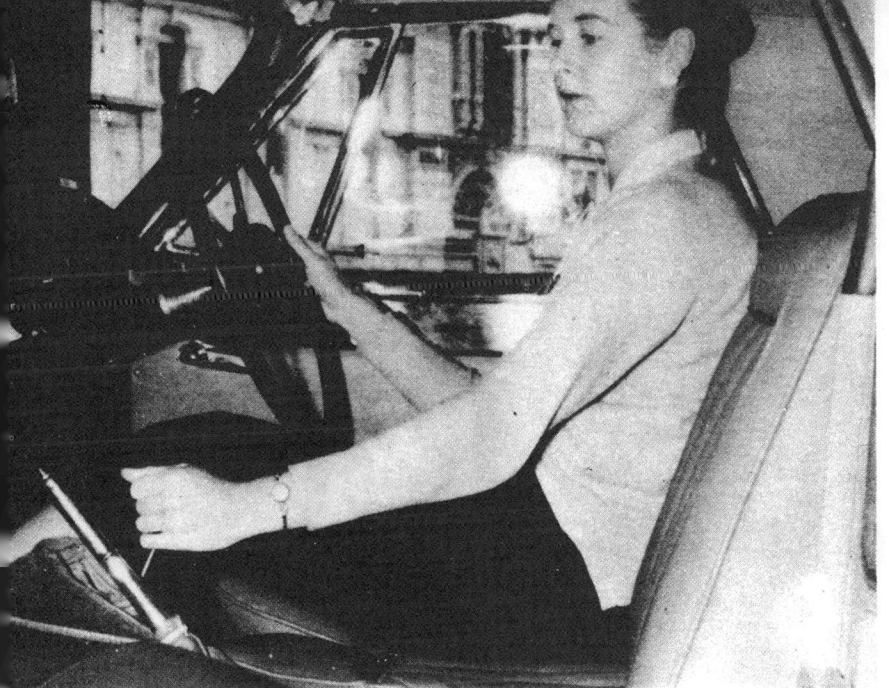

● FLY-OFF handbrake and stubby gear-lever are ideally placed for sporty driver.

rack-and-pinion type has been adopted, with modifications to prevent road shock being transmitted to the steering wheel. Careful use of rubber and bonded rubber mountings absorb any jolts, but at the same time stop any spongy movement.

The bulbous horn button in the centre of the 18 inch, four spoke steering wheel has been replaced with a more practical flat button. Owners of XK120's are always glad to tell of frightening experiences caused through accidentally knocking the cone shaped button.

Still in the front end department, the suspension has been made stronger and slightly stiffer with bigger diameter torsion bars which now have a rate of 154 lb./in. instead of 128 lb./in.

Semi-elliptic springs have been retained to suspend the solid rear axle and bigger telescopic shockers have been fitted all round.

Chassis frame features remain the same. For those not familiar with it, the Jaguar frame is a steel box section, with torsional rigidity supplied by large box sectioned cross members.

The wheel base is eight feet six inches, and the track is four feet three inches in the front and an inch narrower at the rear. The overall length is 14 feet five inches.

The profile of the body is similar to the XK120, but the likeness ends right there. The new model has more chrome, a heavier radiator grille and bigger, more practical bumperbars.

Chrome flashings on the tail seem to give a better proportioned appearance, while the bumpers, front and rear, wrap around the body and have decent sized over-riders, which by the way, do not detract in any way from the car's appearance.

Three alternative bodies are available on the XK140 chassis. They are the open two-seater, the hardtop 2/3 seater coupe and the drophead coupe which will seat two adults and two children or midgets.

Leg room has been increased in all models because the motor has been shifted three inches forward in its frame.

The roadster version still seats only two people comfortably, but luggage space has been increased. A mohair hood, tonneau cover, and glass side curtains are included in the standard equipment.

Jaguars have provided for the family man with the very elegant fixed head coupe, the top of which extends six inches further back than it did on the XK120's. Although the front seat is big enough for only two full-sized people, a third adult can be comfortably seated in the compartment behind the front seats, providing he is willing to sit across the car, instead of facing forward. Alternatively, two children can take his place, this time sitting right way round.

The vehicle which I personally consider to be the most handsome car in the current Jaguar range, is the drop-head coupe. This express chariot offers all the joys of open motoring, but in a few moments can be converted into a snug car, which, from the inside looks like a finely finished saloon.

The seating arrangement is similar to the hard top, but the rear compartment is smaller.

Like all the Jaguars, the instrument panel is joy to see with its large, round dials with black and white markings designed to be read at a glance. I can almost hear some Detroit iron enthusiast saying round dials look old-fashioned.

The current Jaguars are fitted with the most impressive set of headlights I have ever seen. Lucas developed them especially for the Le Mans 24-Hours Race and they proved to be so successful that they are now standard equipment.

Who was it said that racing didn't improve the breed?

Customers who want even more power can order a special equipment edition of any of the XK140 range, at additional cost, of course.

By using a C-type cylinder head with 9:1 compression pistons and a dual exhaust system, the developed horsepower has been stepped up to 210.

Wire spoke knock-off wheels and fog lights are included.

In spite of the immense power which is available from these cars, they are so docile that grandma could use one for a shopping expedition. The Jag will potter along at 10 m.p.h. in top gear without fuss, but at the will of the driver it can be transformed into a snorting machine which can eat half a dozen Detroiters before breakfast.

The prices, including tax are: The two seater, £1974; the drop-head coupe, £2094; and the fixed-head coupe, £2126. ●

● CONVERTIBLE boot offers adequate luggage room for two travellers.

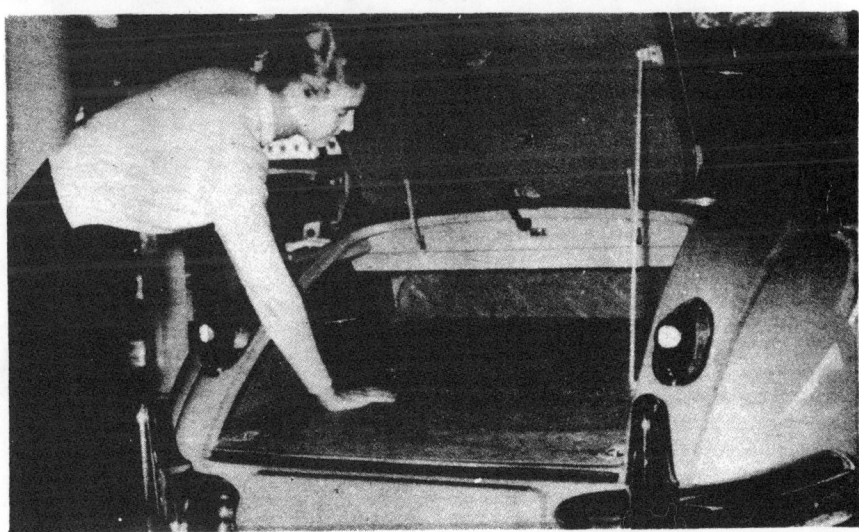

Notes on the 140

The latest race-proved Jaguar combines more power and better handling with the accustomed beauty of the 120

Offered in a hard top coupé, roadster, and full convertible, the 140 will meet the requirements of any driver.

In action, the Jaguar is as competent and controllable on the racetrack as it is on the town boulevard.

By CHARLES C. WALLACE

THERE have been a lot of articles written about the new XK 140, 140M and 140MC Jaguars. Most of them have given the relative performance of the cars, and the graphs have outlined the *overall* performance differences between the 140 and the 120 series.

They have, at the same time left out a good many of the features of the new cars that make the 140 definitely desirable property. In the first place, and unquestionably most important, the 140 is a lot more comfortable than the 120. The engine has been moved forward, and the cockpit considerably enlarged. This is a step in the right direction if you happen to be near the six foot mark, because the old 120 just wouldn't have let you get aboard with that much length. The wheel has been canted slightly too, and the whole revision adds up to a lot more enjoyable car to drive.

While we're on the cockpit, there is a small point that I don't personally mind, but that might be a bit of a bother to the driver not acquainted with the Jag. The throw on the gearshift lever had been increased, and the lever is slightly angled. It is a bit of a problem to be sure that the gear is all the way home in either second or high. There is also the difficulty of getting the gear hung momentarily in the gate on fast shifts too, but this is a small price to pay for a box as rugged as the one in the Jaguar.

Another point directly related to the roomier passenger compartment, due I believe to moving the engine forward, is the better handling characteristics of the 140. The old cars used to stick persistently at the front, and unless you wanted to raise the angle of the front end, would give you a real argument when you wanted the car to go into a drift. This isn't the case with the new ones. I think the added weight at the front end has helped. The car will now go into a drift easily, and it is perfectly controllable through the whole turn.

The brakes are improved on the new cars too. The one we raced at Sebring showed no fade over the entire twelve hours. It seems to hold wonderfully even after a great deal of punishment, and gives you a feeling of safety that is really gratifying.

In general, the 140 lives up to its predecessor's reputation for a reliable and safe sports car at a reasonable price. The engine in all of the new models seems practically unbreakable and the handling and comfort are much improved. The rack and pinion steering is a step toward an even more tractable ride and with the car running in class C, I'm looking forward to one of the most enjoyable seasons of racing yet.

—☆—

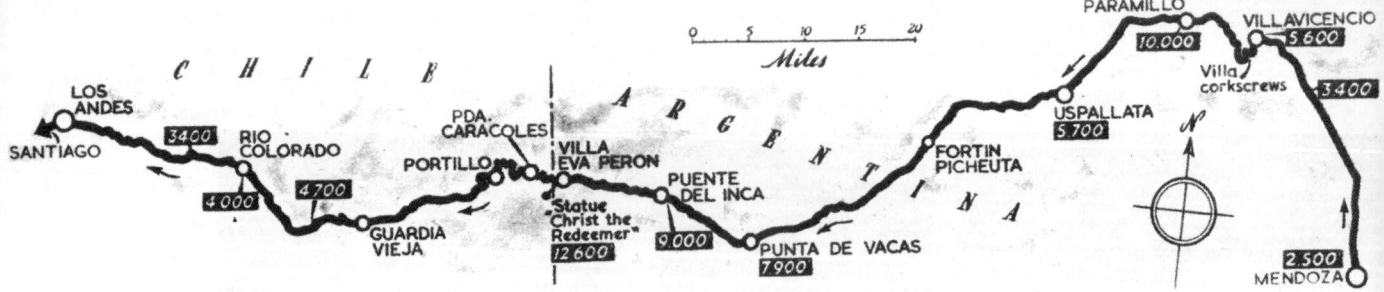

Up in the mountains—route of the Jaguar over the most arduous 160 miles of its journey

JAGUAR OVER THE ANDES

"A Good Advertisement for Coventry"

THE whole thing really started when F3060/8S—to refer to my XK120 Jaguar by its engine number—arrived in Buenos Aires in August, 1954. For some time, however, I had wanted to cross the Andes from Argentina to Chile in a sports car and, once and for all, debunk the old, very firmly entrenched theory that the Andean chain could be climbed only by American jobs of vast litreage, with substantial modifications to brakes, cooling systems, pumps and the like. I had owned a previous XK, and it seemed to me an eminently suitable vehicle for the job, so when my new one arrived, complete with C-type engine and all the modifications catalogued by the factory, I felt that the signs and portents indicated unmistakably that now was the time.

Therefore, having run in 3060, if we are allowed a further abbreviation, my wife and I were all ready to start in February, 1955, which is, of course, late summer in this part of the world. Nothing was done to the car except that, as it has the large, 25-gallon tank which is optional, no room was left for luggage, so I borrowed a rack from a friend's XK, made by the firm of Derrington in England, which proved worth its weight in gold to us.

We were planning to stay at least 20 days in Chile, and would need a fair amount of equipment, so that there was not very much spare room left when the car was fully loaded. Additionally, we took along the most essential spares, unobtainable en route, such as an extra fuel pump, water hoses, spare coil, fuel and oil pipes, plugs, and several other items sent out by the factory with 3060.

We left on February 18, and as the fuel available from pumps in Argentina is of markedly low octane rating, we filled up with 100/130 octane in Buenos Aires, planning to "water it down" with periodic fill-ups during our trip out to Mendoza, at the foot of the Andes, and some 700 miles out from Buenos Aires. We fuelled every 100 miles or so, and fortunately our system worked quite well.

However, the first part of the trip was something of an Odyssey, for during the first 130 miles we had really torrential rain—in which connection let me say that the Jaguar hood and sidescreens proved inadequate as 'flu-preventers, and by the time we had moved out of the rainy area we were so wet that it was difficult to tell whether we'd been using them or not. Luckily the heater worked very well indeed, for it grew quite cold later on.

Once we had left the rain behind, the insect kingdom moved in, and we were pelted by successive hordes of butterflies and locusts, which seemed to take particular glee in carrying out kamikaze charges against my radiator and windscreen. As a consequence, I had to get out every few miles and scrape a mass of insects off the car.

The afternoon was splendid, the road strongly reminiscent of the curate's egg, and thus we eventually arrived in Mendoza at 11 p.m., having driven continuously for fifteen hours, with 3060 pinking badly by now as the lacing of good fuel had gradually become smaller and smaller. In Mendoza, which is a large city, we were somewhat taken aback to discover that there was not a single hotel room available, so that, although we were both exhausted, we had no option but to journey out to Villavicencio, famed for its mineral waters and some 5,600 feet up in the Pre-Cordillera, the chain of foothills before the Andes proper.

The next day we repaired back to Mendoza and contacted a local racing driver named Pablo Gullé, who kindly let us have a few gallons of 100/130, which, mixed about

Heading for the tunnel which road and rail traffic share 11,000 feet up, on the border between Argentina and Chile

50/50 with normal pump fuel gave us 90 octane—about optimum for 3060's 8 to 1 compression ratio. Back to Villavicencio, and next day the fun was to start.

We left at 8 a.m., and in fact the climb was exciting but uneventful. We drove steadily up and through the famed Villa corkscrews, and on to Paramillo (10,000 feet up), Uspallata—scene of a great battle over a century ago —Polvaredas, and so to picturesque Villa Eva Perón, the Argentine customs post, actually some miles from the real frontier.

All this time the scenery had been gradually changing from lush greenery at Villavicencio to bare, sun-baked rock at Eva Perón, while towards the latter part of the trip we caught occasional glimpses of mighty Aconcagua, the highest peak on the American continent (23,000 feet), saw the amazing natural bridge at Puente del Inca, and ploughed through oceans of dust at Polvaredas and Los Horcones.

We took about an hour and a half to clear the customs, and then drove through the tunnel which burrows its way through the Andean rock, located 11,000 feet up—a trip which is an experience in itself as the tunnel is actually for the railway and is just one-track-and-a-bit wide. As a result, the only way to get a car across is to ride with one pair of wheels bumping across the sleepers and the other on the shoulder of the ballasting, the car thus straddling one rail!

What was most nerve-wracking was the fact that the Jaguar ground clearance at the sump just, but only just, proved sufficient to clear the rail, which obliged us to press on extremely regardful at about 10 m.p.h., to avoid the suspension flexing unduly and bumping the bottom of the oilpan against the track face. It took us some 20 minutes to cover the short length of the tunnel, in second gear and hoping for the best. Fortunately enough, nothing untoward occurred.

As we gained an hour through time difference between Argentina and Chile, we thus achieved a somewhat staggering point-to-point average from one customs post to the other!

We went on to a wonderful hotel in Portillo, which must rank as one of the world's best; it is on the shores of a beautiful lake, blue and translucent in the clear mountain air. The Chilean customs are in the hotel, an arrangement which we found extremely convenient, and so we enjoyed a really pleasant few hours' stay, aided by an excellent lunch and the excellent Chilean wines.

Arid, sun-baked mountain slopes border the rocky road leading from the heights down to Chile

In the afternoon we left, and started the descent of the Chilean corkscrews, a really shattering drop. I estimate that in less than five miles one descends some four thousand feet, so it can be well imagined that we did the whole descent in second gear and with the brakes hard on, these components almost boiling when we arrived, although they stood up to the job really manfully.

Eventually we arrived at a place called Salto del Soldado, 6,500 feet up, where we rested ourselves and 3060 before carrying on. From here onwards, however, the descent is rather less like an express lift.

At about this stage vegetation begins again, and the scenery around this part is really beautiful—the barren part is merely awe-inspiring. It rains more on the Chile side, and it was this, together with "highest-peak" considerations, which led King Edward VII to exercise his *divortium aquarium* international limit arbitration in the early years of the century, thus settling a point over which Argentines and Chileans had been bickering for years.

Thus we kept on going down, over the typical rough Chilean roads, until late at night we arrived at the capital, Santiago, looking rather like Abominable Dustmen; the

At sea level, the Jaguar shows no trace of its ordeal in the high places

At 12,600 feet this huge statue marks the border, and the vow of peace between the two neighbouring countries

OVER THE ANDES . . .

dust-sealing is the worst criticism I can make of this wonderful vehicle, the Jaguar XK120—during the whole trip the open cockpit relentlessly sucked it in. We even found grit behind the instrument panel!

This last startling revelation was at Importadora Fisk S.A., who are local Jaguar agents and most helpful and efficient people. When all this distressing business was over, we found that the only attention 3060 required, after its really gruelling test, was some adjustment to a tie-rod which had loosened up—surely a good advertisement for Coventry!

We fooled around Chile for some twenty days or so, visiting friends and exploring the country, finding the roads pretty poor except for one magnificently engineered 90-mile highway between Santiago de Chile and Valparaíso, the world-famous seaside resort, on which we had our first and only encounter with the Chilean police.

Apparently they have imported an American speed trap and set it up between two towns; we were stopped and informed that we had been travelling at 100 m.p.h. where the speed limit was exactly half that! Why they have to hold cars down to 50 on that wonderful road is beyond me, but as foreign tourists we got away with it, and the police were very nice about the whole thing.

So, after surfeiting ourselves with scenery, seafood and wine, we set out on our return trip, the same way as we had come. This time, of course, we were even more heavily loaded, with wines, canned seafood and the like, and there was just not another cubic inch of space left in the car, the passengers' heads protruding from the packages in a manner rather reminiscent of a Doré illustration of Dante's Inferno.

Although Chilean fuel was said to be of 76 octane rating, the Jaguar pinked badly on it, so the real rating cannot have been much higher than on the Argentine side. It is cheap, however, although oil is very expensive. I had to set the ignition on full retard with the vernier adjustment provided on the distributor (an invaluable feature this), but even so 3060 pinked plaintively and continually, although that did not hamper its ability to leave everything else on the road standing. There are few fast cars in Chile, and 3060 has only seven brothers there, plus one or two Mark VII cousins.

Frontier Statue

On the way back we lunched at Portillo again, crossed the tunnel in the afternoon, and then, on the Argentine side, decided to climb to the statue of Christ the Redeemer, on the frontier, and the highest point on our travels—13,000 feet. We reached the statue without any trouble, but it was bitterly cold there and we did not tarry long, except to look around and read the bronze plaque which proclaims, "Sooner shall these mountains fall than the peace between Argentina and Chile be disturbed."

When we stopped the engine, there was neither backfire nor running on—which amazed the lone operator of the wireless station, who said this was the first car which had failed to evince those phenomena after the terribly hard climb from Villa Eva Perón to the Redeemer—this in spite of the execrable fuel and with the ignition fully set back!

In the fullness of time we arrived back in Buenos Aires, having enjoyed our trip to the full, despite dire predictions, and proved two contentions of mine—that the Andes could be climbed with a standard sports car, and that the Jaguar was superb as a real sports car—neither a hotted-up tourer nor a disguised Grand Prix racer. The car came through with really flying colours, as mechanically nothing at all was needed before or after—but, oh dear, the rain- and dust-sealing!

LUCIO BOLLAERT

On the Argentine side of the huge Andean range, the Jaguar stands lonely amid gaunt, stony hills and screes

drive the NEW 1955 JAGUAR

*now more than ever...
the finest car of its class in the world!*

NEW redesigned chassis for even greater roadability

NEW larger diameter torsion bars

NEW rack and pinion steering

NEW high lift cams and 190-250 horsepower

NEW oil ignition coil

NEW enlarged cockpit — increased leg room

Plus smart new refinements of the same sculptured beauty that made Jaguar the world's most admired motor car. Seeing's believing. Drive it yourself. Call your Jaguar dealer today.

XK-140 Super Sports Roadster.. from **$3465***

XK-140 Super Sports Convertible or Hard Top Coupe .... from **$3810***

XK-140 "M". Wire wheels, twin exhausts, 2 fog lamps, windshield washers. $145 additional.

XK-140 "MC". As above with Special Crankshaft damper, "C" type cylinder head. 210 H.P. $295 additional.

"D" competition model, 250 H.P. available soon.

Laycock de Normanville overdrive optional.

*Port of entry. Price includes heater, tachometer, directional lights, electric windshield wipers, electric clock, automatic back-up light.

Distributor West of the Mississippi
CHARLES H. HORNBURG, JR., INC.
9176 Sunset Boulevard, Los Angeles, Cal.

Distributor East of the Mississippi
THE HOFFMAN MOTOR CAR CO., INC.
487 Park Avenue, New York City • 65 East South Water Street, Chicago, Ill.

JAGUAR CARS NORTH AMERICAN CORPORATION
Factory Representatives • 487 Park Avenue, New York City 22, N. Y. •, 9155 Sunset Boulevard, Los Angeles 46, Cal.

A Jaguar coupe gets in the spin of things in a California race.

A long screwdriver lets you set the points without getting burned.

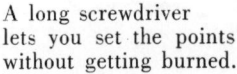

Tune-up testing equipment is used for setting spark.

In checking spark advance look for "leaking" wires.

soup for the Jaguar

By STEVE SPITLER

THE tuning of the Jaguar XK series is not as difficult as it is with many cars, due mostly to the factory's interest in racing. At one time or another, almost every possible setting has been tried on these cars, both in ignition and carburetion so the builders have been able to publish very positive specifications for speed tuning.

With the Jaguar, there are no such instructions as "set the timing to a light ping on the road." Instead, any variation from the setting recommended has been found to give very bad results somewhere in the speed range.

The first thing to consider, and the only variation from a factory setting, is in the spark plugs. The original Champion plugs supplied with the car seldom last more than 500 miles, even if the owner is careful on his break-in period. A good replacement for these is the KLG plug. An FE50 is best for around town use, and an FE80 for competition. Compromise plugs, such as the FE60 and 70, are recommended if a careful check of the plugs shows too much overheating. The FE70, while very good for road use, will load up in town, unless maximum revs are given the engine occasionally.

The variations from factory setting mentioned earlier is in the plug gap. The .022 setting will not give a smooth idle. But if the plugs are gapped at 25 thousandths, a smooth idle can be obtained at 500 for the MK VII model, 600 for the stock XK, and 650 for the modified machines. For competition, the plugs should be re-gapped after tuning to .022, or several hundred revs will be lost in top gear, but only on top, and no power is lost in the lower gears. The Champion equivalent to these plugs have such a narrow heat range that plugs which are usable in town will burn up on the road, and vice versa.

The second department to check in tuning is the one which delivers the spark to the plugs. While not a large department it is very important, due to the fact that ignition wires which look good may still be "leaking" at full load. Any wire which shows signs of corrosion or cracking should be replaced. Another check is to rev up the engine at night, with no light under the hood. Wires which are shorting out will show a blue corona wherever they are passing current to a ground, current which could be used at the plug to much greater advantage.

As for the coil, if an owner suspects that this component has gone sour, the best thing to do is to take the car to a shop with an ignition analyzer. Unless you are prepared to change coils and re-check performance, this is the only

The Jaguar engine is a prime example of precision engineering.

The 140 features a larger amount of chrome fittings.

way of testing for a weak spark output.

For delivering current to the coil, the distributor is the next consideration. A set of points which are grey over their entire surface with no pits, are perfectly serviceable. However, any corrosion or pitting will call for new points, while extreme pitting usually indicates the need for a new condenser. Once again, an ignition analyzer can show up such a fault if the owner does not wish to change components.

For point setting, the recommended .012 inch is acceptable, but a meter which shows a dwell setting of 38 degrees is much more accurate. Also, always set your points *first*, as changing the points setting will alter the timing. On a Jaguar, a very long screwdriver will reach the points easily, without burning an arm, or getting a hand in the way.

Whatever else is done, the factory setting as regards timing should be rigidly followed. For XK120, and XK120M and MK VII models, the timing should be set at 7 degrees or 2½ teeth above the mark on the case. For the XK140 and XK140M cars, an altered distributor gives a setting of 10 degrees or three teeth. These settings can be made with the click adjuster on the distributor, with the engine at idle.

As for the carburetors, the U. S. instruments fitted to the Jaguar should give absolutely no trouble once properly set. On the very late XK120's and on the XK140 models, set the float arm to a distance of ½ inch below the lip on the float chamber cap. On the earlier cars, the setting was ⅜ inch. Here again, attention should be paid to wear on the various parts. In particular wear on the float needle will produce gas leaks and will cut mileage to an alarming degree.

The slides should next be checked for dirt, looseness or wear. The slide caps should never be wiped out dry, but should be washed out to prevent scratching.

The shoulder of the needle should be even with the bottom of the slide. This is not necessarily the center boss, but on a flat (with a ruler, etc.) with the bottom of the slide itself.

Then, with the slides assembled and checked for freeness, the dashpots should be filled with a light oil and the dampers tightened down.

And so to the final stage. With both air cleaners off, listen to the hiss of air in the inlets. With the linkage loosened, set the throttles so that an even hiss is obtained on both carbs, then lock up the linkage and re-check. Once they are drawing evenly at idle, it is a simple matter to adjust the mixture. On all but the early Jags, a vacuum fitting is provided on the rear of the manifold. Slipping off the tube to the windshield washers, any sort of vacuum gauge can give an accurate enough reading to synchronize the mixture settings. With an adjustment of the mixture screws of about 1½ turns down from full stop for a beginning, turn the screws up, for leanness, until a maximum vacuum is obtained. Then back off slightly and adjust the other carb. Adjust first one and then the other, until a maximum reading can be obtained. In the absence of a vacuum gauge, set to the leanest mixture possible, while still keeping a smooth idle. Don't be shocked at a vacuum reading of only about 17 inches. The proper setting on the distributor will only give you about this much, while adjusting the timing to give a higher reading will only cause missing on the upper end.

If, after all the above, you can't get 5500 revs on top gear, it's only because you don't have room . . .

—☆—

JOHN BOLSTER TESTS

THE JAGUAR XK 140

A High-Performance Car of Many Qualities and Amazing Value—100 m.p.h. in 26.2 secs!—Superb Steering, Brakes and Controllability—An Effortless Maximum of Over 120 m.p.h. and 100 m.p.h. cruising on Overdrive

PROBABLY the most famous sports car ever built, the Jaguar XK 120 brought an entirely new conception of ultra-rapid luxury motoring. Of superb appearance, it at once appealed to connoisseurs of high speed machinery, and its very advanced 2 o.h.c., 3½-litre engine ensured that it was even faster than it looked. Yet, it was more flexible than many a luxury limousine and, like all Jaguars, represented amazing value for money. Of course, its phenomenal success is now history.

It was thus with immense interest that one examined its successor, the XK 140. Could this really be a better car than the 120? Now that I have driven it, I can state categorically that it is a great improvement in every important respect.

Having a very solid box-section chassis frame, the Jaguar has independent front suspension by unequal length wishbones, of which the bottom pair are attached to torsion bars. The stub axles swivel on ball joints, and the steering is by a new rack and pinion unit, ahead of the wheel centres. The hypoid rear axle is on underslung semi-elliptic springs, and the dampers are telescopic all round.

The car tested was a "Special Equipment" model, which means that it had a Laycock de Normanville overdrive, racing-type wire wheels, and a C-type cylinder head. All the figures given in this article therefore refer to that particular specification.

The six-cylinder engine has a bore and stroke of 83 mm. x 106 mm. (3,442 c.c.). The inclined valves are operated by twin chain-driven camshafts in a light alloy head. Valve clearances are set by shims beneath the inverted piston tappets. The unit is perfectly straightforward to dismantle, and the instruction book gives detailed directions on cylinder head removal for decarbonization. Throughout the car, all units are accessible for servicing and adjustment. The compression ratio is 8 to 1 and 210 b.h.p. is produced at 5,750 r.p.m.

The gearbox is in unit with the engine. It has synchromesh on the upper three ratios, and a delightful little central lever. The overdrive unit is attached to the rear of the box, and there is a short, open propeller shaft. The brakes have racing linings, which must be run in carefully.

The body is a delightful piece of work. The model tested was a hard-top coupé, though drophead and open models are also listed. The wooden dashboard, full instrumentation, high quality trim and upholstery, and useful pockets and lockers, make this a most attractive car inside. The general appearance is excellent, for the lines are artistically without fault, and there is no unnecessary decoration.

On taking one's seat, it is at once obvious that the driving position is far better than that of the previous model. The accelerator and brake are arranged for "heel and toe", and the clutch pedal has a space on its left to permit the foot to be rested. The steering column is adjustable, and there is more leg room than before for a tall driver. The windows are exceptionally deep, which avoids the claustrophobia that coupés often give, but their curved shape disguises the area of glass.

Above all, the body is exactly the right size. It feels a narrow car to drive, and yet there is enough width for two hefty individuals in heavy overcoats. The rear seats are for children, or for adults on short journeys; they are very handy for occasional use. The luggage boot can be reached from both outside and inside the car.

On moving off, wheelspin is easily induced on any road surface, with 210 b.h.p. under the pedal. The clutch is smooth but can never be made to slip, and the gear lever is ideally placed. The overdrive is on the facia panel, for right-hand operation, and the translucent switch lever becomes illuminated when the unit is in operation.

For use with the overdrive, the normal 3.54 to 1 axle is replaced by a 4.09 rear end. This adds immensely to the pleasure of driving, for the top gear acceleration is really brilliant, and the flexibility notably improved. It is, in fact, perfectly easy to drive at little more than walking pace, and then to accelerate away briskly, all on top speed.

The direct drive gives slashing acceleration up to 105 m.p.h., after which the overdrive can be switched in. The ratio then is 3.19 to 1, which is theoretically a little on the high side. The car travels at very high speeds in a gloriously effortless manner, but peak revs. cannot

"On taking one's seat, it is at once obvious that the driving position is far better than that of the previous model. . . ."

"The body is a delightful piece of work . . . general appearance is excellent, for the lines are artistically without fault, and there is no unnecessary decoration."

be reached under normal conditions, about 4,800 r.p.m. being the limit on overdrive. The timed mean maximum speed of 121.6 m.p.h. could certainly be exceeded with a lower gear. However, it is a matter of academic interest only whether 120 m.p.h. or 130 m.p.h. is the ultimate velocity. What does matter is that 100 m.p.h. can be attained in 26.2 secs., and then held as a cruising speed on overdrive with only a whiff of throttle. I often had an indicated 135 m.p.h. on the somewhat optimistic speedometer.

Perhaps the greatest improvement of all is in the braking department. With the new racing linings, it is possible really to drive on the brakes without inducing fading. Repeated applications from two miles a minute produce a choice scent of hot linings, but this has no detrimental effect, nor is adjustment required after quite a useful mileage.

These brakes, plus the excellent controllability, make possible the full use of all the available performance whenever traffic conditions permit. This is the most effortless car imaginable, the reserve of power for overtaking being most valuable. The exhaust is well silenced, and the engine is particularly smooth. The high compression C-type unit is just fractionally more audible than was the earlier, "softer" version, but it is still flexible almost beyond belief.

I have been asked about the use of a conventional rear axle in a car as fast as this. I would say that, compared

CONTINUED ON PAGE 122

ACCELERATION GRAPH

As the acceleration graph and tabulated figures show, the sheer performance of the car is immense. However, that is only half the story. The new steering utterly transforms the handling, and the suspension has also been revised. The XK 140 is, in fact, quite firmly sprung, and all the "float" of the 120 has gone. There is a wonderful feeling of complete control, and this is one of those very rare cars that seems to help the over-impetuous driver out of his difficulties. The rack and pinion steering gives beautifully precise control, and one can fling the 26 cwt. car around like a 1½-litre machine.

(*Above*) "*The rear seats are for children, or for adults on short journeys; they are very handy for occasional use. . . .*"

(*Right*) "*On moving off, wheelspin is easily induced on any road surface, with 210 b.h.p. under the pedal. . . ."* The engine of the "Special Equipment" model with C-type head.

During the road tests the car was taken to its breeding ground at Le Mans. With adequate space for two, or more if required for short distances, the XK.140 can certainly add grace and pace to its qualifications

JAGUAR XK.140 COUPE

IN October, 1952, the Jaguar XK.120 special equipment coupé was road tested by *The Autocar*; at that time is was not for sale in Great Britain, which must have been extremely tantalizing for enthusiasts who had the purchase price ready. After a time, of course, the XK.120 was available on the home market and the model become very popular, especially amongst those who like to travel fast and far.

At the 1954 London Motor Show the XK.120 was succeeded by the XK.140, and events have proved that the title "Fiercer Jaguars" given to *The Autocar* description of the new models in the issue of 15 October of that year was indeed apt. The trend these days is for more b.h.p. per litre, and Jaguars have never lagged behind in this field. The present standard version of the well-known six-cylinder, twin overhead camshaft engine develops 190 b.h.p. as compared with 160 of the 120 engine, and when it is fitted with the high lift camshafts and 8 to 1 compression ratio of the special equipment model, the power output is increased to 210 b.h.p. at 5,750 r.p.m.

In addition to increased power output from the engine, the chassis has benefited from lessons learnt on the racing circuits of Europe. Road holding, steering, brakes and suspension have been improved, and have helped to make the XK.140 a car in which it is possible to average very high speeds indeed over long distances with greater ease than in its predecessor.

The weight distribution of the Jaguar XK.140 coupé is now 50.3 per cent at the front, and 49.7 per cent at the rear, as compared with 47.5 per cent and 52.5 per cent of the XK.120 coupé tested by *The Autocar* in 1953. This has been achieved by moving the engine farther forward and placing the battery, previously located behind the seat, in the engine compartment. This extra weight on the front wheels is the most decisive factor in the improved cornering ability. It results in a controlled degree of drift such as was achieved on racing cars of the past, when small section tyres were fitted to the front wheels to achieve the same purpose by sliding, without the science of the action being fully understood. The car is fitted with rack and pinion steering, and the front torsion bars have been increased in diameter.

The extra power output has resulted, not unnaturally, in an increase in maximum speed, and the special equipment model—in this case including racing tyres—is capable of 130 m.p.h. in overdrive top gear. At this speed the engine was turning over at 4,900 r.p.m., with overdrive engaged. When the car is fitted with an overdrive, the axle ratio is 4.09 to 1, which gives an overall transmission ratio of 3.19 to 1.

It is probable that by dispensing with the overdrive and having the optional axle ratio of 3.31 to 1, the maximum speed might be increased slightly. But for all normal road use in Great Britain, and fast touring on the Continent, the combination as provided on the test car proved adequate and delightful. In conditions where fast cruising is limited by traffic congestion and inadequate roads, the lower ratios provided by the 4.09 to 1 axle give superlative acceleration and enable very high average speeds to be maintained. The readiness with which 100 m.p.h. can be reached, rather than the absolute maximum, is the car's outstanding attribute.

It is on such roads as the Routes Nationales of France that the car comes into its own. Heading south from the Belgian motor road where the maximum speed figures had been taken, the Jaguar seemed naturally to be turned in the direction of Le Mans, where the marque has achieved such fame.

The 3½-litre engine fills most of the space under the bonnet. The special equipment model is fitted with the "C" type cylinder head and a high-speed crankshaft damper

The interior finish of the body is worthy of that of a car costing twice as much. There is a map pocket in each door, and a very small cubby hole with a lockable lid on the left of the facia panel. The windscreen washer is part of the special equipment, and the wipers have two-speed action

It was the return journey against the clock that made the greatest impression. Maximum speed was used in the intermediate gears, with the change from top to overdrive being made at 5,500 r.p.m. Le Mans was left at 10.20 a.m. and the Jaguar was at Le Touquet airport at 2.28 p.m. Two short stops were included in this time, and the last 90 of the 220 miles journey were on wet roads.

In overdrive the car seemed to don the proverbial seven-league boots, and the tall popular trees lining the long straight stretches of road appeared like a giant fence rushing by. Despite such sustained hard work, the oil pressure was steady at all times and there was never any sign of overheating.

One very noticeable feature of the Jaguar coupé is its comparative silence at speed. The car cruises very happily with the speedometer needle hovering between the 100 and 110 m.p.h. marks, and the crew is able to converse in normal

tor, and after the car has stood in the open overnight one merely switches on the ignition, waits a second or two for the float chambers to fill, then presses the starter button. It was never necessary to press the button a second time, and after a few minutes' running the starting carburettor would cut out automatically as the engine reached operating temperature.

During the road test, when a great number of miles were covered at high speed, no attention was needed apart from maintaining the oil level and no water was added to the radiator.

The car would trickle gently along with other traffic in crowded city streets, drawing attention only because of its attractive appearance. Its hill climbing abilities would appear to be limited only by the need for maintaining adhesion of the 600×16 tyres. If the driver changes down on a main road gradient it is only because he has been baulked by other traffic or because he wishes to indulge his *joie de vivre*.

In two hours on the Continent, the car covered 123 miles, and on occasions such as those the overall fuel consumption of 21.7 m.p.g. was helped to a great extent by continuous use of the Laycock-de Normanville overdrive. Operating only on top gear, the overdrive is brought into action by moving a small switch, illuminated in the "on" position, fitted on the extreme right side of the facia panel. On a number of occasions the overdrive was engaged at maximum revs—6,000 r.p.m.—and the unit came into action with a barely noticeable pause and no sign of clutch slip.

There is little difference between the times taken during the performance tests and those recorded with the XK.120, for increased power output has to deal with an increase in weight of one hundredweight. What should be borne in mind is that the extra weight has meant more room and comfort for the occupants of the car, with a higher maximum speed and improved fuel consumption. The wheelbase remains the same, but the XK.140 is three inches longer, one and a half inches higher, and two and a half inches wider than its predecessor.

The suspension is a happy combination—there is comfort at low speeds with none of the teeth-chattering effect which in the past was associated with a sports car, even over cobbled roads, and with the tyres inflated to the pressures recommended for high speeds, the ride is still comfortable. Indeed it is possible to write a legible hand at over 110 m.p.h. There is no sway or heeling over on fast corners, and the driver knows that there is reserve to allow for any of his own shortcomings. Restraint is required with the throttle pedal on

The smaller radiator grille has made a neater frontal appearance. Flashing-type direction indicators are fitted at the bottom of each wing

tones, despite an audible intake roar in the higher-engine-speed range. There is a complete lack of exhaust boom. However much this might please the out-and-out enthusiast, it can become overpowering in confined quarters. Wind noise also is at a very low level, and the car is restful to travel in.

The major part of the road test was carried out with the car using racing tyres, and the high pitched whine over smooth tarmac associated with this type of cover was noticed because of the general low noise level. Road speed tyres are standard equipment for the XK.140, and the difference in rolling radius of this tyre and the racing type makes a considerable difference to the speedometer reading. In the data panel the corrections given are for racing tyres, which give 20.3 m.p.h. in top gear per 1,000 engine r.p.m. and 25.9 m.p.h. in overdrive. When rechecked with Road Speed tyres the speedometer corrections were as follows:

Car speedometer 10 20 30 40 50 60 70 80 90 100 110 120
True speed   .. 12 20 27 36 45 55 65 75 85 95 105 115

Another remarkable point about the XK.140 is its docility and flexibility in traffic or when travelling slowly. It is quite possible to accelerate from 10 m.p.h. on top gear without protest from the power unit. Not many years ago a twin overhead camshaft engine with an 8 to 1 compression ratio would have been a temperamental beast. Difficult to start, it would have oiled up plugs at low speeds and stalled at inconvenient times.

Not so the Jaguar—it has an automatic starting carburet-

Wire-spoked wheels form part of the special equipment offered for the Coupé. There is a lockable hinged flap over the petrol filler, and strong corner bumpers with over-riders protect the rear of the car

ROAD TEST . . .

wet surfaces, for when carrying out the standing start acceleration tests it was found easy to spin the rear wheels on a dry road.

The improved weight distribution, achieved mainly by repositioning the engine, has eliminated the oversteer noticeable in the earlier XK.120, and the suspension is firm without being harsh. The steering is light yet very positive. Road shocks are felt to some extent through the steering wheel and the best control is achieved by allowing the wheel to "float" in the driver's hands.

The driving seat is tailored to the car's performance. It has a more than adequate fore and aft adjustment, and this, combined with the telescopic steering column, enables drivers of vastly different proportions to achieve a comfortable position. A tall driver does not find he has to peer under the top rail of the windscreen, and one very quickly becomes accustomed to the divided windscreen glass. More room for the right elbow would be appreciated.

The brakes proved entirely adequate for the high speeds involved. Under extreme conditions they did not fade or grab, but each application was accompanied by a rather annoying squeal from the front drums. The brakes call for heavier pedal pressure than usual when an emergency stop is required and some might prefer a measure of servo assistance. The brake pedal is well placed in relation to the accelerator, so that heel and toe gear changes can be made when approaching a corner. The hand brake lever is placed close to the gear lever on the passenger side of the propeller shaft cover.

Room for golf clubs and other lengthy items can be obtained by lowering the hinged flap in front of the luggage compartment. The rear quarter vents in the body can be opened to provide extra ventilation

The clutch transmits the 210 b.h.p. to the rear wheels without protest in the form of slip or judder. It is necessary to depress the pedal completely to achieve a noiseless gear change, and the pedal travel is very long without achieving a light operating load. The gear change is satisfactory, but with a long movement of the lever from first to second. The box itself could be improved if the ratios between first and

Right: This unretouched picture was taken just before the maximum speed was achieved in overdrive and shows the rev counter on the left recording 4,800 r.p.m. and the speedometer on 135 m.p.h.

Below: A flat floor is given to the luggage compartment and it is free from obstructions which might cause damage to soft leather cases

second were slightly closer. First gear is desirable for starting from rest.

Long-distance touring in the grand manner can be enjoyed only if the car is comfortable, and in this respect the Jaguar is ideal for two persons. There is an ample seat adjustment and the passenger is able to stretch his or her legs out. The back rests are not adjustable, but the angle is well chosen for comfort and control. It is possible for one adult to ride behind the driver or passenger with some discomfort on long journeys, or as an alternative there is room for two children. The comfort was impaired on some occasions by a draught around the ankles which came through the body trim below the facia when the window was slightly opened. A recirculation-type heater is part of the standard equipment and this functions well as a windscreen demister, although the fan is very noisy, and quite disturbing at low road speeds.

Lighting is in general good. Yellow bulbs were fitted in the headlamps for Continental use and these were not entirely adequate at high speeds, but experience of other cars with the same type of headlamp using normal bulbs has shown that they permit full use to be made of the car's speed after dark. The twin fog lamps on the test car form part of the special equipment. The interior of the car can be illuminated by lights set in the roof lining and controlled by a switch on the facia; it was felt that they might be brighter. The instrument illumination can be dimmed by rheostat. There is a light built into the luggage compartment lid.

By lowering the hinged flap in the front of the locker, the capacity can be greatly enlarged, but this prevents use of the rear seat. The floor of the locker is hinged, and beneath it are stowed the spare wheel and tools. The quality of the tool kit is in keeping with the car. The one-piece bonnet is released by pulling a catch beneath the facia, and some slight knack is required to find the safety catch on the front of the radiator grille. The supporting stay for the bonnet is clipped in a rather awkward position, especially for a short person.

The number of cars capable of reaching 100 m.p.h. has increased in the past few years. There are very few which can reach this figure in under 30 sec, as the XK.140 does with ease. More important, it can be held in overdrive to become a comfortable cruising speed with very low throttle openings and to record a fuel consumption of near enough 22 m.p.g. That these figures can be achieved in a car whose comfort and safety are superlative implies the highest praise for the team responsible for its creation. When these qualities are related to its price, there is no other car which can approach it in the high performance sphere, and it is a fine advertisement for the British automobile industry.

ROAD TEST: JAGUAR XK.140 COUPE WITH OVERDRIVE

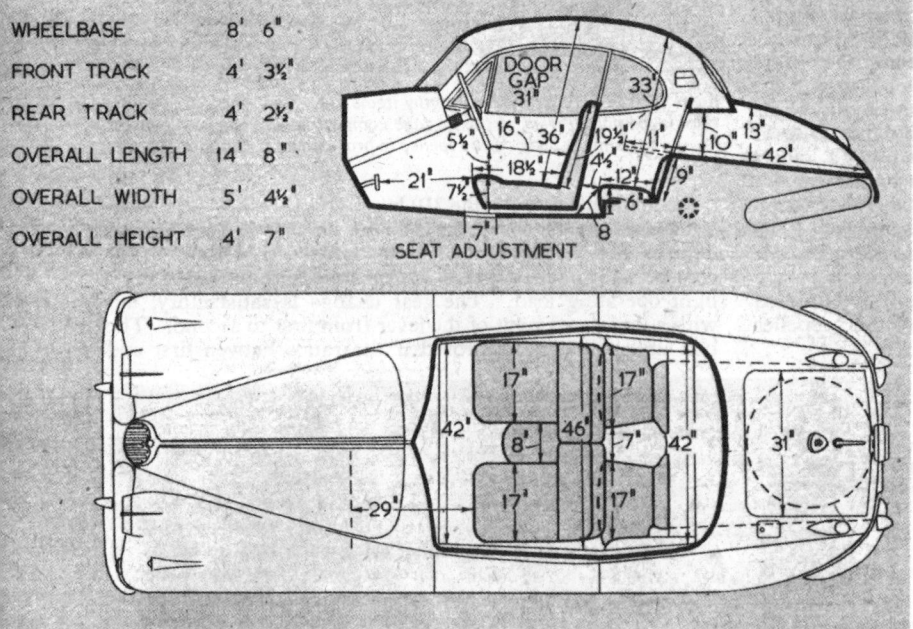

WHEELBASE	8' 6"
FRONT TRACK	4' 3½"
REAR TRACK	4' 2½"
OVERALL LENGTH	14' 8"
OVERALL WIDTH	5' 4½"
OVERALL HEIGHT	4' 7"

DATA

PRICE (basic), with fixed head coupé body, £1,291 5s 0d.
British purchase tax, £539 2s 11d.
Total (in Great Britain), £1,830 7s 11d, including special equipment.
Extras: Radio, £47 5s 3d.

ENGINE: Capacity: 3,442 c.c. (210 cu in).
Number of cylinders: 6.
Bore and stroke: 83×106 mm (3.27×4.17in).
Valve gear: twin overhead camshafts.
Compression ratio: 8 to 1.
B.H.P.: 210 at 5,750 r.p.m. (B.H.P. per ton (laden): 134.7).
Torque: 213 lb ft at 4,000 r.p.m.
M.P.H. per 1,000 r.p.m. on top gear, 19.6.
M.P.H. per 1,000 r.p.m. on overdrive, 25.1.

WEIGHT: (with 5 gals fuel), 28 cwt (3,136 lb).
Weight distribution (per cent): F, 50.3; R, 49.7.
Laden as tested: 31 cwt (3,472 lb).
Lb per c.c. (laden): 1.01.

BRAKES: Type: F, two-leading shoes; R, leading and trailing shoes.
Method of operation: F, hydraulic; R, hydraulic.
Drum dimensions: F, 12in diameter; 2¼in wide. R, 12in diameter; 2¼in wide.
Lining area: F, 95 sq in. R, 95 sq in (121.8 sq in per ton laden).

TYRES: 6.00—16in.
Pressures (lb per sq in): F, 23; R, 26 (normal). F, 30; R, 35 (for fast driving).

TANK CAPACITY: 14 Imperial gallons.
Oil sump, 19 pints.
Cooling system, 25 pints.

TURNING CIRCLE: 33ft (L and R).
Steering wheel turns (lock to lock): 2¾.

DIMENSIONS: Wheelbase: 8ft 6in.
Track: F, 4ft 3½in; R, 4ft 3⅜in.
Length (overall): 14ft 8in.
Height: 4ft 7in.
Width: 5ft 4½in.
Ground clearance: 7½in.
Frontal area: 17.5 sq ft (approximately).

ELECTRICAL SYSTEM: 12-volt; 64 ampere-hour battery.
Head lights: Double dip; 60-36 watt bulbs.

SUSPENSION: Front, independent, torsion bars and wishbones. Rear, half-elliptic leaf springs. Anti-roll bar position, front.

PERFORMANCE

ACCELERATION: from constant speeds
Speed Range, Gear Ratios and Time in sec.

M.P.H.	3.19 to 1	4.09 to 1	5.59 to 1	8.11 to 1	13.81 to 1
10—30	—	—	7.9	5.8	4.2	—
20—40	—	—	7.5	5.7	4.7	—
30—50	—	—	7.4	5.6	4.2	—
40—60	—	—	7.7	5.8	—	—
50—70	—	11.0	8.3	6.2	—	—
60—80	—	12.0	9.4	6.9	—	—
80—100	—	19.1	11.5	—	—	—

From rest through gears to:

M.P.H.	sec.	M.P.H.	sec.
30	3.2	100	29.5
50	7.5	110	37.7
60	11.0		
70	14.2		
80	16.9		
90	22.7		

Standing quarter mile, 17.4 sec.

SPEED ON GEARS:

Gear	M.P.H. (normal adn max.)	K.P.H. (normal and max.)
Top o/drive (mean)	129.25	208.0
(best)	129.5	208.4
Top	100—111	161—177.6
3rd	72—80	116—129
2nd	43—50	69—80
1st	21—26	34—42

TRACTIVE RESISTANCE: 35 lb per ton at 10 M.P.H.

TRACTIVE EFFORT:

	Pull (lb per ton)	Equivalent Gradient
Top	332	1 in 6.7
Third	426	1 in 5.2
Second	560	1 in 3.9

BRAKES:

Efficiency	Pedal Pressure (lb)
88 per cent	100
82 per cent	70
62 per cent	50

FUEL CONSUMPTION:
21.7 m.p.g. overall for 588 miles (13 litres per 100 km).
Approximate normal range 18–23 m.p.g. (15.7–12.3 litres per 100 km).
Fuel, first grade.

WEATHER:
Cloudy, slight breeze, dry surface.
Air temperature, 50 deg F.

Acceleration figures are the means of several runs in opposite directions.

Tractive effort and resistance obtained by Tapley meter.

Model described in *The Autocar* of 15 October, 1954.

SPEEDOMETER CORRECTION: M.P.H. (With Racing Tyres)

| Car speedometer: | 10 | 20 | 30 | 40 | 50 | 60 | 70 | 80 | 90 | 100 | 110 | 120 |
| True speed: | 12 | 20 | 28 | 35 | 44 | 54 | 62 | 72 | 82 | 92 | 101 | 111 |

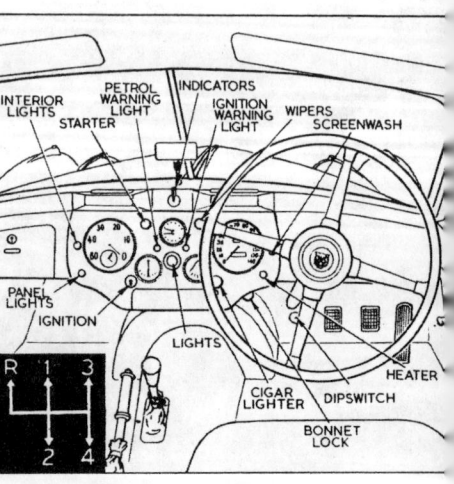

DRIVER'S REPORT
JAGUAR

1956 version of a car produced by one of the World's leading automobile manufacturers upholds its fine car ancestry

THE JAGUAR XK-140 is a car that is not changed materially in appearance from the first XK models introduced in 1949.

Six cylinders, in line, double over head camshafts, independent front suspension with torsion bars, solid rear axle with semi elliptic springs, four speed floor shift gear box with syncromesh on second, third and fourth (Borg Warner automatic transmission is available on the sedan, coupe and convertible coupe), so it's the same car. Or is it?

The Jaguar company, in Coventry, England, has not been content to rest on its laurels. Continuous changes have improved this breed of cat to the point where Jaguar cars are a better buy now than at any time in the last seven years.

Let's take a good look at the car. MOTOR LIFE was loaned a hard top coupe model XK 140 MC by Jaguar Cars of America Ltd. This particular car was not brand new but has been used as a company car and had 6,000 odd miles on the odometer when we picked it up. Extra equipment on the car included the "C" head, which boosts the horsepower from the normal 190 to 210 at 5,500 rpm, overdrive, heater, windshield washers, and center lock knock on wire wheels.

Styling-wise, the Jag coupe is a controversial issue. Either you like it or you don't. We've found very few people who were "in-between" on the subject. In 1955, with the advent of the XK-140, the addition of jump seats in the convertible and hardtop coupe models necessitated a little longer top which we don't think added much to the appearance of the car.

The interior shows excellent quality, typical of Jaguar, and presents a luxurious appearance with its comfortable, well upholstered seats in genuine top grain leather. The wood finish on the instrument panel and window frames seems rather archaic under present design and production methods but nevertheless imparts a certain feeling of elegance not to be found in many cars. Jaguar interiors are, on the entire line, tastefully done and do not dazzle you with chrome or plastic as some manufacturers are prone to do with their automobiles.

Most of the conveniences and extras found in American cars (radio, heater, windshield washers, automatic transmissions) can be had on Jaguars except power equipment, which due to the car's design is totally unnecessary. Compactness of the passenger compartment does not allow for major seat movements (4-way seats) and the seats are light enough so they slide easily fore and aft by hand when the seat lock is released.

Automatic window lifts are not necessary because the driver can reach both doors and all four windows of the car from his seat without really stretching. This is something that would be impossible with large domestic cars because of the seat width.

As we leave the office and proceed through city traffic, several things are noticed about the Jag that cannot be found while sitting still. The close ratio gear box performs smoothly but the position of the gear shift lever was awkward for me, as it was a little too far back. A driver with short legs, who would have the seat forward, would find second gear on the four speed box just about in his right hand pocket.

The location of such a necessary item as the shift lever, can be a real headache to the designer because he is forced to put everything in a position that should suit the majority of people who might buy the car. Obviously he can't satisfy everyone. The seat and the steering wheel locations are both adjustable so that is no problem in this department.

Being one of the long-legged variety, I like to drive with the seat well back. This leaves the rear jump seat on the driver's side useless except for someone with no legs. In fact these seats are only large enough for gnomes or small children at best, and then only for short distances. It did increase the luggage space though if you aren't trying to carry passengers in the rear.

Visibility is excellent with one exception. The windshield post creates a blind spot which gave me fits until I got used to it. This condition would be just as bad on the convertible but much less bothersome on the roadster because of its small windshield frame.

Instruments and switches are all within easy reach of the driver but I would prefer them to be more in the line of sight. The instrument panel in the Jag is in the center of the dash and symmetrical about the centerline of the car, which is thought to be good design in some schools. Probably the reasoning behind

Jaguar trunk compartment is completely upholstered in carpeting of a color that matches the car. When the lower floor is raised it exposes the spare wheel, jack, grease gun, brass hammer for knock off wheels and tool kit.

XK 140 Coupe 190 hp	$3810

This price includes heater and defroster, tachometer, turn indicators, telescopic steering column, backing lights, spare parts kit, hand tools and locking glove compartment.

XK 140 M Coupe 190 hp	$3955

Same equipment as above with wire wheels, twin exhausts, fog lamps and windshield washers.

XK 140 MC Coupe 210 hp	$4105

As above with special crankshaft damper and "C" type cylinder head.

Laycock de Normanville overdrive $160
Available on all Jaguar cars.

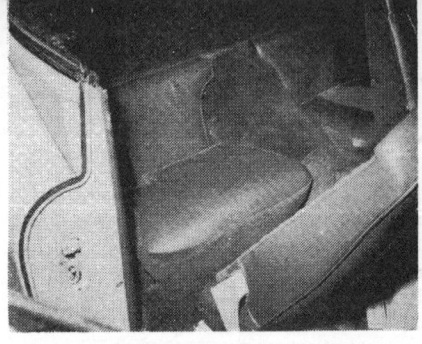

Jump seats in rear of coupe are good for small children on short excursions only, can be removed for carrying luggage.

the Jaguar arrangement is due to the fact that cars coming off the same assembly line are due for shipment to many countries throughout the world.

In England and Australia, all cars have right hand drive. In North and South America and most of Europe they have left hand drive. Therefore one instrument panel will do for any delivery and the only major components that have to be moved are the steering and pedal assembly. But for fast driving, as this car is capable of doing, I still prefer the instruments in front of me.

Steering through rack and pinion, new to Jaguar in 1955, is quick (2¾ turns lock to lock) positive and easy. Handling qualities have been improved, over previous models, by this change.

Even though the ride is a little stiff by American standards, it is quite comfortable. Seating is typical of sports cars, feet out in front, seat low, placed well rearward of the chassis center which not only gives the driver (and passenger) a comfortable seating position but gives him a "feel" of the car that adds materially to his ability to handle the vehicle.

Performance-wise the coupe is respectable, but it does not approach the better times that can be obtained with the roadster version, due to the heavier weight of the coupe.

CONTINUED ON PAGE 122

Above, left, spare parts kit that comes with Jaguars includes complete engine gasket set, fan belt, radiator hoses, ignition points, condenser, valve springs, sparkplugs, and brake bleeder hose. Interior view shows leather seats, walnut instrument panel, floor shift lever, emergency brake handle and carpeted floor.

Jaguar XK 140 MC lines are pleasing to the eye. Modified models can be distinguished from standard models by wire wheels and twin pipes on modifieds.

JAGUAR XK 140 SPECIFICATIONS

ENGINE		GEARBOX	
Cylinders	6	four speed synchromesh on 2nd, 3rd and 4th	
Bore & stroke	3.267 x 4.173	**CHASSIS**	
Displacement	3,442 cc (210 cu. in.)	Wheelbase	102 in.
Compression ratio	8:1	Tread (front)	51 in.
Horsepower M Model	190 @ 5,500 rpm	(rear)	51⅜ in.
Horsepower MC	210 @ 5,750 rpm	Length overall	14' 8"
Valve arrangement	dohc	Width overall	64½"
		Height	55"

When jump seats are not occupied, bulkhead can be let down which allows longer parcels to be carried in the Jag trunk.

Black JAGUAR

An Appreciation of the XK140 Fixed-head Coupe and of What Lies under its Bonnet

ONE of the soundest pieces of advice I have ever encountered is not to drive a strange car fast until you have got the feel of it. "Fast" is relative, of course, and it would have been silly of me to have held an XK140 under the 60 m.p.h. at which my 1½-litre Riley had customarily travelled. None the less I went warily anywhere off the main roads, for it is the unusual camber, the sudden dip halfway round a bend and the stray dog on the minor road that catch you out.

On a fast bend the Jaguar was quite different in feel from the Riley; the Michelin X tyres seemed to have to do a much sterner job in compelling the heavier front end to go where the driver wished. At high speeds the front wheels were much more sensitive to the road. Well, I reflected, before the comparative sensations wore off, this is recirculating ball steering instead of rack and pinion and this is a 3½-litre six-cylinder against a 1½ four. Start learning if you want to stay on the road.

Very soon there was no comparison, and very soon one knew instinctively how fast the car would go round a bend. The restless-seeming steering wheel lost its restlessness and will, no doubt, respond to a couple of fingers at ninety if you believe in that sort of thing. Frankly, I do not. At low speeds or high I prefer a solid twenty-to-four grip on the steering wheel and am loth to relinquish if for any pretext, certainly not hand signalling.

Now the all-round excellence of this machine could begin to make itself felt. To talk contradictorily, it is the most ferociously docile car that one could imagine; and aptly named, for the Jaguar at 30 m.p.h. is the South American feline purring in the Amazonian sun. But when the driver opens the twin throttles wide in second or third the fangs are showing and the car is a black streak, almost airborne.

But Jaguar performance is so well known that it need not be dwelt upon. Where the car is impressive is in its gentleness. You can make a forceful change and hear the r.p.m. of the engine come back to three-five or three thousand in the exhaust note; but you can also move the short, almost delicate, gear lever silently and cleanly, matching the r.p.m. with a sensitive throttle foot, so that the passenger's only awareness of change will be the swing of the rev counter needle across the black dial in its burr walnut surround. As a car to be treasured, the XK140 is driven that way unless professional reasons demand high performance. I count it as a black mark if the front of the car, reaching out ahead of me through the two-piece screen, shows by the slightest tremor that a high-speed change has been less than precisely judged.

By the Abbaye de Grandvaux, near Oyonnax in the Juras

The Laycock-de Normanville overdrive is an obvious choice for such driving. At about 50 m.p.h. the inch-long plastic switch handle (on the facia, convenient to the right hand) is flicked over to the left and the 3.19 to 1 overdrive ratio can be eased in with a slight release of the accelerator. Thereupon the engine loafs around for all the world like those of an airliner on its way down from 15,000ft; you can visualize the lazybones of a crankshaft, idling round in those seven gleaming bearings. The overdrive tell-tale light is extinguished by a change into third, for the gear is not operative on this ratio but, unlike the Bristol, the overdrive remains in circuit on top unless positively switched out. Both arrangements are attractive, and I doubt if a driver would develop a strong preference for either.

One of the best chuckles I have extracted from the 140 came when two workmen passed the car just as I was leaving a park. "That's a damn silly car," said one to the other, and I know just what he meant, for I have the fixed-head coupé which, superficially, might seem to merit the remark. So far as I am concerned, however, the two comfortable, one occasional and four-at-a-pinch seating which this model provides is ideal: there always seems to be a little more room somewhere, yet the compactness of the body is extraordinary. The fixed-head 140 is a quite small car overall, with a steering lock that is really useful. Its normal working complement of driver and navigator have space to spare and to sleep in (the Tulip Rally first proved that) and, if the owner has a typing job to do, it is transformed into a red leather and walnut office that rivals the average board room. All this in a shape that is harmonious in the extreme and oh so logically a descendant of those impossibly long-bonneted S.S. models of so many years ago!

The heart of this black beast is, of course, the magnificent XK engine. The six-cylinder internal combustion engine, if not as old as Adam, is of a respectable antiquity and might have been thought to be beyond the age of surprise, even if it could be improved in detail. Yet the Jaguar XK unit made a terrific impact on introduction. The design team accomplished so many detail improvements, and revealed such a flair in selection of operational methods, that the result was a world-beater, as witnessed by Jaguar victories in sports car racing.

You can describe this engine in orthodox terms: six-cylinder, 83 × 106 mm bore and stroke, 3,442 c.c. Various compression ratios are available (mine is 8 to 1) and the combustion chambers are hemispherical, the valves being operated by twin overhead camshafts. There are two carburettors and the head is light alloy.

But now consider the design in detail. Where decisiveness was needed it was there: "The advantages of the hemispherical head over all other types are so many when carefully analysed that I find it difficult to see why this type of head is not more generally employed" (W. M. Heynes, Chief Engineer). An ex-Riley owner reads such a view with pleasure.

Where patient trial and error were called for in a realm of indecision it was there also: Harry Weslake and Co., starting with the basic principle of a curved valve port with a venturi orifice, measured air flow through full-scale models of either wood or aluminium, which were varied in dimension until maximum flow had been obtained. And as very small changes in port shape can produce large differences in flow, accurate cores were straightway taken from the most efficient design and supplied to the pattern maker.

Cylinder head material is DTD 424, a commercial alloy, and the weight of the bare head is only 50 lb against 120 lb in cast iron, an obvious advantage where the inevitable weight of a big engine is embarrassing; as a guard against handling damage—a risk with light alloy—twenty thousandths of an inch are taken off in a final cut from the joint face.

Somehow the look of the engine conveys the scrupulous care which has been taken with the design and manufacture; it lies, a compact mass with its gleaming camshaft covers, down under the jaw of the Jaguar. There is satisfaction to be got in the contemplation of the two three-branch exhaust manifolds, plunging down to lead the fast-moving exhaust gases out in a resonant organ note from the wide exhaust; in pressing home the dashpot pistons of the two carburettors

Lakeside scenery near the Swiss border, south of Pontarlier

against the slight resistance of the newly replenished oil; in withdrawing the long, balanced dipstick from its snug fit aft on the port side of the engine.

There is more significance to the act than seems apparent. If you overfill the sump of a Jaguar you can lose 20 b.h.p. at an engine speed of 5,000 r.p.m., and this is a reminder of the care taken in devising the lubrication of this engine, for a similar penalty arises from an excess of oil on top of the baffle in the sump. Oil passages therefore were made large in order that flow through the engine should be as slow as possible. Otherwise the oil from the by-pass circuit accumulated on top of the baffle. Why? Engine oil flow increases by 50 per cent at 60 lb per sq in between 1,000 r.p.m. and 5,000 r.p.m. But pump delivery is directly proportional to engine speed and therefore gives a 400 per cent

Oil flow through the engine, and pump delivery. The dotted line is the requirement before the crankpin drilling was modified, the solid line is as the engine went into production

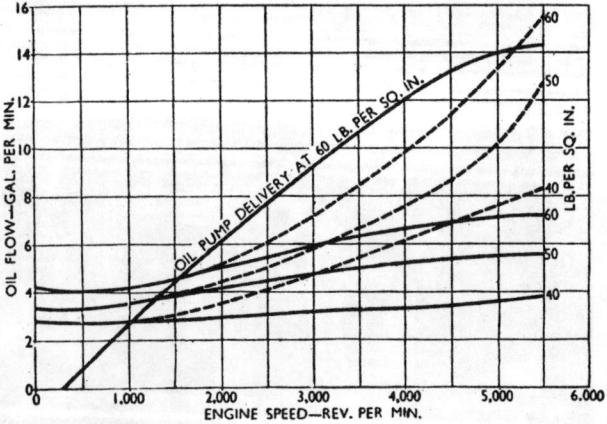

Autoroute halt by the Brussels-Ostend highway

Black JAGUAR . . .

increase, most of which must be by-passed. Oil drillings were countersunk to assist this slowing-down process and the difference (see graph) was quite startling.

I mention these considerations (Mr. Heynes recounted many more in his notable Paper on the engine) because the total of them has had such a tremendous effect in terms of output, smoothness and silence. The crankshaft is another case in point. It is a fairly typical seven-bearing shaft only partially counterweighted, and that mostly at the centre, because full counterweighting, by making the shaft heavier, would increase the torsional vibration, which the Jaguar chief engineer says is probably the cause of more engine failures, directly or indirectly, than any other single factor in racing.

Vibration dampers are the antidote, the Jaguar having the Metalastik unit. But that is only the culmination of a strict assembly routine. The shaft is balanced dynamically on an Avery machine and the flywheel, already micropoise-balanced, is then fitted; the assembly is now rechecked statically and modified if desirable. A further check is made after the clutch has been bolted in position.

At the earliest stages of development a preliminary check of the assembly was made without a damper. From the results sample Metalastiks were tried with various weights and rubber mixes and from the further results the final damper specification was drawn up.

So the meticulous care has been taken, and it is small wonder that owners continue to lavish attention and affection on their engines. I filled up the other day at Humphries' Garage, which lies just to the south of the new town of Bracknell, in Berkshire. The proprietor invited me to go into the workshop and have a look at the engine of an XK standing there. It had been considerably modified—a Scintilla magneto was an indication—but it was its beautiful condition that was so striking; copper tubing gleamed and the top of the header tank was highly polished brass plate.

Those eight gallons of Esso Extra will carry the XK140 just about 160 miles, during which time 80 or 85 m.p.h. will be seen fairly frequently, but not more. Acceleration will be used to the full when needed, but the need will be more infrequent than frequent.

The brakes, also, will tend not to be used to the full except in emergency, when the owner had assured himself that they will be there. In the braking, however, is the one hint that the Jaguar must be watched for treachery. The air scoops on the front drums permit easy entry of water, which may affect one or both sets of linings. If one set, there is a sharp pull to the other side from low speeds; if both, the brake pedal needs a hard shove. So far, these symptoms have applied only at low speeds, and I think high-speed braking generates enough heat to dry the linings out almost immediately. Anyway, if you live with a Jaguar you must be prepared to keep an eye on its claws. I have lived with mine for about 8,000 miles, and I think that each of us is aware that neither of us dominates the other.   MICHAEL BROWN.

ROAD TEST

BELOW: JAGUAR Corner for the Jaguars seems appropriate as the XK140 tours around the Albert Park circuit after road test.

JAGUAR XK 140 IS A REAL GRAND TURISMO

By BRUCE KNEALE

WHEN British racing driver Peter Whitehead was in Australia last year he told friends here that more and more enthusiasts in Europe were coming to regard the Jaguar XK140 hardtop coupe as *the* Gran Turismo car for anyone outside the near-millionaire class.

That this point of view is neither an isolated nor an unreasonable one is apparent from the words of Ken Purdy, author of that sprightly and illuminating tome *Kings Of The Road*, and one of the best-informed as well as the most literate of all American motoring writers.

He said, of the Jaguar XK120 hardtop coupe (and, of course, the comment applies with equal if not more validity to the XK140):

"... the most exciting automobile of the past twenty years? When was there another like it...?" The XK coupe is in the tradition of the great European two-seaters of the 1930s; a snug buttoned-up *voiture de grand luxe* for two people and two only."

It is from such a viewpoint, we think, that any true appraisal of the car must be made. Despite the quite astonishing successes of standard Jaguar roadsters and coupes in the hands of private owners since Sir William Lyons first revealed his sensational baby to a disbelieving world in 1948, the car was designed for high-speed touring — *not* for racing. And that is not to sell short the outstanding results achieved on road and track by privately-piloted cars in absolutely standard trim.

In its current form then, the Jaguar XK140 sports car, in whichever of the three models available you may choose, is designed for long-distance touring at a high rate of knots. Fundamentally, it is the same vehicle that enraptured fans of the *marque* back in '48.

BIG POWER is obtained from relatively small capacity in the Jaguar motor, which is reasonably easy to work on.

There have, of course, been modifications and improvements. The compression ratio has been raised from seven-to-one to eight-to-one; rack-and-pinion steering is fitted as standard; brtke horsepower has been raised from 160 to 190 bhp with 210 available to those who can afford the full C-type modification; front suspension is altogether more rugged with longer, bigger-diameter torsion bars; more leg-room is provided for the driver, with, in the hardtop and drophead coupes, additional small seats for two children or one adult sitting crosswise; luggage space has been considerably increased and heavier bumpers front and rear, with solid over-riders, take care of the humorist who does his reversing staring straight ahead.

How does the car stand up to its claims after this effluxion of time and in the light of the many excellent vehicles that have come (and in some cases, gone) since its introduction? We think, well. But let the facts speak for themselves.

The Jaguar XK140 hardtop which forms the basis of these comments had done approximately 8500 miles when at was decided to make it the subject of a road-test as searching as possible in the circumstances obtaining at the time. The car had been run-in for 3000 miles at gradually increasing speeds, starting with 35 mph in top for its 500 miles.

No special preparations were undertaken other than the fitting of a set of platinum-point variable heat-range plugs and a mild tune-up, including checking of electric fuel pump, the ignition system and carburettors.

Nave plates were removed from the wheels, tyre pressures were raised to 35 lb. to the square inch for the rear wheels with a shade less in front; rear spats, tools, and spare wheel were removed, and the ignition was retarded a little more than one degree.

Maximum-speed runs were made over a flying-mile course (the situation of which must remain our secret) at 7 am on a cold, frosty morning, the car having run 20 miles or so to the test road and being right on its normal working temperature. Electric timing equipment was used to obtain the figures given here and it was checked with stopwatches.

The Jaguar attained the magic 100 mph with almost frightening ease and speed and wound up slowly from 120 mph to its maximum of 131 mph. At 100 mph little more than half throttle was in use.

If you regard these figures are unduly optimistic, so did the test crew at the time and they were checked and rechecked. Four runs, two in each direction, were made for speed maxima, while acceleration tests started with the clutch coming-in in first gear around 2500 rpm on the tachometer. The needle was well in the red during all maximum-speed tests.

Impressive as these figures may be, however, they convey neither the ease with which they were obtained nor the good manners of the car during their taking. At no stage did the driver feel insecure; at no stage

ONLY SLIGHTLY changed since its introduction eight years ago, the XK front remains as attractive as ever. Lights at bottom of mudguards are turn indicators.

did the car deviate from its chosen line. The rack-and-pinion steering was exemplary, precise and accurate, though conceivably some drivers might prefer a heavier "feel" at high speed. Rear-wheel spin was easy to provoke in both first and second gears, and there was a decided "cheep" when the car took off in acceleration tests.

Wind noise was unexpectedly low, a tribute to the Jaguar's low frontal area and flowing lines, and with the windows all but closed it was difficult to believe the car was going as hard as it was.

There was none of that impression of speed that one knows in open roadsters with the wind buffeting and tearing at the cockpit, though the writer was certainly conscious that he was travelling faster than he had done on land before!

The ride is excellent, with a degree of stability and roadholding noticeably absent from lighter open sports cars. Incidentally, the car, with the driver up, and about six gallons in the tank, weighs something like 28½ cwt., which after all is not light.

A weight distribution of approximately 51 per cent front to 49 per cent rear is responsible for a pleasant degree of understeer. Cornering is good on pretty well any kind of surface, though slight roll is present when the car is pushed hard through tight 90-degree turns.

It would be idle to suggest that the Jaguar is without some minor shortcomings, which, of course, is true of any car outside the Rolls-Royce or Bentley class and the Jaguar pretends to be neither.

Immediately apparent to the driver who likes fast going is the absence of any real lateral support. The Jaguar's seats are superb for all normal driving purposes, with good vision and no transference of road shock, but they offer little support for the shoulders during hard cornering. Passengers who enjoy sustained high-performance motoring have made similar comments.

Similarly, the clutch pedal mounting is far from ideal, while the enthusiast who likes to tinker at home and do his own tuning will bemoan the positioning of the distributor deep in the bowels of the works department.

One disappointment with the car tested was that the new close-ratio gearbox advertised by Jaguar Cars Ltd. as being fitted to the XK140 models was in fact absent, as from earlier models imported into Australia. We understand that later models have the box, which is a decided improvement on the old one.

These, however, are minor, and only minor, failings. There is no doubt at all, as Britain's John Bolster has said, that this is one of the finest high-performance cars ever to come off a production line to the middle-income buyer.

In fact, the car lives up to all claims made for it by its makers and exceeds them. Those who doubt that should ask themselves what other marque provides this kind of performance and finish at the price. The Jaguar is not cheap — particularly in the amount of accommodation it provides for the money — but when you look at what else is offering it is an awful lot of car for the money.

In terms of general finish and equipment, this Jaguar is in line with the best that makers have offered in the past. The facia is of handsome walnut veneer, equipped with every wanted instrument, cigarette lighter, and a heating system. Seats, including the occasional seats, are upholstered in fine soft leather and foam rubber, and the floor is carpeted with felt beneath. Twin sun-visors are of polaroid or some similar material and there is a very fair set of tools. No starting handle is provided.

Twin six-volt batteries providing a 12-volt system, sit in special compartments behind the front wheels, access to which is by special doors. Because the batteries are away from heat, they rarely need topping-up.

Ignition is through Lucas oil-coil and Dunlop Road-Speed tyres are fitted as standard equipment. Special equipment models offer foglights, windscreen washers, 210-bhp, and wire wheels, for owners who have the extra money to spend.

For the family man who is reluctant to give up the pleasures of sports-car motoring, the Jaguar XK-140 coupes have one immeasurable advantage over the XK120 — they do offer accommodation, if not specially capacious accommodation, for children. This is a wonderful argument to use upon recalcitrant wives with a yen for living rooms on wheels or other derivations and variations of the Detroit barge.

For those who travel, as Purdy says, *a deux,* this is the answer. The coupe holds an immense amount of dunnage if the occasional seats are not in use. Add to this a 14-gallon fuel tank, an easily-obtained 25 mpg at a steady 50 mph or 18 mpg driving hard, an elegantly-distinctive body considered by many automotive aesthetes to be one of the all-

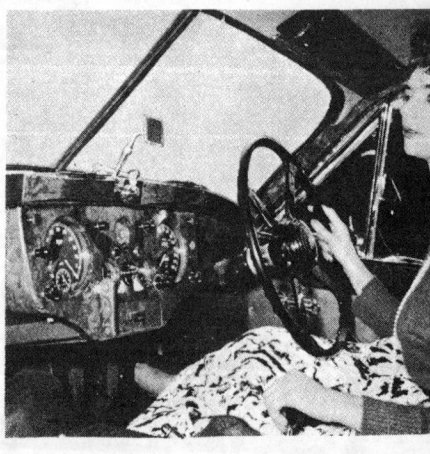

FACIA PANEL is of walnut veneer and has good range of dials, etc. This picture, taken after test, indicates female admiration for these coupes.

time gems of motorcar design, and what more can you ask? Not much, we think. ●

ROAD TEST OF JAGUAR XK140 STANDARD HARDTOP COUPE

TOP SPEED — average of two runs each in opposite directions over measured mile . . . . 131.85 mph

SPEED THROUGH GEARS —
0-30 mph . . . . 3.1 sec.
0-40 mph . . . . 4.9 sec.
0-50 mph . . . . 6.8 sec.
0-60 mph . . . . 8.9 sec.
0-70 mph . . . . 11.6 sec.
0-80 mph . . . . 15.0 sec.
0-90 mph . . . . 19.6 sec.
0-100 mph . . . . 26.0 sec.

BRAKES TO REST —
30 mph . . . . 31 ft

STANDING QUARTER — average two runs in opposite directions . . 16.8 sec.

SPEEDS IN GEARS (at 5800 rpm) —
First . . . . 37 mph
Second . . . . 69 mph
Third . . . . 100 mph
Top . . . . 131.85 mph

ACCELERATION IN TOP —
10-30 mph . . . . 6.4 sec.
20-40 mph . . . . 6.1 sec.
30-50 mph . . . . 6.3 sec.
40-60 mph . . . . 7.2 sec.
50-70 mph . . . . 7.6 mph
60-80 mph . . . . 8.0 sec.
70-90 mph . . . . 9.6 sec.
80-100 mph . . . . 11.0 sec.

CONDITIONS — Cold, frosty autumn morning. Time: 7 a.m. Tyre pressure: 35 lb. sq. in. Plugs: Platinum point, gap .022in. Spark retarded 1 deg. Miles per gallon: 24 at steady 50 mph; 18 driving very hard.

XK "SS"

A Potent New Super Sports Jaguar for Touring or Racing

DEVELOPED from the successful D-type racing sports car, a new 2-seater Jaguar has made its appearance in response to demand from America for a car combining racing performance with equipment and weather protection of touring-car standard. The new Jaguar, to be called the XK"SS" should meet this demand in a most potent and satisfying manner, for it follows the mechanical specification of the 3½-litre Le Mans cars in all essentials, yet has a full-width curved windscreen, folding hood, luggage grid and bumpers. The cockpit is properly trimmed, has well-upholstered seats and a full "touring" range of instruments. Features retained from the D-type include the large tail fuel tank, drilled lightweight steering wheel, and Dunlop disc brakes and light-alloy disc wheels with knock-off hubs. The car is initially for export only, and first deliveries will be made in February to the U.S.A., where the price is $6,900. The XK"SS" is an addition to the Jaguar range and will not supplant any existing models.

SCI ROAD TEST:

Jaguar XK 140 MC

Photographs by Don Typond

Trunk is long and shallow, and added length can be obtained by folding open a flap between compartment and cockpit.

RECENT owner polls and surveys have only served to underline the fact that the Jaguar occupies a unique place among sports cars. Ever since its introduction in late 1949, the XK series has set a worldwide value-for-money standard, and even American production experts have been known to wonder how they do it for the price.

Reasonable cost alone won't sell cars, though, and one tends to search further for the magic touch that has made every sports car larger than an MG a "Jaguar" in the eyes of the public. It's now an institution, on a par with Harris tweed, and its shrewd director, Sir William Lyons, has wrought this reputation by planned activity in several areas. The formula has included racing competition in the most publicized events, a calculated eye for styling and equipment, plus planned and selected sales and service facilities.

One of the most important lessons learned in nearly ten years of association with the American market has been that a good design properly promoted will long remain successful, and that public interest can best be whetted by periodic improvements both inside and out. The original XK series was well established as a sure seller, and had been supplemented by coupe and convertible models, but the domestic machines were catching up in power and speed and had trimmed the original Jaguar margin of 20 miles per hour. Experience on the circuits had taught a lot about handling, while several interior shortcomings were well known. A synthesis of all these findings appeared at the London show in 1954, in the form of the new XK 140.

For several reasons, the long and deep twin-cam six was moved forward three inches in the chassis, and a rubber-mounted rack-and-pinion steering gear replaced the old Burman recirculating ball unit. The previously special M-type high-lift cam was made standard, as was a Lucas oil ignition coil and the output of the stock XK 140 thus

The new Jag cruises comfortably between 85 and 90 mph. Steep positive caster angle at front wheels telegraphs road shocks at low speeds.

RATING FACTORS:

Bhp per cu. in. 1.00
Bhp per sq. in. piston area 4.17
Torque (lb-ft) per cu. in. 1.04
Pounds per bhp—test car 14.5
Piston speed @ 60 mph .... 1835 fpm
Piston speed @ max bhp .... 4000 fpm
Brake lining area per ton
  (test car) .... 137 sq. ins.

PRICES:

Roadster base price .... $3510.
Special equipment (MC)
  Group: .... 295.
Chromed wire wheels .... 150.
Overdrive .... 160.
Radio .... 95.
White sidewalls .... 25.
Service transportation
  charge .... 45.

jumped to 190 horsepower at 5500 rpm. To make best use of this, the gearbox was fitted with closer ratios and a slightly higher rear axle ratio was adopted. The exterior changes are easily seen, and include functional additions such as the much heavier bumpers as well as less immediately useful chrome decoration.

Again with an astute eye toward American requirements, a "Special Equipment" package was made available and was fitted on SCI's roadster test car. The "M" suffix includes dual exhausts, the wire wheels, fog lights and windshield washers, while the "C" indicates use of the C-type cylinder head and a special high-speed crankshaft vibration damper. This whole group thus constitutes the "MC" model. SCI's MC Jag, in handsome dark green, was supplied by Jaguar Cars North American Corporation, who went to considerable trouble to ensure that the car was in good condition for our test. Since many Jaguars seem to be "worn" as sporty roadsters-around-town, rather than being driven as the cars they are, we wondered just how well this suited them, and particularly this new model with its higher ratios and increased power. The answer, of course, is that the Jag will put up with it, but begins to get figuratively hot under the collar.

Thankfully the XK no longer seems to get physically hot in traffic, as a result of a larger, rearward-slanted radiator and water pump refinements. Even when the electric choke was cut in by means of the under-dash switch, starting tended to be sluggish on cold days. When warm there was no trouble, however, and idling was smooth, steady and quiet. A look at the torque curve of the C-type engine reveals a strange flat spot between 2000 and 3000 rpm, and acceleration up to the latter figure is good but not staggering. Best performance around heavy traffic thus requires active use of the clutch and the bottom two gears, which is not as pleasant as it might be.

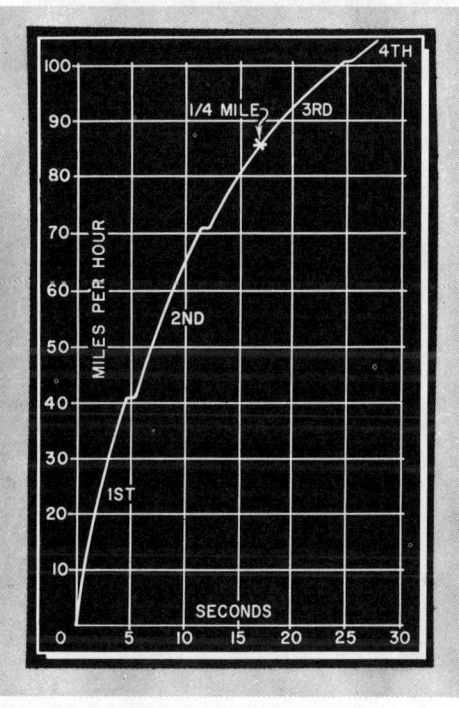

Acceleration chart shows maximum efficient wind-out in gears. Standing quarter was clocked at 16.9 seconds, at a speed of 86 mph.

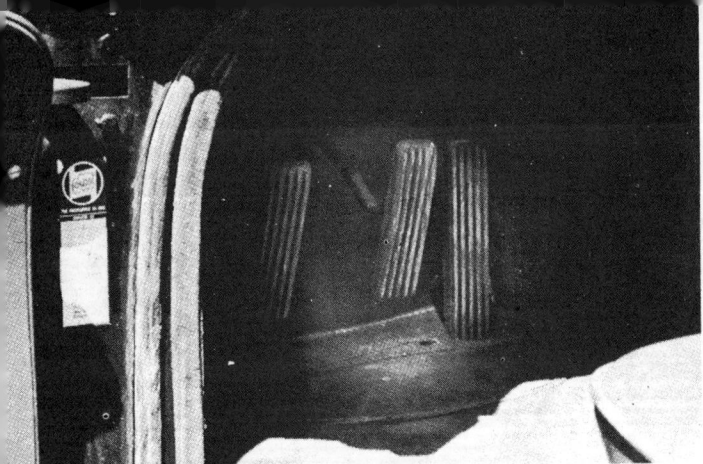

Pads on brake and clutch pedals have full foot length, though angle is a bit awkward for some people. Cockpit is snug, but adequate.

With the side curtains, and the very-hand-operated top in place, the 140 MC is effectively protected.

View of cockpit reveals seating, instruments, and leg room. Note speedometer placed on right which makes 140 excellent rally car.

The clutch pedal angles back sharply, forcing an uncomfortable contortion of the left foot, and disengagement pressure is on the high side. In compensation, the clutch action is silk-smooth and yet free from slippage even when worked hard. The shift pattern is conventional, with a positive and smooth remote control and a not-quite-foolproof spring latch for the left-hand reverse gate. First gear can be engaged silently from rest if the lever is first moved briefly into the second gear synchromesh, and if the car is rolling slowly first can be picked up directly without a sound.

Movement of the short lever to second gear traverses a wide arc, and in combination with a rudimentary degree of synchronization this is a very slow shift. Low gear should be used for smooth starts, and will carry the car well beyond any in-town speed limits, while second will bring you right up to highway cruising speed. If the town traffic is heavy with a lot of stop-and-go driving, you will note that the right foot must be pulled well back to get on the brake, while the special hard linings fitted to this particular car called for markedly high pedal pressure. A screened opening in the backing plate admits air to the front brakes, as well as water during rainy driving, and when the shoes are wet their behavior is anything but predictable. This is embarrassing in close company, and plates are available to seal up these vents when cooling is not a prime consideration.

An overall length of fourteen and a half feet and a weight of a ton and a half point up the fact that the Jaguar is not a small car, and it confers few advantages in maneuvering and parking. It does score highly for its very tight turning circle, which makes it surprisingly potent in gymkhanas. The shift of engine weight toward the front and the retention of the old caster angle on this car of 2½ to three degrees positive have caused the steering feel at low speeds to be distinctly heavy and potentially tiring. There is, of course, no play, and the strong springy return action of old Jaguars is still present.

The high caster, we were told, also contributes to the sometimes annoyingly insistent road reaction transmitted to the wheel by the fully reversible gear. Not restricted to any speed range, this occasionally sets up oscillations way out of proportion to the road ripples, and according to the representatives can be reduced by cutting the caster to 1½ degrees positive and altering the ball joint seating.

At low speeds and in traffic, then, the Jaguar calls for a strong hand behind the wheel, and does not appear at its best. As the road opens out and the lever can be moved across the gate to third, the MC enters its area of greatest competence. Movement between third and fourth is short and neat except for a fallible synchro on third, which is quieter than the other indirects and yet has a pleasingly mechanical whine that is part of the car's appeal. At high revs this is echoed under the hood by the dual cams and their chain drive, which have a similar machine-like whir. The familiar sophisticated Jaguar exhaust purr is heard only under wide throttle, and with some restraint the car's high performance can be used fully without advertising the fact (The old M's *did* sound nice, though).

Fame has deservedly come to the XK engine for its rigidity and smoothness, which derive from the size of the seven main bearings and the stiffness of their supports and the crankshaft. In this department, it is utterly uncanny for an engine of this size, and this feeling of solidity plus the instant response to the throttle encourage free use of the gears and the revs. As mentioned before, this is fortunate since the C-type head doesn't get a real foothold until the 3000 rpm mark is passed. Beyond this point in second and third gears the nose comes up and the roadster begins a relentless rush forward. Third gear with its maximum around 100 is particularly nice and just right for position-

Although its new position is not discernible, twin-cam six was placed three inches forward on chassis. Note inclined radiator, and enameled exhaust manifold. Fuel feed is through two SU's of horizontal design.

SPECIFICATIONS — JAGUAR XK 140 MC ROADSTER

TOP SPEED:

Two-way average	121 mph
Fastest one-way run	124 mph

ACCELERATION:

From zero	Seconds
30 mph	3.0
40 mph	4.5
50 mph	7.1
60 mph	9.1
70 mph	14.8
80 mph	18.8

SPEEDOMETER CORRECTION:

Indicated	Actual
30	29
40	39
50	50
60	61
70	71
80	80
90	90
100	101

FUEL CONSUMPTION:

Hard driving	11.5 mpg
Average driving (under 60 mph)	18 mpg

BRAKING EFFICIENCY

(10 successive emergency stops from 60 mph, just short of locking wheels):

1st stop	66
2nd stop	63
3rd stop	58
4th stop	67
5th stop	63
6th stop	62
7th stop	59
8th stop	63
9th stop	62
10th stop	59

SPEED RANGES IN GEARS:

I	0-41
II	11-70
III	17-101
IV	21-121

POWER UNIT:

Type	6 cylinder, in line
Valve Arrangement	inclined OHV, twin overheads cams
Bore & Stroke (Engl. & Met.)	3.27 x 4.17 in. (83 x 106 mm)
Bore/Stroke Ratio	1/1.28
Displacement (Engl. & Met.)	210 cu. ins. (3442 cc)
Compression Ratio	8 to 1
Carburetion by	2 horizontal S.U.
Max. bhp @ rpm	210 @ 5750
Max. Torque @ rpm	218 @ 1000
Idle Speed	650 rpm

CHASSIS:

Wheelbase	102 ins.
Front Tread	51 ins.
Rear Tread	51⅛ ins.
Suspension, front	Unequal length wishbones, torsion bars
Suspension, rear	Live axle, semi-elliptic leaf springs
Shock absorbers	Girling tubular
Steering type	Rack and pinion
Steering wheel turns L to L	2¾
Turning diameter	33 ft.
Brake type	12 in. pressed drums, 2 LS front
Brake lining area	208 sq. ins.
Tire size	6.00 x 16 (Dunlop Road Speed)

GENERAL:

Length	174 ins.
Width	62 ins.
Height (top up)	52½ ins.
Weight, test car	3040 lbs.
Weight distribution, F/R	50/50
Fuel capacity—U. S. gallons	16¾

XK 140

ing and power out of open back road bends.

From a standing start there is a thumping rear spring windup but commendably little wheelspin. Once in high gear, cruising speed is largely a matter of circumstances, but we found speeds between 85 and 90 miles per hour mechanically comfortable.

For the first time on a production Jaguar, the brakes appear to be consistent and fadeproof under hard, fast road use. They do not yield the highest retardation for pressure exerted, but the combination of hard linings, venting and wire wheels has ensured that they will always be there when you need them. This is uncommon on a car as fast and as heavy as this, and has taken some five years to achieve. A remaining fault is a slight tendency toward nosediving on braking.

Weight Distribution

The forward engine shift changed the Jag's weight distribution from 48/52 to 50/50, and produced a notable improvement in its already good high speed handling. The chassis characteristic is one of very strong understeer, which confers excellent stability both in a straight line and on fast corners at the expense of some low speed responsiveness. As noted by top Jag driver Charlie Wallace in SCI over a year ago, it is now much easier to set up and hold an honest drift, and the steering is fully quick enough to allow precise control. The steering action also lightens as speed increases, and all reactions and responses become rapid and predictable.

Even at high speeds there is noticeable roll when cornering, but it doesn't affect control or intrude on the driver. The unsprung weight of the live rear axle shows up on bumpy corners, where the rear end as well as the rest of the car becomes light-footed and jumpy. Control can be maintained, though, as breakaway will not occur without plenty of warning.

This same sensitivity to small bumps shows up in the ride of the 140 MC, which is fitted as standard with the same one inch front torsion bars that used to be optional in "M" form. The resulting higher suspension rate has helped to improve handling. The ride is, however, comfortable under most circumstances and free from pitching.

A sense of well-being is also derived from the seats, which are much better than appears at a glance. Access to them is quite easy for a sports car, and the passenger can first sit down and then swing his legs into the car. The doors are well-hinged and latched, with a twist lock for the interior cord-type release. In spite of a lack of visible contouring, the seat backs provide good lateral support for the torso. Cushioning just strikes the medium between softness and firmness, and does not tire one on long trips.

The driver sits with his feet unusually high and the wheel right on his lap. Modifications to the interior together with seat and wheel adjustments have made it possible for many more people to drive the Jaguar comfortably, and leg and head room is now ample. In fact, the left foot has to choose between flopping about loose in a bottomless hole or resting gently on the clutch pedal. There is not too much left elbow room for the driver, but he can often make use of

Flap, between trunk and cockpit, in the unfolded position, yields enough room for assembled fishing rod, gear.

the door cutaway. The cockpit in general is adequate but small for a car as big as the Jaguar.

Instruments

Adjustment of the big-slim-rimmed steering wheel is made difficult by the proximity of the instrument box. The gear lever and pull-up handbrake are close at hand, but the clockwork direction signal switch is hidden in an almost inaccessible cranny at the left. Instrumentation is complete, and could hardly be better graduated and marked. In view of this, it's too bad that deep recessing in the dash has caused certain critical dial areas to be hidden from the driver's view. Minor controls and dash lighting are good, but a map-reading light is sorely missed.

Odds and ends can be stored in deep door pockets, whose flaps are heard to open when the doors are closed. The side curtains are stowed tightly in a bag which then fits in a shelf high behind the seats and above the folded top. Erection of this top is a clumsy process that can be refined with practice, and is almost worth the trouble. Fitting between the top and the heavy plexglas side curtains has been much improved and effectively withstands wind and rain. The same can't be said of the area above the windshield, which leaked freely on the test car in spite of three clamps.

As car speed rose above 100 miles per hour, the right side curtain moved and flipped open the right hand top latch. Simultaneously, three side snaps popped open and added to the sound and fury. While these conditions were peculiar to the SCI test car, they seem to be typical of what to expect. The same snaps were inadequate on the tonneau cover, and the owner would do well to install "Dot" fasteners all around. Visibility is much enhanced by raising the rear window flap, but without this the view to the rear is a very short and narrow one.

Body

The trunk itself is long and shallow, and the length can be increased even more by folding open a flap between the trunk and cockpit. With this open and the seat pushed forward, a bundle of skiis could be carried *inside* the car on the right, when the top is up.

Under the long, alligator-type hood the C-type head is an unalloyed joy with its red and polished aluminum finish, and the enamelled exhaust manifolds recall the classic era. The forward shift has made it a tight fit, however, and many electrical and carburetion adjustments are hard to reach from above. The plugs couldn't be easier to service, and the brake master cylinder reservoir is handy.

This latest revision of a time-tested machine is notably improved in the handling and braking departments, and this together with its smooth and surging power make it a delight to drive at high speeds over long distances on fast, winding roads. If used in town it can be difficult to the point of being tiring, but this is not its purpose in life. The steering and the top provide annoyances at present, but these can be dealt with and are just part of getting so much car for such a reasonable price. This is, after all, the crux of Jaguar success, and the XK 140 series has ably enhanced the reputation of its forebears. —*Ludvigsen*

DROPHEAD: (Left) Jaguar's latest sports car, the XK 150, is available in two body styles. A single-piece wrap-around windscreen with slender pillars features. The chassis has single-pad Dunlop disc brakes all round.

★

FIXED HEAD version (below) shows the thicker "waist line" of the XK 150. Bolt-on disc wheels are standard, but centre-lock wire type are fitted on the special equipment model.

THE NEW JAGUAR XK 150

Disc Brakes and 3.4-litre 210 b.h.p. Engine in Successor to the XK 140—Basic Price only £1,175

LATEST model of a famous line, the Jaguar XK 150 goes a stage further towards realizing the modern ideal of the sports car. In the not very distant past, noise, discomfort, and a certain amount of temperamental behaviour were regarded as inseparable from the machine of abnormal performance. Jaguar Cars, Ltd., have already proved that these shortcomings are as out of place in a speed model as in a large and luxurious saloon.

The new Jaguar is immensely fast, one need hardly remark, but it is more roomy and practical as an everyday vehicle than its predecessors, with improved all-round visibility and a distinctly Continental line. On the mechanical side, the engine has better low and medium speed torque, which increases the already excellent top gear flexibility, but most important of all is the adoption of disc brakes, which really permit the full performance to be exploited.

The engine of the XK 150 is the latest version of the 3.4-litre with the B-type cylinder head. This unit is now standard on the Mark VIII and 3.4-litre saloons also. It delivers 210 b.h.p. (190 b.h.p. nett), which is the same output as the previous XK 140 had when fitted with a C-type head. The B-type head has the large valves that originally came from racing, but has slightly smaller ports, and twin S.U. type H.D.6 carburetters. The result is improved torque in the accelerating range. A new 12-blade fan operating in a cowl gives better cooling with less power wastage.

There are three optional transmissions. One can order the four-speed synchromesh gearbox either with or without a Laycock-de Normanville overdrive, or alternatively a Borg Warner automatic box may be specified. Where the "plain" gearbox or the "automatic" are employed, the ratio of the hypoid rear axle is 3.54 to 1, but the overdrive goes with a 4.09 to 1 rear end, giving an overall ratio of 3.19 to 1.

With a wheelbase of 8 ft. 6 ins. and a track of 4 ft. 3⅜ ins., the XK 150 is quite a compact car. Fixed head or drophead coupé bodies are offered, with occasional rear seats and adequate luggage accommodation. Both models have padding to protect the occupants in the event of a crash, but whereas the bodies with fixed heads are fitted with leather-covered instrument panels, the dropheads have anodized aluminium.

Compared with the XK 140, the new model is some 4 ins. wider at shoulder height, with large door pockets. The screen is now a single-piece wrap-around, with commendably thin pillars, and there is a large curved rear window. The bonnet line sweeps down to a lower and wider radiator grille, as on the 3.4-litre saloon.

Unlike the saloon, however, the body of the XK 150 is not integral with the chassis frame. This is a sturdy box-section structure, with independent front suspension by torsion bars and semi-elliptic rear springs. There are Girling telescopic dampers all round and rack and pinion steering.

The single pad Dunlop brakes have 12 in. discs. The operation is hydraulic, assisted by a Lockheed vacuum servo. These disc brakes are standard on all XK 150 models, and are fitted to all four hubs. A normal central hand brake lever operates on the rear discs by a mechanical hookup.

In its least costly form, the car comes with bolt-on disc wheels. However, the slightly more expensive special equipment model has centre-lock wire spoked wheels, and in both cases the tyres are 6.00-16 ins. Road Speed. Other special equipment features are a dual exhaust system, foglamps, and windscreen washers.

A car such as this is primarily intended for long, fast journeys. The comfort of the seats and the driving position are thus of exceptional importance. Full advantage has been taken of the extra width and the larger glazed area to obtain an impression of space inside. There is no sensation of being "shut in", which is sometimes a disadvantage of coupés. The lower bonnet line makes the front mudguard fairings stand out more boldly, and the general impression from the driving seat is of a small, compact car with excellent all-round visibility. The 14-gallon fuel tank is a useful feature for long-distance travel, and the petrol consumption is very moderate for so fast a car.

Prices range from the standard model at £1,175 (£1,763 17s. including P.T.) to the special equipment model with automatic transmission at £1,440 (£2,161 7s. including P.T.).

JOHN BOLSTER.

ABBREVIATED SPECIFICATION

Car: Jaguar XK 150 fixed head or drophead coupé, prices from £1,175 (£1,763 17s. 0d. including P.T.) according to equipment.

Engine: Six cylinders, 83 mm. x 106 mm. (3,442 c.c.), twin overhead camshafts, 210 b.h.p. (gross), 190 b.h.p. (net) at 5,500 r.p.m., 8 to 1 compression ratio. Max. b.m.e.p. 155 lb./in.² at 3,000 r.p.m. Twin SU type HD6 carburetters.

Transmission: (1) Borg and Beck 10 ins. single dry-plate clutch, and four-speed gearbox with synchromesh on upper three gears and short central lever, ratios 3.54, 4.28, 6.2 and 10.56 to 1. (2) Same clutch and gearbox, plus Laycock-de Normanville overdrive, ratios 3.19 o/d., 4.09, 4.95, 7.16 and 12.2 to 1. (3) Borg Warner automatic transmission, ratios direct 3.54, inter 5.08-10.9, low 8.16-17.5 to 1. Hardy Spicer open propeller shaft. Hypoid rear axle, ratio 3.54 to 1, or 4.09 to 1 with overdrive.

Chassis: Box section frame. Independent front suspension by wishbones, torsion bars, and anti-roll bar. Rack and pinion steering. Rear axle on semi-elliptic springs. Girling telescopic dampers all round. Dunlop single pad 12 ins. disc brakes with hydraulic operation and Lockheed vacuum servo. Bolt-on disc wheels, or centre lock wire wheels, fitted 6.00-16 ins. Road Speed tyres.

Equipment: 12-volt lighting and starting, speedometer, rev. counter, ammeter, fuel, oil pressure, and water temperature gauges. Heating and demisting. Two-speed wipers. Self-cancelling trafficators. Plus foglamps and windscreen washers on special equipment models.

Dimensions: Wheelbase, 8 ft. 6 ins.; track, 4 ft. 3⅜ ins.; overall length, 14 ft. 9 ins.; width, 5 ft. 4¼ ins.; turning circle, 33 ft. Weight (dry), fixed head 25 cwt. 3 qrs. 16 lb., drophead 26 cwt. 3 qrs. 4 lb.

1957 CARS

STURDY rear bumpers are used on the XK150, doubtless with the American market in mind. Rear wheel spats are omitted on the new car. This view shows the very neat hood and sizeable rear window of the drophead version. The wire wheels are an optional extra.

The New JAGUA

Two New Coupé Models with Disc Brakes, a New Cylinder Head and Re-styled Bodies Giving Greater Internal Width

DISC brakes all round, the latest B-type cylinder head and re-styled bodies, which give considerably greater interior width without increase in overall dimensions, are the principal features of a new Jaguar XK150 model which is available in fixed-head and drop-head coupé versions. Other important changes include a wrap-around front screen in place of the former V type and much larger rear window area on both the fixed- and drop-head bodies. The overall effect is to provide improved performance, more room and greater stopping power in adverse conditions.

In view of the important part played by disc brakes in the successes of C- and D-type Jaguars at Le Mans and elsewhere, the adoption of this form of brake on the new XK series is of particular interest and, incidentally, is one more example of the old adage about racing improving the breed.

Of the latest Dunlop type (fully described in our issue of October 17 last year), the new brakes are applied to the rear as well as the front and in each case a single pair of opposed pads operates on a 12-in. disc. In addition, the rear caliper assemblies carry an additional pair of manually operated pads for the hand brake, which is of the racing fly-off type.

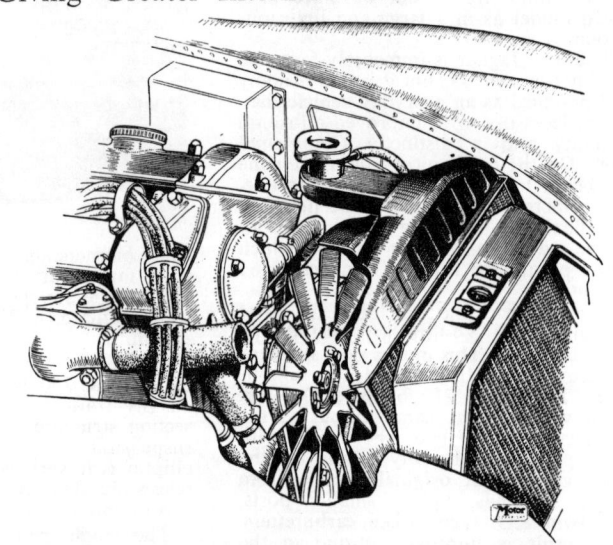

TWELVE BLADES are provided on the fan of the XK150 (in place of eight on previous XK models) in the interests of silence and efficiency. Note also the sharply sloping radiator core and small header tank with extended filler neck.

JAGUAR XK150 COUPES (Fixed-head and Drop-head)

Engine Dimensions
- Cylinders 6
- Bore .. .. 83 mm.
- Stroke .. .. 106 mm.
- Cubic capacity .. .. .. 3442 c.c.
- Piston Area .. .. .. 50.4 sq. in.
- Valves .. Overhead (twin o.h. camshafts)
- Compression ratio .. 8/1 (7/1 optional)

Engine Performance
- Max. Power (gross) .. .. 210 b.h.p.
- at .. .. .. 5,500 r.p.m.
- Max. b.m.e.p. .. .. 155 lb./sq. in.
- at .. .. .. 3,000 r.p.m.
- B.h.p. per sq. in. piston area .. 4.17
- Piston speed at max. power .. 3840 ft./min.

Engine Details
- Carburetters Two horizontal S.U. type HD6
- Ignition timing control .. Vacuum and centrifugal
- Plugs: make and type .. Champion N8B
- Fuel pump .. .. S.U. electric
- Fuel capacity .. .. 14 gallons
- Oil filter .. .. Tecalemit full-flow
- Oil capacity .. .. 15 pints (incl. filter)
- Cooling system Pump, fan and thermostat
- Water capacity .. .. 23 pints

- Electrical system .. .. 12-volt Lucas
- Battery capacity .. .. 64 amp. hr.

Transmission

	STD.	O/D	AUTO
Clutch:	Borg & Beck 10 in. s.d.p.		Torque converter
Gear ratios:			
Top (s/m)	3.54	4.09 (o/d 3.19)	3.54
3rd (s/m)	4.28	4.95	—
2nd (s/m)	6.20	7.16	5.08-10.9
1st	10.55	12.20	8.16-17.5
Rev.	10.55	12.20	7.12-15.2
Prop. shaft			Hardy Spicer
Final drive			Hypoid bevel

Chassis Details
- Brakes Dunlop hydraulic disc with vacuum servo
- Brake disc diameter .. .. 12 in.
- Friction lining area .. .. 31.8 sq. in.
- Suspension:
  - Front Independent, torsion bars
  - Rear .. .. Semi-elliptic
- Shock absorbers Girling telescopic (1¾ in.)
- Wheel type .. Steel disc (wire extra)
- Tyre size .. 6.00-16 Dunlop Road Speed
- Steering gear .. .. Rack and pinion

Dimensions
- Wheelbase .. .. .. 8 ft. 6 in.
- Track .. .. .. 4 ft. 3⅜ in.
- Overall length .. .. 14 ft. 9 in.
- Overall width .. .. 5 ft. 4½ in.
- Overall height .. .. 4 ft. 7 in.
- Ground clearance .. .. 7½ in.
- Turning circle .. .. 33 ft.
- Dry weight:
  - Fixed-head .. .. 26 cwt.
  - Drop-head .. .. 26¾ cwt.

Performance Factors
(At dry weight, f.h. model)
- Piston area, sq. in. per ton .. 38.8
- Brake lining area, sq. in. per ton .. 24.5 (disc brakes)

	3.54 axle	4.09 axle
Top gear m.p.h. per 1,000 r.p.m.	22.6	19.6 (o/d 25.1)
Top gear m.p.h. per 1,000 ft./min. piston speed	32.5	28.2 (o/d 36.1)
Litres per ton-mile	3520	4070 (o/d 3170)

XK150

UNMISTAKABLY Jaguar in outline, the XK150 has an extremely purposeful appearance. A wider car internally than its predecessors, it has a wrap-around windscreen with thin pillars and a very wide rear window.

The main pads are, of course, hydraulically operated and therefore completely self-compensating, whilst they incorporate the ingenious Dunlop self-adjusting system by which a clearance of 0.010 in. is at all times maintained between the pads and the disc surfaces when the brakes are released so that, although there is no possibility of binding, lost motion on the pedal is virtually non-existent.

This desirable condition is achieved by an ingenious arrangement of retractor pins and springs, the former serving an additional purpose of giving a visual indication of pad wear as their ends protrude through the cylinder block for easy inspection. Another point of technical interest is that a heat barrier is provided between each pad carrier and its actuating piston; the only direct contact between the two is via a ball-pointed plug, so that undue heat cannot be transmitted to the hydraulic fluid.

Brake operation is assisted by the latest Lockheed servo of the suspended vacuum type, which has a virtually immediate response. The combination of this and the self adjusting properties already mentioned should result in a braking system which is not only powerful and free from fade, but one which also gives immediate response to the lightest pressure on the pedal.

The new cylinder head is of the B type, as fitted to the latest Mark VIII engines. It represents a modified version of what is usually known as the C-type head and combines the same diameter port throat as the previous head but with the bigger valves of the C type. The result is to provide the same maximum output, 210 b.h.p. gross, as the Special Equipment version of the XK140, but at a speed 250 r.p.m. lower and with a slightly improved maximum torque at 1,000 r.p.m. less. The net effect is a very considerable all-round improvement on the standard XK140 unit and the same maximum output as the Special Equipment XK140 engine, but with greatly improved torque in the middle and lower ranges. The following table illustrates the differences between the three engines in precise detail:—

	Standard XK140	Spl. Equip. XK140	Standard XK150
Max. power (gross)	190 b.h.p.	210 b.h.p.	210 b.h.p.
at	5,500 r.p.m.	5,750 r.p.m.	5,500 r.p.m.
Max. torque	203 lb./ft.	213 lb./ft.	215 lb./ft.
at	3,000 r.p.m.	4,000 r.p.m.	3,000 r.p.m.

The XK150 engine also has the twin HD6 S.U. horizontal carburetters and the new inlet manifold used on the latest Mk. VIII, in which the water-heating gallery is separate instead of being integrally cast in order to give better control of heat transference. Another new under-bonnet feature is a 12-bladed fan in place of the previous eight-bladed type to provide an improved air flow coupled with a reduction in noise.

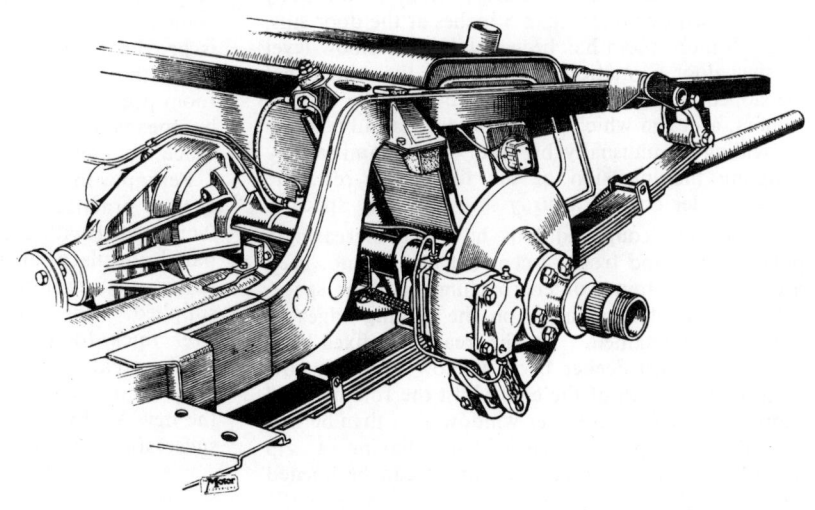

RACING LEGACY.— Dunlop disc brakes are fitted all round on the new XK150. This drawing shows the arrangement at the rear, which includes an additional pair of manually-operated pads for the hand brake, the lever of which has the usual sports-type fly-off ratchet. The main brakes are servo-assisted.

The New JAGUAR XK150

INTERIOR INNOVATIONS on the XK 150 include a leather-covered facia, the instruments grouped on a central panel and a padded crash roll on the scuttle. In the drawing the carpet has been turned back to show the foot-ramp extensions which now figure on the d.h. coupé as well as the fixed-head model. The car shown below has Borg-Warner automatic transmission which is an alternative to a synchromesh gearbox (with or without overdrive), controlled by a short central lever, just visible in the photograph on the left. This also shows the tipping seat squabs with their cut-away backs, and the two rear seats.

In other respects, the XK150 follows the now familiar specification of the XK140 and full details are set out in the data panel. A point to note, incidentally, is that buyers have the option of three forms of transmission, namely: (a) a normal four-speed single-helical synchromesh gearbox with short remote-control central gear lever; (b) the same, but with a Laycock de Normanville overdrive for top gear, operated by a switch on the facia panel (a slightly lower axle ratio being used in this case); or (c) a Borg-Warner fully automatic gearbox with the selector lever mounted on the base of the instrument panel in the manner now familiar on the 3.4-litre Jaguar.

As with the previous models, two versions are available, the standard model and a Special Equipment edition; the latter is fitted with knock-on wire wheels (in place of the pressed-steel type), dual exhaust system, fog lamps and windscreen washers.

Changes in the exterior shape of the car bring it more into line in many respects with the recently introduced 3.4-litre model than the former XK140. The bonnet and radiator grille have been widened considerably and, in place of the wing line dipping in a pronounced slope to the rear of the doors and then sweeping up over the rear wheels, it now follows through almost in a straight line. This has enabled the interior width of the body to be increased by no less than 5 inches at the door sills, whilst still more room has been obtained at elbow level by a new door formation; this enables the trim panel to be sloped considerably outwards towards the base of the doors, a design which has the additional advantages of providing an unusually big door pocket and largely eliminating the intrusion of the fixed arm rest, the window winder and an ashtray into the body space.

Both the new coupé editions have the increasingly popular wrap-round front screen, but this has not been carried to the extreme of encroaching on door space, and hinged ventilating panels on the leading edges of the doors are retained. At the rear, the fixed-head model has a much deeper back window which is now carried the full width of the car, whilst the folding-head version also has a much larger window area than before, the pliable transparent plastic used having a zip surround at the top and sides so that it can be opened

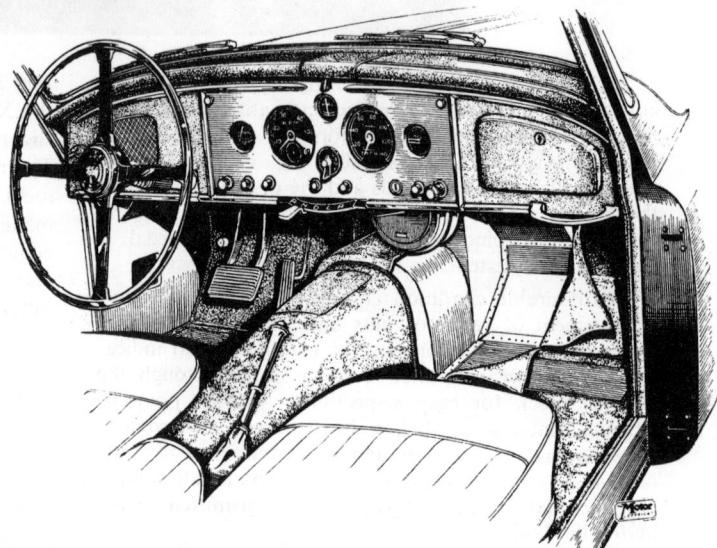

in hot climates. The coupé top of the drop-head model, incidentally, is of mohair and fully lined to conceal the hood mechanism.

The interior of both versions follows the same general planning as before, with separate adjustable seats at the front and occasional seats for one adult or two children at the rear. The increased width has, however, made a very considerable difference to comfort and, in this connection, the fact that a greater width of foot space is provided on each side of the propeller shaft tunnel is worth noting. Another point is that the extra leg room previously provided only on the fixed-head edition by means of foot ramps protruding into the bonnet space has now been applied also to the drop-head body.

Perhaps the most striking departure from usual Jaguar practice is the provision of a leather-covered facia board with the instruments grouped on a central panel in place of the previous figured walnut. As before, a comprehensive range of instruments is supplied. The edge of the scuttle is leather covered over thick foam rubber for passenger protection and similar treatment is applied to the top screen rail of the drop-head model. In other respects, the equipment of the new XK150 models is similar to that of their highly-successful predecessors.

LOOKING IN AT JAGUAR

Some notes on the famous Coventry firm and a description of the new Jaguar XK150

XK150 AND 2.4-LITRE.—Two typical Jaguars, the latest model on the left, photographed outside the link-road section of the famous Coventry factory. The badge on the left is that worn by the new XK150, proudly proclaiming Jaguar's victories in the Le Mans 24-Hour Race in 1951, 53, 55 and 56—although the Jaguar factory has since withdrawn from motor racing.

THE title does not refer to the several occasions on which Jaguar cars have appeared on TV. It refers to a quick visit by MOTOR SPORT to see how the world-famous Coventry factory, which manufactures only cars of the highest performance, has recovered from the unfortunate fire last winter and to examine and photograph the new XK150 which supersedes the so successful Jaguar XK140.

THE JAGUAR FACTORY

The present Jaguar factory lies at the foot of Windmill Hill on the Birmingham side of Coventry and the Jaguar executives have thoughtfully provided huge arrowed signs indicating just where visitors should turn off the ring-road. This factory consists of a 600-yard-long line of buildings, with triangulated glass roofs, divided centrally by the link-road, the latter now roofed over and part of the factory. The fire which broke out in a tyre store last winter destroyed the contents and roof of the left-hand line of buildings, where the assembly lines are situated, as well as some 200 cars. It is now history that Jaguar faced this severe set-back with characteristic vigour and were soon back in production, at first employing all the staff, but in two three-day shifts. About a fortnight after the disaster production was steadily mounting towards normal, and this quick recovery of very vital export trade is largely due to the courage of the workers, who set about helping to clear up the mess in the burnt-out shops and then worked uncomplainingly in the bitter cold of wall-less unheated shops. It is pleasing to pay, even belatedly, this tribute to another triumph of British tenacity in defeating adversity.

To revert to the factory, when Jaguar outgrew the original Swallow premises at Coleshill, following the tremendous sales-appeal of the s.v. S.S.90 and 3½-litre o.h.v. S.S.100 sports cars, they sold out to their neighbours, the Dunlop Rim and Wheel Company. Today, the factory they have occupied since 1952 is leased to them; during the war it was the Daimler shadow factory.

As we have said, the left-hand side is devoted to assembly, being divided from the right-hand section as you face this long factory from behind the office blocks by the entrance road. Here the gallant efforts of many fire brigades stopped the spread of the flames, which was fortunate, because under the link-road is a 500-gallon petrol storage tank! The right-hand side is the engineering section, where engines are built up and tested and bodies arriving from the Pressed Steel Company are painted and pre-mounted on the separate box-section chassis.

It is only fair to explain that in describing the present arrangement of the factory some evidence of the fire still exists. Thus trimming has to be done in an area of the engineering section and seats and cushions are stacked in part of the quietly-elegant reception hall, on one wall of which hangs a painting of H.M. the Queen, reminder of her visit to the Jaguar works. Moreover, part of the one million square feet of the factory area is still "out of bounds" and much of the roof is temporarily repaired and will have to come down. To enable repairs to be effected, a new 250,000 sq. ft. building is being put up to house some of the assembly lines and, after the main factory is fully rehabilitated, it is expected that this will be retained for storage and spares dispatch, etc.

The reduced area of the factory due to fire damage has resulted in some cramping of the assembly lines, which now double back one behind the other so that the fullest possible use can be made of the reduced shop area. However, all 4,000 workers are employed on a full five-day week and Sir William Lyons has led his team rapidly back to nearly full production. We, who live in a country partly dependent on motor-car exports, rejoice and give thanks that it is so.

The chassis frames, which arrive from Rubery Owen, are of box-section channel—except in the case of the XKSS, which has a tubular space-frame. Here it can be said that we saw only the prototype XKSS cars in the factory, for very unfortunately a batch of production SS Jaguars was destroyed in the fire and production had not recommenced at the time of our visit. However, the reception accorded in America to the one SS which was on the high seas at the time and thus arrived intact is well known to Jaguar, and no doubt the first customers' cars will arrive in New York any day now.

Some D-type cars were in the factory but production of these has ceased. Nor do Jaguar intend to take any further part in racing, at all events for the time being, which those who regard with pride the "Le Mans Winner—1951, '53, '55 and '56" plaques on their Jaguars must regret. The explanation is that the load on Chief Engineer Bill Haynes and loss of the ordinary mechanics who used to be taken from the production lines to work on the sports/racing Jaguars can no longer be tolerated. While they were in production 100 each were built of C- and D-type cars. Ecurie Ecosse now "wave the Jaguar flag" but they get only moral support from Coventry.

So production at Coventry is now concentrated mainly on the "2.4," "3.4" and Mk. VIII saloons, which use box-section chassis with torsion-bar i.f.s.

The chassis frames, with engines installed, proceed on trolleys while the bodies are mounted, overhead conveyors bringing seats, wheels, etc., to the assembly point and they then proceed at floor level for final assembly and finishing, two automatic chain-conveyors dealing with "2.4" and "3.4" saloons and a similar conveyor with the Mk. VIIM, Mk. VIII and XK models.

The bodies arrive unpainted and are stacked outside the factory under weather sheets until required. They then go through a long paint oven, lining one side of the body shop, on rotatable jigs, so that paint can be sprayed on adequately during the 13 hours each one spends in the oven. We write "paint" but, in fact, paint and cellulose have been replaced by synthetic enamel. XK bodies are welded-up in the factory, from pressed sheets delivered sub-contract. Castings also arrive from outside supply sources as Jaguar do not have a foundry, and these spend several weeks "in pickle" in the open. By purchasing complete saloon shells and XK body panels from outside suppliers Jaguar dispense with heavy presses, although they have small presses for the manufacture of seat-pans, body brackets, etc. Complete bodies are moved to the assembly lines on overhead electric hoists running on rails. Incidentally, Jaguar provide a weekly tour of the factory for interested individuals and parties, and neat overhead notices signify what each assembly line, or bay, is engaged on.

The engine assembly section of the Jaguar factory is extremely impressive. Here the famous twin-cam six-cylinder power units are built up and thoroughly tested. We were intrigued to see what looked like several hundred of these purposeful power units with their gleaming cam-boxes, stacked until required for installation in a

ONE OF THE JAGUAR PRODUCTION LINES with Mk. VIII saloons nearing completion.

chassis. There is no apparent standardisation in respect of machine tools and Landis, Churchill, Newell, Herbert, Maximatic and other lathes, grinding and lapping machines cope with crankshaft production. The individual care taken is notable. Crankshafts are examined carefully, journals hand-polished if necessary, and each one is dynamically balanced on Avery or Brockhirst electric balancing machines and then dynamically balanced again after the clutch assembly has been fitted. Before this, of course, a careful dimensional check has been made.

All engines are assembled, leisurely and carefully, by hand fitting, on a single automatic chain conveyor-line which starts at floor level as crankshafts are fitted into crankcases and continues on waist-high trolleys as the engines grow. Another chain-conveyor, parallel with this assembly line, carries " dinner-wagons " containing the required parts and components.

Towards the end of the line the gearboxes, with their short rigid levers, are fitted. It is significant that every Jaguar engine is thoroughly tested. A bay beside the end of the assembly line, to which completed power units are taken on 400-volt overhead cranes, is devoted to this testing. As exhaust gas and fluids are led away and fed from beneath the floor this shop is free from noise and fumes, although it is pleasantly warm !

Each engine is first run for $1\frac{1}{2}$ to two hours at 1,500-2,000 r.p.m., some on petrol, some on town gas after being equipped with Mangoletsi gas carburetters. The sump is then removed, flushed out, and refitted for the power check on fresh oil. Some 25 Froude water-brakes are in use for this purpose, and every engine is tested for output in each gear (running with its gearbox in place), carburetter adjustments are made, and finally a flash-reading of maximum b.h.p. is taken. The complete test occupies four hours per engine. If an engine is below power or faulty it is given a red label and rejected. Engines which pass their test satisfactorily are sprayed with lanolin to protect the high polish of their cam-boxes and other parts from damage by sea-air during shipment. This is carried out in a small covered spray-chamber in which inspection is facilitated by four-tier neon lamps.

Quite as a sideline Jaguar machine massive crankshafts for outside firms under contract, using a Hey Engineering lapper installed when they built war-time tank engines.

The thorough testing, following the careful hand assembly, of the car engines bears comparison with the best Continental practice, and it is on account of the time spent on the test-beds that large quantities of engines have to be stacked up, to keep pace with the flow of car assembly.

Each car goes for an 8-10 mile road test, first in the hands of a driver who reports any faults. These are rectified and a different driver, who is not told the findings of the first driver, goes for a further run, so that a double check is obtained. Temporarily the test department is situated in the aforesaid Dunlop factory. Each completed Jaguar is then carefully examined under neon lighting and body blemishes, etc., rectified. Twelve test-drivers and a total of 48 staff are employed in the rectification section.

At present the output is in the region of 69 cars a day, a week's output of some 345 Jaguars being composed, on an average, of 60 per cent. saloons, 40 per cent. sports cars. A board in the link-way giving the output from hour to hour, and indicating which departments are causing a lag, if any, acts as a spur to production.

RUN IN A 3.4-LITRE SALOON

Bill Rankin, Jaguar P.R.O., after taking us round the factory, drove us to lunch in a 3.4-litre Jaguar saloon with automatic transmission and later let us try it for ourselves. This roomy saloon, luxuriously upholstered in leather, with an imposingly deep, full-width walnut-veneer facia made in the factory, is an impressive " business-man's express." The seemingly unlimited supply of power which pours from the outstandingly smooth and quiet twin-cam engine is no surprise to those who have driven an XK model, but the supple yet roll-free ride, powerful brakes, and light steering possessing a taxi-like lock are amongst the pleasant surprises. The " 3.4 " is a very silent car, so that minor body noises are noticed. The Borg Warner automatic transmission embraces a wide brake pedal in lieu of a clutch pedal for those sufficiently dexterous to brake with either foot. The control lever for selecting reverse, low, drive, park, and neutral protrudes from the centre of the facia in a horizontal quadrant and is sensibly lettered. By flicking a switch on the right of the facia-sill middle gear can be held to any desired r.p.m. after being selected by a kick-down change, instead of top re-engaging at about 45 m.p.h. The engine ran-on after being cut at the conclusion of a short, fast drive. This fine 120-m.p.h. car is now available on the home market. It differs from the 2.4-litre in having S.U. instead of Solex carburetters, apart from the difference in engine size. It is distinguishable from the rear by its twin exhaust pipes, from the side by its non-spatted back wheels, and from the front by a wider radiator grille. So great is the prevailing demand for these saloons that there is no likelihood of an open version being introduced. Incidentally, asked if Jaguar care at all for history, Mr. Rankin reminded us that they own a fine example of Austin Seven Swallow saloon, on loan to the Montagu Museum together with a D-type Jaguar.

THE NEW XK150

The XK140 has been superseded by the new XK150, which we examined and photographed but were not invited to drive. This retains the same chassis and wheelbase as the XK140 but has as standard the B-type cylinder head developed for the Mk. VIII, which gives good torque at moderate r.p.m. while providing a maximum of 210 b.h.p. at 5,500 r.p.m., on a compression-ratio of 8.0 to 1, using twin S.U. H.D.6 carburetters. Three transmissions are available— a normal box with ratios of 11.95, 6.58, 4.54 and 3.54 to 1; a box with Laycock overdrive on top gear, giving ratios of 13.81, 7.60, 5.24, 4.09 and 3.18 to 1; or a Borg Warner automatic box giving ratios of 8.16-17.6 to 1, 5.08-10.95 to 1 and 3.54 to 1, selected mechanically. An outstanding feature of the XK150 is the use of Dunlop 12-in. disc brakes on all four wheels. Normally bolt-on wheels shod with Dunlop " Road Speed " 6.00 by 16-in. tyres are supplied, but centre-lock wire wheels are available as an extra.

Inside the coupé body of the XK150, which retains two folding occasional seats behind the two front seats, greater width and better visibility are immediately apparent. A wrap-round screen and partially wrapped-round large back window have altered both the appearance and the pleasure of occupying the body. Luggage space remains the same in area but is enhanced because the front wall of the boot hinges down so that golf-bags, etc., can be thrust through to the rear compartment of the body. The doors have very spacious storage wells and the familiar imposing facia is retained.

The weight of the fixed-head coupé is quoted as approximately 26 cwt. A drophead coupé is also available. With a top speed of approximately 130 m.p.h. and disc brakes as sure as the drum brakes on the very earliest XK120s were doubtful, the Jaguar XK150 should sell even more readily, especially in the U.S., than did the exceedingly popular XK140, which has contributed generously to Jaguar's splendid record of post-war export sales exceeding $52\frac{1}{2}$ million dollars.—W. B.

The XK150.

THE NEW JAGUAR XK 150

Its changes are subtle but surprisingly extensive

IN THE FALL of 1948 Jaguar showed an experimental roadster at the London Show. As is well known, this car stole the show, and by the fall of 1949 it had been tooled up and placed in production as the model XK-120.

Now Jaguar has announced the XK-150, and although the basic chassis is much the same as it has been for the past eight years, there are a number of important detail changes and, as can be seen here, the sheet metal is completely new. Significantly, no announcement has been made regarding the firm's mainstay in the line, the sports roadster, but it is generally understood that an open bodied two-seater will come along later. The important changes in the new line can be summed up as: new bodies, new brakes and a more flexible engine.

The new bodies offer a choice of either a hard-top coupe or a convertible and it is interesting to note that these machines are strictly personal cars, designed to be even roomier and more comfortable than before. The occasional seats for two are continued, and these are capable of genuine occupancy by two children or one adult. At the front end the appearance is almost unchanged except that the wider grille of the 3.4 sedan is used, tilted back somewhat. The new hood (or bonnet, if you wish) is wider at the front and slopes downward somewhat more than formerly for improved vision. Incidentally, this component and the rear deck lid are made of aluminum, whereas the rest of the body is steel.

A new semi-wrap one-piece windshield is used, special attention being paid to elimination of the usual entrance obstruction found in full-wrap windshields. At the sides of the body the fade-away fenders barely "fade," and this alone has made it possible to increase the interior width at shoulder level by 4 in.

Viewed from the rear, the new bodies appear much the same as before although the rear glass of the hard-top is completely new and is a tremendous improvement to most observers. As before the bodies are built by Pressed Steel Co., Ltd.

Interior changes include a switch to the instrument panel layout of the 3.4, but leather covered on the hard-top, anodized aluminum on the convertible. Wood trim has been discontinued and replaced by leather throughout.

As mentioned, the chassis is basically unchanged, with a Rubery-Owen-made box-type frame, a torsion bar front suspension and rack and pinion steering. The Moss gearbox has the same close ratios of the old "C" type, as used in the current 3.4 sedan, but the control lever is the same as formerly used in the XK. Overdrive is optional, as is a Borg-Warner automatic transmission. The Salisbury hypoid axle has a ratio of 3.54 on all models except when overdrive is specified. In such cases the axle ratio is 4.09, giving a 5th gear of 3.19:1, overall.

The new brakes are made by Dunlop and consist of a C-type mounting giving a pair of opposed pads or spots at each wheel. The company states that although they are much simpler than the multiple spots used on the "D" and the "SS," 30 successive stops from 100 mph, at one-minute intervals and at a deceleration rate of .7 g, can be made with absolutely no sign of fade; i.e., there is no increase in required pedal pressure. A conventional Lockheed booster is used to give low pedal pressures and a progressive feel to the brakes.

The engine is the new 210-hp "blue-top" type as used in the Mark VIII and 3.4 sedans. This engine has sealed S.U. carburetors and develops more torque (216 lb-ft) at a lower speed (3000 rpm) than any previous Jaguar dohc engine. It is also notably smoother and quieter than prior models, and a larger air inlet coupled with a 12-blade fan and a Marston radiator should insure improved cooling efficiency.

Although the new XK-150 coupes are in no sense sports cars suitable for occasional competition work, the name Jaguar has come to mean extraordinary performance, good roadholding and excellent value. The SS model takes care of the competition side, and these two new models will adequately carry on the company's tradition of quality at a low price. ●

New hood dips lower to meet canted 3.4 grille.

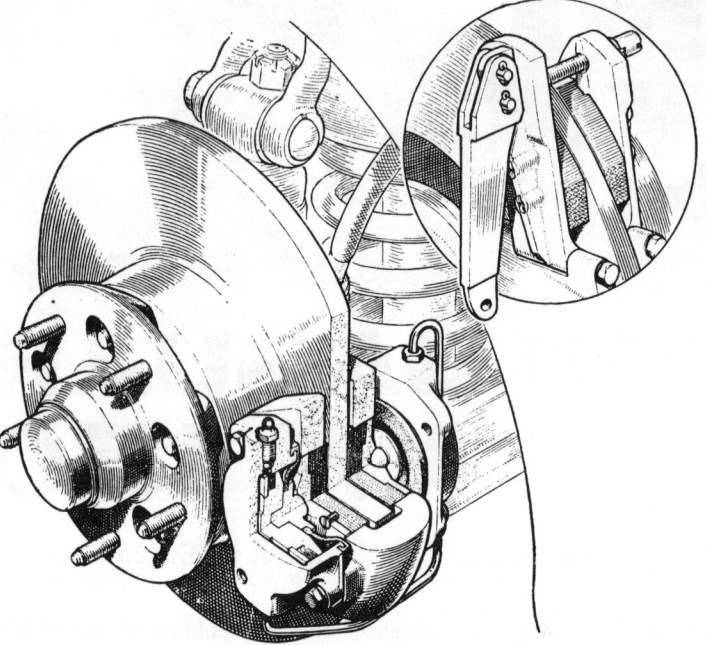

The production-model brakes have one pad on each side of the disc. Pads are self adjusting, and replacements can be installed without bonding or riveting.

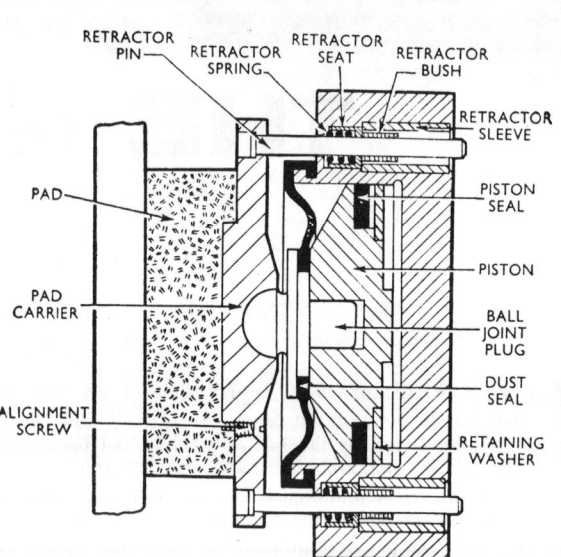

Retractors for the pads, as shown, were not a part of the disc brakes originally tested by Stirling Moss on a C-type Jaguar in 1952.

LE MANS

Ron Flockhart (3) takes checker to lead one-two-three-four Le Mans Jaguar win. Ninian Sanderson (right), was second in classic 24-hour French sports car race. Jaguars averaged 113.8 mph during run—six miles an hour faster than '55 record.

JAGUAR'S 24-HOUR PARADE

By AL BERGER

BRITISH-MADE cars tightened their apparently unbreakable grip on the greatest of all sports car races as Jaguars swept the top four places in the 25th anniversary running of the Le Mans 24-hour endurance race. The dark green sharkfinned D-types of Ecurie Ecosse won first and second places; the Ivor Bueb-Ron Flockhart car, which drove 2,732 miles at a record-breaking average of 113.85 mph, crossing the finish line just ahead of teammates Ninian Sanderson and Jock Lawrence. (Flockhart and Sanderson co-drove to victory last year.)

French- and Belgian-entered Jaguars were third and fourth, and to cap the British triumph, first and second place on Index of Performance went to the 750-cc and 1100-cc Lotus entries. The only other Jaguar, driven by Duncan Hamilton and the U.S.'s Masten Gregory, placed sixth.

There's a corner of France that will be forever English—or so it seems after this year's clean sweep of the Le Mans classic by British cars.

Best showing of an Italian car was fifth place of the Lewis-Evans/Severi Ferrari. The mighty Maserati and Ferrari teams, driving the most powerful sports cars they have ever built, wore themselves out in a furious early-lap duel which saw speed records toppling on nearly every round. The Italian teams were dogged with bad luck from the very beginning, as Stirling Moss' Maserati coupe had difficulty starting, and Peter Collins, who broke away to an immediate lead, lasted just 14 minutes before his Ferrari went out on the second lap with a broken piston.

On the 19th lap Behra, challenging Moss for second place behind Hawthorn, became the first man to achieve a 200 kilometer-per-hour lap. Hawthorn, in response to immediate signals from the pits, answered with a flashing 202.252 kph (126.2 mph) tour. On the straightaway, speeds were becoming frighteningly fast—Gregory was timed at 287.999 kph (179.8 mph).

But the pace was beginning to tell. After two hours and 10 minutes, Moss pulled in trailing black smoke, from a broken line pouring oil over the exhaust. Mechanics discovered that he also had a broken axle, and the coupe was through. Not long afterwards →

With engines screaming and tires smoking, 62 sports cars surge onto the Le Mans circuit at the start of the 24-hour race. Jag victory came after Italian teams blew themselves up in uncalled for speed sprints. The Jag pit controlled their cars like robots.

CONTINUED FROM PAGE 121

→ Maserati's hopes were completely shattered as Behra's co-driver, Andre Simon, brought in the 4.5 with a broken axle. This left World Champion Juan Manuel Fangio, who was being held in reserve until one of the Maseratis was in striking position, to sit out the race in the pits as a spectator. Then Ferrari's chances vanished, as first Musso, then Gendebien went out with the same trouble that had sidelined Collins—burned-out pistons.

Meanwhile a motor racing epic was taking place. In a manner reminiscent of Ralph De Palma's 1912 push-to-the-finish at Indianapolis, Roger Masson was pushing his Lotus, which had run out of fuel near Mulsanne, no less than four miles, back to the pits! As the gallant Masson collapsed, Co-driver Hechard took over the refueled car. Three hours later Masson took the car again, and despite the two-hour delay, finished 16th.

By midnight, Flockhart's Jaguar was in the lead, only 2 mins. 24 secs. ahead of the Aston-Martin driven by Tony Brooks. Then it was Aston-Martin's turn to see its hopes disappear. A 3.7 liter entry had already been retired, the Salvadori/Leston car was having gear trouble, and then, shortly after 2 a.m., Brooks went into the bank at Tertre Rouge, swung broadside to the road, and was hit by Maglioli's Porsche just behind it. Neither driver was seriously injured, but Aston-Martin and Porsche were out of contention.

At the finish, as the Jaguars swept across the line, the Coventry and Hornsey firms had achieved a really remarkable record. All five Jaguars which entered the race had finished, and they had barely missed making it a 1-2-3-4-5 sweep. All four Lotuses had finished, too, thanks to Masson's heroic effort. Of the first 16 places, 12 went to the five Jaguars, the four Lotuses, an A.C.-Bristol, an Aston-Martin and a Cooper. The British cars had conclusively proved that whatever handicap they must give their Italian rivals in top speed, they more than make up in reliability. Since Jaguar first won Le Mans in 1951, only the great Mercedes-Benz cars have ever been able to beat them there, in 1952 and 1954. Since the German firm's retirement from racing in 1955, Jaguar's domination of the 24-hour race has been complete. ●

CONTINUED FROM PAGE 94

with some more complicated and much more expensive cars, the Jaguar does perhaps spin its wheels a little more when getting off the mark, as one would expect. It is also occasionally possible to "feel" the axle on fast corners with a very bumpy surface. Nevertheless, the Jaguar is far easier to drive than some Continental cars with independent rear ends, and in general the chassis design represents a most effective compromise.

If the XK 140 is an extremely fast car, it is also a very docile one. It has absolutely perfect traffic manners, and entry and exit is easy, even for a lady in evening dress. The excellent all-round visibility and compact dimensions are also appreciated in town, just as they are on the open road. Above all, though, this is an ideal long-distance car, and would be sheer heaven for Continental touring.

The C-type engine, reinforced by the overdrive, makes a notable improvement in economy; 17¼ m.p.g. was recorded when driving the car very fast indeed. A more gentle driver could average 20 m.p.g., and still enjoy a 100 m.p.h. burst occasionally.

The Jaguar XK 140 is a very high class machine that has more delightful qualities than almost any other car on the market. I have long ago given up wondering how they make them for the money; for sheer value there is nothing to compare with them in the high-performance field.

SPECIFICATION AND PERFORMANCE DATA

Car Tested: Jaguar XK 140 coupé (Special Equipment Model). Price £1,291 5s. 0d. (£1,938 4s. 6d. including P.T.).

Engine: Six cylinders 83 mm. x 106 mm. (3,442 c.c.). Inclined valves in light alloy head, operated by chain-driven twin overhead camshafts. 8 to 1 compression ratio. 210 b.h.p. at 5,750 r.p.m. Twin SU carburetters. Lucas coil and distributor.

Transmission: Single dry-plate clutch. Four-speed gearbox with synchromesh on three upper gears and short central remote control lever. Laycock de Normanville overdrive, controlled by right-hand switch. Ratios, 3.19 (overdrive), 4.09, 5.59, 8.11, and 13.81 to 1. Open propeller shaft. Hypoid rear axle.

Chassis: Box section frame. Independent front suspension by wishbones and torsion bars with rack and pinion steering. Rear axle on underslung, semi-elliptic springs. Racing type wire wheels, fitted 6.00-16 ins. Road Speed tyres. Hydraulic brakes, front shoes self-adjusting.

Equipment: 12-volt lighting and starting. Speedometer, revolution counter, ammeter, electric clock, oil pressure, water temperature and fuel gauges, cigar lighter, heater and demister, flashing indicators, self-cancelling screen wipers and washers.

Dimensions: Wheelbase, 8 ft. 6 ins.; track, front 4 ft. 3 ins., rear 4 ft. 3¼ ins.; overall length, 14 ft. 8 ins.; width, 5 ft. 4¼ ins. Turning circle, 33 ft. Weight, 26¼ cwt.

Performance: Maximum speed, 121.6 m.p.h. Speeds in gears, direct top 105 m.p.h., 3rd 76 m.p.h., 2nd 52 m.p.h., 1st 30 m.p.h., standing quarter-mile 16.8 secs. Acceleration, 0-30 m.p.h. 3.4 secs., 0-40 m.p.h. 5.4 secs., 0-50 m.p.h. 7.2 secs., 0-60 m.p.h. 10 secs., 0-70 m.p.h. 12.4 secs., 0-80 m.p.h. 16.8 secs., 0-90 m.p.h. 21 secs., 0-100 m.p.h. 26.2 secs.

Fuel Consumption: Driven hard, 17¼ m.p.g.

CONTINUED FROM PAGE 100

It is a remarkable achievement on the part of the designers of the twin cam engine in the Jag to have produced an engine capable of putting out one horsepower per cubic inch, as this one does (210 bhp, 210 cubic inches) and still retain the flexibility of the unit as a whole. The car is docile in city traffic and yet goes like a bomb when you hit the open road at full throttle.

Many people place too much emphasis on the ability of a car to get from 0 to 60. There are many cars on the road that can outrun a Jag for a quarter mile from a standing start but acceleration does not stop at the end of the quarter mile with Jaguar. You keep going, and going, and going until you're doing 120 or better. And this from a car that is primarily designed for a high speed touring car is plenty in our estimation.

No timed top speed runs were made with the car, due mainly to the fact that El Mirage dry lake (where we test the faster cars) was no longer dry. Winter rains had drenched the area and not enough warm weather had come along to evaporate the inch of water on the surface. However, on the way to the desert test strip, speeds of 100 mph were attained with no strain on either the car or the driver.

Some cars when reaching speeds of 70 or 80 mph give you the impression that the body has become detached from the wheels and is more or less floating along over the road, and not necessarily in cadence with the humps and bumps. Not so the Jag. Both the driver and passenger had a complete feeling of confidence in the car. The maximum speeds we attained were dictated by the road conditions (traffic) rather than the limitations of the car.

The overdrive models, as tested, come equipped with a 4.09-to-1 rear end ratio which is reduced to 3.19-to-1 when overdrive is engaged. The Laycock-de Normanville overdrive unit works when the car is in fourth gear only and is engaged by a switch on the left side of the instrument panel. No let-up on the accelerator, or clutching, is necessary when engaging or disengaging overdrive. Just flip the switch and you're in or out of the gear with ease.

There are sports cars on the market now that out perform the Jaguar, there are sports cars that are lower in price, there are many that look better (some that look worse) and some with more quality. But, when the chips are down, it would be pretty difficult to find a car with the quality, performance and versatility of the Jaguar at anywhere near the price. Dean Batchelor ●

Long as ever and even more graceful, the hood now dips lower.

Viewed from above, broad rear-window and overall width are evident.

ROAD TEST JAGUAR XK-150

IT IS NOW almost exactly nine years since the 1948 Earls Court Show was laid on its collective ear by the introduction of the XK-120. The interval has been filled with most gratifying sales, both of the original model and of its derivations. The first all-new car in the XK line (for the general public) is the 150; a high-performing personal coupe or convertible—to be joined much later, perhaps, by a new roadster—it is unmistakably a Jaguar, and a prestige car by anyone's standards. What is not so obvious is its newness. Jaguar owners immediately spotted it, but other sports car drivers did not.

Whether this conservatism in the face of the money spent for new dies has been a wise policy, only the years (nine?) will tell. From a distance of 6000 miles, it is easy to say that a little more should have been spent in order to introduce another sensation comparable to the first XK-120. But there is always the chance that an explosion will backfire.

Although observations on a test car's looks sometimes do not sit too well with readers, here goes: The front end, a close examination of which discloses that every component has changed, retains its classic beauty. The "cab" has an appearance of lightness, correctly symbolizing the improved vision through the wider windshield and rear window. Its 4-inch width gain at shoulder height is too evident, reminding one more of a mature mother cat than a lithe young huntress. The rear, heaven help us, needs customizing! Its collection of chrome clutters the excellent basic shape. (Letters will be answered if time permits.)

Increased interior width is immediately evident on opening the door, as is replacement of all the wood on window sills and instrument panel with leather. We know it was impractical and we know it contradicts what we said in our second paragraph, but it was handsome as all get out and we're sorry it's gone. The panel layout, though not the finish, is now that of a 3.4, with a sponge-rubber-padded brow over it.

The newly curved windshield makes vision effortless and broad despite the long hood, now more sharply sloping. There is no Detroit-type distortion, and no dangling corner post to dodge while entering. Individually adjustable seats provide lasting firm comfort around town and promise the same for a trip. The steering wheel, of traditional four-spoke design, continues adjustable for different drivers or just for pleasant variation in arm position.

A touch, and no more, on the starter button hurls the engine into life, the starting carburetor audibly sucking in air until the thermostat shuts it off. Engine warm-up is neither fast nor slow, and running temperatures were indicated as comfortably cool.

The test car's clutch demanded too much stretch by comparison with the cramped throttle foot position, and gives us an opportunity to voice a loud warning: This was one of the prototype cars, reportedly No. 2, and there are other such around the country. A number of bugs in the prototypes will be absent from production models. Among them are the awkward accelerator and the absence of a rest for the left

Standardization comes to Britain: "Blue Top" engine is that of 3.4.

With all its changes, this is still a top spot for trips of any length.

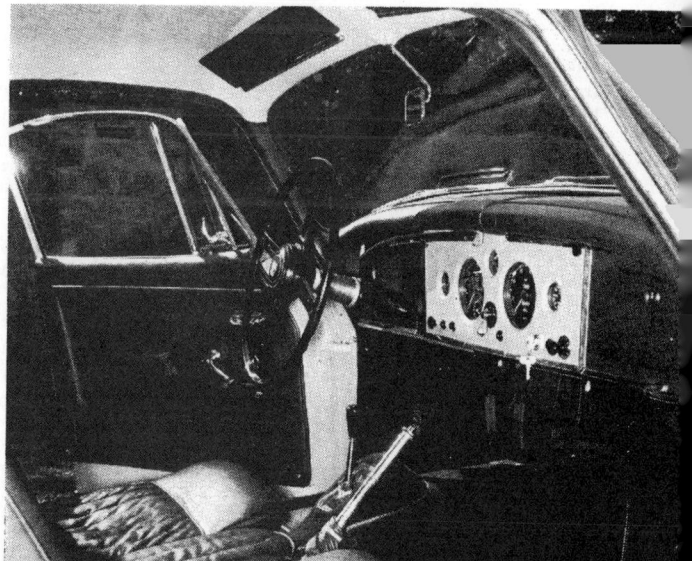

Above the seats is a door to the trunk, so long loads can be carried.

a sports car turns into a Gran Turismo

foot, the latter to be remedied by a convenient-sounding support from which the dip switch can be reached by rocking the foot.

Some clutch slip marred our more rapid take-offs, as did a particularly recalcitrant shift into second; neither should be considered characteristic, for the components are those used in the 3.4, which gives no trouble in these respects. The closely spaced third and fourth ratios come nicely into their element at higher touring speeds, with shifts back and forth just as positive and easy as they should be. The fact that the car is contented in third gear until close to the 100-mph mark can, of course, keep the whole matter theoretical in many localities.

The 150 is available with either the Borg-Warner automatic, in which a manual over-ride switch prevents engagement of the top ratio when the driver wants more acceleration or engine braking; or with the overdrive added to the manual gearbox, in which case selection of overdrive is by means of an electric toggle switch and possible on fourth gear only. With overdrive —to our mind the obvious choice for this car—the 4.09:1 rear axle replaces the 3.54 axle of the test car or the automatic version, and the possibilities of sheer driving pleasure become even more apparent. Not only does the top ratio (overdrive fourth) promise an advantage in lower piston speed with its 3.19:1 ratio; acceleration times will also improve, though shifts will have to be made at lower car speeds.

Referring back to the manual-shift car we had, it seems likely that fine tuning and optimum conditions could have given us up to 10 mph better than we recorded. The 150 was deliberately designed as a 130-mph car, and buyers will undoubtedly record that figure, if not on every try.

At the all-important other end of the scale, the Girling discs (described in the August R&T) were the subject of some controversy among us at first. Pedal pressure even with the power booster is so high as to make necessary a preliminary warning to a first-time 150 driver. The boost is proportional to pedal pressure, yet it took us the better part of a day to adjust to the sheer push that was so unexpected after driving other recent Jaguars. It was certainly no strain after that, and the outstanding record of the new brakes in resistance to fade made the inconvenience well worth while. The booster, by the way, is now mounted in the left front fender.

We should like to see various minor changes incorporated in the 150. Among them are a larger shift knob (and, some day, a synchronized low gear); larger glove boxes; doors lockable from the interior; instruments mounted in front of the driver; door checks, and better-placed ash trays.

The price given is intended only as a guide. Shipping, land freight and crating will vary it from city to city.

ROAD & TRACK ROAD TEST NO. 150

JAGUAR XK-150 COUPE

SPECIFICATIONS
List price	$4530
Wheelbase, in.	102.0
Tread, f/r	51.6
Tire size	6.00-16
Curb weight, lb	3090
distribution, %	50/50
Test weight	3410
Engine	6 cyl, dohc
Bore & stroke	3.27 x 4.17
Displacement, cu in.	210
cu cm.	3442
Compression ratio	8.00
Horsepower	210
peaking speed	5500
equivalent mph	127
Torque, lb-ft	216
peaking speed	3000
equivalent mph	69
Gear ratios, overall	
4th	3.54
3rd	4.28
2nd	6.16
1st	10.6

CALCULATED DATA
Lb/hp (test wt)	16.2
Cu ft/ton mile	92.7
Engine revs/mile	2600
Piston travel, ft/mile	1810
Mph @ 2500 ft/min.	83.0

PERFORMANCE, Mph
Top speed, timed	121.6
3rd (5700)	109
2nd (5750)	76
1st (5750)	47
see chart for shift points	
Mileage range	16/21 mpg

ACCELERATION, Sec.
0-30 mph	3.2
0-40 mph	4.8
0-50 mph	7.3
0-60 mph	9.5
0-70 mph	12.0
0-80 mph	16.0
0-90 mph	20.2
0-100 mph	25.8
Standing start ¼ mile	17.1

TAPLEY DATA, Lb/ton
4th	270 @ 57 mph
3rd	335 @ 50 mph
2nd	480 @ 40 mph
1st	off scale
Total drag at 60 mph, 113 lb	

SPEEDOMETER ERROR
Indicated	Actual
30 mph	31.8
40 mph	41.7
50 mph	51.6
60 mph	61.5
70 mph	70.9
80 mph	80.8
90 mph	90.1
100 mph	99.5
122 mph	121.6

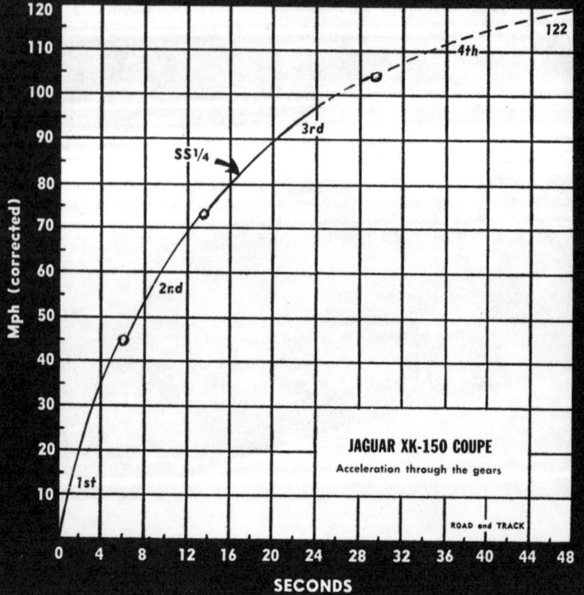

JAGUAR XK-150 COUPE — Acceleration through the gears

A full-bodied sporting coupé for two, the Jaguar XK150 has the well-bred road manners and agility that its lines suggest

The Autocar ROAD TESTS 1674

Jaguar XK150

IN *The Autocar* of 17 October 1952, a Road Test of a Jaguar XK120 fixed head coupé showed that the car would reach 50 m.p.h. in 7.5sec and 80 m.p.h. in 17.1sec. It had a maximum speed in top gear of 121 m.p.h. and weighed 27 cwt. Three years later the XK140 produced comparable figures of 7.5 and 16.9sec; the best speed in direct top was 111 m.p.h., and the car weighed 28 cwt. This car was fitted with an overdrive which operated on top gear, and an ultimate 129.5 m.p.h. was recorded.

The latest version—the XK150—has a slightly lower maximum speed than that of the XK140, but it has noticeably superior acceleration and more room in the restyled body—two valuable assets. The specification of the special equipment model XK150 (costing £117 basic more than the standard model) includes Dunlop disc brakes, wire wheels, a dual-exhaust system and the Blue Top 210 b.h.p. engine. The standard version has drum brakes and disc wheels, and its engine develops 190 b.h.p.

The manner in which this Jaguar goes about its business is impressive. The times recorded for the standing start acceleration tests are among the best obtained by this journal. The concrete surface of the Ostend-Brussels motor road was damp at the time and wheelspin was unavoidable, but the way in which the twin-overhead camshaft engine launched the car into the distance was quite memorable.

Completely smooth, with a turbine-like flexibility right up the speed range, this famous engine proved itself capable of a freak demonstration. Starting from rest with top gear engaged, the XK150 reached 100 m.p.h. in 36.4 sec. A little clutch slip was permitted to get the car rolling and then, as the engine revolutions built up, the car gathered speed quietly with no signs of protest such as pre-ignition or vibration. Exhaust noise is almost inaudible, and in this respect alone the car is very restful when driven fast. On a suitable modern motor road, the Jaguar will cruise steadily at 110-115 m.p.h. in overdrive. On one journey in England 57 miles were covered in the hour.

The Blue Top head of the special equipment engine has the larger valves of the C-type unit, but this does not result in a loss of torque in the lower speed range. Thus the XK150 is a tractable top gear car.

Its extra weight and increased frontal area (18.2 sq ft compared with the 17.5 sq ft of the XK140) are countered by the added power. The ability to surge in top gear from 30 to 50 m.p.h. or from 60 to 80 m.p.h., for example, is very restful. The car will trickle smoothly and economically through traffic without the need for constant gear changing; moreover, driven comparatively slowly on English roads with the maximum speed kept below 80 m.p.h., a very creditable fuel consumption of 22 m.p.g. was recorded. Best economy, with full use of overdrive, was 24 m.p.g.

The use of high cruising speeds on Continental roads, with 115 m.p.h. indicated often on the speedometer, brought the figure to 18.5 m.p.g. For hard driving on winding British roads, using the ready power to rush past slower-moving traffic, consumption was 16 m.p.g.

Cold weather starting was instantaneous, even when the car was covered with thick frost after a night in the open; the twin S.U. HD6 carburettors have an auxiliary starting instrument which cuts in according to engine temperature, and the functioning of this auxiliary unit can be detected as a faint hissing which ceases as normal operating temperature is reached. The mixture became over-rich before the starting carburettor cut out, and it was advisable to run the engine fast for a few minutes to clear it. The engine responds immediately at all times to a suddenly opened throttle, and there is no power roar. The carburettor intakes are effectively silenced by a large air cleaner mounted within the right front wing valance. An S.U. electric petrol pump is located rather inaccessibly for maintenance on the outside

A wide, curved rear window surmounts a tail liberally spread with chromed fittings. The quarter-lights are hinged for ventilation. Twin exhaust pipes betray special equipment specification

Jaguar XK150...

Disc brakes all round and wire wheels with centre-lock hubs are fitted to the special equipment model. To aid forward vision, the bonnet has a pronounced downward rake from a high scuttle

of the right chassis member. The 14-gallon fuel tank has an inadequate filler, which will not accept the full flow from a garage pump. When the tank was replenished, petrol fumes were noticed inside the car.

First gear is normally used to get the car moving from rest; second, into which the lever has a comparatively long travel, has a very potent usable range up to 58 m.p.h., with still a little to spare before the rev counter needle reaches the limit of 6,000 r.p.m.; there is, however, a noticeably large gap between the lower two ratios. Third, with its high maximum, is so quiet that on more than one occasion the driver was unaware that he had omitted to change up in traffic. The movement between the ratios is sweet, but the synchromesh mechanism on the car tested was scarcely adequate. In order to engage a gear silently with the car stationary it was necessary fully to depress the clutch pedal, which has a long travel. The clutch action was light, and there was no sign of unpremeditated slip during the testing. On full throttle standing starts there was no clutch judder, but there were occasional indications of axle wind-up. Normal upward or downward changes with the car in motion required full disengagement of the clutch, and double-declutching was desirable.

Fitted as an extra, the overdrive is worth every penny of its cost. Its function is more that of a fifth gear than what is usually understood as an overdrive. It is controlled by a neat lever switch mounted on the right of the facia, and it can be used at any speed. Occasionally during the performance testing there was a slight lag before the overdrive cut in. In most instances when the switch was moved at full throttle in top gear, the Laycock unit could be sensed rather than felt as it cut in. It enables long distances to be covered with a minimum of effort and fuel consumption.

Disc brakes of Dunlop manufacture are fitted to the Jaguar XK150 special equipment models, fore and aft, and their hydraulic actuation is assisted by a Lockheed vacuum servo. Their behaviour is superb, and the fade-free retardation always available permits an experienced driver to travel very quickly with confidence. The pedal pressures are light for normal use and have a desirable progressive increase up to maximum effect. Brake manufacturers consider that 1 lb of pedal effort per cent braking efficiency is a good design target—and this the XK150 approaches. There is no squealing at any speed.

The car pulled up square on wet or dry roads, completely free from judder or shake. Friction pad adjustment is automatic as wear takes place. Naturally, if the clutch is freed and the engine stalls, there is no vacuum assistance and extra pedal effort is required. The servo as fitted to the XK150 disc brake system does not deprive the driver of sensitivity of control.

Additional pads are applied mechanically on the rear wheel discs by the handbrake lever. Their power was not up to the high standard of the footbrakes, even when applied hard, they would not hold the car on a steep gradient. The lever, of the fly-off type, is adjacent to the transmission cover.

Suspension is free from roll and pitch, and on smooth roads the ride is comfortable at any speed. Even on Continental pavé, with the tyres inflated to high-speed pressures, there is no discomfort. No tyre squeal is heard when cornering fast, and on wet roads the car remains as though glued to the road in a most reassuring fashion. Of course, if the power is applied at the wrong time when cornering the back end will break away, but the driver senses that the car, correctly handled, will take care of him.

On rough roads some feed-back is transmitted through the steering wheel, but not to an unpleasant degree. The first-class steering is positive and reasonably light, with immediate response to the driver's movements; at slow speeds there is little self-centring action. At high speeds, the directional stability adds to the crew's confidence.

Control of the car is assisted materially by the driving

Left: Direct forward vision is unimpeded by the screen pillars. Deep overriders for the substantial bumpers protect the car from aggressive parking tactics. The frontal aspect has been kept agreeably clean and simple. Right: Neatly finished but rather shallow, the luggage compartment can be extended forward when a hinged flap above the rear squabs is lowered. The spare wheel sits in a covered recess beneath the luggage

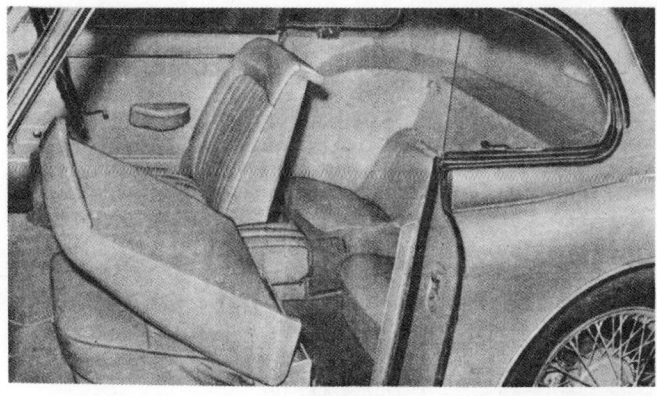

Mainly for children, the rear accommodation also provides extra luggage space. Trim is in leather of first-class quality. A four-spoked wheel with comfortable finger grips has a telescopic mounting on the steering-column. Handbrake and gear lever are adjacent between the seats

position. The four-spoke wheel is set at a near vertical angle, and is adjustable on its column for reach. The driving seat has a wide range of fore and aft adjustment, so that drivers of different leg lengths can be seated comfortably. The back rest is set fairly upright and the range of adjustment enables an alert and comfortable attitude to be adopted. A little more lateral support from both cushion and squab would be appreciated.

One of the important improvements in this latest, more refined XK model, is the increase of body width to give four more inches at shoulder height. The new wide, one-piece curved screen provides excellent visibility with little interference from the raked pillars. The top of each side lamp can be seen by the driver, and the red inset in the back of each lamp body indicates the car's width at night.

The long range beam of the head lamps allows speeds of up to 100 m.p.h. to be reached at night on suitable roads with safety. The roadsides also are well lit, and the dipped beam does not upset approaching traffic whilst providing sufficient illumination for kerbside cyclists. A reversing lamp is provided.

There is no apparent distortion through the sides of the windscreen, but it reflects the leather covering of the facia. High-speed motoring in the rain is made difficult when wind pressure tends to lift the wiper blades off the glass. A more firmly sprung blade arm would surely cure this—now an annoying fault on several fast cars which have curved screens. A two-speed wiper motor is supplemented by an induction-operated screen wash. The wipers do not clear the far ends of the screen.

The speedometer is obscured by the left hand when holding the wheel; apart from this, the instruments are legible and within easy vision from the driving seat although the main dials would be better located in front of the driver.

The twin loud-tone, high-frequency horns are operated by a push-button in the steering wheel boss. It is unusual for a Jaguar not to have a polished veneer facia and window rails, but the matching leather trim of the panel is tastefully carried out. There is a small, open cubby on the driver's side, and, on the opposite side, a similar compartment with lockable lid.

A plated grab handle is provided for the passenger's use, and there is ample seat adjustment on this side. Both the seat backs are hinged to allow access to the small rear compartment, but it seems a pity that the backrests are not adjustable for rake. The doors have no check stays and their lower edges easily become jammed on the average kerb or verge. On level ground, clearance of the tips of the doors is 9in unladen; camber and weight of crew reduce this to only 3 or 4in. It is not possible to lock either door from the inside, and there are no door pulls. A hinged ashtray is fitted low down in each door, and there is a tendency to knock one's knuckles on the open trays when operating the window winding handles.

Included in the standard equipment is a recirculatory heating and demisting system. This proved capable, with the assistance of the somewhat noisy booster fan (with no rheostat speed control) of keeping the screen clear, but the majority of the heat was directed to the driving side of the interior. It is understood that an improved heating system is likely to be in production by the time this report appears. With the front quarter lights open, a draught from the scuttle vents was felt, but this could be avoided to some extent by opening the rear windows. With any window open, the car was remarkably free from wind noise. Hand-operated fresh air inlets are provided at each side.

Behind the seats is space, on two small padded cushions, for two children or, transversely, one adult. Legroom naturally is severely limited—footroom even more so—and this accommodation can fairly be regarded as for emergencies only. The whole floor is trimmed with carpet which fits neatly. Below the rear window is an interior lamp which is lit when either door is opened, or which can be operated by a facia switch. A map light on the facia would be an appreciated addition.

The XK150 has only a shallow luggage compartment, but as the car is primarily a two-seater, the space behind the seats provides adequate extra capacity. A flap to which the rear seat squabs are attached hinges forward to allow lengthy items such as golf clubs to be carried. The compartment floor, which is unobstructed, is covered with a mat. Below is the spare wheel and a space for tools.

The luggage compartment lid has a recessed lamp and is locked by the glove box key. The supporting strut for the lid takes up valuable space in the locker when the lid is closed.

A familiar power unit on the world's sports-racing circuits, the twin-o.h.c. 3.4-litre engine has a splendid external finish. Items for routine servicing are mostly accessible though not the twin batteries in the wings behind the front wheels

Jaguar XK150...

Twelve chassis points require lubrication every 2,500 miles, in addition to the usual checking of oil levels. No starting handle is provided. Beneath the bonnet, the engine oil filler orifice in the exhaust camshaft cover is within easy reach, and the oil reservoirs for the clutch and brake master cylinders are accessible. Two 6-volt batteries are fitted, one in each front wing.

The Jaguar XK150 is undeniably one of the world's fastest and safest cars. It is quiet and exceptionally refined mechanically, docile and comfortable. As with most cars, there are a few body details which could be improved, but we do not know of any more outstanding example of value for money.

JAGUAR XK150

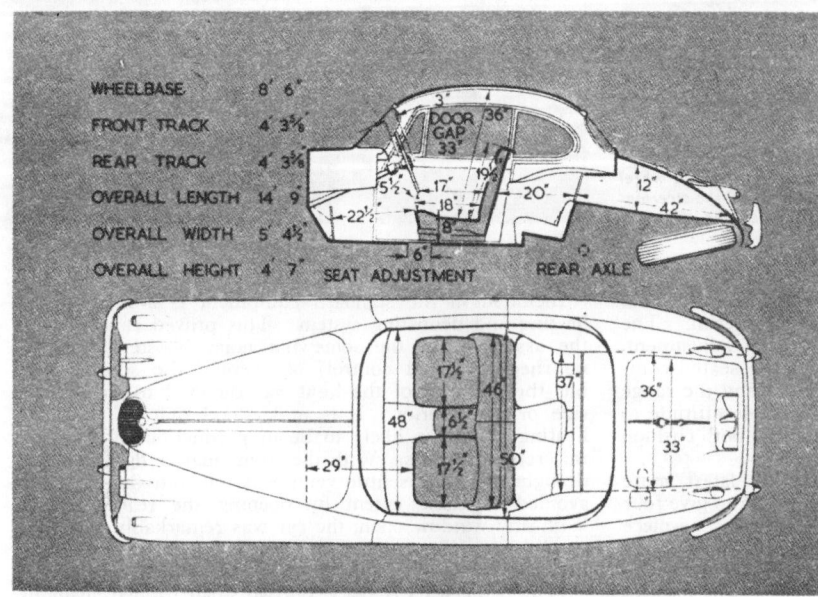

Measurements in these ⅛in to 1ft scale body diagrams are taken with the driving seat in the central position of fore and aft adjustment and with the seat cushions uncompressed

PERFORMANCE

ACCELERATION: from constant speeds.
Speed Range, Gear Ratios and Time in sec.

M.P.H.	*3.18 to 1	4.09 to 1	4.95 to 1	7.16 to 1	12.18 to 1
10—30	—	7.4	5.5	3.5	2.5
20—40	—	6.4	4.7	3.3	—
30—50	—	6.2	4.7	3.5	—
40—60	9.1	6.3	5.0	—	—
50—70	9.9	6.5	5.1	—	—
60—80	11.0	7.1	5.8	—	—
70—90	13.1	8.0	7.4	—	—
80—100	17.4	10.2	—	—	—
90—110	22.9	13.8	—	—	—

*Overdrive.

From rest through gears to:

M.P.H.	sec.
30	2.8
50	6.5
60	8.5
70	11.4
80	15.0
90	19.5
100	25.1
110	33.5

Standing quarter mile, 16.9 sec.

SPEEDS ON GEARS:

Gear	M.P.H. (normal and max.)	K.P.H. (normal and max.)
Overdrive (mean)	123.7	198.9
(best)	125.5	201.9
Top (mean)	114.0	183.4
(best)	115.0	185.0
3rd	70—91	113—146
2nd	45—62.0	72—100
1st	18—33.0	29—53

TRACTIVE RESISTANCE: 20lb per ton at 10 M.P.H.

SPEEDOMETER CORRECTION: M.P.H.

Car speedometer:	10	20	30	40	50	60	70	80	90	100	110	120
True speed:	12	20	29	38	48	56	66	76	86	96	106	110

TRACTIVE EFFORT:

	Pull (lb per ton)	Equivalent Gradient
Overdrive	250	1 in 8.9
Top	344	1 in 6.4
Third	440	1 in 5.0
Second	612	1 in 3.6

BRAKES: (from 30 m.p.h. in neutral)

Efficiency	Pedal Pressure (lb)
31 per cent	25
58 per cent	50
75 per cent	75
94 per cent	100

FUEL CONSUMPTION:
20.5 m.p.g. overall for 950 miles. (13.78 litres per 100 km.)
Approximate normal range 16–24 m.p.g. (17.6–11.7 litres per 100 km.)
Fuel, premium grade.

WEATHER: Bright and frosty, later dull with fog patches, damp surface.
Air temperature, 35–45 deg. F.
Acceleration figures are the means of several runs in opposite directions.
Tractive effort and resistance obtained by Tapley meter.
Model described in *The Autocar* of 24 May, 1957.

DATA

PRICE (basic), with fixed head coupé body, £1,292.
British purchase tax, £647 7s.
Total (in Great Britain), £1,939 7s.
Extras: Radio £35 approx.
Overdrive, £67 10s.

ENGINE: Capacity: 3,442 c.c. (210 cu in).
Number of cylinders: 6.
Bore and stroke: 83 × 106 mm. (3.26 × 4.17 in).
Valve gear: two overhead camshafts.
Compression ratio: 8.0 to 1.
B.H.P.: 210 (gross) at 5,500 r.p.m.
(B.H.P. per ton laden 184.3).
Torque: 216lb ft at 3,000 r.p.m.
M.P.H. per 1,000 r.p.m. on top gear, 19.6.
M.P.H. per 1,000 r.p.m. on overdrive, 25.1.

WEIGHT: (with 5 gals fuel), 28¾ cwt (3,226lb).
Weight distribution (per cent): F, 52; R, 48.
Laden as tested: 32½ cwt (3,646lb).
Lb per c.c. (laden) 1.06.

BRAKES: Type: F. and R., disc.
Method of operation: hydraulic, vacuum servo assisted.
Disc dimensions: F, 12in diameter; 276 sq in swept area.
R, 12in diameter; 276 sq in swept area.
Friction area: F, 15.9 sq in. R, 15.9 sq in.

TYRES: 6.00—16in.
Pressures (lb sq in): F, 23; R, 26 (normal).
F, 30; R, 35 (for fast driving).

TANK CAPACITY: 14 Imperial gallons.
Oil sump, 15 pints.
Cooling system, 23 pints.

TURNING CIRCLE: 33ft (L and R).
Steering wheel turns (lock to lock): 2¾.

DIMENSIONS: Wheelbase: 8ft 6in.
Track: F and R, 4ft 3⅜in.
Length (overall): 14ft 9in.
Height: 4ft 7in.
Width: 5ft 4½in.
Ground clearance: 7⅛in.
Frontal area: 18.2 sq ft (approximately).

ELECTRICAL SYSTEM: 12-volt; 64 ampère-hour battery.
Head lights: Double dip; 60-36 watt bulbs.

SUSPENSION: Front, independent, wishbones and torsion-bars with anti-roll bar. Rear, half-elliptic leaf springs.

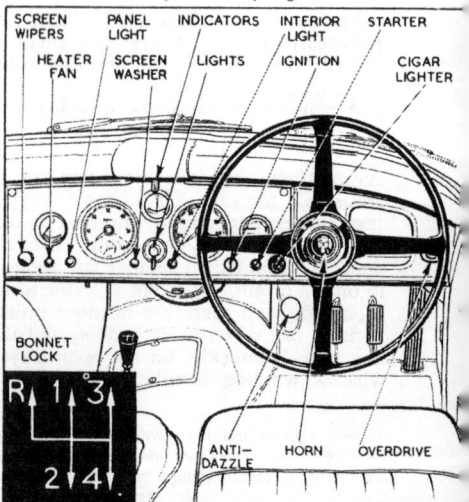

1958 CARS

THIRD BODY STYLE ADDED TO XK150 RANGE

An Open Two-seater JAGUAR

Three S.U. H.D.8 carburetters are used with the new cylinder head and induction manifolds on the S-type engine. Power output is 250 b.h.p. at 5,500 r.p.m. on a 9 to 1 compression ratio, and the engine has lead-bronze bearings for the mains and big-ends.

ALTHOUGH it was as an open two-seater that the original XK120 established the reputation of Jaguar Cars Ltd. as one of the world's leading manufacturers of very fast cars and marked the beginning of all the international sports-car racing successes which have followed, no two-seater model has so far figured in the latest "XK" range. The omission, it can now be revealed, was a result of the serious fire which extensively damaged the factory in February last year.

Both the fixed and drop-head coupé XK150 models were then almost ready for production and the two-seater was due to follow soon after, when production schedules were so rudely disrupted. Rather than delay the introduction of the XK150 range in toto, it was decided to press ahead with the fixed and drop-head versions (which appeared in May last year) and to introduce the two-seater when production permitted. Now the trio is again complete, although the new two-seater is at present an export-only model.

Three Versions

The word "trio" is not, perhaps, strictly accurate because the new two-seater roadster is, itself, offered in three forms, although apart from the wheels, they are of similar external appearance. All follow the general mechanical specification of the other XK150 models but differ in certain important details.

First there is the standard version with the 190 b.h.p. edition of the well-known twin o.h. camshaft "XK" engine. This model has Lockheed hydraulic brakes working in 12-in. diameter drums, with two leading shoes at the front and the large total friction - lining area of 189 sq. in. The wheels are of the bolt-on disc type.

Next comes the Special Equipment model with the B-type cylinder head which, in conjunction with two H.D.6-type S.U. carburetters and the dual exhaust system raises the power output to 210 b.h.p. at 5,500 r.p.m. Both this and the standard model have an 8:1 compression ratio but a 7:1 ratio can be supplied for markets where fuels are of low octane rating. The Special Equipment model has single caliper Dunlop disc brakes with servo assistance and wire wheels with centre-lock hubs. In addition, windscreen washers are fitted as standard.

Finally comes the S-type model which, although not intended as a competition car offers the maximum performance possible from an XK150. The general specification is the same as that of the Special Equipment model apart from the important differences which now follow.

These mainly concern the engine which, in the S-type, has a power output of 250 b.h.p. at 5,500 r.p.m. and a torque of 240 lb. ft. at 4,500 r.p.m. on a 9:1 compression ratio.

New Cylinder Head

These increases are achieved by the introduction of a new cylinder head and induction design in conjunction with three H.D.8 S.U. carburetters. The new cylinder head is known as the "straight-port" head because the inlet ports have a less pronounced curvature in plan view than those in the B-type cylinder head although, in fact, they still follow traditional Jaguar design embodying the Weslake patent of combining a curved port with a venturi entry to give improved filling at high r.p.m. The 2-in. S.U. carburetters are mounted on an entirely new three-section induction system, in which each carburetter serves two cylinders via induction pipes which are curved to combine a smooth gas flow with passages of equal length so that the ram effect in each case is equal. A specially shaped trumpet is fitted to the intake of each carburetter to extend the effective length of the inlet passages, the trumpets

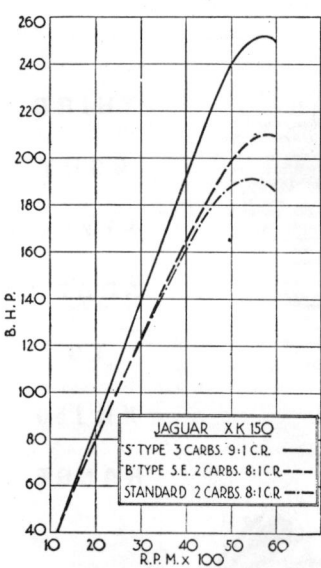

Comparative power curves for the three stages of tune of the XK150 models.

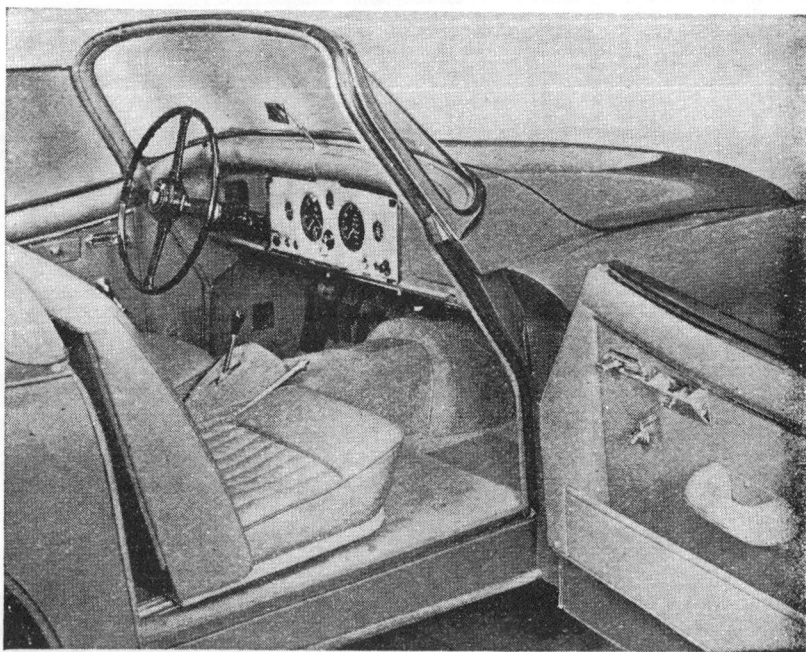

Fittings and finish are to typically high Jaguar standards; the side armrests are shaped as door-pulls, there is a wide pocket across the base of the door and an ashtray at the top. Instruments are grouped on a padded facia panel flanked by cubby-holes.

An Open Two-seater
JAGUAR

taking their supply of air from a steel-mesh, flame-trap type of air cleaner. The whole effect is to provide considerably better torque in the higher speed range. To ensure an adequate margin for the increased loads, lead-bronze bearings are used for the mains and big-ends.

In the transmission, a stronger clutch unit is used to take the extra torque, whilst the disc brakes are of a new Dunlop production type with quick-change pads. In this design, which is based on that used on the Le Mans cars, the pads can be changed simply by removing a single bolt which releases a retainer plate and allows the pads (which are rectangular) to be withdrawn.

In the case of the standard and Special Equipment models, buyers are given three transmission options: (a) normal four-speed synchromesh gearbox with central remote-control and a final drive ratio of 3.54 : 1; (b) the same but with Laycock de Normanville manually controlled overdrive on top gear and a final drive ratio of 4.09 : 1, giving an overdrive ratio of 3.19 : 1; and (c) Borg-Warner fully automatic transmission with the selector lever on the facia board and an intermediate-gear hold switch to prevent automatic changes into top when special conditions dictate; the final-drive ratio is 3.54 : 1. For the S-type, a synchromesh gearbox and overdrive, as in (b) above, is standardized.

The Same Shape

In its general design and styling the new two-seater is identical with the other models except for the hood and a forward extension of the rear panelling to eliminate the occasional rear seats and produce a concealed hood of easily manageable proportions. There are also one or two minor differences appropriate to an open car.

Elimination of the occasional seats has enabled the rear panel to be extended forward 21¾ in. to give a very sleek appearance from the rear. The interior of the boot itself is unaltered and the decked-over space aft of the individually adjustable front seats serves both to accommodate the hood when furled and to provide an extremely useful space for light luggage within the cockpit. Actually, the width at this point is 47 in. and the shape is such that it is possible to accommodate a bag of golf clubs.

The fabric hood offers good headroom and all-round vision. It is attached at the front to the screen by two toggle catches, whilst the rear and side portions are secured by the usual press-studs. Once the drill is known, furling and erection are straightforward and a reasonably practised driver can erect or lower the hood in just about 60 seconds.

An excellent refinement is the use of winding windows in place of side-screens

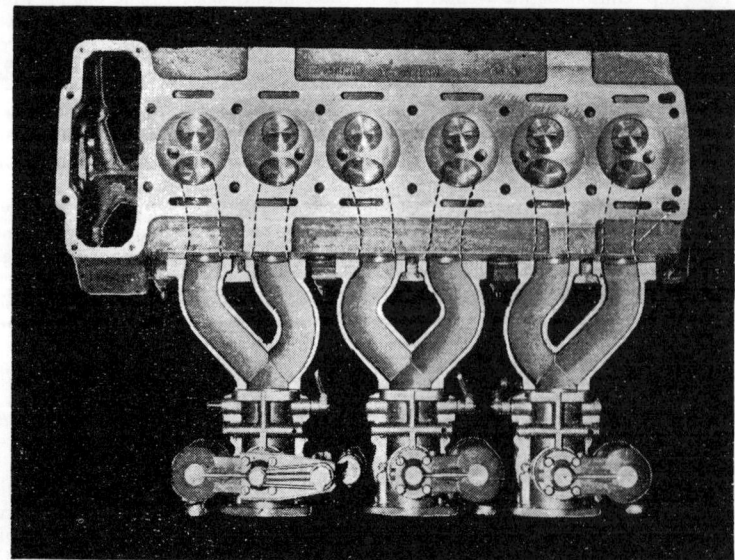

The new S-type Jaguar cylinder head with its three-piece induction manifold cut away to show the inlet passages. The paths of the ports have been dotted in to show the reduced curvature which gives rise to the appellation "straight-port" head.

An Open Two-seater JAGUAR

Easy erection of the hood is a good feature of the new two-seater model, the rear window being of pliable plastic material to assist folding; it can be zipped open to provide extra ventilation in hot weather.

and these are, of course, quite independent of the hood; when wound down, they disappear completely into the doors. The glass is 12⅜ in. deep whilst the fore-and-aft measurement at mid-height is 25½ in. The rear window, which is of pliable transparent plastic to assist folding without damage and can be zipped open for hot-weather driving, is 9¾ in. deep at the centre point and 39 in. wide.

Doors of similar design to the drophead coupé are used, but the interior trim is slightly modified, the ashtray now being placed near the top whilst the padded arm-rest is shaped to act also as a door-pull. There is a deep pocket formed in the lower portion. Another minor internal difference is in the mounting of the mirror, which is now placed in a central position above the padded scuttle.

The whole effect is both sleek and workmanlike, but this new model nevertheless offers a touch of luxury which is in contrast to the somewhat spartan qualities often associated with open two-seater sports cars.

As already indicated, this model is at present being supplied only for export, and no sterling prices are quoted. In U.S. dollars, prices for the Special Equipment model are $4,495 with synchromesh gearbox, $4,660 with synchromesh gearbox and overdrive and $4,745 with automatic transmission. The S-type model is available in "overdrive" form only at $5,020. No prices are yet available for the standard model. It should be noted that the dollar prices quoted do not include variations in delivery charges which occur in the U.S. according to locality.

JAGUAR XK150 2-SEATER

	STANDARD	SPECIAL EQUIPMENT		STANDARD	SPECIAL EQUIPMENT
Engine dimensions			**Chassis Details**		
Cylinders	6	6	Brakes	Lockheed hydraulic (2LS on front)	Dunlop disc with servo
Bore	83 mm.	83 mm.	Brake size	12 in. drums	12 in. discs
Stroke	106 mm.	106 mm.	Friction lining area	189 sq. in.	31.8 sq. in.
Cubic capacity	3,442 c.c.	3,442 c.c.	Suspension: Front	Independent (torsion-bar)	Independent (torsion-bar)
Piston area	50.32 sq. in.	50.32 sq. in.	Rear	Semi-elliptic	Semi-elliptic
Valves	Overhead (twin camshafts)	Overhead (twin camshafts)	Shock absorbers	Telescopic hydraulic	Telescopic hydraulic
Compression ratio	8:1	8:1	Wheel type	Bolt-on disc	Knock-on wire
			Tyre size	6.00-16 Dunlop Road Speed	6.00-16 Dunlop Road Speed
Engine Performance			Steering gear	Rack & pinion	Rack & pinion
Max. power	190 b.h.p.	210 b.h.p.	**Dimensions**		
at	5,500 r.p.m.	5,500 r.p.m.	Wheelbase	8 ft. 6 in.	8 ft. 6 in.
Max. b.m.e.p.	146 lb./sq. in.	155 lb./sq. in.	Track	4 ft. 3⅜ in.	4 ft. 3⅜ in.
at	3,000 r.p.m.	3,000 r.p.m.	Overall length	14 ft. 8 in.	14 ft. 8 in.
B.H.P. per sq. in. piston area	3.78	4.17	Overall width	5 ft. 4½ in.	5 ft. 4½ in.
Piston speed at max. power	3,840 ft./min.	3,840 ft./min.	Overall height	4 ft. 4½ in.	4 ft. 4½ in.
			Ground clearance	7½ in.	7½ in.
			Turning circle	33 ft.	33 ft.
			Dry weight	27¾ cwt. (approx.)	27¾ cwt. (approx.)
Engine Details			**Performance factors**		
Carburetters	Two S.U.	Two S.U. (H.D.6)	(At dry weight)		
Ignition timing control	Centrifugal & vacuum	Centrifugal & vacuum	Piston area, sq. in per ton	36.2	36.2
Plugs	Champion N8	Champion N8	Brake lining area, sq. in. per ton	137 (drum type)	22.9 (disc type)
Fuel pump	S.U. electric	S.U. electric	*Top gear m.p.h. per 1,000 r.p.m.	(a) 22.7, (b) 19.6, (c) 26.4	
Fuel capacity	14 gal.	14 gal.	*Top gear m.p.h. per 1,000 ft./min. piston speed	(a) 32.6, (b) 28.2, (c) 36.2	
Oil filter	Tecalemit full-flow	Tecalemit full-flow	*Litres per ton-mile	(a) 3,280, (b) 3,800, (c) 2,800	
Oil capacity	15 pt. (incl. filter)	15 pt. (incl. filter)			
Cooling system	Pump, fan & thermostat	Pump, fan & thermostat			
Water capacity	23 pt. (incl. heater)	23 pt. (incl. heater)			
Electrical system	Lucas 12 volt.	Lucas 12 volt			
Battery capacity	64 amp./hr.	64 amp./hr.			

*(a) 3.54/1 top, (b) 4.09/1 top, (c) 3.19/1 overdrive

Transmission	**Synchromesh Gearbox** Borg and Beck 10 in. s.d.p.		**B-W Automatic**
Clutch	Without O/D	With O/D	Torque converter
Gear ratios: Top (s/m)	3.54	4.09 (O/D 3.19)	3.54
3rd (s/m)	4.28	4.95	—
2nd (s/m)	6.20	7.16	5.08-10.95
1st	10.55	12.19	8.16-17.6
Rev.	10.55	12.19	7.12-15.2
Prop. shaft	Hardy Spicer, open	Hardy Spicer, open	
Final drive	Hypoid bevel	Hypoid bevel	

S-type Model

The S-type model differs from the Special Equipment model in the following respects:—ENGINE: Compression ratio, 9:1. Max. power, 250 b.h.p. at 5,500 r.p.m. Max. b.m.e.p., 172 lb./sq. in. at 4,500 r.p.m., b.h.p. per sq. in. piston area, 4.97. Carburetters, three S.U. (H.D.8). Sparking plugs, Champion N5. Fuel pumps, two S.U. electric. TRANSMISSION: Supplied only with synchromesh gearbox and overdrive. BRAKES: Dunlop disc with quick-change pads. Lining area 32 sq. in.

JAGUAR XK 150

JAG'WAR, JAG'YOU ARE OR JUH-GWAR'; no matter how one pronounces it, the XK is certainly *the* sports car which first caught the fancy of the general American public. So popular that even today stopping at a light in any sports car whatsoever may still elicit the question, "Is that a Jag?" not to mention the more prosaic "How much did it cost?" and "Wottle she do?"

How did all this come about? Is it the result of thousands of interviews of a carefully balanced cross-section of the American population by a team of Motivational Researchers? Were such answers tabulated, analyzed, studied and pondered upon, the conclusions then being passed on to the design and styling divisions at Coventry?

In a word; No.

The first XK, a 120, was cooked up in the fertile minds of Jaguar Cars, Ltd.'s Engineering Department in the late forties. It was based on their extensive experience pre-war in providing the English with cars which went quickly, looked quicker, and sold even more quickly. Unlike its SS predecessors, the XK 120 had a "real" racing engine with twin overhead camshafts and an independent front suspension sprung by the then new-fangled torsion bars, both features having appeared previously only on the most expensive equipment. The gearbox had four forward speeds, conventional enough in Europe to be sure, but in America quite extraordinary.

When to this triumvirate of engineering details was added a sleek roadster body that exuded speed as no dream car has since, the public's enthusiasm was spontaneous and overwhelming. The announced price of $4000 was too much for the credulity of many and predictions of the forthcoming bankruptcy of Jaguar Cars, Ltd. were freely offered.

Like so many predictions of things to come, this one not only failed to come true, the very reverse occurred. Tantalized by the special inducements offered by H. M. Government to dollar earners (larger than usual allocations of critical materials) and guided by their long experience in

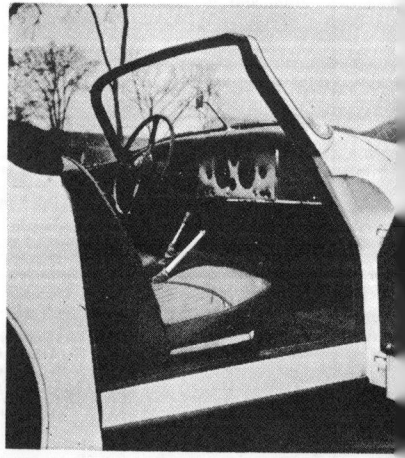

Padded cowl keeps dash light reflection off curved windshield. Grey leather instrument panel contrasts with red seats.

providing a lot for a little, the Coventry firm pushed the car into production.

It soon was skimming cream off the American market, its sales spurred on by the impressive announcement that a "stock" XK 120 had been officially timed at 132.6 mph. Actually it had a full belly pan, a metal tonneau cover and a small racing windscreen — all of them "available options". Convincing proof anyway that the everyday 120 could justify its designation.

No Hollywood starlet's rise to fame was complete without a pose alongside one of these fierce cats, and indeed, several genuine stars used XKs for personal transport.

Such fast machinery was sure to be raced, especially when it cost so little. And raced it was, with great success. It naturally followed that various refinements were introduced, especially in the engine where power increases from the original 160 to 180 and then 210 were offered.

In 1954, six years after its introduction at Earl's Court, the XK 120 was supplanted by the XK 140. The engine had been moved forward five inches, rack and pinion steering was incorporated and handling was much improved. The styling had been, if the phrase may be forgiven, face-lifted.

Another two and one-half years later, the completely restyled XK 150s were presented, but alas, only in coupe and convertible form. Featuring one-piece windshields and — worthwhile improvement — disc brakes all around, they certainly appealed. The coveted roadster, alas, was delayed for a year, its tooling apparently destroyed by that disastrous fire.

Now it is here, and what a change from the wind-and-rain-in-your-ears 120s and 140s. Which is to say it has wind-up windows. In our book this makes it a convertible, the plush XK convert being instead a cabriolet with the lined interior to its top. But never mind, why argue about words?

The roadster of our test is the hottest option, the S-type. The three S.U. carbs, the 9 to 1 compression, and its Gold Top cylinder head boost gross peak power from the Blue Top's 210 to 252 bhp at 5500 rpm.

Equal length passages are provided in the three separate intake manifolds to achieve equal ram effect at each cylinder. Despite this, the three carbs are closer together than the cylinder spacing would warrant in order to fit within the engine compartment. Inequalities in length are avoided by slightly kinking the inner pipes. These bends appear to be if anything, a bit sharper than those of the ports, the latter being straighter than on other XKs to improve the ability to fill the cylinders.

The close ratio Jaguar four-speed transmission is fitted and a Laycock de Normanville overdrive (optional on the normal 150) works on fourth gear only. The effect is to have a five speed box, with literally finger-tip shifts between 4th and 5th. The delightful thing about this particular OD is that you can make shifts without lifting your foot from the throttle. A click of the long-handled switch — it's mounted on the dash just to the left of the wheel — and the revs drop from a roaring 5500 to a purring 4275 — or vice versa. The exhaust note, a strong determined one, reminds us of Brick Reed's Green Hornet, but it shouldn't cause objections. On the normally engined roadster, the OD is optional. So is a Borg Warner automatic transmission.

Our entire Lime Rock shake down "cruise" was run with the top down, folded neatly behind the split seats. With the door windows down (what a luxury!), the curved windshield swept the air past us with a minimum of turbulence. All the comforts of a fast coupe with the splendid out of doors feeling of a raceworthy roadster. Winding up the windows (it's better to do this with the door open, to avoid working the soft rubber seal on the door post) provides even more protection, valuable in the case of strong side winds. For pleasant protection from too-bright sunlight, top up and windows down is the just right combination. But with both up, the designation roadster explains itself, for there are noticeable drafts at the top and rear of the joints between the two.

The foam rubber seats are very comfortable and provide good support. Even more welcome is the "dead pedal" on which to brace your left foot when charging round sharp right bends, as at Lime Rock where we gave the "S" its workout. Steering is just a shade on the strong side, as befits a car of this size and speed. It is precise and quick, two virtues which go well with the ever astounding power available at the rear wheels. This is one of the few reasonably priced sports car in which you can hold a four wheel drift on sharp turns for any length of time without losing most of your headway. And to utilize this ability, you need the quick steering which the XK provides. The clean response of the engine to the throttle helps, too.

The ample torque of the "S" type engine extends over a wide range, despite its peaking rather high at 4500 rpm. It copes more than amply with the roadster's curbside weight of 3190 pounds. Wheelspin can easily be provoked from a standing start and in these rather sophisticated days, it seems to us that better location of the rigid rear axle would more than justify the expense involved. For today's buyer,

Disc brakes all around give the 150-S fantastic stopping power from almost any speed. In 10-stop test—no fade!

Luggage space is more than barely adequate. Spare and tools are hidden under flooring out of the way of cases.

Hustling 150 "S" differs not at all externally from its more docile brother. Difference is all in GO!

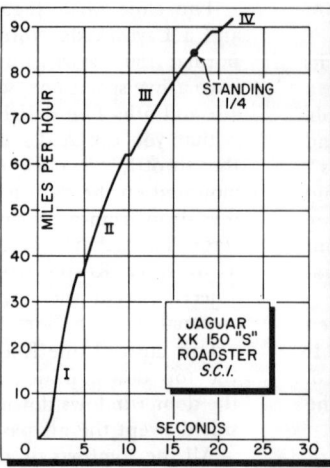

Compare this, the normal XK 150 engine, with the "S" power plant shown on the cover. Latter gives acceleration shown at right but it's not available in XK's other body style, the coupe shown below.

supplementary radius rods (such as Traction Masters) would seem appropriate, though how "stock" this would leave you is a good question.

Once underway, the acceleration is really sparkling, as a glance at the chart and the specs will show. A standing quarter time of 17.3 seconds is no mean feat for a car that would be just as happy trickling down Main Street. Though top speed no longer lives up to the type designation, at least not as we tested it, it's plenty high. We were unable to use our calibrated high speed test stretch; the best we can report being two runs in opposite directions on a fairly straight, level stretch. Both ways we indicated 4850 rpm in "fifth" and 134 mph on the about 10% optimistic speedometer. The former works out to be but 122 mph, the tach itself having been checked out in a lower gear at these revs. Allowing a bit for wheel slippage, this would seem to be just 120 mph. Neither we nor the owners of the car, Jaguar Cars, Inc., were impressed with this figure and the "S" is now in the shop to find out why it didn't go faster. My estimate is that it should do 130 to 135 mph—with the top up, of course. It may be that the "S" is geared just a hair too low (numerically) to reach this without a downhill run in, but nevertheless, this gearing does provide smooth, easy running, which in turn promotes economy and comfort.

Speeds and acceleration of this sort deserve the best in braking, and here the "S" is faultless. Our ten fierce stops from sixty were made with ease, the discs being servo-assisted, and though smoke and a strong smell began to stream through the front spokes toward the last, there was never any difficulty in stopping the car. Thanks to the difference in brake cylinder bores (2⅛" front, 1¾" rear), no wheels locked up, an all too frequent occurrence on lesser cars. There was no loss in pedal, either, the pads being self-adjusting. Stopping distance was strictly a function of tire and pavement adhesion, the pedal pressure required being consistently within reason. For convenience when racing, the pads on the "S" are quick-change.

There's no doubt about it, the "S" *is* intended for the SCCA's Production Sports Car category, where it should polish up Jaguar's glory, now somewhat tarnished from neglect. Our test car is the second "S" in the country, the first (whose engine is shown on the cover) being in the hands of Alfred Momo and Walt Hansgen who have already started polishing. At a NY POE price of $5095, it should soon be joined by many more.

JAGUAR XK 150 "S"

Price at all U.S. POE $5,095
U.S. Importer: .... Jaguars Cars Inc., 32 E. 57th St., New York 22, N. Y.

PERFORMANCE

TOP SPEED:
  Estimated .... 125-130 mph

ACCELERATION:
  From zero to   seconds
  30 mph 3.6
  40 mph 5.5
  50 mph 7.1
  60 mph 9.2
  70 mph 12.6
  80 mph 15.7
  90 mph 20.6
  Standing ¼ mile 17.3
  Speed at end of quarter .... 84 mph

SPEED RANGES IN GEARS:
  I 0-36
  II 11-62
  III 16-89
  IV 20-108
  OD 25-top

SPEEDOMETER CORRECTION:

Timed Speed	Indicated Speed	Timed Speed	Indicated Speed
30	30	70	65
40	38	80	73
50	48	90	82
60	56		

SPECIFICATIONS

POWER UNIT:
  Type .... Water-cooled In-Line six
  Valve Operation .... Dohc, 70° inclined valves
  Bore & Stroke .... 3.27 x 4.17 in. (83 x 106 mm)
  Stroke/Bore Ratio 1.28/1
  Displacement .... 210 cu. in. (3442 cc)
  Compression Ratio ...... 9/1 (8/1 except on "S")
  Carburetion by .... Two S.U. H.D. 8 (H.D. 6)
  Max. Power .... 252 bhp @ 5500 rpm
                          (210 @ 5500)
  Max. Torque .... 240 lbs.-ft. @ 4500 rpm
                          (216 @ 3000)

DRIVE TRAIN:

		optional ratios—Borg-Warner automatic
Transmission ratios	test car	
I	2.99	(2.30-4.95)
II	1.75	(1.44-3.08)
III	1.21	(1.00)
IV	1.00	
OD	0.78	
Final drive ratio	4.09 (3.19 in OD)	(3.54 with B/W or without OD)

  Axle torque taken by ... Rear springs

CHASSIS:
  Frame .... Welded channel sections
  Wheelbase .... 102 in.
  Tread, front and rear .. 51¾ in.
  Front Suspension .... Wishbones and longitudinal torsion bars
  Rear Suspension .... Rigid axle, semi-elliptic springs
  Shock absorbers .... Girling 1¾ in. telescopic
  Steering type .... Rack and pinion
  Steering wheel turns L to L.. 3½
  Turning diameter, curb to curb .... 33 ft.
  Brakes .... Dunlop 12 in. discs, quick-change pads
  Tire size .... 6.00 x 16
  Rim size .... 16 x 5K (16 x 5½K for disc wheels)

GENERAL
  Length .... 177 in.
  Width .... 64½ in.
  Height .... 55 in.
  Weight, as tested ...... 3190 lbs. (plus 300 lbs. crew)
  Fuel capacity .... 17 U.S. gallons

RATING FACTORS:
  Specific Power Output .. 1.20 bhp/cu. in.
  Power to Weight Ratio .. 12.7 lbs./hp
  Piston speed @ 60 mph .. 2130 ft./min (1665 in OD)
  Speed @ 1000 rpm in top gear. 19.6 mph (25.1 in OD)

ROAD TEST TWO JAGUAR ROADSTERS

REFERENCE to our file of back issues discloses that this is the fifth production Jaguar XK-type car we have tested, the first being May, 1951. That first test wasn't really much of a test either, which shows that both R&T and Jaguar have made a few changes in the interim—both have adhered to a basic policy, both have nevertheless made extensive changes.

In the case of the famous XK, the general specifications read almost the same today as they did when the car was first shown nearly 10 years ago. The cold but factual performance figures haven't changed much either, in 10 years. Horsepower has been raised, but the weight has also increased. The net result is a car which in normal form, as sold to the public, still goes from 0 to 60 in close to 9 seconds, and will, under favorable conditions, exceed an honest 120 miles per hour.

But now we have a new Jaguar, the XK-150-S, and that innocent-looking suffix letter makes another story. The XK-150-S will, in effect, replace the ill-fated XK-SS model (Road & Track, August 1957) which was not, and will not be, placed in production. The usual reason given for the dropping of plans for XK-SS production is "because of the fire," but no real production tooling ever did exist and it is much more logical to assume that costs with makeshift tooling proved to be far more than the announced $5600 price tag.

The detail differences between the two new roadsters are as follows:

	150	150-S
Head color	blue	gold
Ports	curved	straight
Pistons	8.0:1	9.0:1
No. carburetors	2, SU	3, SU
size	1.75 in.	2.00 in.
Clutch	std sdp	spl sdp
Bearings	babbitt	lead/bronze
Bhp, SAE	210	250
net	190	n.a.
Valve overlap	30°	60°
Std axle ratio	3.54	4.09
optional	4.09	none
overdrive	opt	std
Auto trans	opt	n.a.

In our opinion the 150-S model makes a lot more sense than the SS; it can sell at a profit for much less money, it is a practical and genuine dual-purpose machine and it will make a lot more friends for sports cars than the SS ever could. The 150-S will be available only in roadster form,

New grained leather, padded dash, and 4 inches more width.

Three SU's on 150-S draw air up through a vertical duct.

PHOTOGRAPHY: POOLE, JANES

TWO JAGUAR ROADSTERS

and only with the 4.09 axle and overdrive as standard equipment. As is well known, the 150-S engine is a production version of the famous D-type unit, with 250 brake horsepower.

As far as driving impressions go, the car seems to ride somewhat better than before, yet despite its being slightly softer it almost never bottoms and roll in tight turns is virtually non-existent. The tire equipment now consists of 6.00-16 Dunlop Road Speeds of a new design designated as the RS-4 (formerly RS-3's were used). As before, these tires have a slight tendency to squeal, even when the pressures, front to rear, are boosted from the recommended 23/26 to 30/35 per square inch. But, adhesion on dry roads is very good and more importantly, the former trait of total loss of adhesion in the wet has been completely overcome.

Rack and pinion steering is unchanged and is superb. However there is still a trace of road sensitivity which transmits itself to the driver's hands on certain types of rough roads.

Also, on very rough roads, and despite an enormously heavy X-type frame, the cowl structure displays a trace of shake which appears to be inevitable with open bodies—every American convertible we have ever tried displays the same fault, several having more noticeable wobble than the Jaguar. In normal to vigorous driving there is definite understeer, but as one approaches the famed "limit of adhesion" the steering characteristic becomes very nearly neutral.

The gearbox is the "C" type, close-ratio unit with no apparent changes. However, for reasons unknown, it shifts much easier and more smoothly than any previous Jaguar—though the synchromesh can be faulted in 2nd and 3rd if snap upshifts are attempted. Downshifts can be effected easily without double-clutching, provided that the lever is moved more deliberately with a slight pause before final engagement. First gear is not synchronized, and seemed a little noisier than earlier models, yet 2nd and 3rd were extremely silent: as good as or better than on any car we can recall.

The disc brakes, which we once erroneously described as Girlings, but which are supplied by Dunlop, are quite innocuous. They seemed, and without question are, completely adequate and pedal effort is very little heavier than for normal servo-shoe vacuum-assisted types. Hard use produced no pungent odors, but if the car was placed in a garage and the doors closed after a hard run, they were evident.

ROAD & TRACK ROAD TEST 179

JAGUAR XK-150-S

SPECIFICATIONS
List price	$5150
Curb weight	3160
Test weight	3460
distribution, %	49/51
Dimensions, length	177
width	64.5
height	54
Wheelbase	102.0
Tread, f and r	51.6/51.4
Tire size	6.00-16
Brake lining area	n.a.
Steering, turns	3.5
turning circle	33
Engine type	6 cyl, dohc
Bore & stroke	3.27 x 4.17
Displacement, cu in	210
cc	3442
Compression ratio	9.00
Bhp @ rpm	250 @ 5500
equivalent mph	141
Torque, lb-ft	240 @ 4500
equivalent mph	115

GEAR RATIOS
O/d (0.78), overall	3.19
4th (1.00)	4.09
3rd (1.21)	4.94
2nd (1.74)	7.11
1st (2.98)	12.2

CALCULATED DATA
Lb/hp (test wt)	13.8
Cu ft/ton mile	82.3
Mph/1000 rpm (o/d)	25.6
Engine revs/mile	2340
Piston travel, ft/mile	1625
Rpm @ 2500 ft/min	3600
equivalent mph	92.4
R&T wear index	38.0

PERFORMANCE
Top speed (o/d), mph	136
4th (5750)	115
3rd (5750)	95
2nd (5750)	66
1st (5750)	38

FUEL CONSUMPTION
Normal range, mpg	14/19

ACCELERATION
0-30 mph, sec	2.5
0-40 mph	4.0
0-50 mph	5.6
0-60 mph	7.3
0-70 mph	10.0
0-80 mph	13.0
0-90 mph	16.4
0-100 mph	21.4
Standing 1/4 mile	15.1
speed at end, mph	87

TAPLEY DATA
4th, lb/ton @ mph	315 @ 48
3rd	400 @ 42
2nd	570 @ 35
1st	off scale
Total drag at 60 mph, lb	100

SPEEDOMETER ERROR
30 mph	actual 31.5
40 mph	40.0
50 mph	48.3
60 mph	57.5
70 mph	67.0
80 mph	76.3
90 mph	86.0
100 mph	96.0

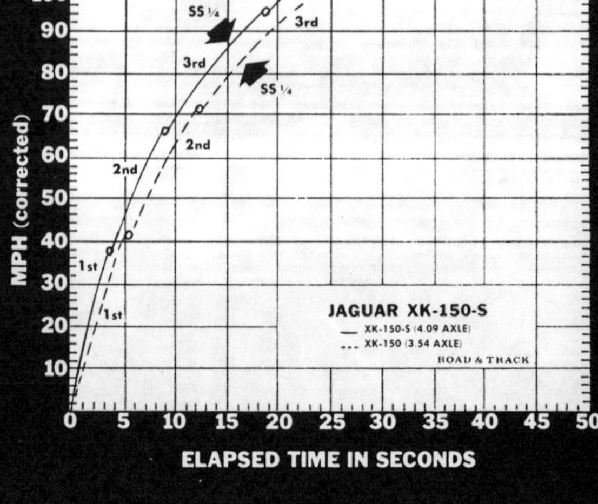

JAGUAR XK-150-S
XK-150-S (4.09 AXLE)
--- XK-150 (3.54 AXLE)
ROAD & TRACK

JAGUAR

Incidentally, these brakes are self adjusting for wear and the 150-S has segment-type linings rather than the circular pads of the 150.

The acceleration figures given in the data panel speak for themselves and were, of course, obtained without using overdrive. In fact, the sole purpose of the overdrive on the 150-S appears to be to make this model into a genuine dual-purpose machine. The extra "5th gear" would never be used in competition, yet it is extremely useful for normal highway driving as can be seen from the *calculated* data, which are based on the use of overdrive. The 4.09 axle gives lower maximum speeds in each gear than in a standard 150 roadster with 3.54 axle. We drove the standard roadster for two days and obtained some spot performance data, which are plotted as a dotted line on the acceleration graph. A brief comparison is as follows:

	150	150-S
Top speed (est)	125	136
Maximum in 3rd (5750)	109	95
Time, 0-60	8.9	7.3
0-80	15.1	13.0
ss ¼	16.8	15.1
Tapley, 4th	270	315
3rd	350	400

A Borg Warner automatic transmission and 2.15 torque converter is optional on the 150, though why anyone would want such a thing is beyond us (we admit some buyers can't drive anything else). The overdrive is a more attractive option since it gives in effect 5 speeds forward with the following overall ratios:

	std	o/d	auto
5th	—	3.19	—
4th	3.54	4.09	3.54
3rd	4.28	4.94	5.08
2nd	6.16	7.11	8.16
1st	10.6	12.2	17.5

Our test car did not have the overdrive, but the 15.5% higher numerical axle ratio would improve the acceleration considerably, probably knocking nearly a full second off our 0 to 60 time and close to .5 sec better elapsed time over the standing quarter mile. Prior experience with the British Laycock de Normanville overdrive indicates that the throttle should always be "eased" when shifting from 4th to 5th, to avoid slip. But driven with reasonable care, the device is truly worthwhile, particularly on long cross-country runs.

Externally the 150 is still unmistakably an XK, but the general lines and appearance have been softened and refined. More importantly perhaps, the seating position has been tremendously improved, the cockpit is roomier, controls are easier to operate and visibility is better.

Jaguar devotees will be pleased to note that the general quality level of paint, finish and trim are considerably improved, not only in first appearance but also in the matter of lasting qualities. No longer is there any varnished wood trim which needs refinishing in six weeks, and the chrome-plated ledge atop the cut-down door is a real boon for the casual arm-out-the-door driver.

The new wind-up windows make the term "roadster" rather incongrous, but they are certainly an improvement over the best of side curtains. The top, at last, has truly graceful lines and it has been carefully engineered to seal properly against water entry, yet to fold easily and compactly behind the seats. Special straps prevent rattles when the top is lowered and a very neat cover fills the space between the seat backs and the rear edge of the cockpit.

The seat adjustment has such a remarkable range that a 6-footer cannot depress the clutch pedal when it is all the way back, and the extra cockpit width inherited from the previous 150 coupes makes it feasible to place a small child comfortably on the padded leather driveshaft tunnel, between driver and passenger. A very small open glove box in front of the driver is useless because everything except used chewing gum falls or blows out and the opposite box, with locking lid, is very little larger. There are, of course, door pockets, and a rear trunk which will hold one medium-size suitcase.

The 150's quoted price ($4550) varies slightly from coast to coast and does not include local taxes and license fees. It does include wire wheels, disc brakes, heater, windshield washers and a tonneau cover. Our test car had chrome-plated wire wheels which cost $250 extra. Other optional extras are automatic transmission $250, overdrive $175 and limited-slip differential at $100. The 150-S roadster is scheduled to cost $325 more, but since overdrive and limited-slip differential are standard equipment, the p.o.e. list price on it will be $5150.

In the final, critical analysis the new Jaguar 150 and 150-S roadsters have a few faults, but among all the automotive connoisseurs we know (and we know quite a few) the Jaguar still rates as the best all-around value in the quality dual-purpose sports car category.

JAGUAR XK150S

LUXURIOUS LIGHTNING

Coventry's latest offering in a long line of superb sports cars is an opulent road machine that has no peer in its price bracket and is a match for many sports cars costing a good deal more.

SPEED AGE EXPERT TEST

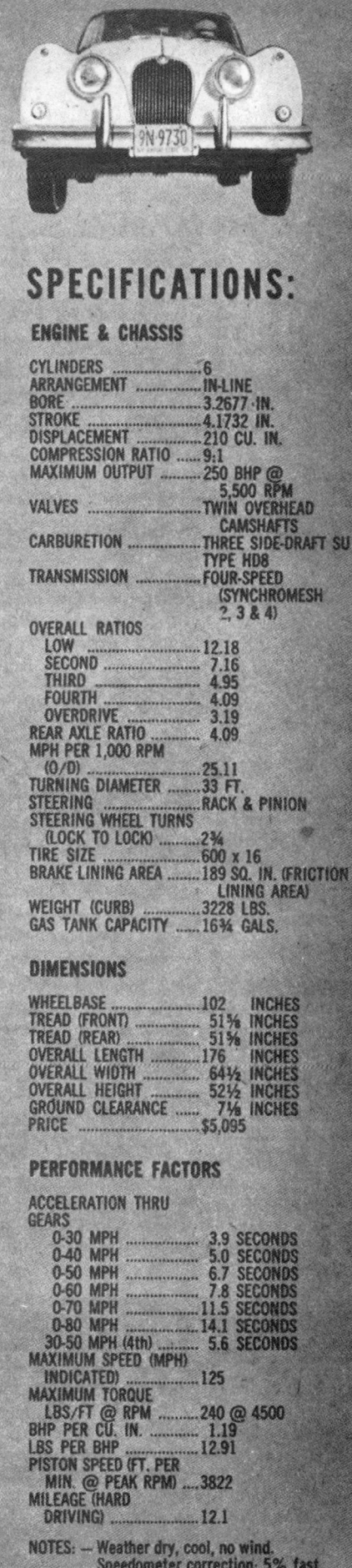

SPECIFICATIONS:

ENGINE & CHASSIS

CYLINDERS	6
ARRANGEMENT	IN-LINE
BORE	3.2677 IN.
STROKE	4.1732 IN.
DISPLACEMENT	210 CU. IN.
COMPRESSION RATIO	9:1
MAXIMUM OUTPUT	250 BHP @ 5,500 RPM
VALVES	TWIN OVERHEAD CAMSHAFTS
CARBURETION	THREE SIDE-DRAFT SU TYPE HD8
TRANSMISSION	FOUR-SPEED (SYNCHROMESH 2, 3 & 4)

OVERALL RATIOS

LOW	12.18
SECOND	7.16
THIRD	4.95
FOURTH	4.09
OVERDRIVE	3.19
REAR AXLE RATIO	4.09
MPH PER 1,000 RPM (O/D)	25.11
TURNING DIAMETER	33 FT.
STEERING	RACK & PINION
STEERING WHEEL TURNS (LOCK TO LOCK)	2¾
TIRE SIZE	600 x 16
BRAKE LINING AREA	189 SQ. IN. (FRICTION LINING AREA)
WEIGHT (CURB)	3228 LBS.
GAS TANK CAPACITY	16¾ GALS.

DIMENSIONS

WHEELBASE	102 INCHES
TREAD (FRONT)	51⅝ INCHES
TREAD (REAR)	51⅝ INCHES
OVERALL LENGTH	176 INCHES
OVERALL WIDTH	64½ INCHES
OVERALL HEIGHT	52½ INCHES
GROUND CLEARANCE	7⅛ INCHES
PRICE	$5,095

PERFORMANCE FACTORS

ACCELERATION THRU GEARS

0-30 MPH	3.9 SECONDS
0-40 MPH	5.0 SECONDS
0-50 MPH	6.7 SECONDS
0-60 MPH	7.8 SECONDS
0-70 MPH	11.5 SECONDS
0-80 MPH	14.1 SECONDS
30-50 MPH (4th)	5.6 SECONDS
MAXIMUM SPEED (MPH) INDICATED)	125
MAXIMUM TORQUE LBS/FT @ RPM	240 @ 4500
BHP PER CU. IN.	1.19
LBS PER BHP	12.91
PISTON SPEED (FT. PER MIN. @ PEAK RPM)	3822
MILEAGE (HARD DRIVING)	12.1

NOTES: — Weather dry, cool, no wind. Speedometer correction: 5% fast. At 57 mph, read 60.

By JOHN BENTLEY

THE last time I road tested an XK Jaguar was three years ago, when I put a well-tuned XK140-MC through its paces and discovered a startling improvement from a few extra horses and rack-and-pinion steering. After that, there was nothing new by way of a production Jaguar until 1957, when the XK150 Coupe made its appearance. The power output of this model was the same as that of the XK-140-MC (210 bhp) but at 250 rpm less (5500.) The 150 Coupe had a breath more torque (216 lbs/ft @ 3000 rpm, compared with 213 lbs/ft @ 4000), but the Girling disc brakes were completely new. Jaguar had finally been induced to discard those antedeluvian cast iron drums in favor of binders that would really stop the car and keep on stopping it.

Front longitudinal torsion-bar suspension and rear leaf springs were retained, but the front end components (the invisible ones) were largely redesigned. And, of course, styling was altogether new, though not as new as might have been expected from an enormously costly retooling job.

No sooner was the XK150 Coupe out, than enthusiasts began asking for a roadster version. At Coventry, they shrugged. Some day soon, hinted Jaguar, when we are not too busy, we'll get around to that roadster.

Well, here it is, complete with winding windows and a huge convex windshield impossible to remove, except with a hacksaw and blow-torch. In fact, up to waist level, the new XK150 roadster is simply the Coupe with the roof and pillars neatly sliced off. But that's only at a cursory glance. Jaguar went far beyond expectations by offering *three* roadster versions, each with additional horses and torque — and, of course, correspondingly higher performance. The menu goes like this: XK150 — 190 bhp @ 5500 rpm. XK150 Special Equipment Model ("B-Type cylinder head") — 210 bhp @ 5500 rpm. XK150S — 250 bhp @ 5500 rpm. It was the "S" that was offered to this magazine for testing by Jaguar Cars Inc., Eastern Jaguar Distributors, and I can truthfully say that I got behind the wheel with a great deal of curiosity.

Naturally, I expected the 150S to be good; you cannot just push an additional 40 bhp out of the exhaust pipe and forget about it. But I hardly expected it to be *that* good, speaking, now, of sheer performance. Taking the XK140-MC as a direct point of comparison, the new roadster (which weighs nearly 200 lbs more) is 1.7 secs. faster to 40 mph; 6/10ths of a second faster to 60; 3/10ths of a second slower to 80 mph. Nothing very

The XK 150S's unadorned silhouette features a large, permanently fixed windshield along wtih the classic Jaguar XK profile. The extra-wide doors permit easy entrance and exit.

Tester Bentley took issue with Jaguar's advertising its Le Mans wins on a medallion set into the chrome strip running down the trunk lid's spine.

Cylinder head on the 150S was formerly used on the D-Jags. Compression ratio is 9:1.

startling, measured by the stopwatch, but the intermediate gear ratios (low, second and third) all are higher on the new model, meaning that results as good or better are being obtained at lower rpm than formerly. Rear axle and overdrive ratios are the same, but the improvements in flexibility and "dig" are startlingly obvious. Second-gear acceleration between 2500 and 4500 rpm is head-snapping; yet the engine will haul away from 15 mph in fourth without ping or protest.

What have they done to the good old XK engine to get all this extra brawn? A number of practical things, several of them derived from racing. For instance, the cylinder head (painted Old Gold) is not the "B-Type" featured on the Special Equipment model, but a straight-port version known as the 35/40 head, because of the valve angle. This is the head formerly used on the racing D-Jag. Compression ratio has been hiked to nine to one. The camshafts offer more valve overlap; ignition timing is further advanced and three whopping two-inch SU HD8 side-draft carburetors with tuned "ram" intakes are installed.

Other logical niceties include lead-bronze racing type main and rod bearings; a special clutch with additional grip; and twin fuel pumps. The clutch is remarkably smooth and almost impossible to slip. But the rear-axle shudder when you try to make a scat getaway against the stopwatch, is a horrible thing to experience. Former XK's had this trouble, but it is now accentuated to a degree where you suspect the whole rear-end is coming apart. The reason is obvious. When you soar to outputs around the 250 bhp mark, with proportionate torque, a modern rear is required to cope with this power. A solid axle slung on a couple of leaf springs is no longer an adequate combination. And what is all this power for, if not to use it?

Obviously, when Jaguar recommends one heat range of spark plug for touring and another for racing, the firm intends the car to be driven in competition. Something should now be done about the rear end, to enable it to absorb the power delivered by the engine. Something, at least, with the function of a torque reaction member.

The test car was prettily finished in white with a contrasting black mohair top and red leather upholstery. The Roadster's bumpers are solid and functional, with backing plates even for the bumper guards.

There is a little too much exterior gook, such as a medallion added to the ornate chrome strip already coursing down the trunk lid. This medallion reads: "Jaguar XK-150: Winner Le Mans 1951-53-55-56-57." Justifiable pride, maybe, but somewhat misplaced. In Europe, everyone knows about Jaguar's fabulous string of racing victories. And over here, who cares? Certainly not Joe Blow in his Golden Sprocket Riviera De Luxe Mushomatic with triple headlights and nine parallel chrome stripes on the rear fenders.

The new Jag has, of course, the

With a whopping 250 bhp @ 5500 rpm under its hood, the XK 150S is loaded.

Although rack-and-pinion steering is a dream, car leans too much on turns

The 150S offers plenty of leg-room, luxurious seats. Headroom is limited.

Typical Jaguar dash-panel — strictly functional — has a business-like beauty about it.

Loads of trunk space make the 150S an automobile perfectly suited to long trips.

same interior roominess as the Coupe, and that is saying a good deal. Although it is strictly a two-passenger machine, each seat offers 324 sq. in. of lounging space (18 x 18 in.), and has a tilting back 20½ inches high. Door-to-door interior width of 51 inches makes it possible to allow a generous 10 inches of elbow room between driver and passenger; and legroom is aplenty, too. Seat height is 7½-in, which means that you really are sitting on something and not on the floor with your legs straight out. In addition, there are six inches of seat travel and the steering wheel (as in the past) telescopes in and out for a wide range of adjustment. With its big 38-inch doors, the convertible roadster is an easy car to get in and out of, no matter what your girth or age may be. The only measurement a shade undersize is the amount of headroom with the top up. A tall driver would absorb that scant 2¾ inches and be unable to wear a hat.

Once installed behind the wheel, you peer out through a vast panoramic windshield providing 737 sq. in. of rounded glass, free from distortion. The 380-sq. in. rear window also is of generous size for a soft top, but as usual with Jaguars, the rear view mirror belongs in a powder compact.

About 11 cubic feet of luggage can be stowed behind the seats and another seven in the trunk, which is certainly enough for two people taking a two-week holiday.

Gone is the elaborate figured walnut woodwork which used to characterize the interior of enclosed or enclosable Jaguars (it disappeared with the XK150 Coupe), but in its place is a pleasing arrangement of leather trim. Gray leather was used to trim the instrument panel of the test car, but all the new Jags have a leather upholstered crash pad filled with rubber, extending right across the dash. The doors, which are opened by push-buttons on the outside and sliding knobs on the inside, feature armrests and oversize map receptacles. The windows wind down neatly out of sight, and the top can be tucked out of sight in a very small space behind the seats.

Instruments are unchanged — a combined 6000 rpm large dial tachometer and clock, and a matching 140 mph speedometer; and the oil pressure gauge and water temperature indicator occupying each a half of the same dial.

The electric overdrive switch is in the left upper corner of the dash; but overdrive (whether switched on or off) is ineffectual below 1500 rpm in fourth gear. The standard XK150 and the Special Equipment model are offered with three transmission options: four speeds with or without overdrive, and a Borg-Warner automatic three-speed shift; but the 150-S can only be obtained with four speeds and overdrive. This system, by the way, affects only fourth gear and has no effect on the ratios of second and third. The 27% raise in ratio means an appreciable rpm drop and piston speed reduction

CONTINUED ON PAGE 159

THE JAGUAR XK150

Road-Test Impressions of a Really Fast, Luxuriously-Appointed Coventry-Built Coupe

THE excellence of the Jaguar is now proverbial and it was a pleasure to drive again behind the famous twin o.h.c. six-cylinder engine, which has won so many sports-car races for the Coventry manufacturer, while road-testing the latest XK150 coupé.

There is no question but that the Jaguar provides very real high-speed performance, not only in respect of a maximum speed exceeding 125 m.p.h. but because roadholding, steering and braking are in keeping, Clubroom accounts of creditable journey times being no excuse for exaggeration where the driver of an XK150 is concerned.

For an outlay of under £1,800 the purchaser of this latest addition to the twin-cam Jaguar family buys more safe speed and convenience than it is possible to obtain elsewhere. It can almost be said that the engine makes the car and the smooth flow of power from beneath the Jaguar bonnet is one of William Heynes' greater achievements. Here is a power unit of 3½-litres capacity, happy to burn normal pump fuels, which delivers its 210 b.h.p. completely unobtrusively and which runs safely to beyond 5,500 r.p.m. in spite of its size. Indeed, the "red" on the XK150 tachometer is between the 5,500/6,000-r.p.m. markings, yet this high-speed racing-type power unit is quite docile and will pull away from under 20 m.p.h. in top gear. The car tested had overdrive on the highest ratio, controlled by a flick-switch on the extreme right of the instrument board, and in overdrive, even at 120 m.p.h., engine speed is a mere 4,764 r.p.m., while 5,500 r.p.m. in normal top gear represents almost 110 m.p.h.

The Jaguar power unit is thus working at all times well within itself. Apart from this application of lazy power there is the continuous surge of acceleration carried high up the speed range. For example, to reach 60 m.p.h. from rest occupies 8½ seconds and 90 m.p.h. is attained from a standstill in under 20 seconds. The "century" is achieved in 25.2 seconds, while speed can be increased from 70 to 90 m.p.h. in a mere 7½ seconds, using third gear, or the XK150 may be accelerated from 80 to 100 m.p.h. in just over 10 seconds, in normal top gear. Such performance, allied to maxima in the gears of 18, 46, 69 and 115 m.p.h., with a genuine 125 m.p.h. available in overdrive top, which steps up the normal 4.09-to-1 ratio to 3.18 to 1, given a clear run, puts the Jaguar amongst the very fastest cars in the land.

A speed of over 100 m.p.h. and super-sports acceleration is not pleasurable under prevailing traffic conditions unless matched by adequate roadholding, braking and general controllability. The Jaguar is more than adequate in these respects.

The steering, very heavy for parking, lightens up at speed, although it is never really light steering, considerable castor-action, which spins the wheel through the fingers after a corner, having to be overcome. But this is accurate, if somewhat spongy, steering, asking 2¾ turns, lock-to-lock, the turning circle being small (33 feet). But it is steering which transmits some kick-back; the four-spoke wheel, with horn-button in the centre, has an instantly-adjustable column, and is set near to the vertical.

The suspension gives a rather dead ride but effectively kills road shock, yet is firm enough not to promote excessive roll when cornering fast. However, there is a sense of vintage-style flexibility about the chassis and although normally not noticeable, over really rough or ripply surfaces the back axle makes its presence felt, reminder that the action of the rear wheels is not independent. This may be because ½-elliptic springs are employed at the back, not the ¼-elliptic springs and ingenious linkage found on the 2.4 and 3.4-litre Jaguar saloons. The hypercritical may perhaps feel that the Jaguar chassis is not so advanced as the splendid power unit.

In general, however, the XK150 handles splendidly, especially in the hands of big-boned, bowler-hatted Britishers. The Dunlop RS4 Road Speed tyres do not protest audibly under rapid cornering, and the car feels safe up to its very high maximum speed. The brakes, in particular, are one of the outstanding features of this outstanding car. They are 12-in. Dunlop disc brakes applied with the aid of a Lockheed vacuum-servo. They really are superb, not only on account of their powerful retardation and complete absence of fade but because they are in no way fierce, stopping the car effectively without the driver having to be sensitive in order not to lock the wheels. There is scarcely any lag in the servo action, although, of course, if the engine stops heavy pedal pressure becomes the *modus operandi*. These Dunlop brakes are so unobtrusive that they might be mistaken for very good drum brakes—until the user gets back into a drum-braked vehicle, when he immediately awards the Jaguar very full marks! Under light pressure the brakes, however, emitted a horrid squeal. The fly-off hand-brake, on the passenger's side of the tunnel, is rather heavy to use but absolutely effective.

Adding to the joy of these excellent control factors is a short, rigid remote-control gear-lever mounted at an unusual but very convenient angle on the transmission tunnel. It is the sort of gear-change the driver operates as rapidly as his hand can move, so it is all the more unfortunate that the synchromesh just cannot compete and a nasty jar intrudes.

Indeed, in matters of detail the Jaguar disappoints, because there are items which seem to lack the touch of experienced drivers in the planning of this fast coupé. The seats, for example, are deep and

SHAPELY COUPE.—The view of the Jaguar XK150 seen so often by drivers of other cars. A medallion on the boot lid proudly lists the Le Mans victories achieved by Jaguar cars.

luxuriously upholstered but the driver would appreciate more support from cushion and squab, and on the test car the seat was insecure in its slides. The pedals are biased to the right, so that the driving position is not entirely natural, while so low is the seat that a driver of average height can only just see both front wings.

The steering-wheel rim is conveniently thin but not sweat-proof. Below it on the right extends a stalk for operating the self-cancelling direction flashers; this might be placed slightly higher up the column, a shade nearer the wheel.

The doors tend to bounce open unless slammed and, open, foul high kerbs. Curiously, they lack "keeps." The luggage boot is roomy if shallow and there is access to it from within the car, although small objects stowed thus soon slide inaccessibly to the back of the boot. The boot lid locks and has a self-propping strut, but it tended not to shut, one corner sticking open. The spare wheel lives below the luggage, under the floor.

Behind the seats, which possess folding squabs, are two (very) occasional seats, useful only for very abbreviated children. Occasionally petrol fumes made the interior of the car objectionable, usually after a spit back from a cold engine. The accelerator action tended to jerky running when opening up from low speeds. The doors have quarter-windows. When fully open, that on the driver's side tended to remove skin from the knuckles of the right hand as the steering wheel was turned, while dazzle from the sun on the plated beading along the base of the instrument panel occurred under certain conditions—minor criticisms, but ones which bear out our statement that as a connoisseur's fast car the Jaguar can be disappointing. The main windows require just over four turns, fully up to fully down. Additional ventilation is provided by toggles enabling the back windows to be slightly opened, and two scuttle ventilators, operated by levers in front of the door openings, are also provided. All this ventilation is a good thing, because the gearbox gets quite hot and blows warm air up its gaitered lever.

Each trailing door possesses a rigid pocket of generous capacity, a drawer-type ashtray and has a sliding interior handle. There are also small armrests, formed as door-pulls. Upholstery is in high-grade leather; on the test car this emitted an unpleasant odour, perhaps arising from some cleaning material.

On the XK150 a polished veneer facia has given place to an upholstered panel. On this the tachometer, reading to 6,000 r.p.m. and figure-calibrated in steps of 1,000 r.p.m., with inset clock, and a 140-m.p.h. speedometer figure-calibrated every 20 m.p.h., with total and trip-with-decimal mileage recorders, are mounted centrally, supplemented by ammeter, petrol gauge marked $\frac{1}{4}$, $\frac{1}{2}$, $\frac{3}{4}$, F, and a combined oil gauge and water thermometer. Normal oil pressure is 40 to 60 lb./sq. in. and temperature remains at 65 to 75 deg. C. under hard driving. The speedometer incorporates the headlamps full-beam warning, and the tachometer the arrows showing which direction-flasher is in operation.

A central facia-sill switch operates the flashers but is a shade inaccessible, the ignition key-hole is separate and the lamps are all controlled from a single central switch marked O, S, H, F. Push-buttons look after panel and interior lighting, other facia controls comprising two-speed wiper knob, cigar lighter, heater fan button and screen washers. The heater fan and screen wipers work, alas, obtrusively. The doors actuate the interior lights when opened, the passenger is provided with a grab-handle, there is a reversing lamp, and the sidelamps on the front wings have red insets. The boot is also lit. On the facia there is a lockable cubbyhole before the passenger and a smaller, open one for the driver. There is soft crash padding on the edge of the facia.

The rear-view mirror could well provide a better view and it is annoying to have to use the ignition-key to unlock the flap of the fuel filler. The petrol gauge incorporates a low-level warning light. Two swivelling, transparent anti-dazzle vizors are supplied.

Some of the foregoing criticisms may seem harsh and we hasten to remind the reader of the very high performance offered by the Jaguar XK150 at what can only be regarded as a very modest price, and of the sheer pleasure to be derived from driving fast this very excellent motor car.

The combination of high speed, very vivid acceleration and safe handling qualities, of which the disc braking is especially praiseworthy, render the Jaguar a superb super sports car, more particularly because the power pours so smoothly from that dependable, docile, quiet and beautifully finished twin-cam engine. The makers request the owner not to exceed 5,000 r.p.m. for any length of time but as this crankshaft speed represents 100 m.p.h. in top gear and nearly 130 m.p.h. in overdrive-top, this cannot be considered a hardship.

The engine picks up speed like a racing-car engine at a touch on the accelerator, yet here the affinity with racing ends, for this is a tractable, quiet power unit, which warms quickly to its work from cold (the twin S.U. type-HD6 carburetters have an automatic enriching unit), and in a test extending over 480 miles consumed no measurable quantity of oil or water. Fuel such as Esso Extra sufficed to suppress all pinking or running-on, while consumption,

---

THE JAGUAR XK150 SPECIAL EQUIPMENT FIXED-HEAD COUPE

Engine: Six cylinders, 83 by 106 mm. (3,442 c.c.). Overhead valves operated by twin-overhead camshafts. 8-to-1 compression-ratio. 210 b.h.p. at 5,500 r.p.m.

Gear ratios: First, 12.18 to 1; second, 7.16 to 1; third, 4.95 to 1; top, 4.09 to 1; overdrive-top, 3.18 to 1.

Tyres: 6.00 by 16 Dunlop "Road Speed" RS4, on centre-lock wire wheels.

Weight: Not weighed. Maker's figure: 1 ton 6 cwt. (dry).

Steering ratio: $2\frac{3}{4}$ turns, lock-to-lock.

Fuel capacity: 14 gallons. Range approximately 310 miles.

Wheelbase: 8 ft. 6 in.

Track: 4 ft. $3\frac{5}{8}$ in.

Dimensions: 14 ft. 9 in. by 5 ft. $4\frac{1}{2}$ in. by 4 ft. 7 in. (high).

Price: £1,292 (£1,939 7s. inclusive of purchase tax). With extras, as tested, £2,006 17s., inclusive of purchase tax.

Makers: Jaguar Cars Ltd., Coventry, England.

SPLENDID POWER-UNIT.—*The well-known six-cylinder, twin o.h.c. engine of the Jaguar which, in the case of the XK150 has four additional fan blades and pours out 210 b.h.p. in Special Equipment trim, functioning with extreme smoothness and efficiency in all its forms.*

driving hard, was better than 22 m.p.g. Thus, with the 14-gallon tank, the driving range exceeds 300 miles.

When the bonnet is propped open this power unit with its polished camboxes, is delightful to behold. From a more practical standpoint, the twin batteries are found to be housed, inaccessibly, in the front wings.

Altogether the Jaguar XK150 coupé is a very acceptable fast car, carrying on a great tradition with dignity and enhanced high performance. It is priced at £1,763 17s. or at £1,939 7s. in special equipment form, with Blue Top cylinder head, as tested, while the overdrive, as on the test car, increased the price to £2,006 17s. For the export market a special triple-carburetter version with the compression-ratio raised from 8 to 1 to 9 to 1 is available, said to be capable of 136 m.p.h.—W. B.

9 DUAL-PURPOSE SPORTS CARS FOR 1959

JAGUAR XK 150S

OF THE SERIES of cars under test, the XK-150 "S" is without doubt the most useable of all on public roads, even when set up for racing. So much so that our sampling was done entirely in Rockland County, a locale which makes up for its lack of private testing grounds with an abundance of rally-worthy blacktop serpentines. Owner Bob Grossman has raced this car extensively all summer but it has undergone only two changes from its original condition. A roll bar was installed and Koni shock absorbers replaced the originals. Though it doesn't interfere with putting up the top, the roll bar does stick through the zip-out back window opening. Perhaps now that winter's here, a bulging back window will be made.

We received quite a few comments from amazed XK-driving readers over our recent test of Jaguar's S-type, so we were pleasantly surprised to find that this car "went" in a markedly different manner from our previous sample. The latter had been driven by just about everybody at the British Press Trials the day before our test and judging from this later sampling, it just hadn't been going the way it was supposed to. Soon we will have full facts and figures, but for now, here are some driving impressions on a much-raced sample.

A little-known standard fitting on the "S" is a Thornton *Power-Lok* differential, an English-built *Positraction* which eliminates wheelspin when the inside rear wheel "lifts". Thus a really comfortable ride can be achieved with fairly soft springs on a somewhat narrow tread without handicapping the car's controlability.

The *Power-Lok* is available on all current Jaguars as an extra-cost option. We recommend it without reservation to *any* Jaguar purchaser. Though it's not easy to explain how it works, it does. Besides, it's cheap, unlike the German Z-F device. Equipped with it, no matter how impossible an angle a car may assume (and as race-goers will testify, XK-150's corner at outlandish ones), the driver can still steer the car with a combination of steering wheel and throttle movement. Though they don't look it, they feel very stable to the driver. So much so that we are now re-evaluating some old ideas. One was that maximum cornering power (measured in units of g) is a goal to be pursued at all costs. Costs of expense or comfort, yes, but at the cost of controlability, we must now say, no. Surely rational control right up to *and past* the peak of adhesion is well worth a slight reduction in the latter.

Since this control is exercised through both the steering wheel and the throttle (or alternatively, the brake pedal), each of these must work in such a way that the driver is constantly in touch with what's going on. In the 150 "S", this is achieved basically through three highly developed systems: the drive train, the steering and the brakes.

The heart of the drive train, the famous XK engine, originally rated at a modest 160 bhp, in this version puts out 250 well behaved horses. Not just sturdy or hairy-legged horses but both strong and well behaved. Theer is no flat spot in the power curve. No matter what the speed nor how hard the car is cornering, movement of the accelerator provides straight forward, direct control over the power output. All too often a highly tuned racing engine is singularly unsuited to being run below, say, 3000 rpm. If you should be so foolish as to drive one that slowly, when accelerating again the urge comes on with a neck-snapping rush that more than likely makes for singularly awkward moments if you're in a corner. Quite to the contrary, the S, though powerful, is silky smooth from about 1000 revs upward. A small detail, perhaps, but important: The accelerator pedal itself operates very smoothly; there is no free play and it never sticks. Like the rest of the engine it seems to feel "exact."

Beneath its polished cam covers (attractiveness of the overall layout was one of the several design criteria initially laid down by Sir William Lyons), the working parts are exact and polished too. The hemispherical combustion chambers (later "invented" by Chrysler, but subsequently abandoned as too expensive!) are machined over their entire surface rather than being left in the "as cast" condition.

Since the introduction of the 140 series, XK steering has been by rack and pinion, a mechanism that cannot be bettered for directness of control and reduction of friction. Through a suitable choice of castor angle in the steering, forces remain relatively light even when taking very sharp bends. One drawback of rack and pinion steering should be pointed out, though. That is its inability to insulate the driver from road shocks on irregular surfaces. But for racing on contemporary American circuits this is a negligible factor.

Thanks to Jaguar's leadership at Le Mans in developing disc brakes into a proven production item, brake fade is now as old-fashioned as wheel tramp. The driver of today is in the enviable position of being able to possess a high-performance sports car which actually has more braking capability than it's ever likely to need. Of course, pads can and do wear out, so on the "S" the quick-change variety are used to speed race-maintenance or preparation.

In the case of Bob Grossman's car, there has been very little of the latter. In addition to the afore-mentioned roll bar and shocks. Bob has added the proverbial gas and oil and just "gone racing." He also races an Alfa in G Production and though it rides on a trailer (boo!!), the S is his personal transportation during race weekends. It is often seen outside one of the nearby night spots, but don't hold this against Bob. He has even lent it to friends the night before a race! How dual purpose can you get?

Just for our benefit, he had the spark plugs changed. After all, they hadn't been out since Watkins Glen. Or was it Bridgehampton? Unnoticed, a brass nipple fell in a plug hole at this time. The clatter resulting when the twin cam six was started caused a lot of head scratching and finally a head was removed (not the mechanic's, the cylinder's). Although this delayed our sampling, all concerned were quite intrigued. Despite some seven or eight races, it seems it had never been off before!

The errant nipple had managed to get caught twixt valve head and piston crown so a fair amount of work was involved and an object lesson learned. Stuff a rag in every open hole.

Early in its career, the Grossman équipe fitted Traction-Masters to the rear suspension but these were soon disallowed by the SCCA Contest Board. They are just trailing arm/radius rods, just like the new Corvette features.

If you want to make your own, use a steering tie rod of the appropriate length (shorten one if necessary). Locate one ball joint on the top of the axle housing above the spring mount and the other one on the frame just above the front end of the rear spring. One on each side, of course.

They will help immensely to eliminate wheel judder when your shocks are tired and axle wind-up at any time. But as Bob and others have demonstrated, the Jag can corner quite well without them. It is hoped that they (or a Coventry version) will at least make the Optical Accessories list for '59.   —*sfw*

Opposite page, owner-driver Bob Grossman leads at the start of LISCA's recent Lime Rock race. At left, he corners "on his ear" in SCCA-NY's Regional at Bridgehampton.

Despite awe-inspiring roll angle, S-type corners quickly. One steers with combination of throttle and steering wheel movement.

THE 1959 L.

CUTAWAY DRAW

The Lister chassis frame.

Although the 1959 Lister has an entirely new body the ge layout of chassis and mechanical components is uncha except in minor details. Front suspension is by equal l wishbones and Girling co-axial coil spring/damper units; c rear the de Dion assembly is located by twin radius arms sliding block. Steering is rack and pinion. The 3.8-litre e illustrated is in unit with a close ratio Jaguar gearbox, and mission is taken through a 3-plate Borg and Beck clutch, Hardy Spicer propeller shaft, to the chassis-mounted Sali final drive unit.

The lines of the bodywork and moulded screen/high tail arr ment bear the hallmark of a Frank Costin design. A C

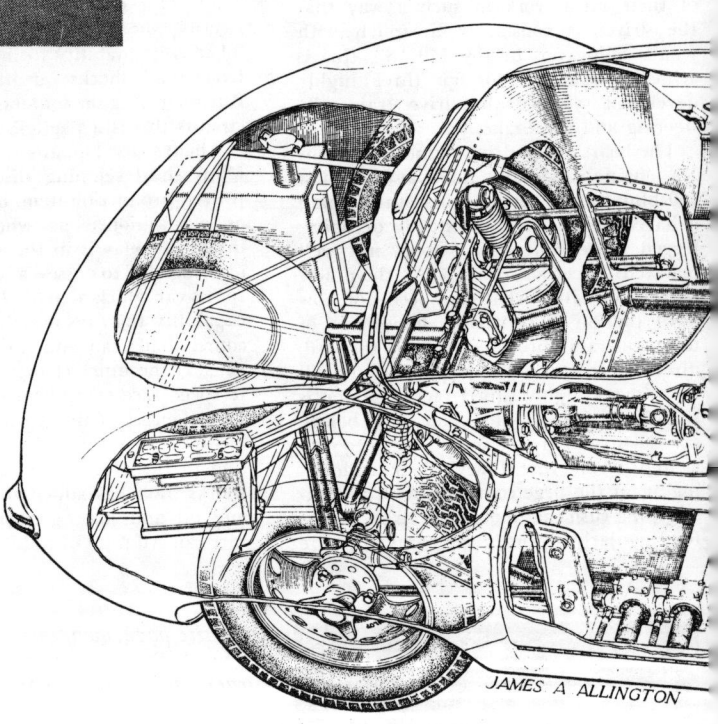

Only very rarely are all these people engaged on assembly at any one time, the general rule being three men per car. It is just possible, if the complement in the fitting shop is doubled, to complete assembly in a week, but such rush work only increases the problems which beset George Palmer who, as Production Manager, is responsible for maintaining a steady flow of components and for seeing that every job is finished on—or ahead of —time. George has been with Listers since 1947 and has been concerned with the development of cars from the time when the firm made its first tentative steps into the motoring world.

When the chief chassis and mechanical components have been fitted the car is wired from a loom supplied by Lucas, the various electrical items finally being connected and tested by the Cambridge Battery Service Ltd. Assembly completed, the car goes to Sitton and Mothersole Ltd., another Cambridge firm, for spraying. The works car illustrated is finished in an impressive shade of dark green with a primrose yellow Lister stripe.

Frank Costin's work on airflow is not confined to bodywork and mechanical components, for the driving compartment of the

Front suspension of the 1959 car features modified wishbones and king pins.

new car, which is far more spacious and comfortable than on previous models, is to be fully air-conditioned. Most notable feature of the cockpit at present, however, is the thick padding of the new seats, which have been specially designed by Cox and Co. (Watford) Ltd. And as well as providing increased comfort for both the driver and a passenger, the 1959 Lister has accomodation for a full-size suitcase in the "boot."

As mentioned above, in basic layout the 1959 Lister is unchanged. In addition to the modified wishbones and kingpins the 1959 cars will be fitted with Dunlop disc brakes—as well as Dunlop wheels and tyres—and the Girling suspension units will continue to be modified by Listers to their own specification. The work carried out on these components involves shortening the whole unit, welding on abutments and making up spring retaining washers. For

its early trials the works car used a somewhat makeshift fuel tank but it is hoped to fit fireproof rubber tanks before the start of the season.

The 1959 works cars will be prepared and maintained in a separate premises by a team of racing mechanics led by Dick Barton. Although small, the works "garage" has facilities for welding and crack detecting, so that preparation can be carried on without any interruption of the production programme.

Don Moore, who has his own workshop in Cambridge, will continue to assemble and tune the Jaguar engines fitted in the works cars; 3-litre units will be used for Championship events—plans for the season include the Nurburgring 1000 Kms and Le Mans —and 3.8-litre engines will be fitted for British (and other) unlimited capacity races. It is noteworthy that Listers have found

ER JAGUAR

JAMES ALLINGTON

...tented tonneau cover, which is essential to the whole conception, will be added later. The only break in the smooth, aerodynamic profile is a blister on the bonnet which is necessitated ... the height of the Jaguar power-unit; it also serves as a con-...ction release for underbonnet air.

Dimensions: Wheelbase, 7 ft 6¾ in; Track—front, 4 ft 4 in—...ar, 4 ft 5½ in; Overall length, 14 ft 4¾ in; Overall width, ...ft 7 in; Overall height, 2 ft 7 in at scuttle, 3 ft 2 in overall; ...round clearance 4¼ in at sump, 6 in at chassis; Turning circle, ... ft; Dry weight, 15½ cwt. The shape of the fuel tank is not ...t finalised, and is not shown in the drawing.

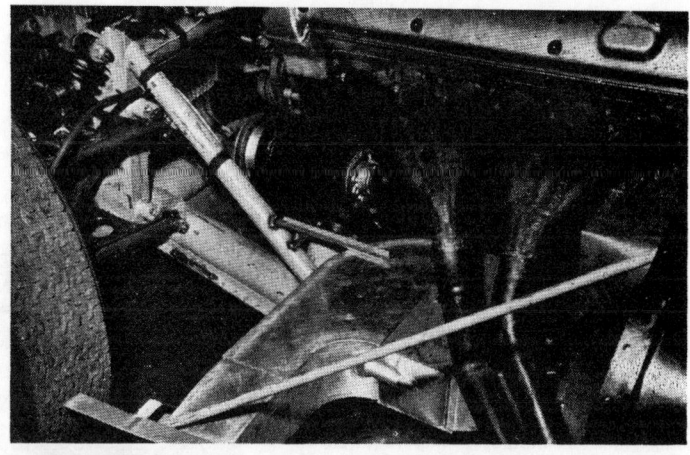

Ducting for the new oil cooler, which has an air intake just behind the nearside front wheel and exhausts into the cockpit.

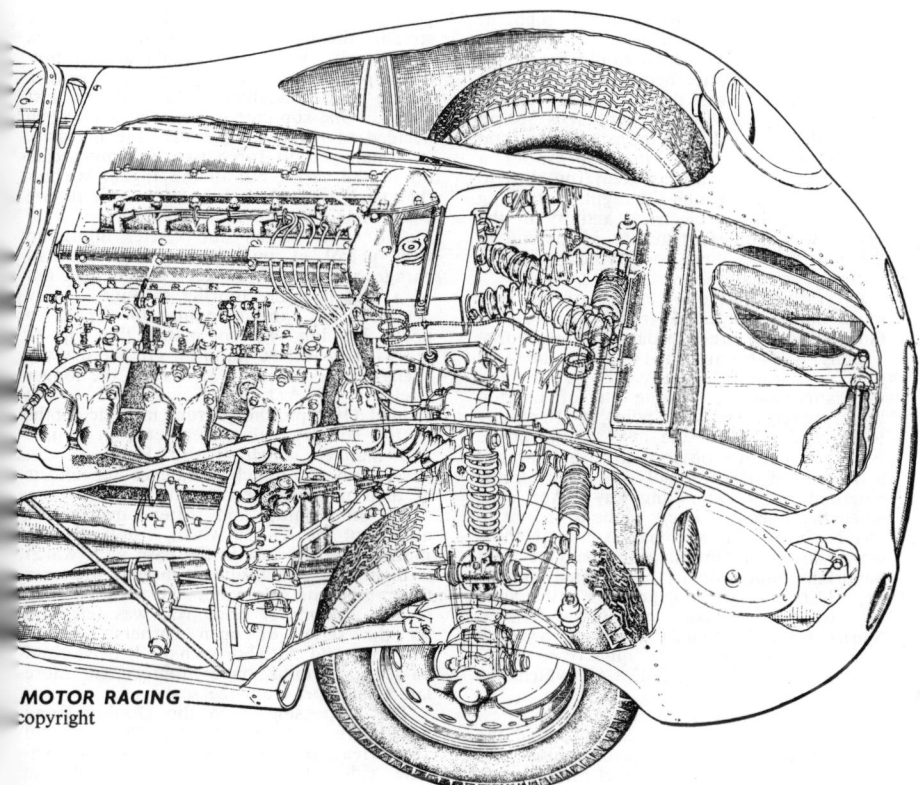

With Frank Costin now employed full-time as Chief Designer, it is reasonable to regard the 1959 Lister as an interim model, to be followed at a later date by an entirely new conception. Despite his association with space frame structures, Costin has a great regard for the twin-tube (or ladder type) frame as employed on the Lister, and considers such a structure vastly safer than an inefficient space frame.

Behind racing—and commercial—success, often given little credit for their efforts, are the men who do the donkey-work. There is a friendly atmosphere at Abbey Road and despite the usual moans and grumbles, one gets the impression that most of the men are happy at their work.

Brian Lister is never slow to give praise for a job well done, and his interest in the men's welfare is shown in the excellent heating system he has installed. In general, he finds, new staff either leave in a few hours or stay for ever. Adaptability is almost as important as a skilled training in any particular sphere, and within a few years the firm has built up a nucleus of employees who can not only "turn a hand" to almost anything, but can do it well. They all show a keen interest in the racing activities of the cars they produce and almost every one of them goes to the circuits at one time or another. They should find their 1959 outings most satisfactory.

the Jaguar engine by far the cheapest, from the maintenance point of view, that they have ever used; the engine maintenance bill for the much-raced 1957 works car was under £50. Brian Lister finds the personnel of Jaguar Cars Ltd. exceptionally helpful, and he, in his turn, has provided Jaguars with an extremely useful means of testing their engines—particularly the 3-litre unit—while their racing programme was in abeyance. Early last season a certain amount of piston trouble was experienced, but this has now been overcome.

In 1959, in addition to the various proprietary components already mentioned, the works cars will use Lodge plugs and BP fuel and oil.

Apprentices play an important part in the work of the Lister organisation, and the experience they gain in working on the cars, and in travelling to race meetings with the works team is obviously going to stand them in good stead in the future; in this way Listers are also contributing to the ranks of skilled racing mechanics, to whom the development of British motor racing owes a great deal.

The first appearance of the 1959 car will probably be made at Sebring, where one has been entered by Briggs Cunningham.

Ducting for the rear disc brakes, which is at present made by Williams & Pritchard.

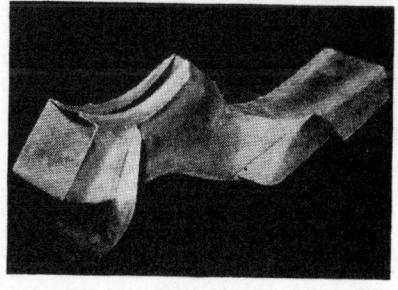

ROAD TEST

JAGUAR XK150

ONE of my memories of early schooldays is the frequency with which, for quite minor misdemeanours, I was required to write out such meaningless phrases as "Manners make the man."

Although still doubting the value of such impositions, I would to-day have no qualms about setting a recalcitrant boy with mechanical leanings the task of writing out a few hundred times "The engine makes the Jaguar." This statement can be applied to all the firm's current models, of course, but to none more than the XK150 coupé, which for fast long distance travel can have few equals.

The smooth, surging power of the engine, which has a maximum output of 210 hp at 5500 rpm, in combination with a torque figure of no less than 212 lb. ft. at 3000 rpm, is matched by the unfailing efficiency of the servo-assisted Dunlop disc-brakes, which are of the pattern now adopted for use on the Formula 1 Ferrari. The remainder of the specification is rather less exciting, but adds up to produce a vehicle capable of cruising in safety—and to the accompaniment of very little noise, other than from the wind—at 120 mph (and well under 5000 rpm) for literally miles on end.

Unfortunate as it may be, facilities for road travel of this nature are not often encountered in the British Isles, and to make an assessment of the suitability of the XK150 for everyday transport the car was used for a journey to Goodwood and for a number of normal trips in and around the metropolitan area, in addition to being driven to Norfolk twice over our "normal" test route.

The first journey to East Anglia coincided with the great Friday night storm which, according to newspaper and radio reports, brought all traffic to a standstill. Visibility, despite the aid of almost constant lightning,

The interior layout. There is ample adjustment for both seats and steering column, but on the test car the driver's seat was not securely held in its slides and, with the steering column in anything but its most forward position, it was difficult to reach the overdrive switch without taking the right hand completely off the wheel. Most drivers would find the seat cushion rather low in relation to the height of the scuttle.

restricted safe speed to about 90 mph, at which the Jaguar whispered along A11, trailing a bow wave which would have been the envy of all concerned with the Sceptre, and showing a marked indifference to the enormous puddles which sometimes spread across the full width of the road. Dry and comfortably secure—at the expense of a misty windscreen—it was great fun thus to be able to rush through the night, marvelling at the amount of electrical activity in the sky; it was a different matter, at the end of the journey, to have to disembark into a virtually flooded garden.

On rather different roads, and in very much more congested traffic, the run to Goodwood, on practice day for the Tourist Trophy, was accomplished in much the same time as it would normally take in far more mundane vehicles. Going out of London there proved to be little point in attempting to force the XK to the head of the queue —it soon became obvious that there wasn't a head—and unfortunately the heavy traffic persisted for a long, long way. And even when there seemed likely to be a chance to change into third and pass some of these slower areas of "mobile chicane," the right hand lane almost invariably became blocked by a heavy lorry using perhaps half a mile of road to overtake one of his fellows. Spirits were lightened, however, when it proved possible to go up quickly to about 105 mph to nip past a police car which was obviously in a hurry.

On the second part of this journey a few short stretches were covered at around the three figure mark, but with traffic and corners very much to be taken into account there was little opportunity to use overdrive, particularly on account of the delay sometimes experienced on "changing down" into top, while the rather widely-spaced ratios did not encourage a change straight down into third. The alternative, of cornering in overdrive, left very little opportunity to "feel" the car round on the throttle, and while the Jaguar was happy to go through gentle bends very fast it needed a little more watching on tighter corners, whatever the gear. Duncton Hill was ascended without either driver or passenger being aware of the gradient, and then, after deliberating for some time (as was the driver of a Porsche just ahead of us) on which side to pass a violently-swaying caravan we nipped past both Porsche and caravan and there we were —Goodwood.

The return journey, on Saturday night, was very fast at first—until we caught up with all those who had left half an hour earlier, and thereafter it proved almost im-

possible to do other than travel with the stream; the car was willing but the roads were weak. Even with Jaguar acceleration it was possible to pass only two or three cars before more headlamps loomed up just ahead. One supreme optimist in a Fiat 600 decided to make the outside lane his own, and managed to force two oncoming cars on to the verge, but in the Jaguar we felt that such manœuvres weren't worth it—we could make up the time later on.

And so it turned out. After filling up with petrol at one of those enlightened garages where you can get ice-cool milk out of a slot-machine, touring through a very deserted City, and stopping for supper in north London, we completed the trip to Norwich in just 90 minutes. In the dry the Jaguar felt completely at ease as the longer stretches of A11 were swallowed up at around 110 mph, this journey into the depths of the country being completed in a time and manner which British Railways can never hope to match, whatever the efforts of their publicity department.

An important, and often overlooked, quality of the XK150 which is noticed on a journey of this sort is the ease with which it maintains straight-line running, whatever the camber or side-wind. On fast bends a certain amount of body roll was felt, and on the series of open corners between Thetford and Attleborough both driver and passenger would have appreciated more lateral support from the seats.

The suspension, with the Dunlop Road Speed tyres at their normal 23 lb. front and 26 lb. rear, provided an extremely comfortable ride and the spaciousness of the passenger compartment — especially at shoulder level—added to the feeling of well-being which is essential for full enjoyment of maintained high speeds on the road. Unfortunately the interior had become somewhat cluttered with luggage, as a man's ordinary suitcase would not fit in the extremely shallow boot, but a great deal of impedimenta can be carried on the rear seats without obstructing rearward vision—which is almost as good as that through the wide, curved windscreen.

On the following day, with the tyres inflated to 30 lb. front and 35 lb. rear for performance tests, there was very little detriment to the ride other than in increased consciousness of really bad surfaces. During the tests themselves awareness of acceleration was diminished by the quietness of the engine, but the rev counter needle rushed round to 5500 rpm very rapidly in first and second gears, first being rather too low for practical use due to an absolute maximum of

CONTINUED ON PAGE 157

AUTOSPORT, JUNE 5, 1959

TEST CAR was fitted with the fixed-head coupé bodywork. The Jaguar's equipment is lavish and its finish luxurious.

The Jaguar XK 150S

An Ultra-High Speed Car That Approaches Perfection

JOHN BOLSTER TESTS

THE 3.4-litre Jaguar engine is one of the marvels of the age. In racing tune, it achieves tremendous speeds, and in normal form it powers a range of cars from six-seater luxury models to the sports XK types. Now, a "hotter" version of this basic engine has been made available, and it is used in the ultra-high speed XK 150S two-seaters.

The new engine is designed to make full use of the latest "super" fuels that are rated at 100 octane or thereabouts. The compression ratio is, therefore, as high as 9 to 1, and Harry Weslake has reworked the twin-cam light alloy head. The venturi-shaped ports have less curve in them than the normal ones in the interest of filling, the necessary turbulence coming partly from the curved inlet tracts. These give an equal length of pipe to each of the six cylinders for ramming purposes, and there are three S.U. constant vacuum horizontal carburetters of 2 ins. bore. Each of these carburetters has a short trumpet-mouthed ramming pipe on the entry side.

The great power potential of this "top end" is easily handled by a very rigid seven-bearing crankshaft with lead-bronze bearings. The output is 252 b.h.p. at 5,500 r.p.m., and there is a useful power increase over the standard engine from the medium speed range upwards. A specially strengthened clutch has been developed to withstand the high loading involved.

The gearbox is the four-speed unit with which we have become familiar, and in this application it is married to a Laycock-de Normanville overdrive. This is used in conjunction with an axle ratio of 4.09 to 1.

The chassis is entirely conventional, a box-section frame being suspended on torsion bars in front and semi-elliptic springs behind. A rack and pinion steering assembly is fitted, and the dampers are telescopic. The Dunlop brakes have 12-in. discs and vacuum servo assistance. Dunlop R.S.4 tyres are fitted to centrelock wire wheels.

Three two-seater bodies are available, a "roadster", a drophead and a fixed-head coupé. The last named was the type which was fitted to the test car. It is a comfortable, roomy body with children's seats behind the main individual seats, and there is a luggage boot of medium size. The equipment is lavish and the finish luxurious. An adjustable steering column ensures a comfortable driving position.

On taking one's seat, one finds that the all-round visibility is good and the bonnet does not seem excessively long. The short central gear lever is conveniently located, and the brake lever is of the "fly-off" type. Very comfortable for long journeys, the seats would be still better if their shape gave more positive lateral location. The pedals are well placed, though the clutch has a fairly long travel.

It is at once obvious that this is a very powerful engine. It has immense torque, giving brisk starts in second gear if desired, and seems even more flexible than the normal Jaguar unit. It is the epitome of smoothness, right up to maximum revs. Even if top gear only is used, the car is sensationally lively, and one can overtake other drivers who are really trying with contemptuous ease.

Perhaps the XK 150S is at its best when driven in this way. The sheer sensual pleasure of feeling the big machine respond to the throttle is one of motoring's most delightful experiences. As the speedometer needle flashes past the 100 m.p.h. mark one lazily flicks the overdrive switch, when one can cruise in effortless silence at three-figure speeds, and exceed 130 m.p.h. on the longer straights. A touch of the brake pedal results in the kind of retardation that only discs can provide, and the knowledge that this immensely powerful fade-free braking is always available adds greatly to the enjoyment of the extremely high performance.

If the XK 150S is regarded as an ultra-high speed touring car, it can be said to approach perfection. If it is handled fiercely, as a sports car, however, it is perhaps open to some slight criticism. There is no synchromesh on bottom gear, and if the up changes are hurried at all, the synchromesh on the other three speeds may very easily be beaten. For the man who likes to make quick, clean changes without a sound at all times, more powerful synchromesh would be a worthwhile improvement.

The acceleration figures are, of course, stupendous, and were no doubt aided by the optional limited-slip differential. Even so, rear axle tramp can be induced if the full power is applied on bottom gear, and on second and third speeds too if the road is wet. Yet, the car is curiously easy to control on wet roads. The entirely conventional chassis may not have the extreme cornering power of some more radical designs, but it scores by giving the driver plenty of warning that the limit is being approached. For this reason, the XK 150S is a particularly safe sports car, and one that may be handled with confidence by any competent fast driver.

As regards the general handling of the

COCKPIT, with an adjustable steering column, easy-to-read instruments, well-placed pedals and conveniently located gear-lever, is set up for serious motoring.

car, I was at first a little disappointed as it tended to be heavy and unresponsive. Later on, I tried higher pressures in the tyres, and at once changed my opinion. The steering became quite light, and the whole "feel" of the car improved. For driving at extremely high speeds it is always advisable to use higher tyre pressures than normal, and I was advised that, as I would be covering a considerable distance at over 130 m.p.h., I should use pressures of 45 lb. (rear) and 40 lb. (front) for that part of the test. Subsequently, I found that the car could be driven normally in surprising comfort with these hard tyres.

A word about the maximum speed. A velocity of 132.3 m.p.h. is obviously beyond the needs of the average owner, and is indeed of only academic interest. It would, however, be possible to travel appreciably faster on racing tyres, when a maximum speed of over 135 m.p.h. would almost certainly be recorded. For a road test, though, it is naturally correct to take the performance figures on the tyres that are fitted as standard. I therefore did this, even though a higher maximum speed figure could have been achieved by making a tyre change.

Of much more value than the maximum speed is the tremendous acceleration. To cover a standing quarter-mile in 15.8 secs., or to accelerate from a standstill to 100 m.p.h. in 20 secs. is to unleash a surge of power that the average motorist can hardly visualize. These figures would be expected of a sports-racing car, but to obtain them from an extremely comfortable and well-equipped closed vehicle is an astonishing experience. The engine makes little sound, the gears are silent, and there is no ostentatious crackle from the exhaust. This Jaguar may be compared with any luxury car or town carriage on the score of silent running and mechanical refinement.

On a long journey, the feeling that the car is never fully extended and always has a reserve of power makes this a most untiring machine to drive. When overtaking has to be carried out, the manœuvre may be completed in the minimum time and distance. Truly a great reserve of performance is one of the most attractive luxuries of motoring.

The Jaguar XK 150S is a very remark-

THE CAR has a sporting appearance yet is entirely suitable for formal occasions (right).

SPECIFICATION AND PERFORMANCE DATA

Car Tested: Jaguar XK 150S fixed head coupé. Price £2,065 including P.T. Limited slip differential, £42 10s. extra.

Engine: Six cylinders 83 mm. x 106 mm. (3,442 c.c.). Inclined valves in light alloy head operated by twin chain-driven overhead camshafts. Compression ratio 9 to 1. 252 b.h.p. at 5,500 r.p.m. Three SU carburetters. Lucas coil and distributor.

Transmission: Specially strengthened Borg and Beck 10 ins. single dry plate clutch. Four-speed gearbox with synchromesh on upper three ratios and central remote control, plus Laycock-de Normanville overdrive. Ratios: 3.19 (O/D.), 4.09, 4.95, 7.16 and 12.2 to 1. Open propeller shaft. Hypoid rear axle.

Chassis: Box-section frame. Independent front suspension by wishbones and torsion bars. Rack and pinion steering. Rear axle on semi-elliptic springs. Girling telescopic dampers. Dunlop brakes with 12 ins. discs all round, vacuum servo assisted. Centre lock wire wheels, fitted 6.00 x 16 ins. Dunlop RS4 tyres.

Equipment: 12-volt lighting and starting. Speedometer, rev.-counter, oil pressure and water temperature gauges, ammeter, fuel gauge, clock, cigar lighter, self-parking windscreen wipers and washers. Heating and demisting.

Dimensions: Wheelbase, 8 ft. 6 ins.; track, 4 ft. 3¾ ins.; overall length, 14 ft. 9 ins.; width, 5 ft. 4½ ins.; turning circle, 33 ft. Weight, 28½ cwt.

Performance: Maximum speed 132.3 m.p.h. Speeds in gears: Direct top, 115 m.p.h.; 3rd, 88 m.p.h.; 2nd, 60 m.p.h.; 1st, 34 m.p.h. Standing quarter-mile, 15.8 secs. Acceleration: 0-30 m.p.h., 3 secs.; 0-50 m.p.h., 5.8 secs.; 0-60 m.p.h., 7.4 secs.; 0.80 m.p.h., 12.4 secs.; 0-100 m.p.h., 20 secs.

Fuel Consumption: Driven hard, 18 m.p.g.

able car. It combines extreme performance with perfect manners to a quite exceptional degree, and it has a sporting appearance that is yet entirely suitable for the most formal occasions. Being a Jaguar, it is really hardly necessary to remark that it represents outstanding value for money.

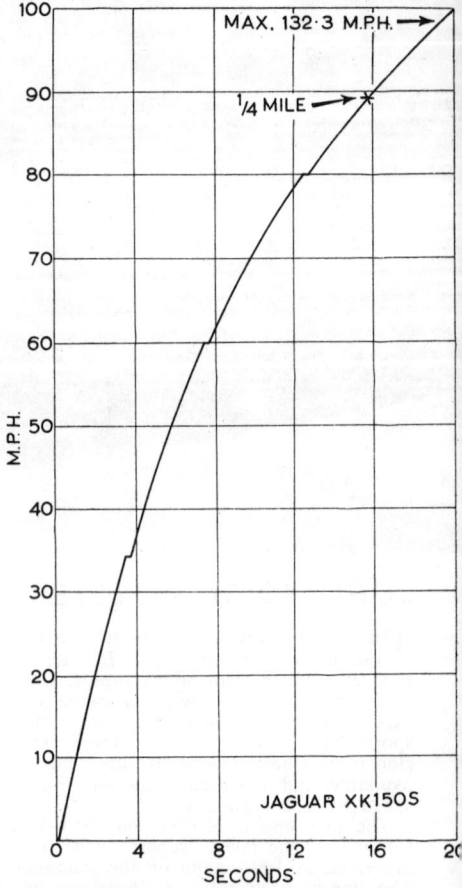

Acceleration Graph

THE ENGINE is one of the marvels of the age, and makes little sound. Over 250 b.h.p. is developed at 5,500 r.p.m.

THE ONLY VIEW that other drivers are likely to have of the Jaguar XK 150S—a sleek and shapely tail.

The JAGUAR XK150S Fixed-head Coupe

An Immensely Impressive Car Which Offers Near-racing Performance in Complete Touring Comfort at a Surprisingly Moderate Price

THE XK150S fixed-head coupé Jaguar is easily the fastest closed car ever subjected to a full-scale road test by *The Motor*. Its mean maximum speed of 132.0 m.p.h. compares with 143.7 m.p.h. recorded with the competition 2-seater Jaguar C-type; but far from detracting from the performance of the XK150S, comparisons of the figures obtained with the two cars show the 150S in even more remarkable light, for whereas the C-type was a very stark model produced in limited series for sports-car racing, this latest fixed-head coupé with S-type engine is very much an everyday motorcar, smooth and flexible, in which people can, and will, go about their normal occasions with complete closed-car comfort and amenities.

With its weight and wind resistance increased by bumpers and fog lamps, as well as the increased frontal area of the coupé top, it is indeed surprising that the 150S should approach the C-type speed as closely as it does.

What is not just surprising, but truly astonishing, is that the 150S recorded exactly the same time, 16.2 seconds, to cover the standing quarter-mile—at the end of which both were travelling at close on 90 m.p.h.—and that the difference in the time taken to reach 100 m.p.h. from rest varied by a mere one-fifth of a second, a difference so small that the performance of the two can be regarded as identical up to the three-figure mark. If the truth of the time-worn tag about the racing car of today being the touring car of tomorrow ever needed proving, these two tests supply all the evidence necessary.

TRIPLE S.U. carburetters identify the S-series Jaguar engine of which the twin-camshaft cylinder head also has improved inlet porting. The long, well-filled bonnet drops away to provide satisfactory forward driving vision.

In Brief

Price (including Powr-Lok limited-slip differential as tested) £1,487 plus purchase tax £623 4s. 2d. equals £2,110 4s. 2d.
Price with normal axle (including purchase tax) £2,065 4s. 2d.
Capacity ... ... 3,442 c.c.
Unladen kerb weight ... 29 cwt.
Acceleration:
  20-40 m.p.h. in top gear   6.4 sec.
  0-50 m.p.h. through gears   6.1 sec.
Maximum direct top gear gradient ... ... 1 in 5.8
Maximum speed ... ... 132.0 m.p.h.
"Maximile" speed ... ... 122.4 m.p.h.
Touring fuel consumption ... 22.0 m.p.g
Gearing: 19.6 m.p.h. in top gear at 1,000 r.p.m. (overdrive, 26.4 m.p.h.); 28.2 m.p.h. at 1,000 ft./min. piston speed (overdrive, 36.2 m.p.h.).

The maximum speed of 132 m.p.h. is so high that some may question its practical value. In the sense that many of those who buy this model will rarely, if ever, attain it, there is force in that criticism; but that argument overlooks the world-wide spread of motor roads, and the fact that there are many occasions on such highways when very high speeds can be held in safety by a driver of experience. We ourselves, having lost time in a maze of city streets, found that along almost the whole of a Belgian motorway a true 100 m.p.h. could be maintained continuously and easily (bar an occasional momentary drop to 90 or so for overtaking), this bringing us back on our busy schedule.

In short, it is the margin of performance available that lends value to the ultimate maximum and it is true to say of the XK150S that it is one of those very rare cars in which even fast drivers find a margin of performance at their disposal under almost any conditions.

Before leaving the question of ultimate maximum speed, a word or two should be said about tyres. Because performance tests of this car would obviously involve a substantial mileage at speeds in excess of 125 m.p.h., it was suggested by the manufacturers that we might care to use racing tyres. It was felt, however, that this would depart from an essential principle of Road Tests—that the car should be driven in the condition in which it is normally sold.

Accordingly, the normal Dunlop "Road Speed" covers were used, but (in accordance with the recommendations of both tyre and car makers) were inflated to 40 lb. at the front and 45 lb. at the rear as a safety precaution for maximum speed trials. This compared with the manufacturer's normal recommendation of 30 lb. front and 35 lb. rear for fast driving and 23 lb. front and 26 lb. rear for everyday motoring.

In passing, it may be remarked that these high pressures (which were retained throughout the performance tests) gave a surprisingly comfortable ride, even over Continental *pavé*, whilst the car remained beautifully steady on both the

THE CURVED tail of the Jaguar makes for a shallow boot but luggage accommodation is nevertheless good for a car of this type and can be supplemented by the rear passenger compartment (right) which has two removable child-size seats. The boot floor lifts to reveal the spare wheel.

The Jaguar XK150S Fixed-head Coupé

actual timed kilometre and round a very gentle high-speed bend taken at something in the region of 130 m.p.h. on the approach run in one direction.

For normal usage, the recommended fast-driving, front/rear pressures of 30/35 lb. struck us as the ideal, because although it shakes a little on "washboard" corrugations, this car is remarkably well sprung for comfort, and low tyre pressures tended both to reduce the responsiveness of the steering and increase the effort required.

At "fast driving" pressures, both handling and comfort reach a very high standard. Corners can be taken fast without appreciable roll and whilst the 150S is not, perhaps, so "tidy" as one or two quite exceptional sports cars we have tried when cornered near the limit, it nevertheless displays cornering qualities which are very much above average and has no unexpected vices to catch the unwary. The rack-and-pinion steering which needs only 2½ turns from lock to lock is pleasantly direct and accurate, giving the driver a useful degree of "feel" which on changing road cambers can be almost excellent yet suffering little from wheel-kick on rough surfaces. Cornering on wet roads, the vast power naturally needs to be used with some discretion.

One of the surprising charms of this Jaguar, a car in which familiar landmarks are apt to appear on the horizon with unexpected suddenness, is the quite remarkable top-gear performance. The maximum gradient climbable in direct top is of the order of 1 in 5.8 and it will climb a gradient of 1 in 7 with a little power in hand at any speed up to 90 m.p.h. or can be slowed right down to 10 m.p.h. Even in the overdrive top ratio, it will cope with a 1 in 10 gradient at speeds up to 90 m.p.h.

If the landmarks come up with exceptional rapidity, the deceleration offered by the Dunlop disc brakes on all four wheels is in keeping with the acceleration. Not only are they powerful, light and sensitive, but they remain so after repeated applications from high speeds so that a driver in a hurry on winding or congested roads can use the car's performance on clear stretches without fear of brake fade.

Before going further, a word or two should be said about the special features of the S-type.

Three-carburetter Head

The engine differs from the normal XK150 design in having the special "straight-port" cylinder head intended for use in conjunction with a three-piece induction manifold carrying three S.U. type HD8 carburetters with trumpet inlets taking air from a steel-mesh, flame-trap type of air cleaner, the whole arrangement designed to give better filling than is possible with two carburetters. In conjunction with a 9:1 compression ratio, the effect is to give the greatly increased output of 250 b.h.p. at 5.500 r.p.m. Other special features include lead-bronze bearings for the mains and big ends.

The only practical penalty that seems to be involved is the obligation to use 100-octane fuel. On the Continent, after we had made our performance tests, no more 100-octane fuel was available, and it was necessary to use the next best obtainable. Although full throttle was avoided to prevent pinking, the effect became noticeable subsequently when the plugs showed every sign of having been "cooked" and a change was made to the harder Champion N3 type as a precaution.

Run on the correct fuel, the engine starts readily on the automatic choke, is beautifully smooth, flexible and quiet (with only a pleasantly restrained exhaust note when working really hard) and displays a surprisingly moderate thirst for petrol. Despite the manner in which the large twin o.h. camshaft engine fills the bonnet, all the points which call for routine attention are easy to reach.

To deal with the greatly increased torque of the S-type engine, a stronger clutch is used, but this calls for no undue effort, although the travel of the pedal is rather long and it must be depressed fully to free the clutch completely. Engagement is smooth and second-gear starts are possible, but these virtues are somewhat nullified by a throttle linkage which is insufficiently progressive in the initial stages so that considerable finesse is necessary to get the car off the mark smoothly.

The gear change, too, could be improved. The remote control gear lever has rather a long travel and the synchromesh is effective only if changes are not hurried. Indeed, the gearbox is the least pleasing feature of the car and cannot be regarded as reaching the very high standard of the rest.

On the model tried, a Powr-Lok limited-slip differential, which is offered as an optional extra, was fitted, and this proved surprisingly effective in cutting out wheel spin when a rapid start was made from rest. It was, in fact, found necessary to adopt a rather different technique when carrying out standing-start tests as the usual wheel spin was absent, and over-brutal driving could produce some axle patter—a phenomenon which could also be induced by accelerating hard in the gears out of a sharp corner.

An excellent feature is a Laycock-de Normanville overdrive, which is applied to top gear only. This gives the very high cruising ratio of 3.18 but such is the smoothness and flexibility of the engine that overdrive can be profitably used when trickling through 30 m.p.h. limits. Engagement and disengagement are by a manual switch effective only if the throttle is at least partially open so that there can be no snatch. The manual switch is situated on the offside of the facia board, behind the direction indicator switch and out of reach of the driver's fingers unless his hand is taken off the wheel.

Good features of the control layout

The Motor Road Test No. 18/59 (Continental)

Make: Jaguar.
Type: XK150S Fixed-head Coupé.
Makers: Jaguar Cars Ltd., Coventry.

Test Data

World copyright reserved; no unauthorized reproduction in whole or in part.

CONDITIONS: Weather: Fine, mainly warm, light wind. (Temperature 52°–72° F., Barometer 29.5–30.3 in. Hg.) Surface: Smooth dry concrete and tar macadam. Fuel: 100 octane pump grades.

INSTRUMENTS
Speedometer at 30 m.p.h.	1% fast
Speedometer at 60 m.p.h.	accurate
Speedometer at 90 m.p.h.	accurate
Speedometer at 120 m.p.h.	2% fast
Distance recorder	2% slow (at fast-driving tyre pressures).

WEIGHT
Kerb weight (unladen, but with oil, coolant and fuel for approx. 50 miles) .. 29 cwt.
Front/rear distribution of kerb weight .. 50½/49½
Weight laden as tested .. 32¼ cwt.

MAXIMUM SPEEDS
Flying Quarter Mile
Mean of four opposite runs .. 132.0 m.p.h.
Best one-way time equals .. 133.9 m.p.h.
"Maximile" Speed (Timed quarter mile after one mile accelerating from rest.)
Mean of four opposite runs .. 122.4 m.p.h.
Best one-way time equals .. 125.0 m.p.h.
Speed in gears (at 5,500 r.p.m.)
Max. speed in direct top gear .. 113 m.p.h.
Max. speed in 3rd gear .. 86 m.p.h.
Max. speed in 2nd gear .. 59 m.p.h.

FUEL CONSUMPTION
(Overdrive top gear)
33½ m.p.g. at constant 40 m.p.h. on level
28¼ m.p.g. at constant 50 m.p.h. on level
27 m.p.g. at constant 60 m.p.h. on level
25½ m.p.g. at constant 70 m.p.h. on level
23½ m.p.g. at constant 80 m.p.h. on level
20½ m.p.g. at constant 90 m.p.h. on level
18½ m.p.g. at constant 100 m.p.h. on level
(Direct top gear)
27 m.p.g. at constant 30 m.p.h. on level
26 m.p.g. at constant 40 m.p.h. on level
25 m.p.g. at constant 50 m.p.h. on level
23½ m.p.g. at constant 60 m.p.h. on level
22½ m.p.g. at constant 70 m.p.h. on level
21 m.p.g. at constant 80 m.p.h. on level

Overall Fuel Consumption for 2,632 miles, 141.8 gallons, equals 18.6 m.p.g. (15.2 litres/100 km.)
Touring Fuel Consumption (m.p.g. at steady speed midway between 30 m.p.h. and maximum, less 5% allowance for acceleration) 22.0 m.p.g.
Fuel tank capacity (maker's figure) .. 14 gallons

STEERING
Turning circle between kerbs:
Left .. 34¾ ft.
Right .. 31¾ ft.
Turns of steering wheel from lock to lock 2⅔

BRAKES from 30 m.p.h.
0.91 g retardation (equivalent to 33 ft. stopping distance) with 75 lb. pedal pressure.
0.63 g retardation (equivalent to 48 ft. stopping distance) with 50 lb. pedal pressure.
0.32 g retardation (equivalent to 94 ft. stopping distance) with 25 lb. pedal pressure.

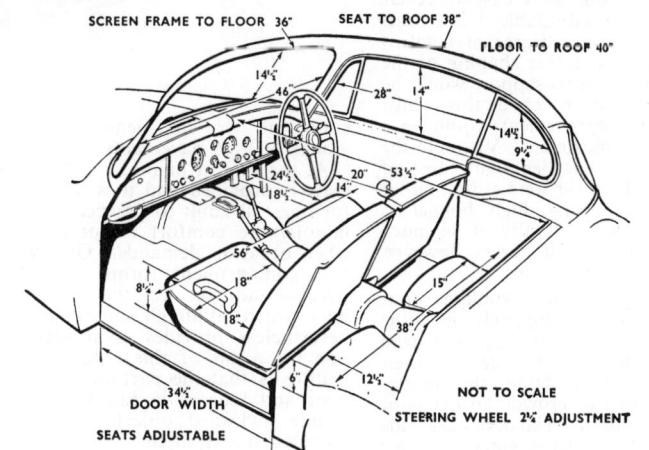

ACCELERATION TIMES from standstill
0–30 m.p.h.	2.9 sec.
0–40 m.p.h.	4.5 sec.
0–50 m.p.h.	6.1 sec.
0–60 m.p.h.	7.8 sec.
0–70 m.p.h.	10.6 sec.
0–80 m.p.h.	13.2 sec.
0–90 m.p.h.	16.5 sec.
0–100 m.p.h.	20.3 sec.
0–110 m.p.h.	25.6 sec.
0–120 m.p.h.	36.2 sec.
Standing quarter mile	16.2 sec.

ACCELERATION TIMES on Upper Ratios
	Overdrive top gear	Direct top gear	Third gear
10–30 m.p.h.	—	6.4 sec.	4.9 sec.
20–40 m.p.h.	—	6.4 sec.	5.0 sec.
30–50 m.p.h.	8.4 sec.	6.1 sec.	4.5 sec.
40–60 m.p.h.	8.5 sec.	6.3 sec.	4.0 sec.
50–70 m.p.h.	9.2 sec.	6.7 sec.	4.5 sec.
60–80 m.p.h.	9.6 sec.	6.3 sec.	5.1 sec.
70–90 m.p.h.	9.5 sec.	6.5 sec.	5.6 sec.
80–100 m.p.h.	10.9 sec.	7.4 sec.	—
90–110 m.p.h.	14.4 sec.	9.1 sec.	—
100–120 m.p.h.	18.9 sec.	—	—

HILL CLIMBING at sustained steady speeds
Max. gradient on overdrive top gear .. 1 in 8.0 (Tapley 375 lb./ton)
Max. gradient on direct top gear .. 1 in 5.8 (Tapley 385 lb./ton)
Max. gradient on 3rd gear .. 1 in 4.5 (Tapley 495 lb./ton)
Max. gradient on 2nd gear .. 1 in 3.0 (Tapley 705 lb./ton)

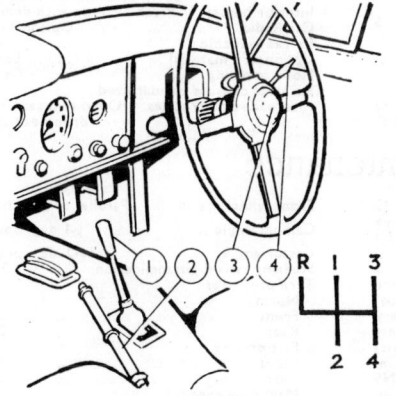
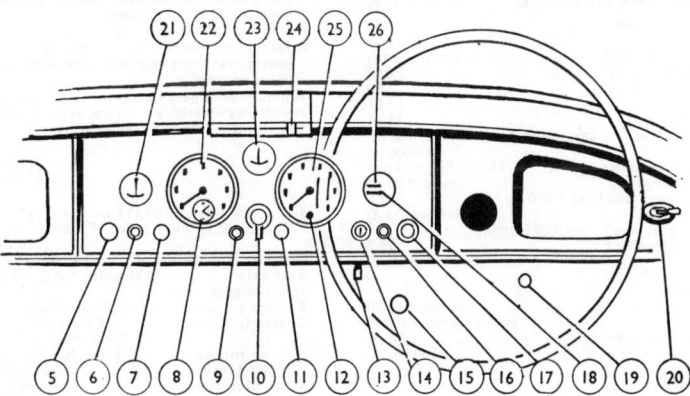

1, Gear lever. 2, Handbrake. 3, Horn button. 4, Direction indicator switch. 5, Windscreen wipers switch. 6, Panel light switch. 7, Heater fan switch. 8, Clock. 9, Screenwasher button. 10, Lights switch (including foglamps). 11, Interior light switch. 12, Headlamp main beam indicator. 13, Trip adjuster. 14, Ignition switch. 15, Headlamp dip switch. 16, Starter button. 17, Cigar lighter. 18, Water thermometer. 19, Bonnet catch release. 20, Overdrive control. 21, Fuel contents gauge. 22, Tachometer. 23, Ammeter. 24, Heater temperature control. 25, Speedometer. 26, Oil pressure gauge.

The Jaguar XK150S Fixed-head Coupé

include room for the driver's foot to the left of the clutch pedal, adjustable steering column for the four-spoke wheel and a central fly-off handbrake which, however, is scarcely as powerful as one could desire.

The instruments are centrally located and have circular black faces with clear white hands and figures, a small detail which is particularly appreciated being that the thermometer and oil pressure gauge share a single dial in front of the driver, their readings so planned that, when both oil pressure and engine temperature are normal, the two hands form a roughly vertical straight line and enable the driver to check that all is well in a single quick glance. The smaller switches are arranged along the base of the central panel in a manner not likely to cause confusion and moderately easy to reach.

The separately adjustable front seats offer a very adequate degree of comfort for long runs, but deeper shaping of the squabs for extra lateral support would be an advantage on such a car as this, whilst another minor improvement would be a less coarse seat adjustment. Vision to the sides and rear is excellent, but most of those who tried the car were at first rather conscious of the long, high bonnet—a somewhat inevitable penalty of so much engine! Average-to-tall drivers, however, can see both front wing tips.

For ventilation, the winding door windows disappear completely into the doors and the usual triangular hinged ventilating panels are provided on their leading edges. In addition, the quarter lights are pivoted to provide an extractor effect when required. The doors are wide and the flat floor makes entry and exit

CONTROL CENTRE for one of the world's fastest closed cars: practical details include a telescopic steering column, padded armrest on the transmission tunnel, cold air vents at foot level, and doors which are hollowed to provide extra elbow room and useful pockets.

easy, but care in opening is necessary alongside high pavements.

At the rear, a pair of small removable seats is provided and it is quite possible for one tall adult to be accommodated—in tolerable comfort if not in luxury—when occasion demands. Otherwise, the rear compartment forms a useful and sizeable adjunct to the rear luggage boot which, although somewhat shallow, nevertheless provides good accommodation for a car of this type. A sensible feature is that the partition between the boot and rear seats can be lowered to enable awkward objects to be accommodated partly in the rear compartment and partly in the boot.

Other details include a fresh-air heater and demister which work adequately if the fan is used . . . two well-placed transparent visors . . . headlights which give an excellent range and are supplemented by two foglights focused to pick out opposite kerbs . . . and stowage for the spare wheel and very comprehensive tool kit in a locker beneath the boot floor.

In all, this XK150S Jaguar is a truly remarkable car which combines a stupendous performance with surprising docility and good manners. To drive it is one of the more memorable experiences motoring has to offer.

Specification

Engine
Cylinders	6
Bore	83 mm.
Stroke	106 mm.
Cubic capacity	3,442 c.c.
Piston area	50.32 sq. in.
Valves	Overhead (twin o.h. camshafts)
Compression ratio	9/1
Carburetters	Three S.U. horizontal type HD8, 2 in.
Fuel pump	Two S.U. electric
Ignition timing control	Centrifugal and vacuum
Oil filter	Tecalemit, full flow
Max. power (gross)	250 b.h.p.
at	5,500 r.p.m.
Piston speed at max. b.h.p.	3,840 ft./min.

Transmission
Clutch	Borg and Beck, 10 in s.d.p.
Top gear (s/m)	4.09 (overdrive, 3.18)
3rd gear (s/m)	5.247
2nd gear (s/m)	7.60
1st gear	13.81
Reverse	13.81
Overdrive	Laycock-de Normanville, manual control
Propeller shaft	Hardy Spicer, open
Final drive	Hypoid bevel
Top gear m.p.h. at 1,000 r.p.m.	19.6 (overdrive, 26.4)
Top gear m.p.h. at 1,000 ft./min. piston speed	28.2 (overdrive, 36.2)

Chassis
Brakes	Dunlop disc all round, servo assisted
Disc diameter	12 in.
Rubbed area of discs	540 sq. in.
Total pad area	31.8 sq. in.
Suspension:	
Front	Independent by torsion bars and wishbones
Rear	Semi-elliptic
Shock absorbers	Girling telescopic hydraulic
Steering gear	Alford and Alder rack and pinion with internal damper
Tyres	Dunlop Road Speed with tubes, 6.00-16

Coachwork and Equipment

Starting handle	Nil
Battery mounting	Twin 6-volt, one in each front wing
Jack	Manual ratchet type
Jacking points	One each side of car (access through apertures in floor)
Standard tool kit:	Adjustable spanner, 6 box spanners, sparking plug box spanner, 2 tommy bars, 4 open-ended spanners, jack and lever, wheelbrace, pliers, copper and rawhide mallet, screwdriver, grease gun, tyre gauge, feeler gauge, distributor screwdriver, valve timing gauge, brake bleeder tube and container, valve extractor.
Exterior lights:	Two headlamps, two fog lamps, two side lights two stop/tail lights, reversing lamp, number plate lamp
Number of electrical fuses	6
Direction indicators:	Flasher type, self-cancelling; separate at front and combined with tail/stop lights at rear
Windscreen wipers	Lucas two-speed self-parking
Windscreen washers	Trico, vacuum-operated
Sun visors	Two of tinted transparent material

Sump: 15 pints, total (13 pints refill) S.A.E. 30 (S.A.E. 20 below 32 deg. F., S.A.E. 40 above 90 deg. F.)
Gearbox and overdrive	4 pints, S.A.E. 30
Rear axle	3½ pints, S.A.E. 90 hypoid
Steering gear lubricant	Grease
Cooling system capacity	23 pints (2 drain taps)
Chassis lubrication	By grease gun every 2,500 miles to 12 points
Ignition timing	9 deg. B.T.D.C. (static)
Contact-breaker gap	0.014-0.016 in.
Spark plug type	Champion N5
Spark plug gap	0.025 in.
Valve timing:	Inlet opens 15 deg. B.T.D.C., closes 57 deg. A.B.D.C. Exhaust opens 57deg. B.B.D.C., closes 15 deg. A.T.D.C.
Tappet clearances (Cold):	
Inlet	0.004 in.
Exhaust	0.006 in.

Instruments:	Speedometer (with decimal trip mileage recorder), rev counter (with inset clock), fuel gauge, coolant thermometer, oil pressure gauge, ammeter
Warning lights:	For ignition, headlamp main beam, low fuel level, direction indicators, overdrive switch
Locks:	With ignition key. Doors and petrol filler. With other keys. Glove locker and boot
Glove lockers:	Two, one with lockable lid, one open
Map pockets	One on each door
Parcel shelves	One behind rear seats
Ashtrays	One on each door
Cigar lighters	One on facia board
Interior lights	Interior lamp (below rear window), panel lights, boot lights
Interior heater	Fresh-air type with demister
Car Radio	Optional extra
Extras available	Radio
Upholstery material	Leather
Floor covering	Carpets
Exterior colours standardized	12
Alternative body styles	Open two-seater and drop-head coupe

Maintenance

Front wheel toe-in	Parallel to ⅛ in. toe-in.
Camber angle	½-1 deg. positive
Castor angle	1½-2 deg. positive
Steering swivel pin inclination	5 deg.
Tyre pressures:	
Normal:	
Front	23 lb.
Rear	26 lb.
Fast driving:	
Front	30 lb.
Rear	35 lb.
Maximum speeds:	
Front	40 lb.
Rear	45 lb.
Brake fluid:	Wakefield Crimson or any other fluid conforming to S.A.E. specification 70 R.I.
Battery type and capacity:	Twin 6-volt batteries (12-volt system) 64 amp./hr.

S.C.W. Quick Test ✓✓✓

S.C.W. drives Australia's

S stands for Glamour since Jaguar rehashed the alphabet.

NO JAGGED SEAMS TO THIS VELVET GLOVE

(Above) Three enormous S.U. carbs with plated dashpots add still more glister to Jag's already lustrous engine bay. (Below) Cockpit is spacious, luxuriously trimmed. Overdrive control is just forward of gearstick.

FOR sheer crowd-stopper potential, Jaguars stand alone — again.

Remember the kerfuffle the first XK-120s kicked up? Shoppers would push and shove and elbow their way into a scrum more hectic than anything the Kangaroos ever created just to get a look.

The early XK was a dream come true, a tangible embodiment of something that had haunted men's dreams for decades. It was long and low and sleek and (for those days) almost unbelievably aerodynamic. It had six cylinders and two overhead camshafts at a time when double knockers were strictly for the Bugattistes. It had a price tag that said it was there to be bought.

And bought it was. The profusion of well-used "Kays" in spectators' car parks and even occasionally in the pits at race meetings all across the country bears ample testimony. The XK 120 put Jaguars in the world competition picture, banishing forever that snide little nickname allusion to the Bentley.

Modifications followed, and with them came a certain slump in exoticism. The 140 was an attractive car, but it looked its age and its ancestry. The 150 was a lot more attractive, but it too lacked something.

Perhaps it was starkness. The 150 looks like the gran turismo machine it is. It seems too comfortable, too secure, too thoroughly tamed to appeal to the fellow for whom the Jaguar badge and nameplate conjure up visions of a lean, feline and above all fiery open two-seater laying tracks of rubber in the wake of its well-oiled operator and his laughing, goldenhaired companion.

The Coventry boffins have snapped back at this gentleman with characteristic brevity in the form of a single letter—S.

first and only XK-150S Roadster

But in the Jaguar alphabet S doesn't stand purely for Sports, or even for Speed. Sir William Lyons has pulled a string or two and worked it so that S can stand for Glamour.

Yes, all the original 120's dash and poise and sex appeal are back in this newest and most sparkling of all imports. So far there's just one XK-150S Roadster in this country, but no sooner had Sydney's Bryson Industries stripped off the shipboard plastic from its shapely cloth top than S.C.W. was on the doorstep begging a swift pedal.

We champed at the bit for nearly a week while Brysons sought permission from the War Veterans' Art Union people (the Jag is part of a £14,500 first prize) and erased a small legacy from the W.W.F. (one dent in the S-type's tail). Then the stage was set.

Standing in the William St. showroom window we caught a brief glimpse of an overalled employee scrambling out of something long and white at the kerbside before the crowd closed in. Shoving ourselves a passage through the melee we just stood and looked, too.

The 150S is even more attractive than its photographs suggest. It avoids the tendency to squatness that characterises the 150 fixed head and drophead coupes, thanks partly to some cunning redesign around the doors and scuttle, partly to a sweeping wraparound windscreen and perhaps most of all to an extremely long tail. From the front it looks brutish. Rearing wingline, hunched shoulders, poised power. From the sides it is just plain glamorous, chrome-plated wire wheels (optional, thank you) and all.

The tail is just a little cluttered. Too much disjointed ornament. But fat twin exhaust tailpipes help carry off a piece of rear-end styling that isn't, perhaps, quite as satisfying as it might be.

The engine compartment is every bit as exciting as it sounds. An audible sigh went up from the crowd as we lifted the bonnet, exposing polished cam boxes, plated balance pipes and three monstrous H.D.8 (two-inch) S.U. carburettors. Differences from standard XK-150 practice lie in the breathing arrangements. Each of the three carburettors feeds into a twin-branch, mildly curved inlet manifold and then through individual ports that are still slightly curved, but much straighter than before. The system follows Harry Weslake's patented venturi-entry principle, but thanks to the modified manifolding and more generous carburetion it gives better chamber filling at high engine speeds.

With these changes and a 9 to 1 compression ratio the Gold Top head boosts gross engine output to 252 b.h.p. at a modest 5,500 r.p.m. (normally 210 at 5,500). Maximum torque rises to 240 lb. ft. at 4,500 against the Blue Head version's 216 at 3,000. Other changes run to a strengthened 10-in. Borg and Beck clutch and quick-change pads for the servo-assisted 12-in. Dunlop disc brakes.

Inside, all is luxury. Trim is in genuine leather, matt finished in the appropriate places to avoid screen reflections. The scuttle rail is thickly padded with rubber that is perhaps a little spongy for real crash protection. The instrument panel, leather covered, has a rubber underlay. Thick, knobbly carpet covers the floor. It is seamed and properly tailored to fit.

The seats are pudgy and comfortable. They have obviously been designed to silence the worryings of suitably ardent young marrieds, but the consequent central perch wouldn't really keep such fortunates in cramp-free ownership of both Jaguar and Little One for more than five years or so—as 12 stone, still bruised Photographer Sandford will testify.

NO JAGGED SEAMS TO THIS VELVET GLOVE

This dual personality robs the seats of the powers of location that are strictly necessary in a car as sporting as the 150S. Any prospective owner who contemplates serious competition work will rip them smartly from their mountings and substitute honest buckets. More docile bachelors (not to mention our newlyweds) will stick for various reasons to the factory's semi-bench dictates.

The driver is nicely placed. He sits up to his work with an adequate range of seat and steering column adjustment waiting to suit his tastes. We juggled ourselves very smartly into a particularly comfy long-arm position that put the wheel just where it was handiest for high-speed twiddling and the pedals at easy leg's reach.

The pedals themselves are ideal. They're the usual long, narrow Jaguar type, light to use and perfectly placed for all the skilled manoeuvres beloved of every enthusiast. Heel-and-toe changes are so easy in this car that a child could handle 'em.

The gearstick is equally well placed. It is heavily cranked forward, but the stick's odd shape doesn't interfere with the slickness of the change. A fly-off handbrake (joy!) nestles between driver's seat and transmission tunnel.

Instruments, in spite of central placement, are surprisingly easy to read.

The engine sets up its even, soundless tickover at a touch of the keyside button. The exhausts burble happily to themselves. We're all set.

First impression is of almost incredible docility. This thumping 3.4-litre punch-packing horse-factory really does feel as smooth and as tractable at town speeds as anything that has yet emerged from Jaguar's Coventry headquarters. Quite literally, there's nothing apart from an unnaturally zestful response to the loud pedal to indicate that this car can develop any more than a domesticated 150 b.h.p., let alone 250. Low speed torque is not frightening, yet it is enough to allow perfectly smooth top gear acceleration from 10 m.p.h. upwards. The standard close-ratio C-type Moss gearbox further disguises the Roadster's tremendous performance at commuting speeds because it combines with engine torque characteristics to set a bottom limit of at least 2,500 r.p.m. even in low gear before things start to happen at bullet speed. The limited-slip diff. fitted as standard doesn't encourage wheelspin.

Unfortunately our tryout car had so few miles up that we hardly felt justified in trying anything that could possibly harm a brand new, barely bench-tried engine. The highest tachometer reading we saw in any gear was 3,000 r.p.m., and that only momentarily. At that speed the car had just begun to reveal its potential. The exhaust note was at the turning point between burble and snarl, the front end showed the first signs of rearing as the nylon Road Speeds on the back wheels bit at the road surface in earnest.

But even if we didn't sample even one mouthful of the Jag's own brand of soup, at least we had the chance to try some other facets of its personality.

We noticed with pleasure that the gearbox, at least in close-ratio form, had lost its old snickiness. Apart from the first-to-second sequence which called for a very determined clutch thrust and a sluggish left hand, the synchromesh seemed ready to withstand anything we liked to hand out in the nature of snatch changes either up or down. The electric overdrive, engaged on r.h.d. S-types through an auxiliary lever just forward of the gearstick, slid in and out of engagement so quietly that almost the only telltale was the tachometer. Overdrive, incidentally, gives a really useful 25 m.p.h. per 1,000 r.p.m. against top's 19.6.

Steering was light and about as precise as steering can get. It seemed a little high-geared for a rack and pinion setup at 3½ turns, and somehow it managed to transmit the feeling that this was, after all, a very heavy sports car at around 1½ tons laden. The steering had handy but not over-strong self-centring. The wheel's rake suited us perfectly.

Roadholding was not as inspiring as we had hoped, due in part to softish spring rates, but it was still mighty good for such a big car. Even on mild bends we were conscious of the Jaguar's bulk and for that reason it hardly seemed appropriate even to think of cornering really quickly (not that we would have done so anyway, considering). Maybe with the aid of all that engine willingness confidence would grow, but the process would probably take time.

The Dunlop disc brakes are superb. They react at a touch without the usual panicky disc brake feeling that the car isn't stopping quite as smartly as it should be—servo assistance seems to pay off!

And that's the Jaguar XK-150S. A supremely attractive car with all the power, both going and stopping, that most enthusiasts could want. We're deeply sorry we couldn't do more with it before our sleek beauty succumbed to the willing hands of many lottery workers and rolled quietly onto its display stand at the entrance to Sydney's Wynyard Station.

Never mind. By way of consolation there's always a 10/- ticket, available from 84 Pitt St., Sydney.

Santa Claus, inveterate gambler that he is, might consider calling early under that sort of provocation. #

—*Doug Blain*

CONTINUED FROM PAGE 148

only just over 30 mph and a marked inclination to promote axle-tramp if anything like a racing start was attempted. The wide gap between second and third was also noticeable, but over 90 mph could be attained in third and the rate of progress was well maintained in top gear, 110 mph coming up from rest in 32 seconds. Surprising as it may be to some, however, the 210 hp 3½-litre Jaguar was not as quick over a standing start quarter mile as the 120 hp, 2-litre AC Ace Bristol tried last month. For performance testing, far more than for normal use on the road, the location of the rev counter on the passenger's side—a design legacy, presumably, from left-hand drive, export cars—is a decided disadvantage.

Rain once again gave the road surface a glassy sheen for the return journey to the metropolis, and although tyre pressures had been restored to normal it proved expedient after a few miles to let yet more air out of the rear tyres—thereby considerably improving tail-end adhesion on a definitely treacherous surface. Only when an attempt was made to maintain "dry road" speeds was tail-end breakaway easily induced, but under such conditions the XK150 required rather delicate handling. It was, on the other hand, possible to slow down—and still get there more quickly than in almost any other car.

FLEXIBILITY

Back in London after completing the performance tests it was noticeable how *slowly* (as well as quickly) the Jaguar would run in third gear, trickling along in traffic and then accelerating without hesitation (other than that accounted for by lost motion in the linkage for the "treadle" accelerator pedal), the engine entirely free of temperament. In town, rather more than on the open road, the very long travel of the clutch pedal made itself felt, and completely silent upward gearchanges were less easily made at 2000 rpm in The Mall than at 5500 rpm on A11. Parking in confined spaces was much easier than had been expected, but more than once the doors jammed on high kerbs; the interior handles are of sliding type and as there are no retaining straps the doors sometimes swung wide open, to the annoyance of passers-by. In addition neither doors nor boot lid shut with the precision which is customary on other Jaguar models.

For shopping the XK150 has two major advantages. It is very easy to get into and out of and it usually earns prompt and courteous attention. But it is not really intended as a shopping car, and my chief memories of it will always be the effortless manner in which it devoured the miles when —late at night—everyone else had gone to bed, and the contemptuous ease with which it rode out the storm on that September Friday evening. For such purposes it would be difficult to imagine a more suitable means of transport.

—D. P.

PERFORMANCE DETAILS

Acceleration

0-30 mph	3.0 seconds
0-50 mph	6.8 "
0-70 mph	11.8 "
0-100 mph	25.0 "
Standing Quarter Mile	16.8 "
Maximum Speed (overdrive top)	125 mph

Speeds in Gears

First	31 mph
Second	60 "
Third	90 "
Top	112 "

Fuel Consumption	18 mpg

A VERY FAST CAR!

To Scotland and the Lake District in a Jaguar XK150S.

THE PERSONIFICATION OF SPEED AND CONTROLLED POWER.—A frontal view of the sleek, very low Jaguar XK150S, capable of a maximum speed of 133 m.p.h. combined with superb braking by Dunlop discs all round and outstandingly docile running.

IT was a happy coincidence that resulted in a Jaguar XK150S coupé being available for test at a time when we were committed to cover the recent R.A.C. International Rally, because we thus had an opportunity of trying this very fast British car over long distances to tight schedules.

In a week of intense motoring which took us up to Scotland and at night through the more steeply inclined areas of the Lake District this XK150S proved to be an extremely good motor car, docile yet exceedingly fast, comfortable, safe and handsome. You cannot well demand more from a car.

A full road-test of the less potent Jaguar XK150 appeared in MOTOR SPORT in October 1958 and in general layout the XK150S resembles that car. It is under the bonnet that the exciting differences are found. For example, the engine has the straight-port cylinder head (painted old gold for purposes of identification) with a 9 to 1 compression-ratio, triple 2-in. S.U. DH8 carburetters, a lightened flywheel and lead-bronze lined big-end bearings. These modifications result in a power output of 250 b.h.p. at very smooth 5,500 r.p.m., hence the use of the term "exciting." In keeping with this useful power output there is a high-pressure clutch, twin petrol pumps and Dunlop disc brakes all round with brake pads of the quick-change pattern.

Overdrive is provided on top gear, controlled by an electrical flick-switch convenient to the right hand on the test car but replaced on later cars by a lever, operating mechanically, and placed ahead of the remote-control central gear-lever.

Stationary, this Jaguar coupé is low-hung and eager-looking, its very low roof-line stylish and impressive. In action it combines immense acceleration and a maximum speed of M 1 potential with velvet-glove smoothness and commendable quietness. The 250 b.h.p. engine emits a subdued roar when it is opened up but is otherwise in no way obtrusive, while the absence of wind-noise round the body at speeds well over "the ton" is truly commendable.

It was into the capacious luggage boot of this Jaguar that we packed the paraphernalia inseparable from going away to watch a day-and-night rally and slid out of London just before the worst of the rush-hour traffic got off the leash. As the November daylight faded and the myriads of lights began to twinkle on the skyline of the Metropolis under banks of sombre clouds that suggested a night of rain, the XK150S thrust its way onto the Barnet By-Pass, aiming for the Motorway. While Londoners prepared to vacate office and factory and fight their way home to enjoy numerous leisure pursuits we in the Jaguar headed north, covering miles in the time it took the maelstrom behind us to cover as many yards.

Comfortable if not 100 per cent. perfect seats, a very efficient heater, and the whispering power of the turbine-smooth 3.4-litre twin-cam engine combine to render this 130 m.p.h. coupé a very restful form of fast transport, its tremendous resources of acceleration from the lowest speeds to near its maximum being both insurance against emergency and an effective means of getting through slow-moving traffic.

On the Motorway the Jaguar settled for 120 m.p.h. on its only mildly-optimistic speedometer, hardly fell below 100 m.p.h., and went to 5,000 r.p.m. in overdrive top gear, or some 128 m.p.h. not allowing for tyre growth at this speed—suffice it to say that in half-an-hour after entering M 1 we were back on A 5, a Motorway average of fractionally under 114½ m.p.h.

This sort of sustained high-speed cruising does not disturb the equanimity of the Jaguar's water or oil temperature, nor did the nylon Dunlop RS4 tyres appear to become more than normally warm. However, one of the exhaust flange gaskets had begun to blow when the car was delivered and this high-speed cruising made it worse so, after having spent the night in Chester, we had this repaired by the Jaguar agent in Blackpool the next day. The efficient way in which this was done while we watched the Rally competitors doing evolutions on the sea-front, and the courtesy extended, suggests an excellent understanding between the Jaguar Company and its agents, which is reflected in a happy and worthwhile customer relationship.

Now we settled down to follow part of the Rally in earnest, confident that the performance of the XK150S would get us where we wanted to be in ample time. So it proved, for we were able to eat a satisfactory dinner at the "Traveller's Rest" at Ulpha before spending the night observing at a choice r.h. bend at the foot of Wrynose Pass!

There is no need to deal in detail with the control arrangements and appointments of the XK150S because these resemble those of the XK150 coupé already road-tested by this journal. Suffice it to say that there is the same excellent gear change, so pleasant to use, a fly-off hand-brake set to the left of the considerable propeller-shaft tunnel, that both front wings are visible to an average-height driver but that the screen pillars seem somewhat thick to a tall occupant, and to permit the very low roof line the seats are set low. The passenger has a rather shallow cubby-hole, the lid of which can only be kept shut by locking it with a key, which is a minor irritation.

THE HEART OF THE XK150S.—This beautifully finished, very smooth, triple-carburetter 3.4-litre engine of this Jaguar gives 250 b.h.p. at 5,500 r.p.m., and will run up to over 6,000 r.p.m. quite readily.

THE JAGUAR XK150S

Engine : Six cylinders, 83 × 106 mm. (3,442 c.c.). Inclined overhead valves operated by twin overhead camshafts. 9-to-1 compression-ratio. 250 b.h.p. at 5,500 r.p.m.
Gear ratios : First, 13.81 to 1; second, 7.6 to 1; third, 5.24 to 1; top, 4.09 to 1; overdrive, 3.18 to 1.
Tyres : 6.00 × 16 in. Dunlop " Road Speed " RS4 on centre-lock wire wheels.
Weight : Not weighed. Maker's figure : 29 cwt. (kerb weight).
Steering ratio : 2 turns, lock-to-lock.
Fuel capacity : 14 gallons. (Range approximately 238 miles.)
Wheelbase : 8 ft. 6 in.
Track : Front, 4 ft. 3¾ in.; rear, 4 ft. 3¼ in.
Dimensions : 14 ft. 8½ in. × 5 ft. 4½ in. × 4 ft. 6¾ in. (high).
Price : £1,487 (£2,110 4s. 2d. inclusive of purchase tax).
Makers : Jaguar Cars Ltd., Coventry, England.

Performance Data

Speeds in gears at 5,500 r.p.m. :
   Second ... ... 59 m.p.h.
   Third ... ... 86 ,,
Acceleration :
   0-60 m.p.h. to 5,500 r.p.m.
     in third gear ... ... 9.8 sec. (9.9 sec.)
   0-60 m.p.h. to 6,000 r.p.m.
     in second gear ... 8.6 ,, (8.9 ,,)
   0-100 m.p.h. ... ... 24.4 ,, (24.7 ,,)

(Figures in parentheses are mean of runs in both directions.)

The driver has an adjustable steering column and room for his left foot beside the clutch pedal. The 140 m.p.h. speedometer is somewhat blanked by the steering wheel rim but the dial possesses trip with decimal and total mileage readings and the needles of the Smith's rev.-counter and speedometer move steadily round their big dials. The instruments are set on a leather-padded panel and the facia possesses crash-padding. Normally the water temperature remains at 70 deg. C., oil pressure at 40 lb./sq. in., as shown on separate dials.

The beauty of driving this fine car is that it is always well within itself. By this we mean that the engine is by no means under-geared. It is unnecessary to go " into the red " on the rev.-counter to obtain all the acceleration normally required, and if 5,500 r.p.m. is used in third gear there is a useful maximum of 86 m.p.h. In second the maximum at this speed is 59 m.p.h. By using overdrive, as has been seen, the engine runs well below peak speed, even approaching the Jaguar's maximum of over 130 m.p.h.

The bonnet-ful of highly impressive and beautifully-finished machinery is something over which the most blasé owner will enthuse and the legendary smoothness and quietness of the Jaguar twin o.h.c. power unit is well maintained in this 250 b.h.p. version.

The steering is perhaps on the spongy side but is quick and responsive, while road-holding is eminently satisfactory, providing the necessary discretion is used with the throttle out of bends on slippery roads.

Coming south from Scotland, traffic conditions made it impossible to average 50 m.p.h. in spite of vastly improved roads below Abington and the many miles of dual carriageway on A 1. However, average speeds very close to this target were achieved in complete safety, at night. Here tribute must be paid to the Dunlop disc brakes, which slow the Jaguar from 100 m.p.h. to a crawl without conscious pressure on the pedal, and, what is more, enable the driver to obtain extremely sensitive and progressive retardation when required.

Our dash south from Scotland was interrupted when it seemed expedient to investigate a noise which had developed in the near-side back wheel. Again a Jaguar agent, this time S.M.T. in Carlisle, gave us willing and courteous attention. The trouble was traced to worn splines on the wheel hub, probably accentuated by demonstrations of the car's remarkable " step-off " from a standstill. Replacing the suspect wheel with the spare improved matters and our high-speed journey continued.

In due course this XK150S was returned to Jaguar's, after proving an ideal car in which to travel far and fast in the November nights. It covered, in fact, over 1,750 miles in our hands and was returned with real reluctance.

Petrol consumption of 100-octane fuel worked out at a commendable 17.05 m.p.g. over 1,000 of the faster miles. Oil thirst was less satisfactory—altogether 14 pints were consumed and according to the dip-stick another three or four pints would have been welcome at the end of the test. Consumption was thus less than 900 miles a gallon.

A quick check of acceleration, after speedometer correction, gave 0-60 m.p.h. in third gear in 9.8 sec. or, holding second gear to 6,000 r.p.m., 8.6 sec., 0-100 m.p.h. (to 5,000 r.p.m. in top) taking 24.4 sec. on the best run.

There are few cars made anywhere in the World which combine the speed, acceleration, economy of petrol and docility of the three-carburetter Jaguar XK150S and none which offers better value-for-money, at its list price, inclusive of purchase tax, of £2,110.

This potent Jaguar justifiably takes its place amongst the great high-performance motor cars of the present day and age. And if, like some correspondents to MOTOR SPORT, you are hard to please, you can now obtain it with the 3.8-litre power unit . . . .—W. B.

CONTINUED FROM PAGE 141

at high cruising speeds, but normal third and fourth are very close together and ideally chosen to invite fast up and downshifts between these two gears. As in the past, the shift lever and quick-release racing type handbrake are centrally located. Shifting is fast and positive with a short travel, yet it is not too difficult to over-ride the synchromesh cones.

Which brings us to the $5,095 question: how does the XK150-S ride and handle? It rides and handles neither better nor worse than the XK140-MC, which means well enough from the standpoint of comfort, but not well enough from the standpoint of competition. A decade ago, the XK150 would have been a marvelous sports-racing machine, neutral-steering, viceless and dependable; but not today. Something should be done about getting rid of a chassis frame built from the main girders of Westminster Bridge, and something should also be done about the rear end. When cornered fast — really fast — the XK150's tires set up the same banshee-like wail for which its predecessors were famous; and though the rack-and-pinion steering is a dream, the car leans too much on turns.

Slip in a tubular frame and a torque-reaction device for the rear end, shed about 600 lbs and you will have an unbeatable Class C production sports-racing car. Too, that enormous windshield should be removable, and much weight could be saved (in competition) with aluminum doors devoid of winding windows, and the use of aluminum for the hood. That is, if Jaguar are at all serious about racing. If the XK150S is merely intended as a Gran Turismo machine, capable of effortless, silent and opulent highway speed, then it has no peer in its price bracket, nor in several brackets above. It is a splendid sports car, docile, fast and impressive, exhibiting in every last detail the usual high quality for which Jaguar is famous. But it is not, by any stretch of the imagination, a racing machine as well. ●

ATTRACTIVE. *The XK 150S is as attractive to look upon as it is exciting to drive, with 3.8-litre engine and disc brakes on all four wheels.*

JOHN BOLSTER TESTS
The 3.8-litre Jaguar XK 150S

LAST year, AUTOSPORT tested the 3.4-litre version of the Jaguar XK 150S. It has therefore been extremely interesting to sample a similar car with the 3.8-litre engine, which is now available on demand at a moderate extra cost. Irrespective of engine size, the "S" series Jaguar has a straight port-type cylinder head which is painted old gold for identification. It carries three 2 ins. SU carburetters, and gives a compression ratio of 9 to 1. Other differences include lead-bronze bearings, a lighter flywheel and a special clutch.

The chassis follows the lines of previous XK models. The frame is an extremely rugged box-section structure, with torsion-bar independent front suspension and rack and pinion steering. At the rear, a rigid axle on semi-elliptic springs is retained, the drive from the four-speed gearbox going through a conventional open shaft. Thus, the design is certainly well tried and of classical simplicity.

One of the most important features of the car is the braking system. Dunlop discs are installed all round with servo operation, and the hand brake is of the "fly-off" type. Centre locking wire wheels are fitted with Dunlop RS4 tyres. Although the machine is compact, it is of extremely solid construction and no attempt at weight reduction has been made.

The fixed-head coupé body is a thoroughly practical type. It has very wide doors containing useful pockets, and the whole interior is well padded, including even the instrument panel. I much prefer this functional interior treatment to the earlier polished wooden facia, and from the point of view of safety the improvement is obvious. The discreet smell of real leather underlines the general air of quality.

The two main seats are separate, and can be adjusted for the tallest driver, though they might with advantage provide more positive lateral location. The rear seats are really intended for children. Though the luggage boot is not enormous, it has quite a useful capacity.

The driving position is a fairly "flat"

PADDED FACIA. The new functional padded dashboard replaces the earlier polished wooden facia. Real leather upholstery underlines the general air of quality.

one, but very comfortable for long journeys. An adjustable steering wheel is a much appreciated feature and the controls are conveniently arranged. The windscreen seems a little shallow by modern standards, but in fact the visibility is good and the bonnet is not aggressively long. The test car, which was finished in dark green, was certainly as attractive to look upon as it was exciting to drive.

As with previous Jaguar models, I found that the normal tyre pressures were far too spongy for anything but the most gentle driving. The handling was generally "soft" and, though the ride was most luxurious, some more air was found to be advantageous before the full potential of the car could safely be displayed.

It then became apparent that the 3.8-litre engine is in a different world from the 3.4-litre. Let's face it, the 3.4-litre Jaguar is a tremendous car, but the 3.8-litre has that extra torque just where it matters most. For example, the acceleration from 100 to 120 m.p.h. is not noticeably less brisk than that from 80 to 100 m.p.h., and the car continues to surge forward even after the overdrive has been engaged at 115 m.p.h.

The maximum speed of 136.3 m.p.h. was timed with all equipment in place, including fog lamps, radio aerial, etc. Obviously, a little "cleaning up" would put a genuine 140 m.p.h. "in the bag", and in fact that speed may be touched under favourable conditions with the car

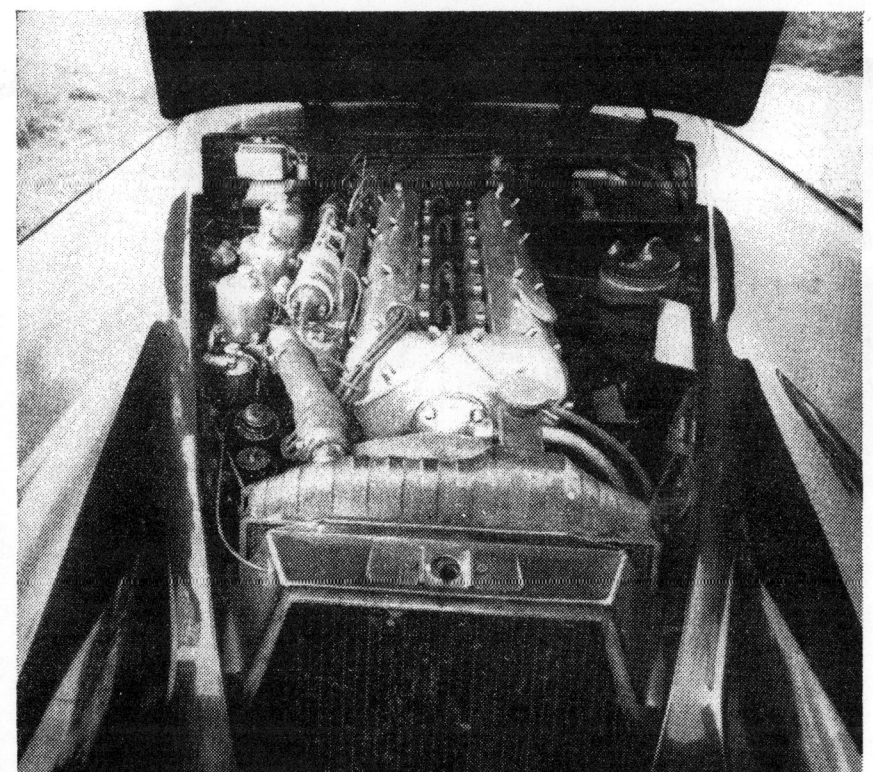

OVER 265 b.h.p. propels this luxurious touring car at speeds in excess of 135 m.p.h.

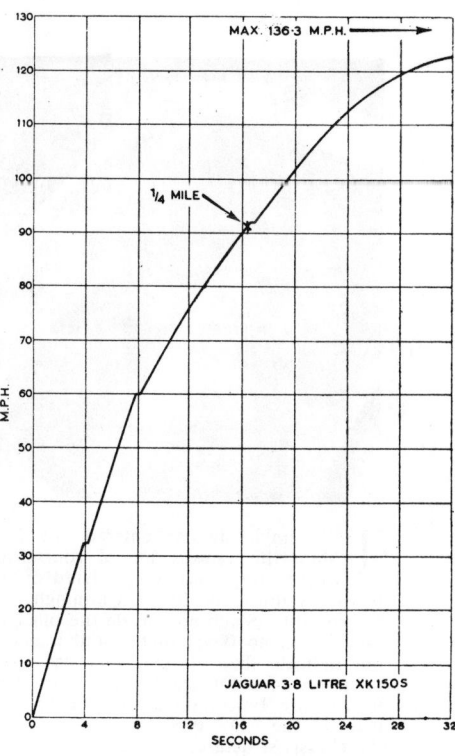

ACCELERATION GRAPH

in normal trim. This is an enormous velocity for a luxurious touring car, and in practical terms it means that there is spectacular acceleration available for overtaking, even at a Motorway cruising speed of 100 m.p.h. or more.

The acceleration is of the kick-in-the-back variety right up the scale, but the potential figures could not be recorded because of wheelspin on the getaway. The 3.4-litre which I tested had a limited-slip differential. Such a component was presumably fitted to the "3.8", yet propeller shaft torque caused the right-hand rear wheel to spin all too easily. In consequence, the initial acceleration was inferior to that recorded for the earlier car, but only because the power could not be transmitted to the road. I would guess that a standing quarter-mile in 14 seconds, and other figures of a similar order, could easily be recorded if independent rear suspension were adopted.

Once the car has been "unstuck" the bigger engine gives a noticeably livelier performance. For example, it reaches 120 m.p.h. in 4.2 seconds less time than the XK 120 took to achieve 100 m.p.h., and not so long ago the XK 120 was regarded as just about the ultimate in potency! There is a wonderful sensation of having almost unlimited power under one's toe, and provided that this immense reserve is never abused, it can be regarded as a very real safety factor in time of trouble.

In their way, the Dunlop disc brakes are just as dramatic as the sheer engine power. The way in which they subdue three-figure speeds, over and over again without any trace of fading, is something which renders the vast performance a practical proposition. A purist might claim that the brakes lack "feel" at town speeds, but once the car is really moving they are sensitive and responsive in a manner which approaches perfection. As is sometimes found with an all-disc design, the hand brake is not at all powerful, though it has a pleasant "fly-off" lever.

The high-speed stability of the car is excellent, and the driver may remain relaxed at over 136 m.p.h. Bumps, changes of camber, and an appreciable curve were deliberately essayed at this velocity without any drama. The Jaguar runs naturally straight and true, in which respect it greatly excels the earlier XK models.

Having regard to its substantial construction and conventional chassis design, the XK 150S corners very well. It rolls less than the saloons of the same make, and is not addicted to screaming its tyres. Furthermore, the 3.8-litre engine may be called upon to provide a modicum of drift on even very fast curves. Its behaviour is always predictable, and there is nothing unusual about its handling. In brief, this is a very fast touring car rather than a tamed-down racing car, and should be treated accordingly, when extremely safe motoring will be the result.

So far, we have tended to speak of the XK 150S in terms of ultimate performance. Yet, it has an even greater charm when not fully extended. Using top gear alone, it will laze along at 25, 50 or 100 m.p.h., and a gentle depression of the pedal will send it scurrying past any ordinary car. The engine is quiet, smooth and utterly responsive to the driver's smallest whim. One may drive all day without really pressing with the right foot, and yet the knowledge that 265 b.h.p. is there for the asking is one of motoring's finest luxuries. A Jaguar driver ought to be a good driver, because he need never be in a hurry.

The Jaguar XK 150S is an extremely fast luxury car that is even more delightful to handle when powered with the 3.8-litre engine. Naturally, it uses more petrol in this guise, but the extra cost is certainly paid for in performance and flexibility. If one must find fault, the steering tends to be heavy for parking and the synchromesh is not particularly potent. Yet, all in all, it is a superbly comfortable car with an almost incredible performance, and if £1,000 were added to the price it would still represent excellent value.

SPECIFICATION AND PERFORMANCE DATA

Car Tested: Jaguar XK 150S fixed head coupé, price £2,065 4s. 2d. including P.T.

Engine: Six cylinders 87 mm. x 106 mm. (3,781 c.c.). Inclined valves in light alloy head operated by twin chain-driven overhead camshafts. Compression ratio 9 to 1. 265 b.h.p. at 5,500 r.p.m. Three SU type HD8 carburetters. Lucas coil and distributor.

Transmission: Specially strengthened Borg and Beck 10 ins. single dry plate clutch. Four-speed gearbox with synchromesh on upper three ratios and central remote control, plus Laycock-de Normanville overdrive. Ratios 3.19 (O/D.), 4.09, 4.95, 7.16 and 12.2 to 1. Open Hardy-Spicer propeller shaft. Hypoid rear axle.

Chassis: Box-section frame. Independent front suspension by wishbones and torsion bars. Rack and pinion steering. Rear axle on semi-elliptic springs. Girling telescopic dampers. Dunlop brakes with 12 ins. discs all round, vacuum servo assisted. Centre lock wire wheels, fitted 6.00-16 ins. Dunlop RS4 tyres.

Equipment: 12-volt lighting and starting. Speedometer, rev.-counter, oil pressure and water temperature gauges, ammeter, fuel gauge, clock, cigar lighter, self-parking windscreen wipers and washers. Heating and demisting.

Dimensions: Wheelbase, 8 ft. 6 ins.; track, 4 ft. 3⅝ ins.; overall length, 14 ft. 9 ins.; width, 5 ft. 4½ ins.; turning circle, 33 ft. Weight, 28½ cwt.

Performance: Maximum speed, 136.3 m.p.h. Speeds in gears: direct top, 115 m.p.h.; 3rd, 92 m.p.h.; 2nd, 60 m.p.h.; 1st, 32 m.p.h. Standing quarter-mile, 16 secs. Acceleration: 0-30 m.p.h., 3.4 secs.; 0-50 m.p.h., 6.2 secs.; 0-60 m.p.h., 7.6 secs.; 0-80 m.p.h., 12.8 secs.; 0-100 m.p.h., 19 secs.; 0-110 m.p.h., 22.2 secs.; 0-120 m.p.h., 27.8 secs.

Fuel Consumption: Driven hard, 13 m.p.g.

The LE MANS

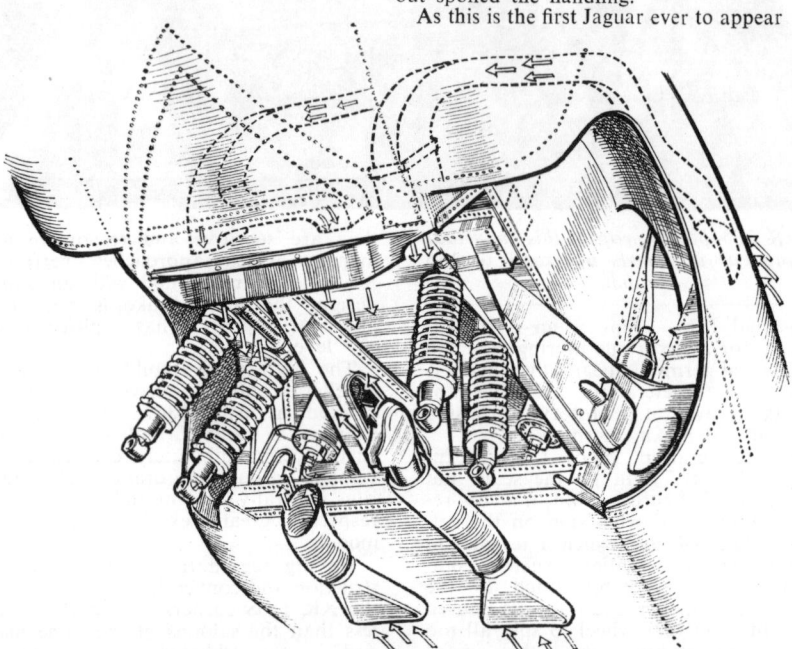

Both wipers and screenwashers have been developed to work at 160 m.p.h. and the screen, of course, is glass. The washers are screened both from the air blast and, more important, from flies that are found to block the jets. The lower wiper is the main one but if it fails the upper one can be brought into use by calling at the pits and inserting a fuse.

THE single Jaguar entered for Le Mans this year is not, of course, a works entry, but was ordered as a private venture by Briggs Cunningham, the entrant. Standing outside the official line, it has no type number and it does not indicate that the company has any intention of returning to racing in the near future. Essentially a logical development of the "D" type competition cars, the chassis structure, rear suspension and engine all show interesting departures from the earlier model.

The engine combines a larger bore (85 mm.) than the 3.4-litre engine with a special crankshaft giving a stroke of 88 mm., and running in seven main bearings in a new light alloy block and crankcase which is the principal innovation. The crankcase finishes on the centre line of the main bearings, which have steel caps, each held on by four bolts in line, and is ribbed for stiffness on the outside surfaces. The liners, pressed into the bores, are almost but not quite dry; between the siamesed cylinders, where there is no space for water circulation, slots are formed in the light alloy near the top of the bores which allow some water to contact the liners directly. Cylinder-head studs and other important bolts thread into heli-coil inserts in the light alloy casting which effects a saving in weight of no less than 80 lb.

Lucas petrol injection into the ports is used in conjunction with a "D" type induction system which has slide throttles operated by a rack and pinion system from the accelerator pedal, and the cylinder heads, which are still basically hemispherical, have been modified to provide some squish area.

It will be recalled that earlier "D" types had a monocoque centre-section formed from riveted light alloy sheet with tubular sub-frames bolted on as extensions at front and rear. The new chassis is very similar, with the main strength residing in the large box members which run under the doors at each side and are bridged by the immensely strong scuttle structure at the front and by the bulkhead box at the back which is shaped to form backrests for the seats, and which contains the flexible bag fuel tank. It differs in that the monocoque structure now extends to replace the rear sub-frame, with the rear body sides and wheel arches providing the cantilever strength to support the tail and the compulsory "luggage boot" which contains the spare wheel and tools. All the principal loads and thrusts from suspension and brakes are transmitted to the car through the final drive unit, and the drawings show how this is mounted to the main structure by special triangular members cantilevered back from the strongest parts of the centre-section (the side boxes and the propeller shaft tunnel).

At the front a tubular steel sub frame is retained; fully triangulated in both plan and elevation, it is bolted to the centre section at four points each side. As previously, the front suspension is by fore and aft torsion bars and unequal length forged wishbones of which the lower ones are joined by a substantial anti-roll bar. Steering geometry conforms with the conventional Ackerman layout, and the rack and pinion gear is bolted solidly to the front cross member. In course of development a rubber-mounted rack, as used on the XK 150 models, was tried but spoiled the handling.

As this is the first Jaguar ever to appear

The upper drawing shows the cantilever members which support the rear of the differential assembly and the mounting of the suspension units. Two ducts run underneath to cool the front of the brake discs, and the two ducts shown dotted, which are fed by side intakes, are for the brake callipers and the transmission oil cooler. Projecting downwards can be seen the "pots" or sumps of the fuel tank. The lower drawing shows the single-pad discs, the anti-roll bar and the front mounting of the unit.

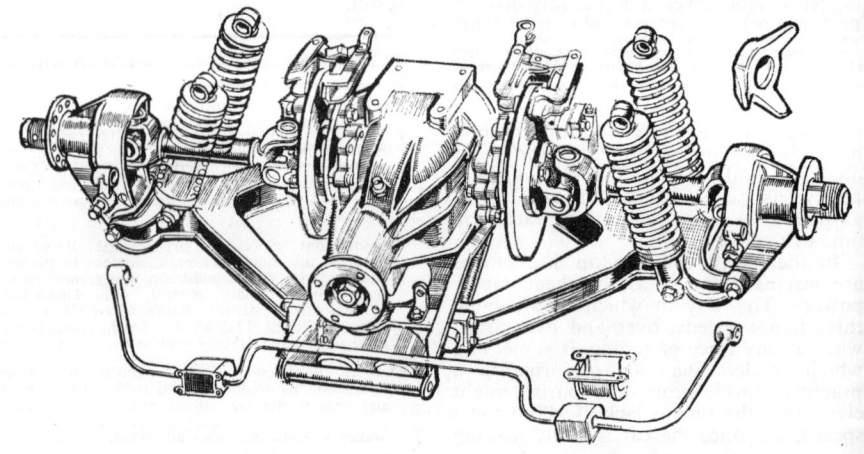

JAGUAR

A flexible clear plastic cover, not shown here, fits over the passenger's side of the new car's cockpit. Note the small rotating ventilator fitted in the Perspex sidescreen and the air intake just behind the door. The body was wind-tunnel developed at Loughborough College.

with independent rear suspension, considerable interest attaches to the design which is clearly shown in the drawings. The large fabricated steel wishbone is attached to the differential housing by widely spaced taper roller bearings at its inner end and to a cast light alloy hub carrier at its outer end with similar bearings. The fixed length halfshafts, with double universal joints, act as radius arms and the actual suspension is by pairs of Girling coil spring/damper units which pass each side of the drive shafts and attach to the wishbones. Geometrically therefore, this is equivalent to an ordinary double wishbone system with the lower wishbone longer than the upper one (the halfshaft). In rear elevation the lower member slopes downwards towards its outer end so that the roll centre is raised an inch or two from the ground. Structurally, as the drive shaft is only capable of reacting loads along its axis, the main wishbone is partly responsible for lateral location and camber control of the rear wheel, and wholly responsible for the control of wheel direction and the transmission of fore and aft loads due to acceleration and braking. As the latter forces act at hub level, they apply a large twisting movement to the wishbone which, together with the need for the utmost rigidity, explains its massive construction. Despite this, it was interesting to learn that a slight tendency to weave at high speed was eventually traced to the ends of the wishbone deflecting forwards under full power and giving some toe-in. To counter this, and to cancel the side thrust caused by 1° of negative camber, the rear wheels are now set with ⅛ in. static toe-in.

The rear suspension, which is completed by a quite flexible anti-roll bar, gives a total wheel travel of about 6 in. With a rate of 165 lb./in. at the wheel, giving a static deflection in the region of 3 in. under full load, it must be classed as relatively hard.

As usual, various difficulties had to be overcome in course of development. It was found that fuel starvation due to surge occurred with sustained cornering at 0.8 g side thrust when the fuel level dropped to 3 pints in one direction or 16 gallons in the other direction (more than half full). Petrol injection systems are particularly sensitive to air in the line as there is no equivalent to the normal float chamber to act as a separator, and special baffling had to be developed for the small "pots" below the flexible tank from which fuel is drawn by the high-pressure pump.

A further trouble, which first appeared on the experimental de Dion-suspended "D" type, was rapid destruction of the differential oil seals by heat inflow from the inboard brake discs. In three successive stops from 140 to 30 m.p.h. the temperature of the latter rose to over 1,000° C., and the oil seal temperature to 330° C. Special air cooling ducts have reduced the disc temperatures to about 800° C., but much investigation was needed to isolate the heat conduction paths to the seals. Interposition of several partial air gaps has now reduced their maximum temperature to about 140° C. which is comfortably less than they can stand.

It is not surprising, however, that a combination of radiant heat from the discs, conduction through the flanged shafts and poor cooling due to the submerged position of the differential unit can raise the transmission oil to temperatures at which rapid carbonization occurs. By switching on the simple but effective circulatory cooling system illustrated, the driver can now counteract this as soon as the temperature gauge rises above a reasonable level.

Although a privately entered car has a difficult task in taking on the factory teams, the Jaguar should be capable of matching any opposition at Le Mans.

The special cooler for the differential oil is fed from one of the side intake ducts. A standard S.U. pump can be switched on by the driver when the oil temperature gets too high, and oil is circulated through the cooler which brings the temperature down to not more than 80° C. A similar duct the other side feeds cooling air to the brake callipers.

JAGUAR SPECIFICATION

ENGINE
- Cylinders .. .. 6.
- Bore and stroke .. 85 mm. × 88 mm. (3.346 in. × 3.464 in.).
- Cubic capacity .. 2,997 c.c.
- Compression ratio .. 10/1.
- Valvegear .. .. Twin o.h.c.
- Carburation .. Lucas petrol injection fed by high-pressure pump, from 26½-gallon tank.
- Ignition .. .. 12-volt coil.
- Lubrication .. Dry sump system with 4-gal. total capacity.
- Electrical system .. 12-volt 40 amp. hr. battery.
- Maximum power .. 295 b.h.p. at 6,800 r.p.m.

TRANSMISSION
- Clutch .. .. Borg and Beck 3-plate, 7¼ in. dia.
- Gearbox .. .. 4-speed with synchromesh on all 4 ratios.
- Overall ratios .. 3.31, 4.23, 5.44 and 7.10; reverse 7.26.
- Propeller shaft .. Hardy Spicer open.
- Final drive .. .. Salisbury hypoid bevel.

CHASSIS
- Brakes .. .. Dunlop disc (twin system). No servo.
- Wheels and tyres .. Dunlop light alloy pin drive disc wheels with centre lock fitting and 6.5×16 Dunlop Stabilia tyres.
- Steering .. .. Rack and pinion. 2½ turns from lock to lock.

DIMENSIONS
- Length .. .. Overall 14 ft. 2 in.; wheelbase 8 ft.
- Width .. .. Overall 5 ft. 3¾ in.; track 4 ft. front and rear.
- Height .. .. To top of screen, 3 ft. 8¾ in.; ground clearance 6¼ in. To top of fin 4 ft. 5¼ in.
- Turning circle .. 38½ ft.

SPECIAL: THE XK SERIES JAGUAR

THE MEMORABLE INTRODUCTION of the Jaguar XK-120 roadster at the 1948 Earls Court Automobile show created much more than a local sensation. It created a general appreciation of flowing, functional body lines; fostered a budding suspicion that sheer glitter might not make the car, after all; and went straight to the heart of every sporting spirit with its thrilling, eager performance. In short, the Jaguar XK-120 promised to make driving fun, and then proved it. To many, the price of automotive one-upmanship came to equal the price of a new, or used, Jaguar roadster. The subsequent presentation of the XK-140 and the XK-150, together with the various modifications of each, brought even better performance and reliability.

The following reports, on the Jaguar XK-120, XK-140 and XK-150 roadsters, are abstracted from material current when the cars were introduced. As did the Road Tests on the T-series MGs (*Road & Track,* June), they attempt to convey the feeling of the times, and present the original material more adequately.

XK-120

1951 — The performance, smoothness, appearance and price of the Jaguar XK-120 make it one of the best sports car values on the market today. It has been rumored that Mr. William Lyons, General Manager of Jaguar Cars Ltd., was personally responsible for the design of the XK-120 Jaguar, but regardless of whose drawing board gave birth to its flowing lines, the car is a paradox. The performance alone makes it a man's car in the truest sense, yet its concours design and feminine appeal make it equally attractive to women.

Perhaps the greatest charm of the Jaguar lies in its response to the driver's skill and proficiency, for this is a car with a dual personality. Driven hard, and using the upper 3 (synchronized) gears to the full, acceleration is far better than will ever be needed in the fiercest stoplight GP. On the other hand, the 6-cyl dohc engine will give smooth acceleration in 4th gear from 15 to over an honest 120 mph, and a lazy driver can even putter around town in high gear, using 2nd only for starting up from traffic lights.

The Jaguar XK-120 has proven to be extremely popular in the U.S., but there are those who have questioned its high-speed ability. For this reason, we were particularly anxious to obtain an accurate top-speed figure. Our test car was completely stock, with no engine alterations, underpan or tonneau cover, and used the standard 3.64:1 rear axle ratio. However, we did remove the windshield and fitted an "aero-screen" (optional extra), a concession to performance which resulted in both the driver and photographer turning a deep blue in the morning desert cold. It was necessary to make numerous runs to obtain the figure we felt was optimum for the car.

At 123 mph (there were two men in the car during the runs), the Jaguar had a steadiness usually associated only with race cars, and occasional gusts of wind had very little effect on its stability.

The brakes proved to be excellent, fading slightly only under the most extreme abuse. However, pedal pressure was a little too low for our own taste.

Around town, the XK-120 is sheer pleasure. Third gear is a better ratio for city traffic than 4th and, on the open road, is just right for passing, with a 60–80 time of just 6.6 sec. Even over 90 in 3rd, the engine felt smooth and strong. Though it did tend to overheat in traffic, cooling was adequate under highway conditions.

The suspension of the Jaguar is all that could be desired in a very fast, long-distance touring machine. It is very stiffly sprung, when compared with current U.S. family cars, and has much less roll. We found it to be entirely comfortable during long drives, and particularly appreciated the excellent seating position and the luxurious leather seats. Luggage accommodations are somewhat less than

ample, though the trunk took two fair-sized suitcases.

The car has a rather awkward appearance with its far-from-weatherproof top in place, and looks even more homely with the fender skirts installed but, in spite of these points, we predict that the styling and performance of the Jaguar XK-120 will bring it immediate and lasting success in the U.S. market.

ROAD TEST
JAGUAR XK-120

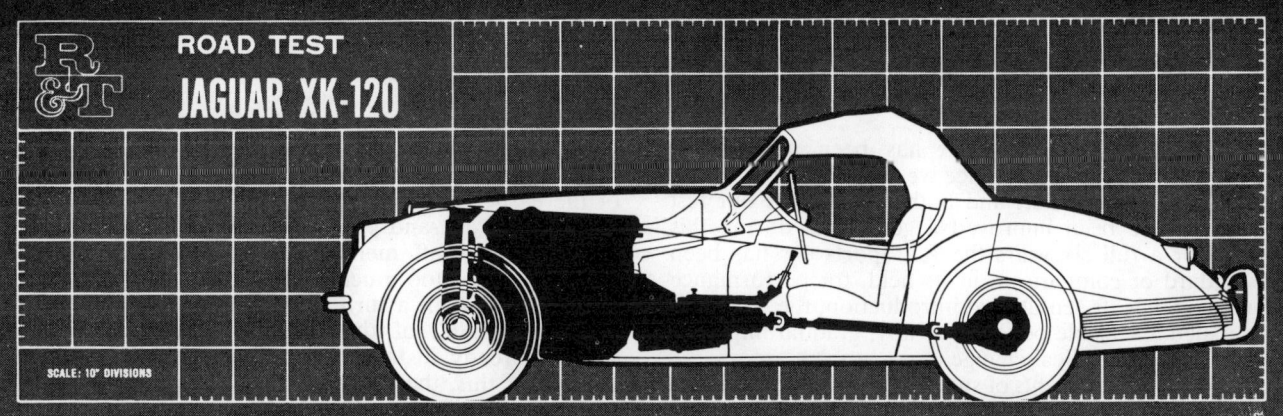

SCALE: 10" DIVISIONS

DIMENSIONS
Wheelbase, in 102.0
Tread, f and r 51.0/50.0
Over-all length, in 173
　width 61.5
　height 52.5
　equivalent vol, cu ft . . . 324
Frontal area, sq ft 18.0
Ground clearance, in 7.1
Steering ratio, o/a . . . . . . n.a.
　turns, lock to lock 3.2
　turning circle, ft 31
Hip room, front 43.0
Hip room, rear . . . . n.a.
Pedal to seat back 40.0
Floor to ground 15

CALCULATED DATA
Lb/hp (test wt) 19.7
Cu ft/ton mile 104.5
Mph/1000 rpm (4th) . . . 22.1
Engine revs/mile 2715
Piston travel, ft/mile . . . 1885
Rpm @ 2500 ft/min . . . 3600
　equivalent mph 79.5
R&T wear index 51.2

SPECIFICATIONS
List price $3945
Curb weight, lb 2820
Test weight 3160
　distribution, % 48/52
Tire size 6.00-16
Brake swept area 340
Engine type . . . . . 6 cyl, dohc
Bore & stroke . . . . . 3.27 x 4.17
Displacement, cc 3442
　cu in 210
Compression ratio 8.00
Bhp @ rpm . . . . . 160 @ 5400
　equivalent mph 119
Torque, lb-ft . . . 195 @ 2500
　equivalent mph 56.2

GEAR RATIOS
4th (1.00) 3.64
3rd (1.37) 4.98
2nd (1.98) 7.22
1st (3.38) 12.29

SPEEDOMETER ERROR
30 mph . . . . actual, 27.0
60 mph 55.8

PERFORMANCE
Top speed (4th), mph . . . 121.6
　best timed run 123.2
3rd (5750) 93
2nd (5750) 64
1st (5800) 38

FUEL CONSUMPTION
Normal range, mpg 16/22

ACCELERATION
0-30 mph, sec 3.2
0-40 . . . . 5.4
0-50 . . . . 7.5
0-60 . . . . 10.1
0-70 . . . . 13.2
0-80 . . . . 16.6
0-100 . . . . 27.5
Standing ¼ mile 18.3
　speed at end 84.0

TAPLEY DATA
4th, lb/ton @ mph . 270 @ 55
3rd . . . . 380 @ 47
2nd . . . . 520 @ 40
Total drag at 60 mph, lb . 110

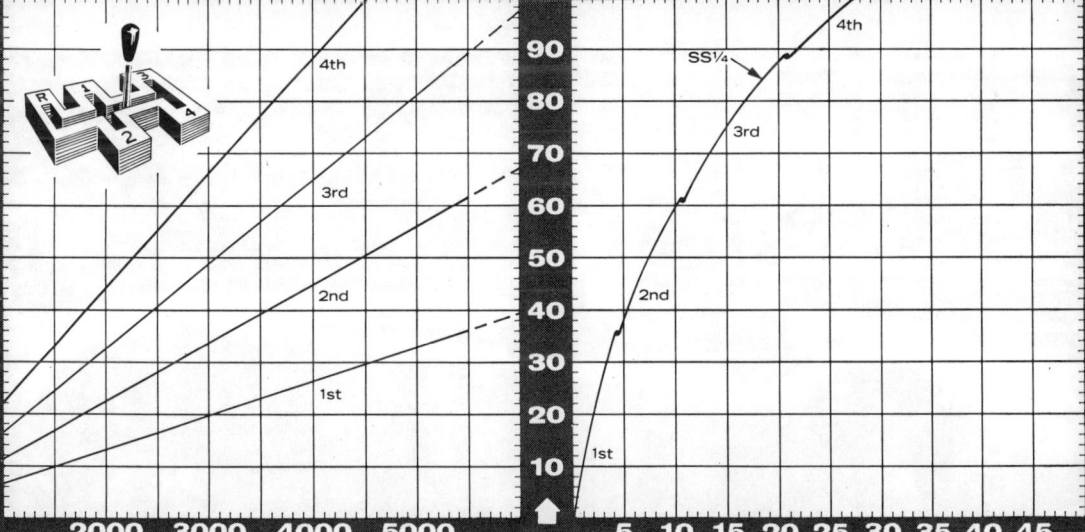

XK-140

1955 — It has been nearly four years since we tested a Jaguar roadster, and both the car and our test procedure have been improved a good deal during this period. For a full six years the XK sports car has been the standard of comparison, in its field, for performance and value. Since its sensational introduction, the company has pursued a sensible policy of steady, gradual improvement rather than radical change.

One of the great benefits of such a policy is that, whereas the original price of about $4000 seemed high to the average American, the price today—after its spectacular 1953 drop of up to $800—is not only lower in dollars, but is also an especially good value when compared with the fantastic prices now being asked for "middle-priced" U.S. cars. In addition to this, of course, there is Jaguar's remarkable record of consumer satisfaction, which stems not only from good service, but also from the fact that absence of model change has kept depreciation remarkably low.

We elected to test the latest roadster in its most de luxe form, the XK-140-MC. The M stands for modified (including wire wheels, and dual exhaust) and the C for the C-type cylinder head. These options added $295 to the list price (included in our data panel price), as well as 20 bhp to the power output of the car. An overdrive is also available as optional equipment.

The long interval between tests made it difficult to make objective comparisons. We did feel, however, that the 1955 car was a little easier to drive in traffic, and that there was a little more leg room than on previous models. The shift lever was somewhat easier to manipulate, but the bias of the pedals to the left felt awkward for a while.

The great increase in horsepower (boosted from the original 160 to 210 bhp) is accompanied by more smoothness and quiet, with the exception that full throttle seems to bring a certain amount of roughness. When we floored the throttle at very low rpm, however, there was a faint tinkle, indicating that the engine tuning was all but perfect for local conditions and premium fuel.

Our test car, to our disappointment, had the old-type gearbox installed, as did most of the early 1955 models. It was adequate, but the excessively high ratio low gear seemed to use too many revolutions for a brisk traffic start. The new close-ratio box is expected to be a considerable improvement. However, we did have the latest M-type exhaust system, which all but silences the engine. This may be something of a disappointment to those enthusiasts who took pride in the rap and crackle of the earlier mufflers.

The new rack-and-pinion steering cannot be criticized, though some staff members felt that the caster return action required too much force at the steering wheel rim to hold the car in a turn.

For 1955, all of the Jaguar models use the stiffer springs already installed for some time on the M-type. In view of this, the excellence of the ride was somewhat surprising and, in fact, the front end oscillations per minute seem to be almost unchanged. This result was achieved by moving the engine about 5 in. farther forward and tilting the radiator to fit under the hood. We found that adjusting tire pressures upward to 30 psi in front and 35 psi at the rear made the tires stop protesting each time we cornered vigorously. The higher pressures made very little difference in the ride.

For a sports car, the Jaguar does have considerable roll in a corner. The extra comfort of the springing which allows this roll, however, will be appreciated by all but the toughest diehards. Also, the beginning of a noticeable roll is a reliable indication of safe cornering speed, and we feel that the Jaguar is one of the easiest and safest automobiles to drive being built today.

The data panel figures tell much of the story on performance. Obviously, only today's cars costing at least twice as much as the XK-140 can improve on such times—but what the figures do not show is the utter ease of obtaining almost exactly the same figures again and again. High speed runs were made with the top up and curtains installed, and we found that wind noise put an end to ordinary conversation at about 75 mph. There were some drafts, which could be eliminated by a little judicious bending of the curtain frames, and visibility to the rear was very poor.

Purists will undoubtedly take offense at the more massive, and substantial, bumpers, but all should agree that the larger luggage compartment is an improvement.

All things considered, in our opinion the "standard of the world" has been, and still is, the Jaguar—in the sports car category.

ROAD TEST
JAGUAR XK-140

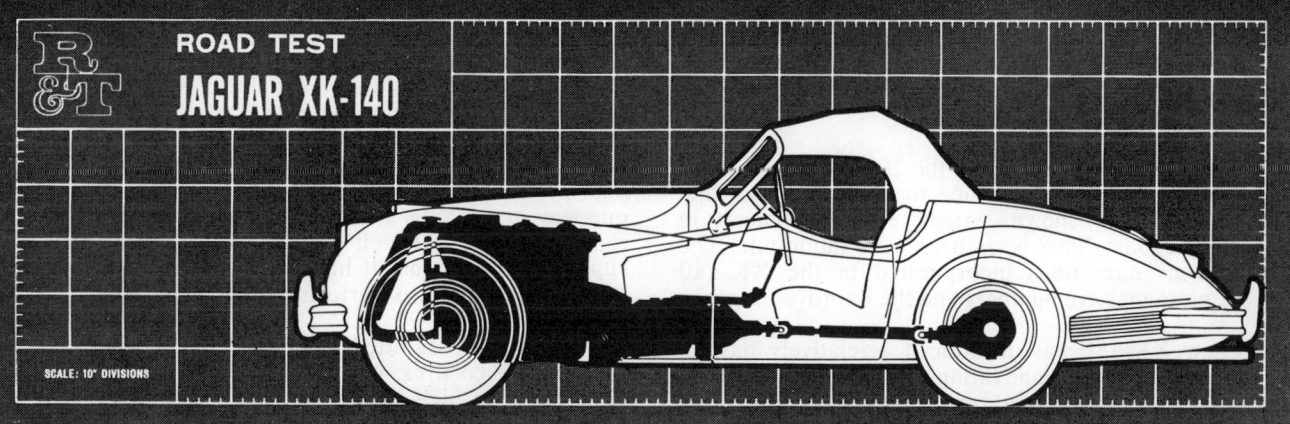

SCALE: 10" DIVISIONS

DIMENSIONS
Wheelbase, in	102.0
Tread, f and r	51.0/50.5
Over-all length, in	177
width	61.5
height	52.5
equivalent vol, cu ft	331
Frontal area, sq ft	18.0
Ground clearance, in	7.1
Steering ratio, o/a	n.a.
turns, lock to lock	3.5
turning circle, ft	33
Hip room, front	43
Hip room, rear	n.a.
Pedal to seat back	40
Floor to ground	15

CALCULATED DATA
Lb/hp (test wt)	16.7
Cu ft/ton mile	94.0
Mph/1000 rpm (4th)	23.1
Engine revs/mile	2600
Piston travel, ft/mile	1810
Rpm @ 2500 ft/min	3600
equivalent mph	83.1
R&T wear index	47.1

SPECIFICATIONS
List price	$3745
Curb weight, lb	3135
Test weight	3500
distribution, %	49.6/50.4
Tire size	6.00-16
Brake swept area	340
Engine type	6-cyl, dohc
Bore & stroke	3.27 x 4.17
Displacement, cc	3442
cu in	210
Compression ratio	8.00
Bhp @ rpm	210 @ 5750
equivalent mph	133
Torque, lb-ft	213 @ 4000
equivalent mph	92

GEAR RATIOS
4th (1.00)	3.54
3rd (1.37)	4.83
2nd (1.98)	7.01
1st (3.38)	11.95

SPEEDOMETER ERROR
30 mph	actual, 30.1
60 mph	57.6

PERFORMANCE
Top speed (4th), mph	125
best timed run	121.1
3rd (5800)	98
2nd (5800)	68
1st (5800)	39

FUEL CONSUMPTION
Normal range, mpg	16/18

ACCELERATION
0-30 mph, sec	2.7
0-40	4.2
0-50	6.5
0-60	8.4
0-70	12.1
0-80	15.7
0-100	26.5
Standing ¼ mile	16.6
speed at end	82

TAPLEY DATA
4th, lb/ton @ mph	280 @ 65
3rd	400 @ 52
2nd	550 @ 45
Total drag at 60 mph, lb	116

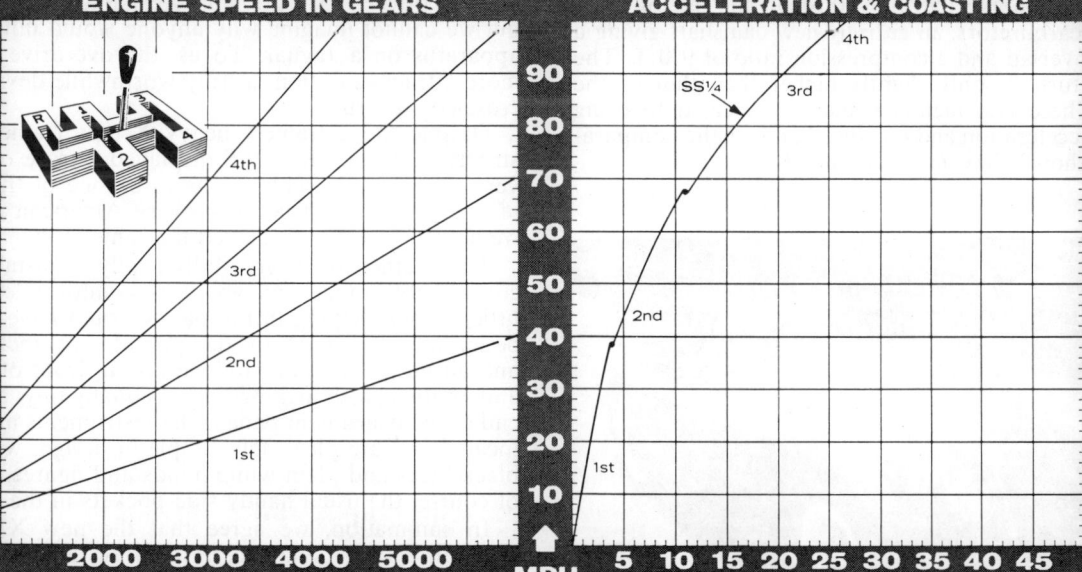

XK-150

1958 — In the 10 years which have passed since the XK-120 was first shown, extensive body changes in XK-series Jaguars have been held to a minimum. The most obvious alterations incorporated in the XK-140 were the more massive bumpers and the improved luggage space.

The new XK-150 has introduced a relatively daring, for Jaguar, series of innovations, including a general softening of the body lines, an improved seating position, a roomier driving compartment, and replacement of the wood on window sills and instrument panel with leather (and a chrome-plated ledge atop the cut-down door of the 150-S!). The 4-in. gain in width at shoulder height adds considerably to riding comfort, but is all too evident from outside the car, and causes the rakish front and rear fender line that distinguished the previous XK models to be all but lost.

Few, however, will lament the passing of the former drafty and leaky side curtains, although the wind-up windows do seem a little incongruous in a roadster. We had no opportunity to subject our XK-150-S test car to a real frog-strangler, but the new and much better looking cloth top obviously has been carefully engineered to prevent the entry of water. It folds easily and neatly into the area behind the seats, has special straps to prevent its rattling about behind the passengers, and is hidden by a neat cover which snaps over the space between the seat backs and the rear edge of the cockpit.

Until the advent of the XK-150-S, Jaguar XK performance figures had not shown any startling rise or decline. True, the horsepower increased, but the weight of the car rose right along with it. Performance has always been good, of course—any stock model, direct from the showroom, could be reliably expected to go from 0 to 60 in about 9 sec and, under favorable conditions, to reach or exceed an honest 120 mph.

As an examination of the data panel will show, however, the XK-150-S has changed all this. The "gold-head" engine (a production version of the famous D-type unit) produces a whopping 250 bhp, through the use of three 2.0-in. SU carburetors, an entirely new camshaft giving a 60° valve overlap and a compression ratio of 9.0:1. The weight, in turn, is only slightly higher than that of the XK-150. These two factors could be expected to bring improved acceleration and top speed and, as the comparative graph shows, they most certainly do.

Driving comparisons are sometimes misleading, especially after a year or two between models, but it seemed to us that the 150-S ride was somewhat better than before. Hard cornering produced very little roll, and the unchanged rack and pinion steering is superb, in spite of the trace of road sensitivity transmitted to the driver's hands on certain types of rough roads. Upper-limit speed runs in high-performance automobiles are always memorable in one way or another, some good, some bad—some downright dangerous. At high speeds, however, the 150-S was superb—one felt that it had been designed expressly for this purpose, and was performing easily and under perfect control.

Our test car was fitted with the new RS-4 design Dunlop Roadspeed tires, which we promptly boosted to the recommended high-speed driving pressure of 30/35 psi. The ride was excellent at these pressures, and we lost most of the tire squeal experienced at the standard pressures of 23/26 psi. Adhesion on dry roads is very good, and it is claimed that the former disconcerting trait of total grip loss on wet pavement has been completely eliminated. In normally vigorous driving there was definite understeer, but steering became very nearly neutral as the limit of adhesion was approached.

The 4-wheel Dunlop disc brakes are entirely able to cope with performance of the 150-S. They are powerful, light and sensitive, and seem entirely immune to fade. Self-adjusting segmented linings are used on the XK-150-S, instead of the circular pads of the 150.

The 150-S is available only with the 4.09 rear axle, and with overdrive as standard equipment. The overdrive is Laycock de Normanville, with a very low cruising ratio of 3.19, and operates off high gear only. A manual switch, located on the instrument panel, is used to engage overdrive.

No apparent changes were made in the "C" type, close-ratio gearbox. However, it operated much more smoothly and easily than those of previous XK-model Jaguars. Our only real complaint is that the synchromesh faults too easily in 2nd and 3rd during fast upshifts. On the other hand, it was not necessary to double-clutch during downshifts if the shift lever was allowed to pause slightly before being pushed home into gear. Second and 3rd gears were extremely silent, but first seemed a little noisier than on previous XK models.

A Borg Warner automatic transmission with 2.15 torque converter is optionally available for the XK-150, but we cannot imagine why anyone would inflict such an apparatus on a Jaguar. To us, the overdrive is a much more attractive option, a truly worthwhile device on long cross-country runs.

Despite the extremely heavy X-type frame, the cowl structure of the XK-150-S displayed a trace of shake on very rough roads. This seems to be one of the penalties of open body construction—every American convertible we have driven has displayed the same fault.

The leather seats are individually adjustable over a considerable range and are very comfortable, though a little deeper shaping in the backs would have given us a better lateral support. Inside appointments include a tiny, and all but useless, open glove box in front of the driver and another, with locking lid but equally tiny, at the other end of the instrument panel. The instruments are centrally located and are pleasingly simple in design, with circular black faces and plain white hands and figures. There are, of course, the usual handy side-pockets in the doors.

In summation, we agree that the new XK-150 and XK-150-S Jaguars have certain minor faults, as had their predecessors in the XK series before them, but we must go along with the many sports-car connoisseurs who maintain that the Jaguar still is the best all-around value in its portion of the sports-car field.

ROAD TEST
JAGUAR XK-150

SCALE: 10" DIVISIONS

DIMENSIONS

Wheelbase, in	102.0
Tread, f and r	51.6/51.4
Over-all length, in	177
width	64.5
height	54
equivalent vol, cu ft	357
Frontal area, sq ft	19.4
Ground clearance, in	7.1
Steering ratio, o/a	n.a.
turns, lock to lock	3.5
turning circle, ft	33
Hip room, front	50
Hip room, rear	n.a.
Pedal to seat back	40.5
Floor to ground	15

CALCULATED DATA

Lb/hp (test wt)	13.8
Cu ft/ton mile	82.3
Mph/1000 rpm (o/d)	25.6
Engine revs/mile	2340
Piston travel, ft/mile	1625
Rpm @ 2500 ft/min	3600
equivalent mph	92.4
R&T wear index	38.0

SPECIFICATIONS

List price	$5150
Curb weight, lb	3160
Test weight	3460
distribution, %	49/51
Tire size	6.00-16
Brake swept area	540
Engine type	6 cyl, dohc
Bore & stroke	3.27 x 4.17
Displacement, cc	3442
cu in	210
Compression ratio	9.00
Bhp @ rpm	250 @ 5500
equivalent mph	141
Torque, lb-ft	240 @ 4500
equivalent mph	115

GEAR RATIOS

O/d (0.78)	3.19
4th (1.00)	4.09
3rd (1.21)	4.94
2nd (1.74)	7.11
1st (2.98)	12.2

SPEEDOMETER ERROR

30 mph	actual, 31.5
60 mph	57.5

PERFORMANCE

Top speed (o/d), mph	136
4th (5750)	115
3rd (5750)	95
2nd (5750)	66
1st (5750)	38

FUEL CONSUMPTION

Normal range, mpg	14/19

ACCELERATION

0-30 mph, sec	2.5
0-40	4.0
0-50	5.6
0-60	7.3
0-70	10.0
0-80	13.0
0-100	21.4
Standing ¼ mile	15.1
speed at end	86

TAPLEY DATA

4th, lb/ton @ mph	315 @ 48
3rd	400 @ 42
2nd	570 @ 35
Total drag at 60 mph, lb	100

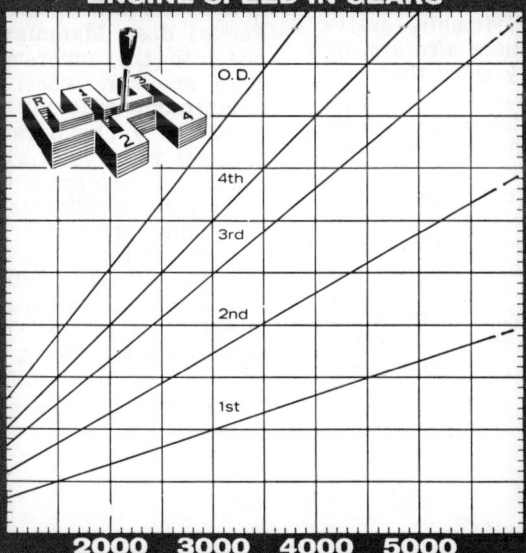

ENGINE SPEED IN GEARS

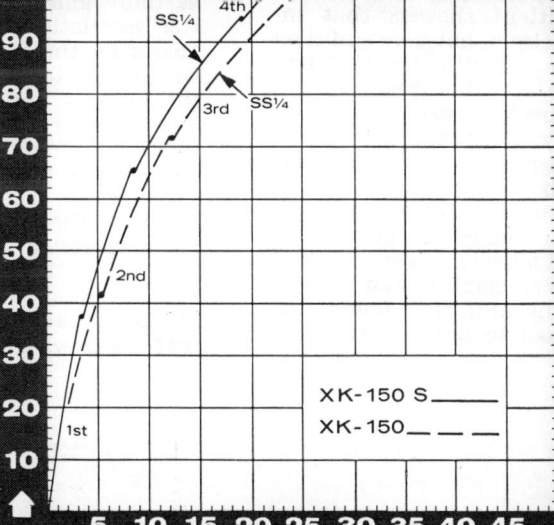

ACCELERATION & COASTING

CONTINUED ON PAGE 55

department than the normal XK. When the 120 was first designed its builders were concerned only with producing a fast *touring* car. And when owners began to use the XK in real competition it was discovered that its beautiful streamlined contours and disc wheels effectively protected the brake drums from any of those nasty drafts. Result: two fast laps and you were free-wheeling. The reason the Modified comes with wire wheels is to provide a little more fresh air for the brakes. This has seemed to work out a bit better in competition and certainly, in ASR's road test, there was never any indication of fade despite some 15 minutes of continuous hard use on a fast-dropping mountain grade.

THE SUITABILITY of the M-type for normal touring and town use is dependent in large part on how it is tuned, as was demonstrated when the test crew picked up Bill Breeze to make the acceleration runs. Breeze, a veteran Jaguar competition driver and now operator of Sausalito's Sports Car Center, took the coupe through a couple of sprints and wasn't satisfied that it was giving its all. A look under the hood and—surprise! — the throttle was only set to open three-quarters of the way. Also, the mixture was cut a bit lean and the plugs were too hot—fine for stop-and-go town driving but tending to miss at really high r.p.m.

With richer mixture and full throttle the coupe wasn't nearly as docile at idle but, my, how it would lay down nice twin stripes of black rubber on the take-off! The acceleration times were not the best that might possibly be obtained, due to intermittent showers that induced wheelspin, but were sufficient to indicate that the Jaguar Modified coupe has few peers in the realm of performance.

Certainly there are few if any production cars in the world today that can boast the combination of easy cruising at better than 100 m.p.h. with complete docility around town—and all with virtually Detroit standards of comfort and ease of control. The ASR crew found that the Jag had to be watched fairly closely to keep the speed within legal bounds; if you let the car go at what seems a reasonable and moderate rate—the rate it naturally wants to run—you are going to get a nasty jolt when you look at the speedometer. It will be reading in the 80's.

The virtues of the XK-120 engine have been recounted too many times for repetition here but we might mention one fact that usually isn't stressed: because this 3½-litre engine employs double overhead camshafts (which look fearsomely complicated) it tends to hold its tune much longer than the pushrod o.h.v. type. There are fewer wear points in the overhead cam type and less inertia in the valve gear. Even after a real beating during acceleration tests the engine remained as crisp as ever and engine heat barely climbed above the normal level.

DESPITE its racing performance, even the Modified Jaguar is primarily a high-speed touring car and so its furnishings and fitments are particularly important. The upholstery, as usual, is well-tailored leather. The two bucket seats, though low enough, are not mere pads on the floor. The instrument panel, of polished walnut, has a really satisfactory array of black-faced dials with white numerals: big, circular tachometer and speedometer; gas gauge (which indicates oil level when a button is pressed), ammeter, oil pressure gauge.

The provision for ventilation is particularly complete: narrow front quarter-windows swing partly open as extractors or open wide as air scoops; rear quarter-windows open partially and give virtually draft-free ventilation. There also are air scoops on the body sides that can be opened to circulate air about the driver's and passenger's feet, plus the normal heating and defrosting system.

The coupe has a bit more luggage space in the trunk than the roadster, since the top doesn't fold down. For a sports car this is quite commodious, sufficient to take at least two fair-sized suitcases. The coupe also has a package shelf behind the seat backs with a concealed package trough under its front half; under this trough are the two 12-volt batteries.

ABOUT HERE we ought to rise and say an unpleasant thing or two: (A) the driving position: The Jaguar steering column is nearly horizontal and the steering wheel is big—no matter what your stature or how you sit you are going to hit your right thigh against the rim of the wheel when you shift from throttle to brake. True, the wheel is adjustable; you can push it in or out. But even if you tuck it under your chin you're STILL going to thump your thigh. The only cure for this is to either shrink the wheel to saucer size or change the angle of the steering column—and that means major changes in the steering system up front.

Which brings up to (B) the horn button: ever since the first XK-120 Jaguar has furnished a horn button that comes jutting out of the wheel like the nose of a B-36. The company apparently expects its customers to adopt the Grand Prix position, with arms extended almost to full length. But if you just happen to like the wheel fairly close you're going to bruise your forearms plenty every time you spin the wheel. The old Mark IV Jag had a nice, flat horn button; the company ought to see if there aren't some of these still kicking around the stockroom.

Adding it all up, you have to give the Jaguar Modified XK-120 coupe top marks. It is a driver's car, with all that implies in instant response, road-holding, braking, steering accuracy and acceleration. But doesn't make him work at it as, Ferrari does. Mamma can take down to the super-market easier than she can wheel the Super Sludgepump Automatic Eight. It is relatively, a cheap car—when you consider what you have to pay for equivalent performance in anything else. And, despite its potency, isn't high-strung or unreliable you can jab the starter button every morning with the full expectation that it will go "bra-a-a-a-a-p-p-p" and take right off. Only thing won't do is fold down into a bed. ●●

End of an era

John Miles gets "that quite special feeling" behind the wheel of Mike Franey's partially restored Jaguar XK150S

MILES Behind the Wheel

THE XK150 was a significant car because it was the last Jaguar to be built using a conventional chassis. In triple carburettor "S" form it was also the most powerful (and civilised) XK ever produced. Approximately 9,400 XK150Ss were built between spring 1957 and autumn 1960, starting with the 3.4-litre coupé and drophead models, and followed by the Oh, so desirable two-seat roadster in spring 1958, production of that car having been delayed by the famous factory fire. What is more illuminating is that of approximately 2,400 3.4-litre roadsters all but 92 were left-hand drive. Jaguar historian Paul Skilliter's researches also show that an additional 36 3.8S roadsters were built towards the end of production, so if we assume that at least half this number went abroad, a genuine right-hand drive XK150 3.8S roadster is a rare machine indeed.

So when the opportunity arose

Good XKs are no longer cheap to buy, and if Franey's experience was anything to judge from, even when you pay for a "good one" it still needs a thorough rebuild. The previous owner had fitted new sills, rear wings and door hinges, but the car clearly still needed a lot of work on both body and mechanical components. In the end it was a complete rebuild. WM Autodevelopments looked after the engine, Forward Engineering rebuilt the close ratio gearbox, overdrive and rear axle. Others involved were Vale Cottage Motors for the excellent paintwork, Ramond Radiators, Auto Sparks for the wiring loom, Robert Stewart for chrome, and many others, including Jaguar expert Aubury Finburg of Classic Autos, who helped over much of the detail work. The owner rebuilt the suspension and cleaned and painted the chassis. The only departure from original are the 15in. (instead of 16in.) E-type chrome wire wheels shod with

restoration is still under way, although the engine, gearbox and rear axle have already been rebuilt, and the car rewired

Above: The car is now running on slightly smaller E-type wheels and low-profile tyres, which marginally reduces the overall gearing

Left: The leather seat surfaces are showing serious signs of wear, and lack much location. The three-spoke steering wheel is wood rimmed

to do a few fast miles in one so lovingly restored as Mike Franey's presented itself, the thing to do was accept. With the same 100in. wheelbase as the FHC, the roadster traded rear seats for luggage space behind the occupants, and a rear body section coming further forward to meet the front seat backs, arguably a more attractive looking rear end than the 2+2 fixed head and roadsters.

Consider that in 1960 the Road Tests of the day had the 265 bhp XK150 3.8S doing 135 mph in top, with the superb bottom end flexibility that has always gone hand in hand with the Jaguar straight six, in all its forms — even the D-type.

205/70 section Pirelli P5 tyres which combined to reduce overall gearing from the standard car's 26 to 23.5 mph per 1,000 rpm.

This was the first time I had ever sat in a "traditional" Jaguar. By today's standards the driving position is almost Vintage in character. The cockpit floor is flat. You sit near to it, legs outstretched (rather than downward pointing) faced by an enormous three-spoke steering wheel which has the "collar type" reach adjustment found on today's Jaguars. Leather covered seats are rather flat — even convex — and devoid of much lateral location.

A few laps of a private test track facility prove that an XK150 has tremendously enjoyable handling. What starts out as understeer, gradually diminishes as cornering forces and power are increased. Once off the straight, the steering is heavy and low geared. If you want to burn expensive rubber you can hold the car in a low speed power slide, otherwise it's pretty neutral at the limit. In spite of quite considerable roll angles the car is always giving plenty of feel and warning.

For a powerful car the XK150S has a wonderfully light clutch. Like all Jaguar Moss gearboxes of the day, the gearchange is narrow gated, and unless you are lucky or much more practised than I was, gears would always "snick" on the first to second change. On the open road, so to speak, such trivialities are forgotten with the bellow of the twin pipe exhaust and in the way this car goes. Given the chance the rev counter (a beautifully steady electric instrument reading) zips round to 5,000 rpm in the lower gears, and soon gets there in overdrive top (around 120 mph). It hums along without fuss at 100 mph, eating up more prosaic machinery. Hood up there is still lots of wind roar, but the car is rock stable, taut and rattle free.

To point that long, curvaceous front end and the Jaguar motif down a long stretch of straight road gives one a quite special feeling of power. The XK 150 3.8S roadster may not have the space, but to recall the other two attributes in latter day Jaguar advertising, it lacks neither grace nor pace. □

Re-Acquaintance with an XK120

The Editor Drives Again the kind of Jaguar He first sampled 37 Years Ago

IN the late 1940s the Jaguar XK120 was an exceeding exciting new sports-car and most of us were avid to try one. In fact, I seem to remember that, for some reason, critical MOTOR SPORT waited longer than most for the priviledge. But at last the day came when I was summonsed to Henly's at the top of Gt. Portland Street, the place where all the used cars deemed to gravitate, racing cars among them, and was dispatched in a new XK120 (Reg No KHP 30 — and where is that one, today?) by "Lofty" England himself. As I had expected, I was impressed, even though, used hard, the brakes faded into utter oblivion, my wife was rendered car-sick for the first time in her life due to the roll on corners when the XK was driven fast along the twisting road from Odiham to Alton, and after I had donned Sidcot suit and flying-helmet and was enjoying a dice round Brands Hatch, the new wonder-car was whipped away from me for filming by the Shell Film Unit, with Stirling Moss at the wheel... I never saw it again and, apart from a short spell with the Ian Appleyard Alpine Rally XK laid on for Jenks and me by Andrew White some years ago, I have not driven one of these sleek and still very attractive Jaguars since.

Reverting to that road-test of 37 years ago, the car had the 3.64 to 1 axle-ratio and achieved 120 mph in top, 90 mph in third gear, and I see that its 0 to 60 mph acceleration figure was only half-a-second slower than that of the Ford Sierra XR4x4 in which I drove to the Midland Motor Museum at Bridgnorth to try again a Jaguar XK120. This car (Reg No PPE 101) belongs to Michael Barker, Director of the Museum, and is also a 1951 model. A very handsome example, finished in the expected Jaguar white, it was supplied to a Mrs Grant-Norton by Weybridge Autos, who had got it from Henly's in London. That was in March 1951 and it was not until 1959 that the car went to its second owner, Mr A. M. Preston, from whom Mike bought it in February 1974.

In its formative years it had done the 1951 Alpine Rally in the hands of W. Grant-Norton and D. Loader, finishing 5th in class, the 1952 London Rally, driven by Grant-Norton, sharing the Team Prize with Sears and Richardson, that year's Brighton Rally, and the 1953 RAC Rally, in which Grant-Norton again shared the Team Prize, with Appleyard and Coombes. Since then Mike Barker has rallied the car and used it for Jaguar OC races, etc, but he was too modest to list his performances. In fact, they include the following between 1983 and 1985: JDC Rally, Telford / Bridgenorth Cavalcade, Display at "MOTEC", JDC Race Meeting, Silverstone, Press demos at HSCC Day Donington, XK Day at Hagley Hall, MMM Stand at Burwarton Show, JDC Concours — 2nd Sports Class, JDC Anniversary Rally Stratford, 1st & 2nd in driving tests MHB & GB, Wolverhampton / Bridgenorth Cavalcade, BMW Meeting at Newtown, Welsh Rally Demo Cardiff, XK Day at Hagley Hall, JDC Rally, "Coronation" Rally Best Mixed Crew, Demo for film on Shropshire, Parade at Coventry, RAC Rally Demo Sutton Park, Second Demo for film on Shropshire.

This XK120, chassis no. 660643, is virtually a standard car. It has 2" carburetters, now has a B-series cylinder head, and standard gearbox and drum brakes, although the engine has been mildly "souped" by changing the valve-seat angles and things of that kind. The one-time Cinturato tyres have given place to 6.00 x 16 Dunlop Racing covers, and these tyres are run at 24/26 lb./sq. in. The present axle-ratio is 3.77 to 1, useful for road motoring. Driven as Barker drives, fuel thirst is around 15 mpg, which was about what I got in 1951, but oil consumption is a bit fierce (as the scraper-rings were removed from the pistons to gain a bit more power), about 50 mpp, and Newtons HD40 Special lubricant is specified for the straight-six twin-cam, 3,442 cc engine. In 1951 you could buy a brand-new XK120 for just over £1,263 including purchase-tax — we insured the MMM car for £20,000 . . .

DEBATE continues as to the source of William Lyons' inspiration for the lines of the XK120, but the result is unquestionably beautiful.

SMALL BUMPERS and separate sidelight castings identify the early cars.

I enjoyed my two-day drive in showery May weather in the car, although there is no hood. It handles well once one is used to it, and there is no scuttle-shake, or dithering of the long tapering bonnet. The big steering-wheel has grips for one's fingers and while it exhibits some free movement and is heavy for hauling the car round sharp corners, and things become somewhat lively if you allow the big tyres to ride the cat's-eyes, the Jag was always under control. Moreover, the excessive cornering-roll I remembered has been eliminated, and because wire wheels are fitted, brake fade is experienced only under racing conditions, and is not then final, I am assured. They are certainly well up to fast road sorties, but pulled a bit when applied hard, reminding one of a spirited horse.

The leather-covered separate seats are comfortable, without being in any way squidgy, the typical XK120 windscreen obviates the need for goggles, and the controls delight. For example, the fly-off centre hand brake could not be more convenient and to the left of it, the rigid little gear lever is exactly to hand. The synchro-mesh on the three upper forward gears can be over-ridden if one is too hurried, but a double-declutch between 3rd. and top obviates this and downward changes with normal double-declutching are a joy, except for the 2nd speed slot being a bit elusive in the narrow gate at first stab, and considerable revving being called for to get smoothly into this gear. Reverse, beyond 1st, presents no problems.

I found that the Jaguar would cruise unconcernedly at almost any speed within its compass, accompanied by a crisp rasp from the twin exhaust tail pipes. There is little need to play outside the 2,500 to 3,000 rev-band in top gear, in ordinary motoring, and for the lazy the engine will pull away from very pedestrian rotational speeds in the higher gears. Indeed, the legal pace came up almost everywhere and I was distinctly impressed when well over the ton was attained up hill, but

ROADSTER version is the most desirable of the XK120 range.

XK SERIES engine has continued right up to the present day in the XJ 4.2, the last model to use it. The new XJ40 saloon will pack the AJ6 unit already seen in the XJ-S.

then I remembered that the owner had told me the speedometer reads fast. . . .

It seems sensible that the big Smiths' tachometer, in which there is a little clock, is in front of the driver, red-marked from 5,200 rpm, whereas the matching speedometer is for the passenger's interest. . . . The sober leather-trimmed fascia carries the instruments that were on the car from new, with an oil-thermometer added on the extreme right. This said 90 deg. C but if you were racing and it showed 120 it would be wise to come in. . . . Water-heat was normally at around 60-deg., oil pressure 50 lb/sq. in., in the combined Smiths dial, and the ammeter was working. Instrumentation is completed by a petrol-gauge incorporating a sump-level oil-gauge. The engine starts at once after the ignition has been turned on with the detachable key and a plated button on the dash has been pressed. Four-star fuel is put in through a lock flap on the top of the tail, with no filler-cap, and another key unlocks the boot, which is full of 15-gallon petrol tank, the spare wheel and the tools.

So here is an immaculate 37-year-old Jaguar XK120 able to provide enjoyable open-air touring (and certainly not hold up modern traffic!) and yet be useable in Club racing and other forms of competition driving. It brought back memories for me, and it fits in well with MOTOR SPORT's new Classic concept; indeed, it had just returned from representing its Museum at a Classic Car Show at the NEC in Birmingham. — W.B.

THE CLASSIC ALTERNATIVE

Time was when you could buy a new Jaguar XK140 for under £1700. That was in 1954, when a Triumph TR2-engined Morgan Plus 4 cost £565. Nowadays, a well-kept XK140 — if you can find one — is worth Morgan money, especially if it's a drophead. But, apart from their 190 bhp outputs and separate chassis construction, these cars are chalk and cheese.

Jaguar's engine codename was XK, and the first car to exploit its power was called the XK120 — whose digits accurately referred to the top speed. Thus began the Jaguar XK series, a sports car range that sold in thousands and spawned five Le Mans winners.

When the Jaguar XK120 appeared in 1949, the all-enveloping streamlined body and resultant 120 mph performance caused a sensation. It was another five years before the evolutionary XK140 appeared. Technically superior, this car had more power, rack and pinion steering and telescopic dampers, but unfortunately it was also heavier and fitted with bigger bumpers for the American market. Production lasted only three years, when the car was superseded by the XK150.

Today's Morgan has had a rather longer life — the Plus 8, the most powerful model, is now more than a decade old. It may be an old design — and it still continues to use the 75-year-old sliding pillar front suspension that was once fitted to the company's three-wheelers — but it is still improved on from time to time. Three years ago the Plus 8 acquired the fuel-injected 190 bhp V8 engine from the Rover Vitesse and, more surprisingly, rack and pinion steering for the first time.

A brand-new Plus 8 will set you back £16,364, give or take a little extra for luxuries such as the optional door handles.

After a staple diet of mass-produced mid-Eighties saloons, both cars serve as a reminder of Fifties-style motoring. The Jaguar's straight-six snarl sounds the more aggressive, but the performance is only average by current standards.

A tested maximum of around 130 mph bears witness to the power of the 3.4-litre twin-cam, especially in "special equipment" 210 bhp form, obtained with high-lift cams and an 8.0:1 compression ratio. Whether the ordinary production cars were capable of these speeds I cannot say, but the car I drove would still amble along at 70 mph — under 3000 rpm in fourth — with barely a murmur.

Hood down, it was a surprisingly civilised machine which still feels taut and rattle-free 30 years on. Of course, you cannot completely ignore the fact that it is an old car. Despite the huge four-spoke wheel, the steering is very heavy, as are the brakes (no matter, this car sports non-standard front disc brakes and a servo). And any attempt to rush the four-speed Moss gearbox (as fitted to early 3.8 E-types) is rewarded by synchromesh grating sounds from below; double-declutch downshifts are essential.

Used sensibly, the Jaguar can still provide a smooth, rewarding driving experience. The ride is much softer than expected and there's some roll when cornering, yet the telescopic dampers prevent bounce or wallow. Driven harder than I was prepared to, I'm sure the leaf-sprung live axle would have caused the back end to hop and skip when powering hard round bumpy corners — but it's far more composed than I had expected. Some of this can be put down to the use of modern radial tyres, since the cross-ply originals were notorious for "tramlining".

The antiquity of the car is very apparent when you look around the narrow cockpit but, for its era, this Jaguar was very sophisticated. It boasted proper wind-up windows, a heater, timer-controlled indicator cancelling, a reversing light and a valve radio for those who could afford this expensive £47 optional extra; there was even air conditioning for the US market.

The brand-new Morgan provides more of a vintage car feel than the real thing. There's the same sensation of sitting low on uncompromising seats with a big steering wheel in close proximity (not necessary on the Morgan for the steering is lightweight). The flat screen and row of circular Smiths instruments nestling in the leathercloth-covered facia add to the illusion. So does the smell of wood and leather.

It provides a completely different driving experience, starting with the muted "woffle" of the big V8 and continuing with the slick change of the Rover SD1 five-speed gearshift. Despite having similar power to the Jaguar, there is no comparison between their performance. The Moggie weighs just over half that of the leviathan XK140, and when you prod the right pedal you know that the horsepower is for real.

And then there's the ride. It may be a product of the late Eighties, but this is no wimp's car. It needs a confident driver to tackle bumpy roads at Porsche-type speeds — the poor pilot has to really hang on as the car pitches, bucks and weaves. Much of the suspension's work is done by the flexing chassis, and it's a considerable handful when the going gets rough. But in fairness, the once notorious bump steer is all but eliminated, and there are no rattles and groans from the body to detract from this masochistic thrill.

The Plus 8 has the kind of brutal acceleration that takes your breath away. Zero to 60 mph takes a supercar-bashing six seconds, and you can reach nearly 100 mph in a quarter of a mile. Brush the brake pedal and the unservoed disc/drum system hauls the speed down with reassuring ease — it has only 880 kg to cope with. And despite the ride, the handling and grip levels reflect the enormous progress that tyres have made during the past 30 years.

Compared with the Jaguar though, the Morgan is a crude and spartan sports car. You have to remove the single-skin canvas hood and stow it behind the seats — the hood doesn't fold — and there's no boot. You peer through scratch-prone Perspex sidescreens and fumble beneath the dash for the fly-off handbrake. There's no radio, for the simple reason that you would not hear it.

Which to choose? The Morgan provides the ultimate undiluted driving experience for those prepared to accept the discomfort and impracticality of it. But the Jaguar is still swift and highly impressive relative to other cars from its era.

Either way, ownership is difficult. You face a four to five year wait for a Morgan or the near impossible task of locating and restoring an early XK Jaguar. Which would I choose? Unfortunately, neither; I'm still hooked on E-types. . . .

Our thanks to Keith Vincent, Registrar of the Jaguar XK Enthusiasts Club, whose 1956 XK140 is featured here.

MORGAN PLUS 8 v JAGUAR XK140

Rocker switches have replaced the toggles, and there's padding where there didn't use to be, but the Morgan facia has changed little. Injected Vitesse V8 gives aural excitement

Sports car or grand tourer? Wood-and-leather Jaguar was a bit of both; note vast four-spoke wheel. XK140 has more powerful version of 3442-cc XK straight-six first seen in XK120

PROFILE
Jaguar XK120, XK140, XK150

Ten years after the launch of the original XK120, Jaguar launched the XK150, instantly recognised by the broader grille and higher waistline. In the S form, this was the fastest XK yet

JAGUAR'S JEWEL

One of the great British classic sports cars of all time must be the famed Jaguar XK series, concours examples of which now fetch high prices. Mark Gillies and Mike Walsh explore the legend

Sensational is a much over-worked adjective when it comes to describing motor cars, but the appearance of the Jaguar XK120 at the 1948 Earls Court Motor Show must surely have merited its use. Britain was slap in the middle of an era of austerity, when beans on toast was the staple diet at a posh hotel like the Strand Palace, when a banana was unknown to most schoolchildren, when rationing was so tight that everything in shops was on a first come, first served basis. If you were very lucky, you might have a new car, but more likely it would be a pre-war Morris, Austin or Wolseley.

What a time to introduce a 120mph sports car, clad in a body of such voluptuous curves that pre-war cars — and contemporary Singers, MGs and the like — looked positively antediluvian! Jaguar took the plunge, and the new car displayed at the show (with type designation derived from the XK engine and the speed) was to become an export leader in the USA.

The XK story dates from before the war, when William Lyons, Bill Heynes, Walter Hassan and Claude Bailey set out to design a new high performance saloon car. The heart of the car was to be the magnificent six-cylinder twin ohc XK engine, a unit which incorporated all of Heynes' thoughts about high performance production engines. The bottom end had a seven-bearing fully counterbalanced crankshaft, the block was light and heavily webbed, and wet sump lubrication was employed. The *pièce de résistance*, though, was the aluminium cylinder head, with efficient hemispherical combustion chambers and a cross-flow design, the gas flow work carried out by Harry Weslake. The twin overhead camshafts were driven by duplex roller chain, and the engine used twin 1¾in SU carburettors. In initial guise, the XK engine displaced 3447cc and gave 160bhp at 5400rpm. It was mated to a four-speed Moss gearbox.

Heynes was determined that the engine's appearance should reflect some idea of the thought that had gone into the unseen internal parts: there were polished cam covers, enamelled exhaust manifold and polished inlet manifold. The engine, of course, was later to power Jaguar to five Le Mans wins, to countless other race victories, and two of the most successful sports cars ever made (the XK series and the E-type). It is still used in modified form in the XJ saloons. In short, it's a classic engine design.

Originally, this unit was intended for Lyons' high performance saloon, but as both it and the Mark V/VI chassis neared completion, it became obvious to Lyons that a worthy successor to the SS100 sports car was possible. As he said: "Such a car with the XK engine would not fail to out-perform easily everything else on the market by a wide margin, irrespective of price". It would also provide a good opportunity for the firm to test servicing conditions.

The XK120 chassis was essentially that of the Mark V saloon, slightly narrowed with 18ins cut out of the centre of the box section frame, and the cross bracing removed and replaced by a single box section cross member. Front suspension was independent by top and bottom wishbones carrying ball-jointed stub axles, with springing by longitudinal torsion bars, while a live axle was carried on long semi-elliptic springs at the rear; there was a front anti-roll bar. Girling lever arm dampers were employed at the rear with Newton telescopics at the front.

Lockheed hydraulic drum brakes were fitted all round — this was a future bug-bear of the model, as there was always a problem dissipating the heat built up under heavy braking, a problem exacerbated by the all-enveloping bodywork and disc wheels. A Burman recirculating ball steering box was standard.

The body mounted on this frame was a shock to those brought up with traditional British sports cars with long bonnet, two small seats and a short stubby tail with spare wheel exposed at the rear. The all enveloping XK120 possesses a rare purity of line from all angles. Incredibly, it took less than two weeks for the shape to progress from idea to reality, with a skilled panel worker shaping the body to fit a skeleton frame under Bill (later Sir William) Lyons' guidance. As on this prototype, the first batch of cars was to be produced with aluminium bodywork. The front bulkhead and firewall, inner wings and part of the boot interior were in steel, and the panels all hung on an ash frame.

As would be normal on all the XKs, the 120 as it first appeared was well trimmed, with wide leather seats (too wide and lacking lateral support, as it turned out), leather trimmed doors and dashboard. There was a full complement of instruments: speedometer, ammeter, fuel gauge, water temperature/oil pressure, and rev counter. It was strictly a two-seater, and for £998 basic provided pre-war racing performance at a (luxury) saloon price.

At first, the flow of cars out of the factory was slow, the flood gates opening only after the change to steel bodies in May 1950. Only 60 cars were completed in 1949, by which time Jaguar had proved the new machine at Jabbeke in Belgium in May and in the *Daily Express* Production Car Race at Silverstone in August. With a slightly higher back axle ratio installed, Ron Sutton managed 132.596mph in front of journalists brought to Jabbeke for the occasion. Silverstone brought a triumph for the works entered team, Leslie Johnson and Peter Walker finishing 1-2.

Rave review

That year also saw the first press review of the model, and *The Motor* was accorded the privilege. The magazine's testers were impressed. Not only did the acceleration and top speed leave them eulogising, but the immense flexibility of that engine and the car's controllability were praised. They 'maxed' it to 124.6mph, covered a standing quarter mile in 17secs, and 0-60mph in 10secs: 'There is no embarrassing sudden response to the accelerator pedal, but rather a docility of the power unit and a smoothness of the clutch which makes for a delightful willingness to crawl in tightly packed traffic.' Moreover, when it came to the handling, they found that 'the car's precise controllability is not always fully appreciated at first, but once it is realised that only small wheel movements and finger-and-thumb are needed it is instinctive to negotiate winding roads at really high speeds.'

Gearbox and brakes were not criticised in the slightest — both were hammered in future road tests — and the excellent stability at speed was noted. The only real reservations were that the seats lacked support for fast cornering, and the headlights were not up to scratch. Overall, though, they concluded that the XK120 'is a car which is superb even at this early stage in what should be a long and honourable career.'

The change to steel bodies in April 1950 marked the introduction of a totally different internal structure, with hollow-section mild steel sills replacing complex wood and single-thickness composite structures. There were welded mild steel door shut faces and a boxed-in door hinge area, plus a new bulkhead. Externally, the headlight nacelles protruded more, there was less slope towards the grille on the front wings, and the rear wing shape was different — bonnet, bootlid and doors were still in aluminium, though the bonnet was heavier. Also new were the chrome-plated windscreen side pillars.

The Autocar was the second English magazine to get its hands on a 120 and the testers were equally impressed. Although their car was appreciably slower through the gears, top gear acceleration was roughly the same. Standing start acceleration figures probably reflect the less brutal approach of *The Autocar* staff, and the heavier (by about 1cwt) steel bodied car actually was not that much slower. Again, there was little criticism and much praise: 'There is a temptation to draw from the motoring vocabulary every adjective of the superlative concerning the performance, and to call upon the devices of italics and even the capital letter.'

An XK120 racing success: Peter Whitehead leads Tony Rolt in the Daily Express *Production Car Race at Silverstone in 1950*

Dewis's special-bodied XK120 did 172.412mph at Jabbeke

Road and Track *and* Motor Sport *also loved the car, but both were critical of some aspects.* R&T *found the car had a tendency to overheat, driving position for tall drivers was cramped, there was inadequate lateral seat support, a lack of indicators, poor dust sealing and an overly long gear lever travel. Bill Boddy, writing for* Motor Sport*, found out about those brakes, and was one of the few testers actually to recognise this shortcoming for many years.*

The late John Bolster, writing for *Autosport*, was rather more precise about the handling than most: 'The XK120 will drift a bend in a delightful manner, but it resents being flung about while it is doing so'. He pointed out that initial mild understeer could be converted to oversteer by sensible application of the throttle.

Jaguar introduced the Fixed-head coupé XK120 in 1951, with optional wire wheels and Special Equipment performance. The coupé, yet another stunning looking creation, appeared in March. As perfectly balanced as the roadster, it was an object lesson to any stylist. Still a two-seater, there was a luggage ledge behind the rear seats, better trim, and many small footwell ventilators (this feature was incorporated on the roadster at the same time). The coupé had wider doors than the roadster, and despite its extra weight was little slower.

The Special Equipment option boosted power to 181bhp, and the Burgess straight-throught silencer gave the XK engine the most gorgeous howl at high revs. Stiffer front torsion bars and rear springs were Special Equipment handling modifications. On cars with wire wheels, the rear spats were omitted as the knock-off hub spinners would otherwise have fouled.

Superb tourer

The coupé was a superb long distance tourer. 'The outstanding impression after having driven this car for more than 2000 miles is the way it goes, and keeps on going' said *The Autocar*. In Special Equipment form, it was actually faster than the original 'ali' bodied roadster, 0-60mph coming up in 9.9secs. This test car was fitted with self-adjusting front brakes, which cured the problem of overly long pedal travel after a few miles of fast motoring.

By now, the XK120 had covered itself in glory in competition. A 20-year-old called Stirling Moss was victor in the 1950 TT at Dundrod, Ian Appleyard won his first two Coupe des Alpes on the Alpine Rally (he was to win four in succession, becoming the first driver to collect an Alpine Gold Cup in the process),

An XK120 driver thanks his lucky stars for straw bales . . .

Leslie Johnson was fifth in the '50 Mille Miglia, and an XK120 nearly won Le Mans in '50, the Johnson/Hadley car retiring when in third place with three hours to run. In '51, of course, the Coventry firm had returned to the Sarthe with the racing version of the XK, the C-type, and carried off the honours, the first of five victories there. Also noteworthy was the 107.46mph averaged over 24 hours by Moss/Johnson at Montlhéry in October '50, and the 131.2mph average for an hour the following March. After 1951, XKs would seldom win major events (except rallies), but they gave many drivers a start in racing, and made up club fields for many years to come.

An XK120 to suit all tastes appeared in April '53 — the Drop-head coupé. Civility was one of the advantages of this model, for the hood was light and easy to operate, beautifully made in mohair and with a fully lined interior. Interior trim was similar to the Fixed-head, and there were the wide doors and wind down windows. This car, which JVB rated so highly ('A long run in this car is a pleasure that is difficult to put into words'), cost all of £1616 2s 6d.

Rare dropheads

Very few Drop-heads were made — only 1760 compared to 7600 roadsters and 2700 Fixed-heads — basically because Jaguar introduced its successor, the XK140, at the Earls Court Motor Show in October '54. This model marked the development of middle-aged spread for the marque's previously lean sports car, as the XK140 had no real performance gains, only the improvement of creature comforts. The concept was swinging from sports car to Grand Tourer.

The most important change was to position the engine 3ins further forward, giving the possibility of 2+2 seating and introducing more understeer into the handling. On the Fixed-head coupé, the two six-volt batteries previously mounted under the parcel shelf were repositioned in the front wings, the bulkhead swept round the engine on either side, the windscreen was brought forward, the roof extended back 6¾ins and the doors further widened so that two occasional seats could be fitted. On the Drop-head coupé, the bulkhead was just moved forward by the 3ins allowed by the repositioned engine, a single 12 volt battery placed in the wing, and two occasional rear seats added. The roadster did not have any extra seats, only additional luggage space and seat movement, while the scuttle line was lifted by an inch to give more thigh space for the driver. The 190bhp Special Equipment engine was fitted as standard, with the new optional unit — using a cylinder head similar to the C-type's — being rated at 210bhp. Cooling was improved by the use of a new, inclined radiator and an eight-blade fan. Also under the skin was the substitution of Alford and Alder rack and pinion steering for Burman (giving more accurate and responsive steering) and the option of Laycock-De-Normanville overdrive.

External changes included a new die-cast alloy radiator grille with thicker and fewer slats, improved headlights with a 'J' monogram in the centre, separate wing-mounted flashing indicators, a chrome strip down the centre of the bonnet and bootlid, the fitment of the number plate between the front quarter bumpers and new quarter bumpers at the rear giving 3ins extra length compared to the 120.

Even with its middle-aged spread, the XK140 proved the quickest XK yet in road tests, which might have had something to do with the press being loaned Special Equipment cars. So the US magazine *Sports Illustrated* managed to record an 8.4secs 0-60mph time, though they felt that more 'go' hadn't been matched by more 'whoa'. The new cooling and steering were praised. Their verdict was that 'the debits against the XK140MC are insignificant beside the credits. It is a wondrous machine — docile, fast, quiet, flexible, comfortable and easy to drive.' The American sports car buyers also felt the same way as 83 per cent of XKs were left-hand drive, most destined for the States. *The Autocar* remarked upon the greater comfort and civilisation of their fixed-head coupé, found the handling to be improved, and considered the brakes to be entirely adequate . . .

Final flowering

Competition wise, the XK140 was never as prolific as the XK120, and was only really competitive in club events. David Hobbs started his long racing career behind the wheel of a 140 in 1960. Increasing softness was marked by the availability of automatic transmission from October of 1956.

May '57 saw the final flowering of the XK theme — the 150. It was 'either the pinnacle of development of the XK series, or the spoiling of a near ideal concept of a sports car which had been born in 1948, according to your viewpoint' in the words of Jaguar historian Paul Skilleter.

The most important revision on the car was the adoption of disc brakes all round, at last giving the car the stopping power to match its speed. At first there were the XK140 power options and fixed-head and drophead coupé styles, but with the coming of the XK150 roadster in '58 Jaguar introduced the 'S' engine, with triple carbs and a new head, giving 250bhp. This was the fastest XK yet. Externally, the 150 reverted to a thin slat grille, and gained a semi-circular dip in the front bumper, more chrome and a wrap-round rear bumper. A one-piece screen became standard, and the scuttle and waist lines were slightly raised.

Road and Track clocked a 150S roadster at 136mph, with 0-60mph in 7.3secs. This was indeed a high speed motor car, and one in which the drivers felt safe: 'Upper limit speed runs are always memorable in one way or another; some good, some bad — some downright dangerous. At high speeds, however, the XK150S was superb — one felt that it had been designed expressly for the purpose.'

A number of people, however, were by now noticing the rather dated chassis behaviour. Bill Boddy claimed that there was 'a sense of vintage style flexibility about the chassis — the hypercritical may perhaps feel that the chassis is not so advanced as the splendid power unit'. Boddy was testing an XK150 coupé, and several detail points — front seats, driving position, lack of keeps on the doors and ridiculously small occasional seats — were felt to prevent the car from being listed as a top GT car. The brakes were praised, but the cart-sprung rear axle was now having to work hard to transmit all that power smoothly . . .

The Motor and JVB also noticed the power transmission problem, especially as their test cars were S versions, with an extra 40bhp to play with. However, it is worth bearing in mind that the standard fixed-head coupé cost £1175 in 1958, £125 less than the Lotus Elite, and the S cost less than half the price

XK 140 OPEN TWO SEATER SPECIAL EQUIPMENT

SPECIFICATION

Engine	In-line 'six'
Construction	Iron block, aluminium head
Main bearings	Seven
Capacity	3442cc
Bore × stroke	83mm × 106mm
Valves	Twin overhead camshafts
Compression	9:1
Power	210bhp @ 5750rpm
Torque	213lb ft @ 4000rpm
Transmission	Four speed manual (overdrive optional)
Final drive	3.54:1 (overdrive: 3.19:1)
Brakes	Drums/drums
Front suspension	Ind by wishbones, torsion bars, anti-roll bar, telescopic dampers
Rear suspension	Live axle, semi-elliptics, telescopic dampers
Steering	Rack and pinion
Body	Separate chassis and body
Tyres	6.00 × 16

DIMENSIONS

Length	14ft 8ins
Width	5ft 4½ins
Height	4ft 4½ins
Wheelbase	8ft 6ins
Weight (unladen)	28cwt

PERFORMANCE

Maximum speed	121.1mph
0-60mph	8.4secs
Standing ¼ mile	16.6secs
Fuel consumption	16-18mpg

of a Ferrari 250GT while providing virtually the same performance. The S was something of a stop-gap as Jaguar were on the way to producing the monocoque construction E-type when the 3.8-litre version of the S appeared in 1960.

The 3.8-litre XK150 gave 220bhp in standard guise, and 265bhp in S form, enough for JVB to record 136.3mph and find that the car really needed an independent rear end to transmit that power properly. It isn't unknown for the friction plates on the optional Thornton limited slip diff to wear out quickly. The transformation of character was complete, now, as he felt the car was a very fast tourer and not a tamed racer, a sentiment that sums up the difference between the 120 and 150. Despite the fact that the 150 still has impressive performance by present day standards, it is very much less of a sports car — the type of car equally at home on track, rally or road — than its distinguished predecessor. Indeed, the 150 feels very dated compared to its successor, the E-type, despite no real performance differences.

The XKs are great cars. They were the first very high performance sports cars to be retailed at a sensible price and produced in any quantity; 30,504 of all models were produced before the last XK150 left the line in January '61. One XK120 averaged 110.31mph for seven days and seven nights in 1952, and that ability to sustain high cruising speeds in complete safety for hours on end is just one of the attractions of the car today, along with that tremendous ability to accelerate past a queue of traffic without the need for frantic gear changing. It's smooth and svelte, and the lines still create a sensation.

Quite simply, an XK has style.

Production history

The first 240 or so XK120s were produced with alloy bodies, but from chassis numbers 660059 (rhd) and 670185 (lhd) steel panels were used, with a different internal structure incorporating new sills, door shuts and hinge areas. There was a different shape transmission hump and chrome-plated 'screen side pillars.

March '51 saw the Fixed-head coupé, and August '51 the arrival of Special Equipment packages for the roadster (fhcs had to wait until September '52 for SE options). A new cam profile, straight-through exhaust and lighter flywheel all helped to give 181bhp, and handling-wise there were stiffer torsion bars and seven leaf rear springs. Wire wheels of 5ins width became an option that year, the disc wheels being uprated to 5½ins in '52. Small footwell ventilators let into the side of the wings before the doors on roadsters were adopted from 660675 and 671097.

Late '51 saw self-adjusting front brakes, and tandem master cylinder and supply tank arrangement. The XK120 line-up was completed in April '53 with the arrival of the Drop-head coupé, with wide doors, wind-up windows, plated metal door frames

Jaguar XK150 in drophead configuration compares with . . .

. . . fixed-head version offering similar 2+2 accommodation

quarter lights; like the fhc there was a parcel shelf behind the seats, which also gave access to the batteries underneath. Also new was a Salisbury rear axle in place of ENV. Close ratio gears could now be specified, as could the C-type head.

XK140s (from October '54 and chassis numbers 800001 and 810001) had the engine moved 3ins forward, so 2 plus 2 seating was in for fhcs and dhcs, with additional seat movement and luggage space for the Roadster. Fhcs have a longer roof, wider (38ins) doors made in steel, indicator switch placed centrally on dash, and batteries in wings. Dhcs had one 12 volt battery in n/s wing, raised facia (by 1in) and 3ins extra front seat adjustment. Roadsters had raised scuttle line, 'ali' doors and vertical dash mounting.

All 140s have external differences (large front bumpers, rear quarter bumpers, different grille, indicators, 'J' monogrammed headlights, larger rear light units, chrome bonnet/boot strips, push button bootlid handle, number plate mounted between rear bumpers) plus the rack and pinion steering, altered centre chassis X-member (for overdrive), cranked universally jointed steering column, stiffer front torsion bars, Girling telescopic dampers at rear, and reversion to single brake master cylinder. All engines uprated, 190bhp standard and 210bhp Special Equipment. There was a new rad and eight-blade fan, and a pressed steel sump.

Production changes were few: a Reynolds hydraulic chain tensioner and Hoburn Eaton eccentric type oil pump, and from October '56 Borg Warner auto 'boxes could be specified. As with 120s an S prefix for chassis number denoted Special Equipment models.

The XK150, from May '57 on, came as fhc or dhc only, from chassis numbers 824001 and 834001 on. Major change was four wheel disc brakes with servo assistance, and nylon interleaving in the rear springs. Two engine options available, 190bhp standard, with 210bhp SE option using the new B-type cylinder head. 60 spoke wire wheels standardised in June '58. Externally, there were thinner grille slats, wrap-round rear bumper, semi-circular dip in the front bumper, a one-piece 'screen and raised scuttle and waist lines. Inside, for the first time on a dhc or fhc, there was no figured walnut trim, only leather, and interior mirror now roof mounted. March '58 saw availability of S engine and the Roadster XK150; 250bhp 'S' engine had 'straight port' head and triple 2ins SU carbs, a 9:1 cr, lead bronze bearings and stronger clutch assembly. The roadster had improved mohair hood, wind-up windows and chrome plated edge across the top of the doors. Twin SU pumps now standard as were quick change brake pads. S engine was available with other body styles from February '59; overdrive and S chassis number prefix standard.

Last major production change was in October '59: the 3.8-litre (3781cc) engine was rated at 220bhp in B-type head, twin 1¾ins SU form, and 265bhp in straight port triple 2ins SU guise. S models had a T chassis number prefix, VA engine number is standard 3.8, VAS 3.8 S type. A Thornton limited slip diff was standard on S models.

The last XK150 left the production line in January 1961, and a total of 30,504 were produced. See accompanying table for full breakdown.

XK PRODUCTION NUMBERS

Model	Years	Numbers
XK120 Open Two Seater	1948-54	1175 (rhd) 6437 (lhd) 7612
XK120 Fixed-head Coupé	1951-54	194 (rhd) 2484 (lhd) 2678
XK120 Drop-head Coupé	1953-54	294 (rhd) 1471 (lhd) 1765
XK140 Open Two Seater	1954-57	73 (rhd) 3281 (lhd) 3354
XK140 Fixed-head Coupé	1954-57	843 (rhd) 1965 (lhd) 2808
XK140 Drop-head Coupé	1954-57	479 (rhd) 2310 (lhd) 2889
XK150 Roadster	1958-60	92 (rhd) 2173 (lhd) 2265
XK150 Fixed-head Coupé	1957-61	1368 (rhd) 3094 (lhd) 4462
XK150 Drop-head Coupé	1957-60	662 (rhd) 2009 (lhd) 2671
Total		30,504

Ian Appleyard was fabulously successful in rallies in his XKs; here he is coming second on the '56 RAC in his 140 coupé

Seven days and seven nights at 100.31mph; some feat

A classic photo; Appleyard in XK120 on the Alpine Rally

Buyers spot check

Talk to recommended XK specialists and it soon becomes apparent that a car in the XK range is perhaps the most difficult of classic Jaguars to buy. The XKs have always had a strong cult following, and consequently many surviving examples have been victims of short cut cosmetic restorations and suspect mechanical rebuilds. Make no mistake, Jaguars are expensive, and even buying a rusty XK could turn out to be the most difficult and most expensive way to acquire the type.

Having decided which XK you want to buy, take great care regardless of the market you are considering. When purchasing restored cars always study the company's work closely — most reputable restorers now provide photographic evidence of progress throughout the task. Do not be shy of seeking a second opinion, something which the best XK specialists are only too willing to accept. Any short measure during the rebuild can lead to prohibitive correction costs at a later date.

At the bottom end of the market rebuild projects are available from time to time, but more common are unfinished restorations. Be very wary of the latter, as a project may be incomplete because of impossible problems. If the car is lacking detail finish, the restoration could prove very expensive — many spare parts are very costly simply because they are pitched against the value of XKs in general. It is also worth noting the difference in the cost of restoring a 120 roadster and a 140 Drop-head — possibly as much as £3000 for a total rebuild — because the former lacks the XK140 Drop-head's creature comforts like wood veneer dash, heater and wind-up windows.

Mechanically the XK is not a real problem. Many of the engine parts are interchangeable with their saloon counterparts. However, the early 120 blocks are completely different from the later cars, and very few components are common. An easy date check is the engine mounting. The 'prototype' 120s have gearbox mountings behind the main block, and these are very prone to cracking. The later 140 and 150 cars have no such gearbox chassis mounts. The timing chain tensioners differ throughout the model's life, from a blade on earlier models to a hydraulic design on the later cars.

When checking the engine listen for any ominous timing chain rattle. Valve guides are the most common source of engine wear, tell-tale signs being excessive smoke from the crankcase breather and the exhaust. The cylinder head is prone to corrosion particularly in the waterways, and it is essential that anti-freeze is used all year round. Also check the exhaust manifold for cracks at the securing bolts, a particular weakness of the design. The XK engine is generally idiot proof with regard to rebuilds, but it is recommended never to 'ring' a worn Jaguar engine. A full rebore is the only worthwhile practice.

The gearbox is generally noisy in first and reverse, with weak synchromesh right through the gate, and does not like fast changes. It is very expensive to rebuild as many of the parts are simply not available. It is not unknown for a Mark IX box to be fitted to the XK, and an E-type clutch will fit exactly. Parts are no longer available for rack and pinion or the steering box, although original parts can be reconditioned.

At the rear the early ENV axles are a very weak design and it is now impossible to find spares, but the later Salisbury design can be fitted to the 120 with a little modification. The rear springs take a great deal of stress, and broken leaves are quite common, while the differential is generally trouble free. Wire wheels can be a problem on a car weighing at least 24cwt, for 60 spokes are not strong enough. It is also essential to check the spline condition.

The chassis is extremely strong, but not completely rust-free. At the front end, consistent water leaks from the radiator can cause the roll-bar mountings to delaminate, so check for bulging metal. Most of the body outriggers can be checked from the underside, but they generally stand up well to rust attack. The front mounting on the rear spring shackles can rot badly, and the last two feet of the rear chassis is very exposed to corrosive road salt. It is essential to check that the chassis is straight. A tell-tale point is just behind the front shock absorbers — the thinnest and weakest point — and any frontal impact will cause a 'concertina' effect. Another quick visual check is to look under the bonnet to make sure the torsion bars run parallel with the chassis side members. If the spacing is unequal on either side, it could well mean the chassis is a write-off.

No consideration was made at the design stage for protecting the internal sections of the bodywork from the corrosive horrors of winter motoring. The sill is a particularly crucial area, as both the front and rear body halves are supported by it. A badly rotted sill will cause door shut pillar problems and would indicate that the front inner wing sections and bulkhead side members will need extensive restoration work. The sill may look sound from the outside, but should be carefully checked from underneath. Another body problem is the catalytic reaction between aluminium panels and steel body sections, particularly on a 120. The steel spur for the aluminium boot is prone to this form of corrosion. Most panels are readily available but tend to be expensive (front wings can be more than £500) and fitting requires expertise.

When checking complete cars look for filler around the headlights, sidelight bases, below the bumper valence, and along the bottom of the front wings. During production, panel fitting was certainly not perfect, and the big slab sides were often very ripply when new.

The laminated ash frame is expensive to replace, and an ill-fitting boot is a tell tale sign that the frame needs correction. It is a particular problem on Drop-heads.

Rivals when new

Rivals? What rivals! Throughout its production life, the XK series of cars was in competition with machines that might have been faster or handled better, or were cheaper, but none combined such stunning good looks with such exceptional handling and scintillating performance at such a low price.

In 1949, there was literally nothing to touch it, and even with the advent of the Aston Martin DB2 in 1950 (not as fast and £650 more) and the Allard J2 (faster acceleration but not as high a top speed, as comfortable, or as good looking, and over £200 more), it was still an unbelievable motor car by the standards of the day.

Later rivals would include the Mercedes 300SL, with 150mph capability and more of an out-and-out sports car, various Ferraris and Maseratis, the BMW 507, the Aston Martin DB2/4 and DB4, the Chevrolet Corvette and Ford Thunderbird. The last named never handled as well as the XKs, but were slightly cheaper on the US market, while all the rest were vastly more expensive, even if they were faster, handled better and were more out-and-out sports cars. For instance, while an XK150S (3.8-litre) cost £2175 in 1959, a 300SL was £5313, a 250GT coupé Ferrari was £5951 and a DB4 Aston was £3755. Even an AC Ace Bristol, providing nothing like the standard XK150's performance, cost over £100 extra! The only car offering a similar ratio of performance per pound was the MGA Twin Cam at £1195 for 110mph. Even by this stage of the XK's career, when it was becoming more and more a Grand Tourer, lacking the chassis behaviour to keep up with all independently sprung rivals, it was still without equal for its price.

Clubs, specialists and books

Much of the information contained in this section is duplicated from the Jaguar E-type Profile in the November 1983 issue of C&S. Needless to say, many of the books and Jaguar specialists listed in that Profile are equally applicable to the XKs, with one or two notable exceptions.

One thing that does not change, however, is the owner's club. With membership at around the 8000 mark and growing, the Jaguar Drivers Club is not only *the* club for Jaguar owners, but also one of the leading one-make clubs in the country. A year's membership currently stands at £15 with a £5 joining fee and the club may be contacted at Jaguar House, 18 Stuart Street, Luton, Beds LU1 2SL (tel: Luton 419332).

Within the club is a thriving XK Register run by John Bridcutt of The Post Office, Market Lavington, near Devizes, Wiltshire (tel: Market Lavington

An historic photograph. This is the first meeting of the JDC's XK Register held in Surrey on January 21, 1968

Seventies racing saw quite a few XKs hacked about

Drag racing with an XK140 and 150 at Santa Pod

(038 081) 2267). As with all the Jaguar Registers, the XK section of the club has a regular monthly column in *Jaguar Driver*, the JDC's monthly magazine, and various social events throughout the year are crowned by the International XK Day, to be held this year on July 1 at Hagley Hall.

The specialists catering for XK Jaguars are, as mentioned earlier, largely the same as those for the E-type. Consequently, it is best to provide once again the latest list of members belonging to the Jaguar Specialists Association. An up-to-date list is available from Harry Phillips of Phillips Garage (address below): simply send him an SAE for your copy.

Having said that, there are a number of first-class Jaguar specialists who, for one reason or another, do not appear in the list but who nevertheless provide a more than adequate service. At any rate, here are the Association specialists:

Southern Classics of Chertsey Mead Garage, Chertsey, Surrey; British Sports Car Centre Ltd, 299-309 Goldhawk Road, London W12; Roger Bywater Engineering Ltd, Unit 4, Hillgate Ind. Estate, Carrington Field Street, Stockport, Cheshire SK1 3JN; Classic Autos, 10 High Street, Kings Langley, Herts; Classic Power Units, Tile Hill, 18 Trevor Close, Coventry; D.K. Engineering, 10-16 Hallowell Road, Northwood, Middlesex; Coventry Auto Components, Gillingwood, Waste Lane, Berkswell, near Coventry, Warwicks and Deetype Replicas Ltd, South Gibcracks Farm, Bicknacre Road, East Hanningfield, Chelmsford, Essex.

Forward Engineering Ltd, Barston Lane, Barston, Solihull, West Midlands B92 0JP; Alan George, Plot 11, Small Firms Compound, Dodwells Bridge Ind. Estate, Hinckley, Leicester; A.W. Hannah, Central Garage, Snaith, near Goole, Humberside; Bill Lawrence Esq, 9 Badgers Walk, Dibden Purlieu, Hampshire, and Contour Autocraft, Station Road, French Drove, Gedney Hill, near Spalding, Lincs.

Phillips Garage, 103-7 New Canal Street, Digbeth, Birmingham B5 5RA; R.S. Panels, Kelsey Close, Attleborough Fields Ind. Estate, Nuneaton CV11 6RS; S.S. and Classic Restoration, Cemere Green Farm, Cemere Green, Pulham Markets, Diss, Norfolk; S.S. & L. Automobile Engineers, Home- farm, Holmlea Road, Datchet, Berkshire; Suffolk and Turley, Unit 7, Attleborough Fields Ind. Estate, Garrett Street, Nuneaton, Warwicks and Swallow Engineering, 6 Gibcracks, Basildon, Essex.

It is worth repeating that George Nolan's shop for new and used Jaguar parts at 1 St. George's Way, London SE15, is a veritable Aladdin's Cave of elderly Jaguar bits, along with the back-up knowledge to make the most effective use of them. Warren Pearce Motors, 59 South Street, Epsom, Surrey KT18 7PX is also helpful where XK matters are concerned.

Potential XK owners are similarly well served by reading matter. Of the numerous works available on the subject, one stands head and shoulders above the rest, Paul Skilleter's superb *Jaguar Sports Car* (Haynes) — highly recommended. Skilleter has also penned *The Jaguar XK*s, one of the excellent Collectors Guide series, and his *Jaguar Driver Yearbook* from 1977 contains a section on XKs.

Andrew Whyte's *Jaguar Sports Racing and Works Competition Cars to 1953* is another highly recommended volume, while Brooklands Books publish two useful road test reprints, *Jaguar Cars 1948-1957* and *Jaguar Cars 1957-1961*.

Two worthwhile titles by Chris Harvey are *The Jaguar XK* and *Jaguars in Competition*, the latter covering the XK's competition history.

Prices

Of all the cars that *C&S* has profiled, the XK series perhaps subject to the greatest price variation. wreck can cost under £1000, while one immaculate 120 Roadster recently sold for over £20,000.

Middle bracket cars can prove a dilemma; you can pick up good sound cars for around £6000 if you work through personal contacts and are prepared to do some tidying work. Dealers' cars in the £6-10,000 bracket have usually been subject to cosmetic restoration and are probably best avoided.

Cars completely restored by reputable specialists are expensive (expect little change out of £10-15,000) but along with middle bracket *known* cars are probably the best route. Roadsters tend to command highest prices, while there seems to be little variation between 120s and 140s and 150s.